Object Orientation

The KISS Method®

Object Orientation

The KISS Method®

FROM INFORMATION ARCHITECTURE TO INFORMATION SYSTEM

GERALD KRISTEN

Kristen Information and Software Services

ADDISON-WESLEY PUBLISHING COMPANY

Wokingham, England • Reading, Massachusetts • Menlo Park, California • New York
Don Mills, Ontario • Amsterdam • Bonn • Sydney • Singapore
Tokyo • Madrid • San Juan • Milan • Paris • Mexico City • Seoul • Taipei

Cover designed by Op den Brouw, Design & Illustration, Reading and printed by The Riverside Printing Co Ltd.
Line diagrams drawn by Margaret Macknelly Design, Tadley.
Typeset by Meridian Phototypesetting Limited, Pangbourne.
Printed and bound by T. J. Press, Padstow, Cornwall.

First printed 1994.

ISBN 0-201-42299-9

British Library Cataloguing-in-Publication Data is available.

Library of Congress Cataloging-in-Publication Data
Kristen, Gerald.
    [KISS-methode voor object oriëntatie. English]
    Object-orientation: the KISS method: from information architecture to information system/Gerald Kristen.
      p. cm.
    Translation of: KISS methode voor object oriëntatie.
    Includes bibliograpical references and index.
    ISBN 0-201-42299-9
    1. Object-oriented programming (Computer science)   I. Title.
QA76.64.K75 1994
005.1'1--dc20

94-28561
CIP

Trademark Notice
ADA is a trademark of the ADA Joint Program Office, DoD, US Government.
C++ is a trademark of CNS Inc.
Eiffel is a trademark of Interactive Software Engineering Inc.
GemStone is a trademark of Servio Logic. Corp.
KISS DOMINO is a trademark of KISS b.v.
KISS method is a trademark of KISS b.v.
Objectivity is a trademark of Objectivity Inc.
Objectory is a trademark of Objective Systems SF AB.
ObjectStore is a trademark of Object Design.
Paradigm Plus is a trademark of Protosoft, Inc.
POET is a trademark of BKS Software GmbH.
Simula is a trademark of Simula AS.
Smalltalk is a trademark of Xerox Corporation.
SQL is a trademark of Oracle Corporation UK Ltd.
Versant is a trademark of Versant Object Technologies.
Windows is a trademark of Microsoft Corporation.

Preface

The background to this book on the KISS method of object orientation is found in my own background as a industrial engineer and my experience with, on the one hand, designing and building technical systems, and on the other, implementing information systems in organizations.

In the early years of my career, using the engineer's viewpoint developed during my study years, I worked at producing energy analyses for production installations. An energy analysis is a study of how much energy is used by plant to carry out a certain amount of work. To do this in a simple and effective manner I would first make a model of the production installation. Then I would use this model to analyse further the details of the energy and production flows. This 'model' was then used for calculating and indicating the amount of energy increase or decrease to be gained by an adjustment in the management of the production installation, or by investing more in energy-saving measures, such as extra heat exchangers, smaller engines or heat/power cogeneration.

Only when the necessary savings have been calculated, was it possible to make decisions on how much should be invested in introducing energy-saving measures. In order to implement these measures, a project plan was drawn up defining the activities to be carried out in the various phases, and indicating the critical activities. This made the sizing, planning and implementing of energy-saving projects predictable and manageable.

Having worked for several years on strongly technical-oriented projects, I felt the need to gain experience in the other subjects I had studied at university. I started work for a multinational company in the Netherlands as an organizational adviser. In this capacity I was included in an extremely important project to implement a standard package to improve the logistical processes in production firms. The purpose of the project was to implement the 'standard package' because this package would reduce lead time, production, inventory and computing costs.

To be able to gain an insight into the details of the logistical process, I first produced an analysis of it. During the analysis I called upon my previous experiences with energy analyses and my modelling of technical production installations. To my dismay, when I tried to use the results of the analysis to review the usability and suitability of 'standard packages', I discovered a communication chasm between the organization and its computing specialists.

One of the main questions needing to be answered to determine the suitability of the 'standard package' in the model of the logistical organization was: "What is the underlying model or information architecture of the 'standard package'?" Based on this I would then be able to make a comparison between the model of logistical organization and the model of the 'standard package'. One of my conclusions was the extent to which the logistical organization and the 'standard package' needed to be adapted to each other.

It became obvious that it was impossible for the computing specialists to provide me with any insight into the underlying model of the 'standard package', to enable me to make the comparison with the model of the logistical process. One of the main reasons for the failure of the project was thus inherent in it.

The poor communication between the organization and the computing staff became apparent on several fronts. The computing specialists insisted on placing themselves in the shoes of the logistics manager, because they felt the logistics managers were unable to understand what it was 'all about' and 'how great' the system would be once the 'standard package' was installed and in production. In such a situation the computing specialist fails to perceive that the organizational processes have grown over time and seem to work in practice. They attempted to use the installation of the 'standard package' as a crowbar to force a change in the current situation without being able to indicate what the expected result of such a change might be.

Being involved in computing projects was a culture shock for me. In a technical environment I was used to evaluating, sizing and implementing projects based on energy analyses and simulation and calculation models. The level of reliability and ease of implementation of these projects was good, despite the extreme size and complexity of the problem area. My original expectation of an extremely advanced computing environment was that this high level at least would be achieved.

The reality was in fact quite different. Computing projects would seem to be unmanageable, unpredictable, cost inflating, increase the rigidity of the organizational structure, and not least to cloud the organization's chain of command. In addition, the automation of systems itself became the goal of the organization and no longer the means of achieving the legitimate goals.

Many of the above-mentioned problems lay in the grey area between the organization and its information system. To be able to find solutions for these problems I returned to my experiences with energy analyses for designing and implementing energy-saving systems. I attempted to discover why it was possible for technical production installations to be manageable and predictable, while this is not possible for information system and computing projects.

One of the first things I noticed was that there are many concepts and conventions used in computing that, together, do not form a complete whole that is inherently consistent. This threatens to cause a Babel-like confusion during the many phases from the creation of a model of the real world through to the use and maintenance of automated information systems. There is a danger that everything becomes much more difficult than is necessary.

A second point to note is that the concepts used are based too much on solutions offered by a specific technology. In addition, these concepts often have an informal and intuitive nature. This makes it impossible to draw up exact specifications.

A third point is that methods for modelling information systems often have such a strongly dogmatic nature that the computing department becomes isolated from the outside world. In such cases the computing specialist must be presented with methods and techniques allowing him or her to communicate with users, clients, project managers and other such persons.

During my search for a solution to the communication problem and a straightforward methodology, I have made use of several fundamental concepts established by other authors. The methodology makes use of several different techniques in an integrated manner. I therefore do not profess to be original in everything I have written. I would, however, like to make clear that the approach and premises of the KISS method deviate strongly from those of conventional methods.

Authorities on methods and techniques will, while reading this book, notice that I use the method of notation from the Extended Entity Relationship method written by Peter P. Chen. This method is applied when defining the conceptual data models. In the second step, I use formal transformation rules to create the database structure for an information system. An important shortcoming of the Extended Entity Relationship method is that it does not support process models.

To be able to model the dynamic aspects I have introduced 'KISS models'. A KISS model describes the life of an object based on the sequence in which the actions on it can be performed. The sequence is defined by 'Iterations', 'Selections' and 'Sequences'.

The introduction of KISS models meant that the existing Extended Entity Relationship method needed to be considerably expanded.

Consequently, while we use the method of notation, the definitions and methods of thinking and working are no longer comparable with our method.

Authorities on Michael Jackson's JSP and JSD methods will almost certainly observe that there are similarities between KISS models and JSD models. The KISS method provides an extension to Michael Jackson's publications. The strength of the JSD method lies primarily in its modelling of the dynamics of the real world. We are, therefore, able to generate systems, based on the JSD models. The extra dimension of the KISS method is the greatly increased semantic value of the models, making the models clearer and easier to understand. In addition, the KISS method incorporates many extra concepts that enhance the clarity of the models.

Based on my own experience and the experiences of other authors I have developed the KISS method into a mature object-oriented systems development method that uses several completely integrated models and techniques. An additional premise of mine was that the models should be readable in natural language so that they could be used in the communication process between end users, information analysts and programmers.

I have chosen to focus the book on the problem domain of the organization and its information structures. Chapter 2 describes the relationship between the organizational system and the information system. This chapter indicates the way in which a division can be made between the information architecture and the management of an organization. The fundamental principles of management and systems implementation are further supported by the *KISS paradigm* for object orientation. Chapter 4 elaborates on the grammar rules of the communication process and on the way in which these rules are used to define an information architecture.

In Chapter 5, I discuss the basic concepts used to create KISS models, object-interaction models and hierarchy models. The main structure of the information system is thus defined.

Chapter 7 lays the foundation of concepts needed to define the encapsulated attributes of objects. The measurement process described in this chapter also defines the fundamentals for object orientation.

Chapter 8 indicates the manner in which attribute types, operations and object conditions are specified with the help of attribute models and action models.

It is shown in Chapter 9 how the transformation rules then allow us to specify the implementation of the system, taking into consideration the restrictions of the database management system or programming language.

Chapter 10 explains how functionality can be added to the information architecture without disrupting the already defined information architecture, while Chapter 11 contains an example that brings together all the concepts described earlier.

The concluding chapter elaborates on how the management of projects can be influenced by the use of various other techniques, the way in which techniques are implemented in the organization, and by the utilization of CASE tools to better manage information systems.

This book is intended to be read sequentially in order of the chapters. Throughout the book there is a build-up of concepts that extend the scope of the KISS method. Skipping chapters may lead to only a partial understanding of the concepts and underlying philosophy of object orientation.

Finally, I would like to thank all the people who have supported me while I was writing this book, both those who acted as critics, and those who encouraged me. I would especially like to mention Eric Laane, Erik van Dongen, Jean-Pierre van den Broeck, Michel van Lieshout, Esther Minderhoud (KISS), Jan van Lente (Philips), Michel Bedel (Lapeyre), Jan Diepenhorst (Dienst Recreatie Rotterdam), Piet Verleijsdonk (BSO/Origin, ILS), Daan Assenberg (BSO/IS), Stefen Hegge (BSO/Origin, ISON), Peter Slagt (Vezeno-Insurance), Wim Vermeulen, Ray Stapel, Rob Tan (OHRA-Insurance), Nigel Backhurst (Swiss Banking Corporation, IE), and all the others who directly or indirectly contributed to the contents of the book. Although I have largely tried to follow all of this guidance, I have undoubtly been negligent in some areas; none of these individuals should bear any responsibility for that.

I also thank Andy Ware, Alan Grove, Melanie Paton and Yvonne Zaslawska of Addison-Wesley for their professional help in the production of this book in a very short period of time.

I especially thank Monique Veltman (Petone, New Zealand) who translated the Dutch text through her knowledge derived from a personal interest in object orientation. Many difficult parts of the text were only translatable because of her personal interest in and knowledge of the KISS method.

I very much look forward to seeing much more of my wife Mirjam and my three sons Gert-Jan, Jasper and Thymen, of whom I saw precious little during the period of writing this book.

Gerald Kristen
Kervellaar 10
5467 BK Veghel
The Netherlands

About the author

Gerald Kristen is general manager of Kristen Information & Software Services. He gained a degree in Industrial Engineering at the University of Eindhoven, the Netherlands, in 1982. Following this, he worked for several years designing and implementing technical production installations. Since 1985, he has developed an interest in systems development methods and techniques. He became a Master of Business Administration at the Catholic University of Leuven, Belgium, in 1988. In 1990 he formed his own company, Kristen Information & Software Services, in order to develop further his ideas on methods and techniques to efficiently and effectively utilize automated information systems in organizations.

Gerald Kristen lives in Veghel, the Netherlands. He and his wife have three sons: Gert-Jan, Jasper and Thymen, who are still too young to read this book.

Introduction

The following text and diagrams are a summary of the rationale and also the symbols used in the KISS method.

The KISS method: project stages and deliverables

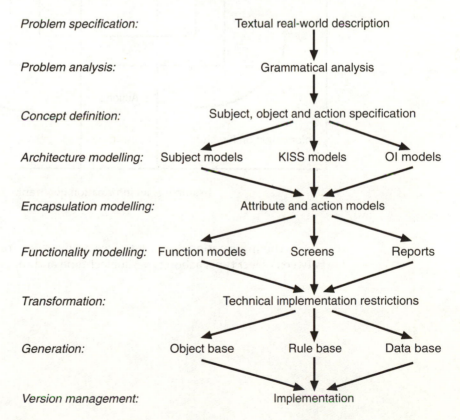

Problem specification:	Textual real-world description
Problem analysis:	Grammatical analysis
Concept definition:	Subject, object and action specification
Architecture modelling:	Subject models KISS models OI models
Encapsulation modelling:	Attribute and action models
Functionality modelling:	Function models Screens Reports
Transformation:	Technical implementation restrictions
Generation:	Object base Rule base Data base
Version management:	Implementation

The information quadrant

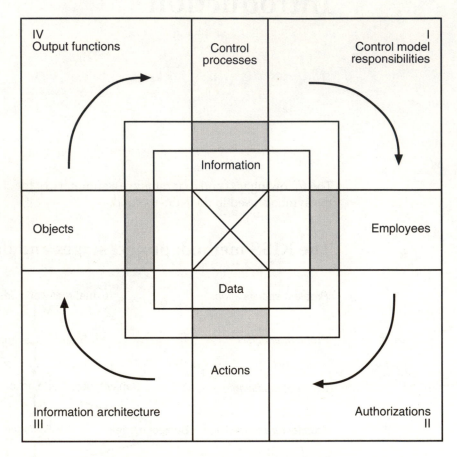

Example of an information quadrant.

The information quadrant gives an overview of the associations between object type, action type, subject type and function.

Symbols of the subject-communication model

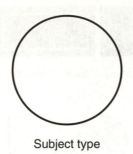

Subject type

Message type

Form

Diskette

Tape

Attributes of work-flow analysis for business process redesign

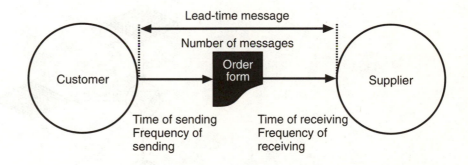

Lead-time message

Number of messages

Customer

Order form

Supplier

Time of sending
Frequency of sending

Time of receiving
Frequency of receiving

The KISS model

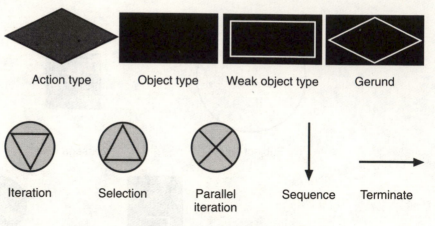

Action type   Object type   Weak object type   Gerund

Iteration   Selection   Parallel iteration   Sequence   Terminate

Symbols used in the KISS model.

The KISS model describes the life of an object at the generic-type level by placing the action types in an Iteration, Selection and Sequence structure. The KISS model instantiates new objects by the first action type in the KISS model as shown by this example from a bank situation.

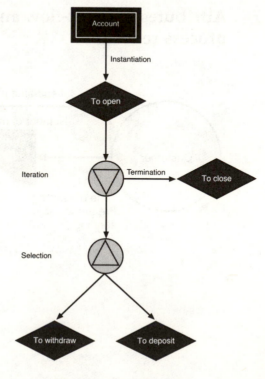

Example of a KISS model.

The object-interaction model

The type level describes the generic life of individual objects, whereas the class level represents the state of objects on which they can be classified into groups.

The synchronization between object types is specified by the action type. The synchronization at the class level is by the ISA symbol, representing a classification.

At both the type and class level the symbols can be dependent upon no, one, two or more object types. The parent is indicated by a double arrow in the direction of the object types instantiating action type or the ISA symbols. The ISA symbol will be connected with a single arrow to the parent type.

The ISA symbol is responsible for the coordination at the class level.

The object class is used for classifying objects only upon attribute values.

The specialization is used for modelling metamorphism and concurrent roles.

The category is used for modelling the asynchronous use of action types, what results is reuse of the action type and a polymorphic behaviour of objects.

The hierarchy model is derived from the object-interaction model by taking out the action types and ISA symbols and replacing them by hierarchy relationships represented by a dotted double arrow into the direction of the parent type.

	Synchronization	No parents	One-parent object type	Two or more parents
Type level	Action type	Object type	Weak object type	Gerund
Class level	ISA symbol	Object class	Specialization	Category
	Coordination	Classification	Metamorphism	Polymorphism

Diagram depicting symbols of the object-interaction model.

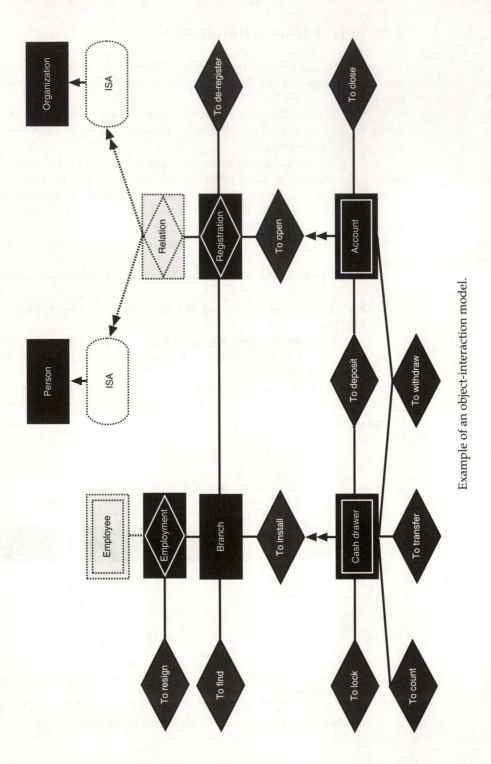

Example of an object-interaction model.

The hierarchy model

The hierarchy model determines in which way the object types and object classes are dependent for their existence on other object types. The hierarchy model is the starting point for defining the class hierarchy.

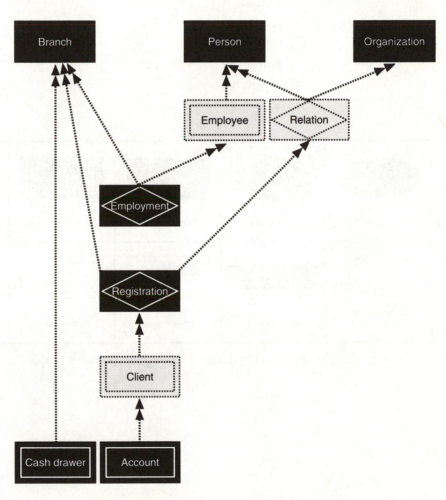

Example of a hierarchy model.

The attribute model

The attribute model specifies the attribute types of the symbols of the object-interaction model by applying the principals of the measurement process and/or declaration process.

The encapsulated attributes can be specified at five different scale types:

(1) Classes;
(2) Ranking scale;
(3) Interval scale;
(4) Ratio scale;
(5) Absolute scale.

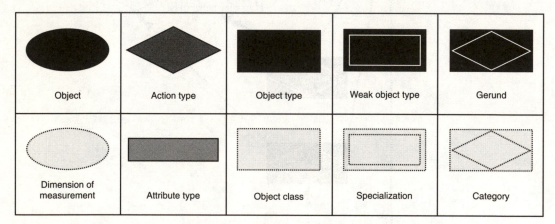

Diagram depicting symbols of the attribute model.

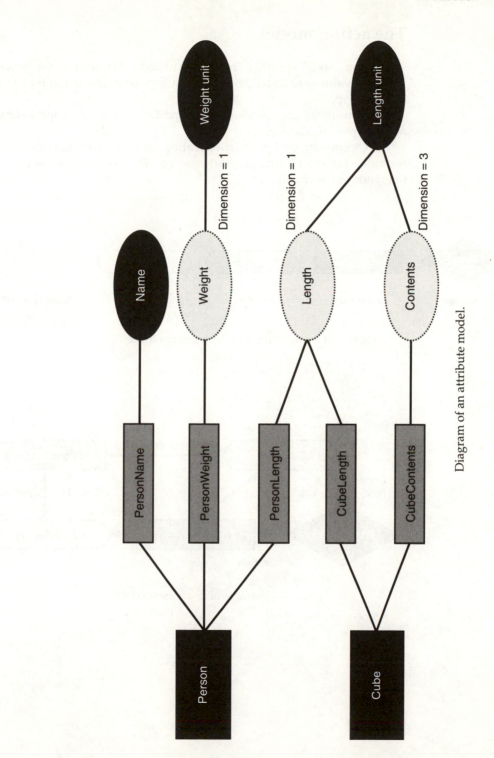

Diagram of an attribute model.

The action model

The action model specifies the encapsulated behaviour of the actions. Attribute values are initialized by a data flow from the action type to the attribute type.

Conditions are specified with condition flows when operations or action types are allowed.

Operations and abstract operations specify, with data flows, the formulae for calculating attribute values. The data flows contain the operands of the calculation.

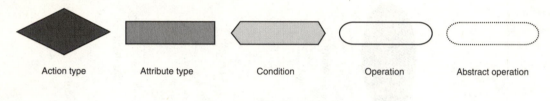

Diagram of the symbols used in the action model.

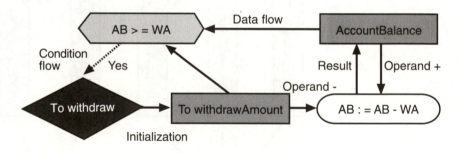

Example of an action model.

The function model

The function model specifies the way in which the end-user communicates with the information system. Every function is under responsibility of one or more subject types. The structure of the function model is similar in structure to the KISS model.

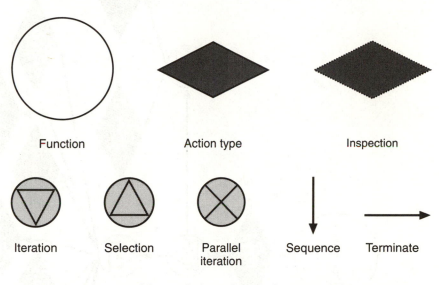

Diagram of the symbols used in the function model.

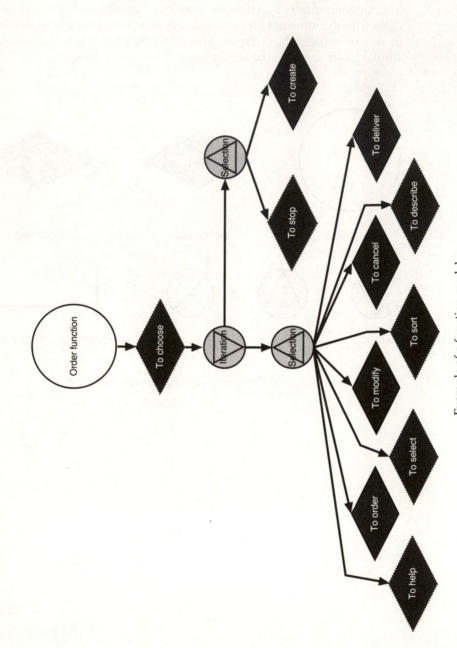

Example of a function model.

Contents

A note on language
For reasons of simplicity the pronoun 'he' is used to relate to both male and female throughout this book.

To Mirjam, Gert-Jan, Jasper and Thymen, who were without me for so many evenings.

1 Introduction to object orientation

1.1 Introduction

In recent years, the provision of good information is something that, for most managers and organizations, has become a mirage in an information desert. The high expectations of computer systems have generally been met only in part or not at all. Frequently described problems are that information systems are difficult to maintain, badly documented, negligibly user-friendly and too costly. In addition, the development of information systems takes too long and the development process, even after so many years, is too unpredictable in terms of completion date and cost. Often the end result is not that which was requested. Alongside these issues there is a general feeling that the manageability of information systems has decreased rapidly over recent years with the introduction of new technologies.

The natural reaction by many information managers has been to separate for as long as possible new developments from existing information systems. The result is an 'unchangeable' environment of information systems in which the unexpressed requirements and wishes of the end user steadily increase. This escalates inevitably until the end user or client becomes dissatisfied and creates his own solutions.

In reaction to this, the search for solutions to the management of the necessary changes continues. It is carried out on a number of different fronts. Since the introduction of computers, limited improvements in management have been gained by utilizing planning methods for the development process, methodologies for systems development, standards for system documentation, assisting organizations during system implementation, and modifying procedures in the organization. More technically oriented solutions are the use of better and faster technical tools such as hierarchical, network, relational, semantic and object-oriented databases, 3GLs, 4GLs and OOPLs, data dictionaries, and CASE tools and repositories.

Despite these efforts, the general picture of systems development is one of an immature speciality unable to produce programs to support the integrated provision of information for organizations in an effective and efficient manner. Consequently, an enormous gap can appear between the information requirements of employees and the current manner in which the organization is supported by automated systems and procedures. A department manager who wishes to take advantage of the opportunities and prepare himself for the threats of the external environment will often decide to provide information for himself and his department by creating a departmental system with little reliance on the central information system. It thus becomes essential to move towards an integrated information system as the external environment demands faster and better information on the business processes.

To be able to manage the provision of information, an integral approach must be taken whereby solutions to some aspects can be assessed and planned, based on their effect on other aspects, without acceding to a less than optimal solution. The approach forms the blueprint for the definition of the total provision of information.

In the provision of information we can differentiate between three poles of change which are constantly kept in balance in a field of tension. These poles of change (Figure 1.1) are:

- Organization;
- Technique;
- Information requirements.

Organizational changes happen on a regular basis in every organization. When you look back 10 years at your own organization, you see that a lot of changes have taken place. For example, new people in the organization, a different structure, new tasks, and so forth.

Technical changes of the past years have been enormous. In the early days of using computers we used radio tubes. Nowadays we use very large integrated circuits for processing data. We have also seen tremendous changes in the storage of data, going from paper, magnetic drums, tapes and disks to optical disks.

Changes in information requirements and the supply of information have also created revolutions. Character-based terminals are being replaced, with increasing speed, by windows-based workstations. We can expect in the near future a further integration of sound, voice, video graphics and such like into information systems. We will see that informatics integrate into current consumer products like television, telephone, fax, CD, video, photography, and so on.

Organizational, technical and external changes make it necessary to assess the modifications and additions to the existing information

Figure 1.1 Poles of change.

system. To obtain a manageable system, each pole of change must be seen not in isolation, but as an interacting part. The interaction between the poles requires communication and consultation between them.

In recent years the computing specialist has concentrated primarily on representing the technical aspects of information systems. This has resulted in a large number of methods and techniques for representing the *technical and logical structures* of information systems.

Methods and techniques developed in the past were in many cases defined by the technical restrictions of the specific implementation technique, such as the facilities of a programming language or database system. The main shortcoming of all these methods is that the progression from one family of techniques to another is not supported because technically-oriented methods are not sufficiently generic. The modelling techniques for information systems are not suitable for the integration of new techniques like sound, video, photographs and such like into existing applications.

An additional problem with the technically oriented methods is that they are not sufficiently adequate to allow organizational changes and changes in information requirements to be translated into information systems. Before we move on to the discussion of object-oriented methods, we shall review the older methods.

1.2   Methods of system development

The widespread application of third-generation languages (3GLs) such as COBOL, BASIC and FORTRAN in the 1970s required the use of structured methods for systems development. The impulse toward a structured method of work came from many research institutes. The greatest need to apply systems development methods came with large-scale projects for military systems and space projects. These large projects involved complex applications and utilized large numbers of programmers. Managers quickly identified the need to structure the method of work in these large projects, to measure the progress and to keep a check on the quality of the resulting products.

At the start of the 1980s we were concerned with three different approaches to the development of software. They were:

- Structured approach;
- Data approach;
- Event-driven approach.

1.2.1   Structured approach

The collection of methods and techniques based on functional decompositions and data-flow diagrams is known as the 'structured' approach. Well-known authors of this approach include Ed Yourdon, Tom DeMarco and Larry Constantine.

The oldest approach is functional decomposition. The basic premise of functional decomposition is a program that receives input, performs a function and produces output. Each function can be divided, in a top-down process, into sub-functions, which in their turn can be divided into sub-subfunctions, and so forth.

The functional decomposition approach is focused on the procedural steps the program itself takes in order to transform the input into output. At a later point in time the functional decomposition models are modified and re-presented as data-flow diagrams. Although there are 'data stores', 'data sources' and 'data sinks' included in the diagrams, the emphasis is on modelling the process and not on modelling the data. This is understandable given that structured methods were developed at a time when there were only procedural programming languages available. The aim of structured methods is to provide a logical model that can be implemented by procedural programming languages such as COBOL.

1.2.2   Data approach

When databases began to play a greater role in the development of software, the structured approach was found to be insufficient because it was focused on modelling function structures. Consequently, a different group of researchers began to develop data-directed development methods. With data-directed development we start by analysing the logical data groups, also known as entities, that must be recorded in the database. Secondly, we describe those programmatic procedures that modify the data. The data approach is often grouped under the general title of the entity–relationship approach. Well-known names on this subject are Charlie Bachman, Peter Chen and James Martin.

A second data approach, which provides a transition to the event-driven approach, is the Jackson System Development method (JSD). This method was developed at the start of the 1980s by Michael Jackson as a logical progression from the Jackson Structured Programming method (JSP). The JSD method emphasizes the description of the behaviour of entities in the real world, while the JSP method provides a basis for structured programming. Both Jackson methods complement each other, but as far as the problem areas to which they can be applied and as far as the manner of access is concerned, they are completely distinct from each other, although they carry almost the same name and use the same method of notation.

1.2.3   Event-driven approach

The event-driven approach is the third collection of methods we mentioned. Event-driven methods were developed at the start of the 1980s and focus on the description of events and the responses they give. These methods have been elaborated by authors such as Michael Jackson, Paul Ward and Steve Mellor. The core of event modelling lies in the construction of event models and state-transition diagrams. The Ward–Mellor approach is frequently used when designing technical real-time systems and process installations in which the recording of data plays very much a minor role. The JSD approach is, on the other hand, used in administrative situations where the recording of data is relevant.

1.2.4   Object-oriented approach

There has been much attention given in recent years to object orientation. One of the reasons for this is that object-oriented languages, such as C++,

Eiffel and Smalltalk, and object-oriented databases, such as GemStone, Versant, Object Store, Onthos, Poet and Objectivity, offer us facilities far better than those of conventional procedural languages and database systems. Using these object-oriented environments we can simply and easily graph user interfaces as well as record complex structures, such as photos and video images, in a database.

One of the characteristics for an object-oriented implementation environment is the representation of an object on a generic level, called a class. Objects are instantiations of classes describing their generic characteristics. The attributes of every object are encapsulated, which indicates that the data of an object can only be changed by its own operations. The operations are implemented in an OO language by a so-called 'method'.

A second characteristic is that the attributes and methods of the objects can be inherited from objects defined as superclasses. A third characteristic of object orientation is that objects are completely independent and communicate with each other by sending messages. The message will be received by objects and invoke the execution of methods that change encapsulated attributes of the object.

The structure of the object-oriented environment is so dissimilar to that of conventional environments that it requires different modelling methods. Rapid technical developments in recent years, in the area of object-oriented programming languages, have made the need for sound object-oriented systems development methods more urgent. Subsequently, in addition to the methods already in use in conventional environments, separate and distinct methods for object-oriented systems development have been introduced. See Booch (1991), Coad and Yourdon (1991a, 1991b), Shlear and Mellor (1988), Jacobson *et al.* (1992) and Rumbaugh *et al.* (1991). What the object-oriented methods of these best known authors have in common is that they are heavily based on the abilities and limitations of the technology, in our case the object-oriented target environment. The target environment is strongly influenced by the 'class' concept. Because of this it is, in my opinion, better to talk about *class-oriented* methods rather than *object-oriented* methods because all these methods focus on modelling the implementation to classes.

The other characteristic that most of the above writers have in common is that they base their methods on three base models. These are the models for 'functions', 'data', and 'events'. In nearly all cases the models make use of modelling techniques that are available and have been known for many years. The modelling techniques were in general only in minor respects adapted for modelling classes and objects.

The method to which a lot of other methods converge to is described by Rumbaugh *et al.* (1991). The method described is called the 'Object Modelling Technique' (OMT). It is comprehensive in describing the actions one has to take for modelling an object-oriented information system.

The OMT-method described by Rumbaugh *et al.* is based on three main models:

(1) *Object model.* The object model is very similar to data modelling with the entity relationship technique that was extended by the end of the 1970s with generalizations, specializations, aggregations, and so on.

(2) *Dynamic model.* The dynamic model of OMT is similar to the state-transition diagramming technique, though it is described in the OMT book in a confusing and inconsistent manner.

(3) *Functional model.* The functional model is identical to data-flow diagramming!

From the above summary of OMT we can conclude that it does not make use of any new modelling techniques. All the modelling techniques used are already known and have been in use for more than 10 years, in for example, the conventional Structured Analysis/ Structured Design method (SA/SD). The distinction between OMT and SA/SD is that the procedural cookbook approach is reversed in OMT. In OMT we start by modelling the data structures of the classes and then model the state-transition diagrams per class and data-flow diagram of the information system.

SA/SD starts with the data-flow diagram, followed by the data model and optionally the state-transition diagram. The other distinction from SA/SD is that the terminology of OMT has added concepts like class, object, and so on, that are related to the implementation of object-oriented languages.

From experience with the SA/SD method we know that the biggest problem is the specification of the coherence between the three different models. Because all three models are modelled independently, no formal consistency can be found between them. In the old days this caused a lot of problems with the three distinct models.

In OMT, and the other object-oriented methods, no fundamental integration of the different types of models has been realized. We can thus expect that these object-oriented methods have exactly the same serious problems as SA/SD. In this book we describe how the KISS method gives a fundamental solution to ensuring consistency between different types of models by making use of a '*linking pin*' principle.

Booch (1991) explains his OOD method by using examples of direct system implementations in C++, Smalltalk, Object Pascal, LISP and Ada. Booch's main distinguishing feature is that he leans heavily towards the programming environment and offers only limited support for the design phase and vague support for the analysis phase.

Coad and Yourdon in their first book offered a very limited description of the object-oriented development process. In their second edition they have further defined the concepts, but still lean strongly towards the structured approach (1991a) and data-flow diagramming. The emphasis of the book is on a popular treatment of the object-oriented analysis phase.

Shlear and Mellor (1988) give an approach to object orientation that is basically very similar to that of OMT. It is also based on the three basic modelling techniques that do not link to each other. From the three models you have to interpret its coherence in an informal way. The emphasis of Shlear and Mellor though, is on real-time modelling. The emphasis is on modelling with state-transition diagrams, with less emphasis on data modelling.

Jacobson *et al.* (1992) have written a book about the Objectory method. The method was developed on top of the work done for the standardization body CCITT in the telecoms industry. One of the subject areas covered in the book is the standards for SDL, a programming language. Large parts of the Objectory method bear resemblance to the specification problems of communication systems and real-time problems. The way in which Objectory approaches object orientation thus has its root in the procedural thinking for real-time communication systems. The result is that the data part is treated very slightly.

Despite the large number of advantages gained by using object-oriented programming languages and methods, such as reuse of specifications, better insight and ease of maintenance, they nevertheless have a great disadvantage consistent with the conventional approaches: both types of approach lack the ingredient of independence from the method of the target environment. In fact all methods of analysis and design are to a greater or lesser degree dependent on the eventual programming environment. When describing and then modelling the real world and the problem area we implicitly build in the restrictions of the facilities offered by the technology of a particular (object-oriented) environment.

A second common denominator of the above-mentioned object-oriented methods and conventional methods is that the models in both types of method are only weakly interlinked, and very often the diagramming techniques used are similar. In order to introduce the 'object orientedness' into a method, in most cases only the method cookbook on 'how to use the well-known and existing models' has been changed. The fundamentals of object orientation are given very often in an informal way in these methods.

Object-oriented methods that focus on the implementation technique of object-oriented languages continue to experience the problem of communication with the end user. Likewise the maintenance aspect of object-oriented systems continues to be a problem in exactly the same way as for conventional environments because of lack of formal models.

The advantage of object-oriented programming environments is that they allow us to complete systems faster than before. Even so, when we have insufficiently thought through the internal structure of an object-oriented system, and when the documentation is minimal, we miss out on the time-saving benefits of object orientation, namely the reuse of objects and inheritance. An object-oriented programming language does not dismiss the need for the programmer to produce a good analysis and design of the problem area before commencing object-oriented programming. To date, object-oriented methods support him in this only to a limited degree, since they focus strongly on object-oriented programming languages and databases.

1.3   The KISS method of object orientation

The basic premise of the KISS method for object-oriented development of information systems differs from that of the above-described methods in the sense that the KISS method begins by describing the reality in an information architecture, without taking account of the restrictions of a specific programming environment. Because of this, the KISS method for object-oriented development is entirely conceptual. The 'KISS technique' can implement an object-oriented information architecture in conventional and object-oriented languages and databases. With KISS, the object-oriented design is created independently of the implementation technique.

Because of the fact that the specifications are independent of any implementation environment, the KISS method is easily applicable for technical and real-time as well as administrative and decision-support systems. The emphasis of this book on object orientation is focused on developing administrative information systems.

The details of the object-oriented design are recorded in the KISS method in an information architecture that can be discussed intensively with the end users. The information architecture forms the basis for the information system as well as for all the changes that take place in the organization's procedural system. Object orientation offers, in this manner, a solution to the problems, mentioned in the introduction, of the management of software and the influence of changes on the organization. With the KISS method, object orientation goes further than being simply a technique which models and designs graphical user interfaces, inheritance between classes or messaging between objects.

The basis of object orientation lies in its divergent methods of thought and work. Object-oriented thinking and working cannot be enforced simply by learning the syntax of object-oriented languages.

Object-oriented thinking is not something automatically gained by programming in C++, Smalltalk, Eiffel, Clos or Simula. This is no more the case than in the past with structured programming: structured systems were not the automatic result when we programmed in a structured language such as COBOL.

It is therefore necessary to first understand the underlying concepts before commencing with an object-oriented way of thinking and working. Then, we can apply these object-oriented concepts to perform object-oriented analysis, design and realization of information systems.

1.3.1   Route map for the KISS method

The KISS method for object orientation is described in the book in an incremental way. Later parts of the book are built upon parts that are discussed in earlier chapters. Very often the best way to learn the concepts of the KISS method is to reread earlier chapters, when missing links are picked up from the text.

The KISS method of designing information is composed of three main building blocks. Each takes into consideration the viewpoint of:

- The organization;
- The information architecture;
- The information system.

All three are strongly related to each other and cannot be seen separately.

The *information quadrant* is a technique that is used for relating the organizational functions, objects, actions and employees or systems to each other. Based upon the initial relations, the management gets insight into the coherence between the related aspects and can order the chronology of the project.

The *subject-communication model* is used for getting insight into the structure, quantity and frequency of communication between individuals, departments and systems. The subject-communication model is the underlying technique for execution of a *work-flow analysis*, which results in a more optimal structure of the communication. This is placed first because in the KISS method we do not want to invest in building information systems for a communication problem, but to solve an existing problem.

The link in this book between the organizational viewpoint and the information architecture is the *grammatical analysis*. With the grammatical analysis of a textual description of the activities of the organization we determine the initial candidate objects, actions and subjects, along with a lot of other concepts. The grammatical analysis is essential for the KISS method and is used throughout all the modelling concepts. The premise is that for good communication between humans/systems we need the grammar of our own language.

The *information architecture* describes the main structure of the way in which objects in a problem environment are associated. The information architecture is described in visual representations of the grammar concepts of our natural language. The models of the information architecture are the *KISS model, object-interaction model* and *hierarchy model*. These three models validate and check each other in a formal way. The KISS model describes the life of an object at a generic level, called an object type. The object-interaction model describes the way in which independent KISS models interact. The hierarchy model describes the existence dependencies and inheritance between objects. All models can be written back into readable English so that the information architecture can be communicated to end users.

The *encapsulated characteristics* of the information architecture are described by the attribute model and action model. These models make use of the global structure defined by the previous models. The encapsulated characteristics fit into the already defined structures and validate previous models.

The *attribute model* describes the attribute types of the objects and actions based upon the principles of the measurement process. The measurement process is an important component of communication. Without measuring attribute values we will not recognize the characteristics of objects and actions in the real world.

The *action model* describes the way in which attribute types are changed by operations, the sequence of execution of operations and the conditions under which operations can be executed. The action model details the previously-defined actions in more detail.

The working *information system* is the implementation of the information architecture into a specific programming language, database management system and user interface. The implementation is done by so-called transformation rules. In general we have two distinct groups of transformation rules for the different environments: the relational and the object-oriented transformation.

The *relational transformation* is based upon implementing the relationship between objects of different records, tables or classes by a newly-introduced combining set, combination table or class association. In the relational transformation we thus will not get only one new implementation concept for an object type newly added to the information system. We will also get additional physical structures for the relationship. The relational transformation creates a high level of maintenance and instability.

The object-oriented transformation is based upon relating the objects by the static and dynamic interaction described by the object-interaction model. The addition of a new object-type results in the implementation environment of only one new record, table or class.

For the KISS model we specify how we apply different transformation rules for implementation of the *dynamics* of objects in both conventional and object-oriented languages and databases.

Finally the end user has to communicate with the information system. The interface between the objects in the information system and the end user is defined by *functions*. The function model therefore describes the communication sequence of the end user with the system.

The important aspect of functions is that the more knowledge about objects encapsulated in the information architecture, the less interesting and leaner the functions will become. The implemented information system develops more characteristics of knowledge bases and of artificial intelligence.

The function itself is always executed under the *responsibility* of a subject (this is a person or system). The function can thus be seen as encapsulated within the subjects that are already modelled in the subject-communication model. The function model describes the internal communication of the subjects whereas the subject-communication model describes the communication between subjects.

The communication between subjects is recorded on forms, disks, file transfer, images, sound, movie and/or photos. These message-types are automatically the input and output of the functions for which subjects are responsible, and about which subjects want to, or have to, communicate.

With the described models we have created a coherent information system for the support of the organizational activities. The communication process is described with the subject-communication model from an organizational viewpoint. When we take into consideration that different persons and systems (subjects) can be working at different locations, we have also defined, with the subject-communication model, a base upon which we can decide how to implement, for example, a centralized information processing architecture or a client/server architecture.

Every methodology is as good as the comprehension of the persons who have to use it. In order to improve the understanding of the KISS method we discuss the 'KISS DOMINO' game. With the KISS DOMINO game we make modelling itself into a communication process between analysts and end users, and vice versa. KISS DOMINO is also supported by real domino pieces with the KISS symbols on them.

The main phases and products that have to be delivered will be discussed in the chapter on system management. The emphasis on project management will be less than in conventional approaches. In contrast to conventional approaches the KISS method pays much attention to checking and validating the *quality* of the specifications and models.

The validation of the quality can be done automatically when using a proper object-oriented CASE tool. This is possible because of the very tight integration and formality of all the different models of the KISS method. From the models we can *generate* large parts of the final information system by applying the transformation rules.

The structure of the book is such that it can be used as a reference to system development. I have tried to avoid syntactical aspects of specific programming languages. The reason is that in my opinion it is important to understand the true concepts of object orientation before programming real object-oriented systems. When you understand object orientation you can even realize object-oriented information systems without needing to use an object-oriented programming language. This is in line with the saying that object orientation first has to settle between your ears before you will get it in your fingers.

1.3.2   The KISS concept of object orientation

Whenever we explain the principles of object orientation to non-computing people, they find them (more often than not) self-evident. This is because the basic principles of object orientation relate closely to the world of experience of the end user. However, a computer specialist with many years' experience in strongly procedure-oriented structured analysis and development methods will find object-oriented modelling and realization of independent objects during development of information systems to be a complete turn-around in his manner of thinking and working. The transition to this manner of thinking and working does not happen automatically. The KISS method provides the systems developer with a framework of ideas and modelling techniques that allow him to define an information architecture which in turn allows an object-oriented information system to be incrementally realized (Figure 1.2).

Rapid developments in the areas of hardware and software have provided a great stimulus for object orientation. These developments extended the initial limited possibilities and increased the complexity of systems. Conventional programming could not handle the complexity, which meant that solutions needed to be found for the increasing complexity of the management of software. Object-oriented software is inherently easier to manage because systems can be constructed of free-standing objects. The strong integration normally found in

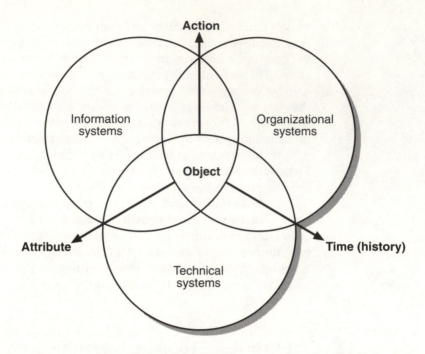

Figure 1.2 Integration of the technical, organization's procedural and information systems by means of objects.

conventional systems is found to be much reduced in object-oriented systems. It is for this reason that the object-oriented approach brings additional facilities closer to the end user, facilities that were previously not available with the procedural thought-boundaries of the 1960s.

New developments which are supported by object orientation are, for example, GUIs (graphical user interfaces) such as windows-type applications, CAD (Computer-Aided Design), multimedia systems that integrate data, sound, pictures and movies, and object-oriented programming languages and databases.

While new technical possibilities are being offered, we also see that a large number of questions crop up in the field of object orientation, which we had not previously seen. The increasing abilities of hardware, along with much reduced costs, lead to the situation whereby economic cost–benefit analyses increasingly point towards the use of more technology to support the end user in performing his function.

The logical consequence of this is that the extent and degree of integration of the information system will increase. This occurs together with the autonomous increase in abilities offered to the total organization by, for example, the standard management, network, database and application software. All these developments demand the use of better methods and techniques to manage the inherent complexity in a planned manner.

We can visualize the dimensions in which the complexity must be managed by allowing the three poles of change to interact with each other.

The common denominator of the interaction between the organization pole and its information system pole is the *action*. The performing of an action demands information, and the performing of an action generates information.

The interaction between the information system pole and the technique pole consists of the recording, processing and presenting of *attributes*, utilizing technical tools.

The interaction between the organization pole and the available technical tools consists of making agreements on how the technique is to be used and how it can support the organization in a procedural manner, in performing its activities. The result is visible in the *course of time* of the changes, where we speak of present, past and future.

The common denominator of the three dimensions, action, attribute and time, is the object. The object is important to the organization in that it records and inquires on attributes, it performs actions, and it explicitly or implicitly defines certain objectives and can find agreement on procedures specifying how objects may be altered, in time.

Using the object as the basis for management, we can make the information system pole, the organization pole and the technical system pole manageable. It is essential to have insight into the way changes in the various poles affect the total environment, in order to be able to find the optimal route for the organization to follow.

The continual downward trend of hardware costs and the increasing abilities offered have the effect of, for example, steadily reducing the technical restrictions facing the analyst and the programmer. Technical restrictions present in the 1960s (such as available memory capacity of maximum 2kB) have long since been surpassed. Programmers are no longer bound by a system-limited technique. The analyst and the programmer exist in an age where, technically, the possibilities are boundless. It is precisely these boundless possibilities which require us to make use of unambiguous concepts and methods of working when reaching agreement on how to utilize information technology in organizations.

In general we can declare that at present, technology is no longer a restricting factor. Areas of concern that exist now, when introducing information technology in a predictable manner, lie much more with being able to make information automation understandable and possible to be grasped within the organization itself. In this sense, the 'predictableness' concerns not only aspects of analysis, design, building and managing information systems, but the impact of information systems on the organizations themselves.

1.3.3   The KISS method of working

The KISS method of object orientation makes use of a method of working which can be described as 'out-of-the-middle'. This method does not supplement a 'top-down' or 'bottom-up' approach to the problem area such as is the case for structured and data-directed approaches. See Figure 1.3.

The reason for the out-of-the-middle approach is that modelling and understanding of things and events in the real world of nature take place by observation. After the phenomena have been observed we can decompose them or group them. The observation itself is a random starting point without the restraint that the description must be global, where this is possible.

To achieve harmony between the automated information system and the organization, we must ensure that the information system can be understood by its users. A method of work based on the description of *observation* of things, objects and events in a *natural language* easily allows the end user to verify the description. Additions to the original specifications allow the description of the objects to become more complete, over time. Independent objects can then be added incrementally to the information architecture.

Another important aspect of the addition of new specifications to those already existing is that the new specifications validate the existing specifications. In this way we have a very tight quality check on the specifications during the whole process. The result is that the end result

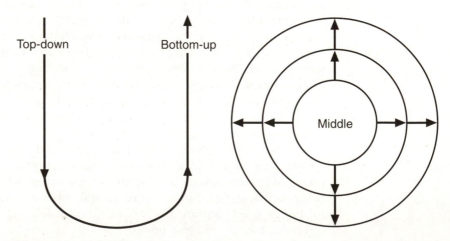

Figure 1.3   The difference between the top-down/bottom-up approaches and the KISS method.

has a high quality standard that is reached by implicit and automatic quality loops in the analysis and specification process.

The KISS method offers a method of working with a collection of techniques which predict how the content of the information automation will be filled in by the information architecture. The information architecture provides the foundation for the analysis, design, building and managing of information systems in relation to the organizational and technical systems.

Information systems set up with the KISS method therefore have a general structure consisting of autonomous objects, which, by performing actions, change the state of the object itself.

By encapsulating the details of its attributes and operations into its innermost layer, the object can conceal these from the outside world.

To be able to represent their internal state, objects make use of information or output functions, each of which shows a specific view of the object. Actions that change the state of an object are steered by input functions. In this manner we end up with a general structure of an information system consisting of three layers (Figure 1.4). Each layer communicates via messages with the adjacent layer. The outside layer, which communicates with the outside world, is the function layer.

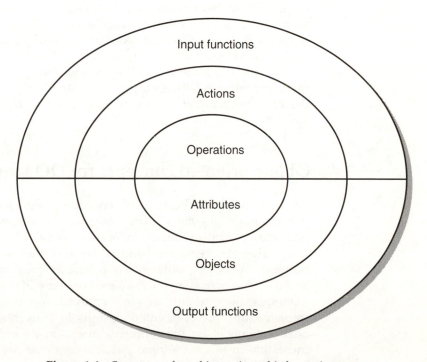

Figure 1.4   Structure of an object-oriented information system.

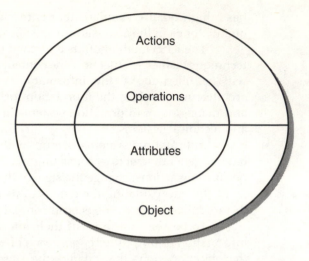

Figure 1.5   Encapsulation of attributes and operations.

The layer containing objects and actions is the structure layer. At this level we concretely define the information architecture. By encapsulating the attributes and operations in the core, we can direct our attention to the information architecture when making our model (Figure 1.5). This defines the main structures of the information automation, the contents of which are specified by the core.

At a later stage we add input and output functions to the information architecture. These input and output functions do not influence the structure, but they do define the desired content of the information system.

1.4   Object-oriented concepts for OO languages

At present, the collection of concepts used with object-oriented programming languages is increasing in size. We will discuss the most important concepts without elaborating on them.

These concepts are handled because they are often used when building systems with object-oriented programming languages and database management systems, but many of these concepts are not automatically present in conventional programming languages. Implementing object-oriented designs in conventional programming environments is, on the contrary, an option we often take. An implementation in a conventional environment does in fact demand extra facilities which then allow the benefits of the object-oriented design to be fully taken advantage of. For this, we create an extra implementation environment beside the conventional implementation environment, for objects, before we move on to object implementation.

Object-oriented programming languages contain a number of concepts which cause them to be given the title of object-oriented programming languages. Key words are:

- Modelling objects;
- Object instantiation and identification;
- Encapsulation;
- Communication between objects by use of messages;
- Inheritance of objects' attributes and operations;
- Implementation of objects in a class;
- Polymorphism.

The first basic premise of object orientation is that we view objects as independent things, and we implement them each with their own behaviour. The behaviour of objects is modelled by describing the changes that an object can undergo or cause. Each object has its own identity and can be uniquely identified by its characteristics.

The behaviour and attributes of objects are encapsulated so that the outside world cannot see the details of the objects, and to allow the main structures to be clearly recognizable.

Autonomous objects communicate with each other by sending messages (Figure 1.6). When receiving messages, objects know implicitly which behaviour to exhibit. This is encapsulated in the object in the form of the specification of operations.

Besides the feature that objects communicate with each other via messages, there is also a structural relationship between objects. The structural relationship between objects arises when, for example, we place certain characteristics in a generic object, and then allow them to be reused by other objects through inheritance. We speak of single inheritance when there is only one generic object, and of multiple inheritance when the attributes of two or more objects are reused. Not all object-oriented programming languages support multiple inheritance. The effect of inheritance is that we ultimately have less to program in comparison with conventional programming languages.

Objects are implemented in the implementation environment in a generic manner by the use of a class. A class is a generic implementation description of the attributes of a group of identical objects. The characteristics and behaviour of objects are described in a class, in a general manner. The concept of class is essential for the use of an object-oriented programming language. Specifically, objects are created for the class by instantiation.

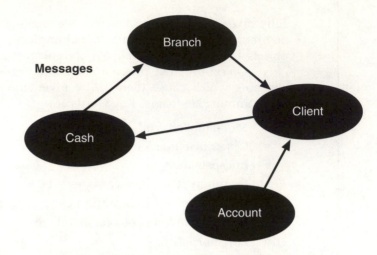

Figure 1.6 Communicating objects.

Finally we shall discuss polymorphism, the concept that shows that in a group of objects, each can react completely differently to one and the same message sent to the entire group.

1.5 KISS in relation to the evolutionary model of information automation

Not every organization experiences information automation problems to the degree described in the preceding paragraphs. The degree to which these problems are experienced is strongly dependent on the growth phase in which an organization finds itself. The extent to which the KISS method offers an immediate solution is therefore also dependent on the growth phase of the organization.

Richard Nolan was one of the first researchers to look at the development of information automation in organizations. He was able to relate the development of information automation to the costs of computing. The results of his first studies, at the end of the 1970s, were staggering in the sense that he discovered a definite law for the computing cost curve over time. One of the conclusions was that the computing costs followed a course directly related to the growth phase in which the organization found itself.

On the basis of his research Nolan (1979) defined six phases (Figure 1.7):

(1) Initiation;
(2) Dispersion;

(3) Management;

(4) Integration;

(5) Data management;

(6) Maturity.

In the *initiation phase* an organization begins to absorb computer technology. Employees with a feeling for technology start to utilize isolated computing tools.

In the next phase, a strong dispersion of applications takes place. The objective of this phase is to build and implement applications as rapidly as possible. The second phase is characterized by programmers who are oriented toward the end user.

In the third phase, the technically-oriented computing specialists reflect on the manner in which systems should be made and documented. In this phase, they gain insight to the fact that isolated applications built with 3GLs or 4GLs consist to a large degree of redundant data and programs. Besides this, it becomes apparent that applications often provide little support to the organization for making decisions spread over a number of information systems and functional areas.

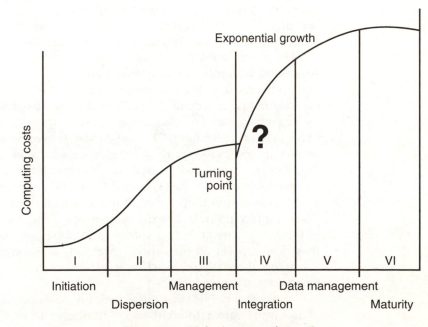

Figure 1.7   Nolan's stages of growth.

The solution to the problems of the first three growth phases can be found close at hand. Nolan indicates that we must first integrate existing applications. Subsequently we must organize the management of the data.

Finally we look at the phase in which, according to Nolan, the entire organization can be supported in a mature manner by automated tools.

Nolan noted that computing in the first three phases is strongly driven by the abilities of the machinery and the software. The computing employees perform their functions based on their technical background and experience. The implemented systems are built in relative isolation and are reminiscent of a group of islands. Sometimes this is accentuated by giving the island systems Greek-sounding names. The islands themselves are usually bound to the organizational structure, resulting in a large degree of instability during organizational changes. In this way, of course, an information system becomes highly dependent on the changes in the organization's structure.

Nolan understood that the entire organization is characterized in the last three phases by steady growth to a maturity of automation and provision of information. By achieving a mature provision of information, the end users, in Nolan's view, are fully supported by the systems they need to carry out their work.

According to Nolan, an organization must progress through each and every phase. One of the striking points Nolan made was that an enormous conversion process is needed to move from the management phase (phase 3) to the integration phase (phase 4).

Growth towards a situation whereby the organization is supported with integrated information systems is, in fact, the cause of big problems. The biggest problem is that integration of systems is no longer just a technical problem, but is also influenced strongly by organizational aspects. These aspects have to do with reaching agreement on procedures. The standardization of data definitions is the subject of these agreement-reaching processes. In this integration phase, therefore, we can no longer separate the organizational aspects from the computerization. We must combine them into a whole.

This means that the methods and techniques of the first three phases, directed firmly towards systems modelling and the application of technology, are no longer sufficient for the integration phase because they do not cover all the aspects. Methods and techniques needed for the integration phase must wholly reflect the organizational and technological aspects.

Another point is that the technically-oriented staff of the first three phases must learn a different way of thinking and working in order to be effective in the integration and data-management phases. The motivation of employees must also take place in a different way. The reward system used in the dispersion phase, the rapid delivery of applications, becomes in the integration and data management phases entirely counter-productive. In the integration phase, one of the main activities must be to reduce redundancy between systems, and in the data management phase rewards must be given for the reuse of specifications and program source code.

The need to integrate the autonomous departmental systems comes about at the very moment that people in organizations realize that there is great redundancy of data between the systems, because the data is stored in different independent island systems. This causes a problem with maintaining consistency between the various island systems.

From the research carried out by Nolan in the 1970s, it became clear that computing costs grow exponentially from the moment that an organization transfers from island systems to integration. The escalation of costs takes place over the entire range of hardware, software, and maintenance, as well as for the organization itself. An escalation with a factor of five to ten is more the rule here than the exception.

The cause of the exponential escalation of costs lies with the exponential growth of complexity of the total information automation. At a particular moment, everything in the system is linked up, with much organizational effort needed to manage the whole affair. This exponential growth of costs is, for most organizations, an unscalable barrier to achieving integrated information systems, if only because the existing computing budget does not allow for further escalation of costs. One logical consequence of this is that only organizations making extremely high profits can take the exceptional excursions into the area of integration of island systems. Organizations that cannot permit this for economic reasons are almost doomed to continue with island systems.

1.5.1   Cause of the complexity

In the period of Richard Nolan's research – at the end of the 1970s – many organizations used a few structured methods for systems development which today we label as conventional. These methods are functional decomposition, data-flow diagramming, logical data modelling and Bachman models, among others.

The main characteristic of these methods is that they model the data and the processes separately, and frequently are based on the technical restrictions of a specific implementation environment. In this form, these systems development methods are relatively quickly adopted by technical specialists who dominate the first three phases of the Nolan growth curve.

The result of modelling information systems in a conventional manner is that the way of working leads automatically to an exponential growth in complexity with an increase in the size of the information system.

The exponential increase in complexity occurs when we join the data structures to the function structures at a technical specification and implementation level (Figure 1.8). This conforms to the effect measured by Richard Nolan (1974) at the transition from the management phase to the integration phase. The explanation for this is given by the use of a calculation example. The calculation uses a fictitious complexity factor related to the number of data and function structures in the system (Table 1.1). When we speak of small island systems, we have a trifling number of data and function structures. This is shown in the calculation: $3 \times 3 = 9$. If an organization has a large number of island systems with a complexity factor of 9 the overall complexity within the organization does not increase – it just has a lot of complexity of systems.

When we perform the calculation for a medium-sized system with 30×30 structures, we end up with a complexity factor of 900. This is 100 times the island administrations, in theory!

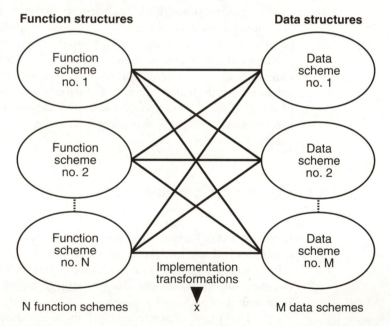

Figure 1.8   The exponential growth of complexity using conventional methods.

Table 1.1   Complexity factors using conventional methods.

System size	No. of data structures	No. of function structures	Complexity factor
Small system	3	3	9
Medium system	30	30	900
Large system	300	300	90000

The technical specialists have naturally found solutions whereby a high complexity factor can be prevented. A limited summary of these is:

(1) An easy way of keeping the complexity factor under control is to build information systems with a limited number of data structures. The result is generally that the information system produced does not have a normalized data structure. This leads automatically to an unnecessary and increasing use of storage space, whereby additional storage space is required for the extra periodic updates. Combined, this means that extra overhead must be built in for the management of correct data.

(2) A second way to manage the complexity of an information system is to purposefully set up small island systems. The price that must be paid for this is the duplication of data and function structures between the various information systems. In time, we find we cannot fully support the organization in its use of data with these island systems. This can lead very quickly to organizational problems.

1.5.2   Object modelling: the solution!

One of the main characteristics of object orientation is that data and function structures are no longer modelled discretely, but are seen as a whole. The big difference from conventional methods for systems development is that the complexity is not defined by the relationships between the function and data structures, but that the whole is encapsulated in the object model of an autonomous object. By definition, the number of components of an object is far fewer than the number of structure elements of a conventional system, making the complexity of the autonomous object models easier to manage.

A calculation of the complexity factor for a direct implementation of the object models in an object-oriented programming language produces Table 1.2.

Table 1.2   Complexity factor using object-oriented implementation.

Size	No. of objects	Complexity factor
Small	3	3
Medium	30	30
Large	300	300

The dramatic reduction in complexity obtainable with object models is lost when the object models are not implemented in an object-oriented target environment. Reasons for implementing design objects in a conventional environment may be, for example, that the hardware is not powerful enough, that too much memory is required, that the investment needed is too big, that current investments are not yet written off. In these cases, the choice must be made to implement the system in a conventional target environment using, for example, 3GLs and network or relational database management systems.

The differentiating characteristic of the KISS method for object orientation is that it can be used to create an information architecture which is independent of the specific target environment. A basic premise of the KISS method is that the specifications are created in a manner such that we can translate them using transformation rules into an information system for an arbitrary target environment.

In the KISS method we differentiate between two levels:

(1)   Information architecture;
(2)   Information system.

We model objects at the level of the information architecture. An object must be seen as an autonomous thing or concept in the real world of the end user, which can interact with other objects. An object in the KISS method undergoes changes through actions.

The object models provide the information architecture with the material for the conceptual level. The object models describe the static as well as the dynamic aspects of an information system independent of a specific database or programming language.

With the KISS method we can reduce not only the complexity of the design, implementation and maintenance of object-oriented information systems, but also the complexity of information systems implemented in a conventional environment.

The information system that results from transforming the information architecture to a conventional environment will consist of transformed object models. The objects described in the information architecture will, in a conventional implementation, be implemented partly as procedural code and partly as a database. The information system can be expanded incrementally by the addition of newly-transformed object models. The KISS method in practice also allows for incremental system development.

The complexity factor of an object-oriented design, produced by the KISS method, increases in proportion as the size of the information system increases. A conventional implementation requires, in actuality, twice as many transformations as an object-oriented implementation because we must implement both the data and the function structures (Table 1.3).

Table 1.3   Complexity factors for OO architecture applied to a conventional environment.

System size	No. of data structures	No. of function structures	Complexity factor
Small	3	3	6
Medium	30	30	60
Large	300	300	600

In Table 1.2, we see that compared to Table 1.1 there is an extreme reduction of the complexity factor for large-scale systems. The information systems produced from an information architecture are quicker to specify and quicker to implement. The result of the reduction in complexity is that the total management of information systems is substantially simplified (Figure 1.9).

In addition to better controllability, the introduction of an information architecture with object models provides a guideline for achieving, in a series of steps, a completely integrated information system.

The effect of utilizing an object-oriented information architecture is the defeat of the Nolan growth curve and therefore the gain of a competitive advantage over the organization using conventional methods of system integration. System integration can be realized in an easier way with the help of object orientation.

The maintenance backlog for information systems can be reduced in steps by reducing the complexity of these information systems. This can be done by specifying parts of the existing information system at the level of the information architecture, which are then transformed to the system environment.

Through the utilization of an object-oriented information architecture the integration of autonomous departmental systems comes within the financial grasp of a much greater number of organizations (Figure 1.10). This achievement is then no longer the exclusive right of organizations with copious amounts of money to spend on computing. Also a client/

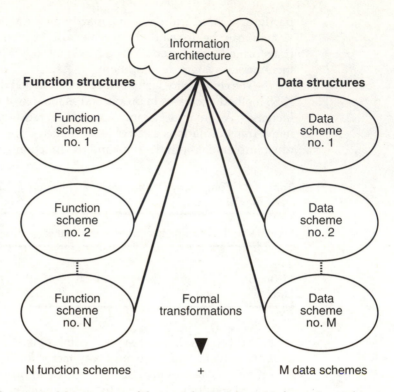

Figure 1.9   Management of the complexity using an information architecture.

server implementation can be engineered better and more easily by using object orientation as the way to design and build information systems.

1.5.3   Repository management systems

Richard Nolan (1979) writes that organizations, when they have been through the integration of the autonomous departmental systems phase, must then spend some time thinking about the management of data.

In the recent past, larger organizations in particular have been expending great financial and organizational effort to achieve control over their definitions of data. The result is, in general, disappointing. The management of data gets no further than, most of the time, the administration and documenting of new data definitions at the time of delivery of information systems. Reuse of data definitions is not achieved; neither is a reduction of concealed redundancy.

The biggest problem facing the data administrator is (most often) the lack of an organizational framework in which the definition,

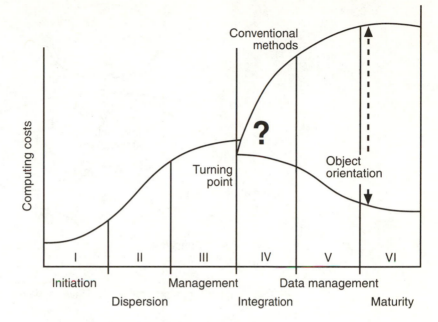

Figure 1.10   Reduction of costs caused by object orientation.

specification and control of data elements for objects becomes a natural activity. A second problem is that the data have no real meaning when the object structures in which they are used are unknown.

The solution for data management is to move to 'object management' for the information architecture. Adding to, changing and removing objects or parts of objects can then be fitted into the framework of the information architecture more easily. The reuse of existing objects can also be demonstrated at an early stage.

The framework for the total control of an object-oriented information system can be set up by a so-called repository management system, in which all aspects of an information system can be managed. A repository management system thus has three principles (Figure 1.11):

(1) Management of the information architecture based on object models defined without a single technical restriction;

(2) Management of the implemented information system using the transformation rules, allowing for the technical restrictions of the implementation environment;

(3) Management of the impact of organizational changes on the information system viewed from the information architecture with object models.

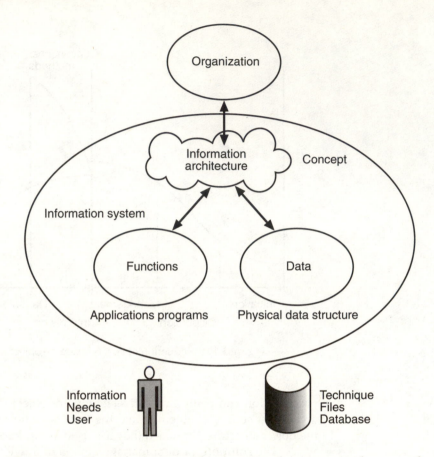

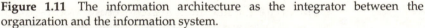

Figure 1.11 The information architecture as the integrator between the organization and the information system.

A controllable repository management system is obtained when we use the object models of the information architecture as a basis for the repository management system.

The information architecture with its object models provides the repository management system with an understandable description of the work procedures of an organization together with their interrelationships. The personal skills needed to set up an information architecture without technical restrictions are business oriented and no longer technically oriented. This means that we require other skills in the integration and data management phases than were required in the first three phases of the Nolan growth curve. Introducing a different way of thinking and working is a conversion process which must take place with the necessary support. The conversion must go further than simply following a training course in another method. This conversion will have to take place together with correct steering and management from the organization. Only then can we reap the rewards to be gained from the use of this technique.

1.5.4 Communication with end users

The maturity phase defined by Nolan is achieved when the structure as well as the content of the information system is so simple that the end user can understand them quickly. There must be no cause to train the end user to the level of an experienced COBOL or SQL programmer. To be able to do this, we must present the meaning and the structure of the information system to the end user in an understandable manner. The information architecture plays an important role here.

The condition that an information architecture must meet in order to be understood by the organization is that the relevant meaning of the objects and events of reality must be represented in the words and ideas of the employees. The importance of the information architecture is that its content is easily understood by the employees. The information architecture must be understood quickly, and be susceptible to only one explanation; this is, among other things, necessary for the validation of the object models during the analysis, design and building of systems.

According to Nolan, the organization becomes integrally supported by its information automation during the maturity phase. It is precisely in this phase that it becomes important for the organization's employees to learn, in a simple and understandable manner, what the structure of the information system is.

The role of the computing department will change to one of a service organization enabling the end users to send information to the system, to extract information from the system and even to create their own functions.

The description of the objects in the information architecture must be meaningful. End users must be able to read the information architecture as if the sentences were plain English with subjects, verbs, prepositions, direct objects, indirect objects, adjectives and so forth.

In this manner, we can learn about the information system in the grammar of our spoken language, instead of that of the database or programming language, which enforces a very limited grammar upon us. The use of the rules provided by the grammar of our natural language leads to a new grammatical direction within systems development, which is expected to make greater strides than those made by the relational approach and even those made by the object-oriented (class) approach.

1.6   Summary

In this chapter we have shown that information automation can no longer be seen from an isolated technical viewpoint. Changes in the organization and information requirements make it necessary for information automation to be approached in a more integrated way.

New object-oriented methods must integrate the three poles of change in such a way that they provide real support for the management of the information automation.

The methods of the past 25 years are strongly related to the developments in technological innovations of each specific period. In this way, the structured approach is related to the future of structured programming languages, the data-directed approach is related to the future of database management systems, and the event-driven approach is related to the rise of 4GL systems. This is also true for a number of object-oriented methods which are restricted by the class and inheritance facilities of OO programming languages.

The aim of the KISS method for object orientation is to define a completely conceptual model of real world problems, independently of the technical abilities of any implementation environment. The basic premise is that the description takes place based on natural language grammar, using an approach which is out-of-the-middle.

The three dimensions of an object are 'action', 'attribute' and 'time'. We describe an object using these three dimensions and thereby obtain the basis for the management of information provision.

An object-oriented information system is built up in three layers. The outside layer is the 'function layer', containing input and output-functions. The middle layer is the 'structure layer', containing actions and objects. The inside layer is the 'core' and contains attributes and operations.

Making use of Nolan's evolution model, we indicated that continuing in the direction of the technology itself does not provide the solution for current information automation problems. If we continue in this direction with conventional methods, we will end up with an exponential growth in complexity and a rapid increase in costs.

The solution to this problem must be found in the creation of an information architecture with no technical restrictions built into the model. Conventional methods of systems development are not appropriate because they use the modelling of the technical restrictions as a starting point.

A second condition for the information architecture is that it is implemented using transformation rules, in an arbitrary programming language and/or database, allowing for the technical restrictions of the language/database.

With this information architecture we can now lay the basis for the management of changes in the organization, as well as the technology and information requirements. The information architecture will form the basis for communication between end users, information system and the computing department.

1.7   Questions

(1)   Discuss why the supply of information cannot be seen as an independent discipline isolated from the organization.

(2)   What kind of system development methodologies can be recognized? Describe their characteristics.

(3)   What is meant by 'class-oriented methods'? What is the distinguishing factor of the KISS method?

(4)   Describe how the supply of information becomes manageable with KISS object orientation.

(5)   What are the main object-oriented concepts of most languages?

(6)   The stages of growth as described by Nolan were the result of empirical studies at the end of the 1970s. Discuss in what way new approaches to software development will alter the results found. Describe the influence of new technologies on end users, software developers, hardware, application software, software development and finance.

(7)   What is the role of the information architecture for the quality, comprehension and maintenance of information systems?

2 Information management

2.1 Introduction

Our ability to control the provision of information in an organization improves as we make the relationships between the organization, the technique, and the information requirements easier for the management to understand. The presentation technique we use for information management is the information quadrant. This presents the relationships between the components of the organization's procedural system, that is, the organization's structures and procedures, and the techniques and tools to be used, denoted as the information system.

Before we start work on a computing project for an entire organization or part of it, it is useful to gain a good insight into (that part of) the organization and the scope of the information system. To define the boundaries of the project, we can indicate in the information quadrant the way in which the information system and the organization's procedural system are related to each other. In the information quadrant we show, globally, how the primary activities are controlled in an organization. In this chapter we also go into detail about how the information quadrant provides an insight into the relationship between the organization's procedural system and the information system, together with the controlling of the organization.

2.2 Information quadrant

The two related parts of an information quadrant are the organization's procedural system and the information system. Both parts of the information quadrant are inseparably bound to each other and influence each other to a high degree. As a result of this, we need to establish how changes in the organization's procedural system influence the information system and vice versa. The details of the organization's procedural system and the information system will now be dealt with, in depth.

The *organization's procedural system* consists of all the departments, employees, organizational functions, tasks, responsibilities and authorities together with the associated procedures and agreements. An organization's procedural system is set up to enable tasks to be performed to fulfil the organization's one or more goals. The goals themselves can differ greatly between organizations. Organizations which aim to make a profit have different goals from non-profit making organizations and societies. Despite this, in order to function correctly, each organization must have a foundation in the form of an information system to adequately provide information to support the organization and its employees.

An information system is an integral part of the organization and, from this standpoint, cannot, therefore, be implemented as something distinct from the organization.

The *information system* consists of the tools and techniques currently used by the organization to reach its goals. The information system supports the organization in carrying out its operational, tactical and strategic tasks. Strictly speaking, a computer standing idle in an air-conditioned space is not an information system or part of one. It is in fact not used by the organization. The computer is, in this case, only a piece of unused technology.

If we look back in history, we see that the first information systems existed in cultures where a definite form of task division had appeared. And for this, they needed a correct registration to enable activities to be handed over to others and to allocate responsibility for them. They needed to register, for example, how much grain was produced by the land, and how much had to be paid to the feudal lord. Administration was also done in situations where the people could not memorize all the information: this led to information systems being set up which recorded and stored data.

The oldest information systems stem from the time of Babylon. The clay tablets with their cuneiform characters were revolutionary for their time and also extremely effective: their users could maintain a precise administration and consult it over a long period of time to find out the quantities, the responsibilities, the time and the quality of delivered, produced, and stored goods. The disadvantage of clay tablets as a practical method was that their volume and cumbrousness made them difficult to use. In the course of the centuries the clay tablet was replaced as a carrier of information by handier carriers such as parchment and papyrus.

In these modern times we also make use of information carriers. We can think, for example, of synthetic CDs on to which information is placed with small dots that can only be read and interpreted by laser beams, or of the magnetic ferrous crystals on plastic tapes, hard disks, diskettes, cards and suchlike, that can only be read and written by special magnetic read/write heads, or of silicon memory chips, and not least, the many sorts of paper on to which we record information using techniques such as printing, writing, punching and copying.

Similarities that exist between the clay tablets in the time of Hammurabi (18th century before the modern era) and the hard disks of modern computer systems are that:

(1) There is always a personal or organizational goal for which we wish to record data. If, at a point in time, the goals or parts of the goals are cancelled, then we see as a consequence that the information systems become an issue to be looked at;

(2) Agreements and conventions are established in order to present in a comprehensible way the things we observe in the real world, and which we find sufficiently relevant to want to record. It is precisely these things and phenomena, in reality, that we try so hard to represent and record in an information system so that we have, for the future, an exact and accurate image of what has taken place in the past;

(3) Agreements on the interpretation of the symbols used. It is only in combination with the grammar of the cuneiform language and its associated vocabulary that we can read and write in cuneiform in a meaningful way. This also applies to reading the inscriptions on a CD, and to characters used in a book.

Object orientation offers a good base for making agreements, because the things and phenomena of the real world form the basis for agreements in object-oriented information systems. The things and phenomena of the real world are thus modelled as 'objects' and 'actions'. The background for this is that objects and actions in the real world are independent of a specific language. The objects represent the status of things in the real world and the actions describe how the objects experience changes.

To be able to draw up an information quadrant we must therefore make an inventory of the objects and actions in the real world. The objects and phenomena are described as much as possible in a natural language independent of a specific programming language. In this way our ability to understand and our insight into information management are improved.

The objects implemented in an information system must represent the actions the organization performs and observes on the objects as faithfully as possible. As the disparity between the objects of the real world and the objects of the information system increases, so the reliability of the data in the information system decreases. To be able to support the organization in its decision-making, the information systems must supply up-to-date information on the status of the objects inside the information system itself. Each information system, then, has output, from which the organization can obtain information for controlling its business processes. The information output eventually takes on a form able to be interpreted by people, such as screens, graphs, reports, letters, listings, images, or sound. The information system thus becomes a technique used by an organization's employees as a support for their short- and long-term decisions.

An information quadrant can be created by relating four relevant areas of interest from the real world to each other:

- *Controlling processes*. By this we mean all the management activities for the operational as well as the long-term decisions and deliberations;

- *Employees*. When we group the employees into their similar functions or departments, this is sufficient to include them in the information quadrant;

- *Actions*. The actions indicate the actual changes that the organization causes to happen to the objects it finds relevant;

- *Objects*.

We form four separate quadrants in the information quadrant which relate to these four areas of interest. The individual quadrants are respectively:

(1) Organizational control model;

(2) Input functions;

(3) Information architecture;

(4) Output functions.

The relationship between the quadrants is shown graphically in the information quadrant in the following way (Figure 2.1): elements of the real world are noted next to the arrows; and the elements representing the real world by means of an information and organization system are shown in the diamonds.

In an information quadrant we make a distinction between the changes carried out on objects by an organization, and the way in which the organization influences and controls the changes.

Globally viewed, the information quadrant makes a distinction between the controlling side and the operational side of an organization. The controlling part of the information quadrant is found at the top, while the operational part is found at the bottom. The operational part is further split into an organizational part and the information architecture.

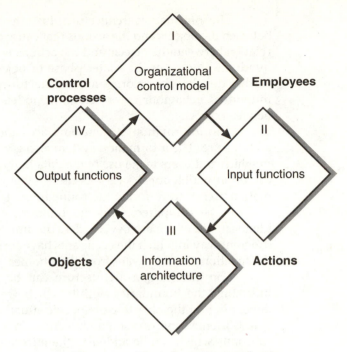

Figure 2.1 The information quadrant.

In the organizational part we allocate authority to employees for carrying out actions which change the status of objects. In an information system this translates to input functions enabling the changes to objects in the real world to be entered into the information system. To obtain information, the output functions of objects in the information architecture are queried.

2.3 Information architecture

An object-oriented information architecture is formed by the relationship between objects and actions. The objects reflect the situation of the relevant things in the real world, while the actions indicate the changes to the situation. Objects in an organization may be, for example 'product', 'customer' and 'person'. The employees of the organization must control the statuses of the objects in the real world from within the organization. In fact, the areas of activity that change the objects of an organization are the reasons for the organization's existence. Therefore the information system must provide the correct insight into the statuses of the objects.

The information architecture illustrates the structural relationship between the objects and the actions that cause changes to the objects. The relation between the objects and the actions is shown in the information quadrant by crosses. In a later phase of object-oriented modelling we further develop the information architecture into models showing the individual behaviour of objects and models showing the interaction between objects.

The information system embraces more than the information architecture. The information system also gives meaning to the manner in which end users make use of the data in the information system. This can differ widely for the various users, even when the very same information architecture forms the foundation. The principle lying behind this can be compared with the building of houses, architecturally identical, but which are nevertheless dissimilar owing to the completely different way in which the occupants have furnished them, according to the functionality they want from their home.

The information architecture can be viewed as a framework indicating the boundaries within which we can define the content, depending on the objective or specific situation. This will result, for an object-oriented information architecture, in a great diversity of output functions which can be added to the information architecture without affecting its structure.

The stability of the information architecture is derived from its reliance on the actual changes carried out by the organization on the objects relevant to it. The information architecture is based on two concrete things which are visible and highly stable, namely the objects and the actions on them. The relationship between objects and actions is shown in a simple way by describing the activities of an organization in English sentences. The starting point for the creation of an information quadrant is, therefore, a description in English of the business activities.

In summary, an information architecture provides insight into the way in which actions and objects are related to each other. The structure is expanded into a detailed information architecture in a further phase of the modelling process. The information quadrant provides a separation between the core of the information automation in the form of an information architecture, and the highly changeable controlling part of an organization.

We gain insight into the control of an organization by relating the business processes to the employees responsible for them. The result forms the basis for the more detailed controlling model of the organization. The input and output functions themselves form the interface between the information architecture on the one side, and the organizational control model with the employees on the other side.

2.4   The creation of an information quadrant

We tip the information quadrant to the right for practical reasons, to end up with a composite matrix (Figure 2.2). For a better comprehension, we will deal with each of the four quadrants in detail, step by step. Finally, we will look at the relationship between the individual quadrants.

Quadrant I:
the control model
— responsibility

The organizational control model indicates who in the organization is *responsible* for the management of one or more business processes. A business process is, for example, creditors' control, delivery of goods, production planning, purchasing, billing, or sales.

In general, we can speak of a regulating business process as a collection of activities which decomposes into a larger number of

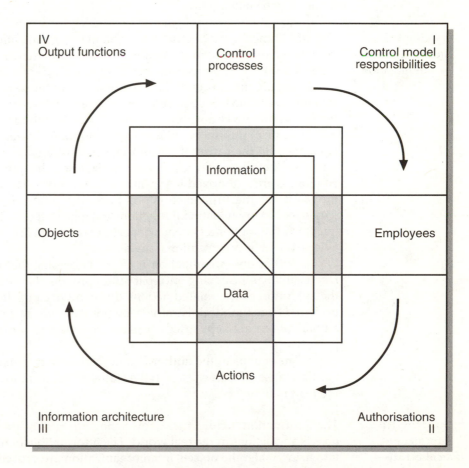

Figure 2.2   The information quadrant.

activities more elementary in nature. Besides this, the execution of a business process is highly variable and dependent on any number of things, for example, how the market requires goods to be delivered, how bills are to be paid, or what must be done when purchasers are given greater or lesser freedom in their choice of suppliers and products.

The organizational control model serves the purpose of managing the performance of operational tasks and of effectively adapting to the opportunities and possibilities presented by the environment. Each element of rigidity which enters the organizational control model leads to the bureaucratization of the organization and a reduction in competitive strength. The control model therefore requires maximum flexibility in the provision of information. The management thus requires an information system that provides insight, and can be adjusted rapidly, for and by the manager.

Quadrant II: the input function — authorization

The input function matrix indicates who in the organization is *authorized* to carry out defined actions. An authorization requires that the responsibility is taken by the employees who are in turn responsible for managing the regulating processes and defining the organization's objectives. An employee who is responsible for a reasonably large number of activities and is no longer able to carry out all the operational duties himself will, because of this, most often delegate part of his duties to operational employees. In their turn, these employees must answer to the manager for these operational duties. The authorization schematic shows which employees are authorized to perform which actions. The actions change the status of the organization's objects. We allow, in general, only employees or organizational functions to be included in the information quadrant, but for homogeneous departments we can include the name of a department or organizational division.

Within one organization it is not necessary that a person with responsibility for carrying out a particular process also be responsible for the execution of the related actions. In many organizations, it is often preferred from the administrative viewpoint that the responsibilities and authorizations are kept strictly separate, in order to prevent fraudulent practices.

The actions in the authorization schematic are elementary activities that cause a direct change in the status of one or more objects, at any moment in time.

Quadrant III: the information architecture — structure

The information architecture shows the *structural relationship* between objects and actions in the real world. The information architecture comes into being when the objects in an organization are caused to change by actions. The actions themselves happen at one point in time according to defined procedures and agreements, and cause change to one or more objects.

Owing to the interrelationship between various objects, the information architecture develops into a representation of the structural relationship between objects and actions. The relationship between the actions and the objects is shown in the information quadrant by a cross.

In quadrant III, there are two entry points we can use to model the information architecture in more detail. The entry point from the object shows in vertical columns by which actions an object can be changed, while the entry point from the action shows in horizontal rows which objects interact with a specific action.

By further modelling the objects and actions we eventually end up with an information architecture represented by KISS models and object-interaction models. At a later stage these models can be matched perfectly with the information quadrant, thereby allowing verification of the information quadrant. The quality of the information system will be increased in this way. Also, the information quadrant can continue to be used as an information management tool, during both the modelling process and the realization of the information system phase.

Quadrant IV: the output functions — information

For the management of business processes, we must have access to the correct *information* on the status of objects. The information on objects must be relevant and readily and easily accessible. The data with respect to objects are queried by using output functions, allowing the regulating processes to be carried out. We must view the output as a tool which enables us to inquire on the status of one or more objects, to compare them, to make calculations, to print them onto forms, present them graphically on a screen, and so forth.

Theoretically, there are endless possibilities for the manipulation of object data. The condition that must be met by the data itself is that it is correct and gives a just representation of the things and phenomena in the real world. The information architecture must therefore have a solid base, so that the correctness and integrity are not jeopardized at the moment when reports are produced. The integrity of the data is, in fact, controlled much more effectively at the time of data input.

2.4.1   Data and information

We make a distinction in the information quadrant between information and data. At the top of the information quadrant we place information because it is desirable that decisions are made based on information that is meaningful to the decision-maker. The data that is queried by the decision-maker has a specific information value and thus becomes information.

On the other side of the operational part of the information quadrant we place data, because here we are dealing with the registration and operational part where no decisions are made that might influence the manner in which the organization's activities will be performed.

It is not necessary that there be any informative value to operational employees at the time that data are input to the system. However, the syntax of the data must be correct. Also, the information architecture must always give a meaningful representation of the things that happen in the real world. This is a condition that must be met before information can be obtained and queried from the system in the correct manner.

2.4.2   Interrelationships between the quadrants

The relationship between the four quadrants is formed by the axis lying between employees, actions, objects and regulating processes.

The cooperating structures between employees with responsibilities and authorizations is generally given by an organizational schematic. Depending on the organizational form we speak of an hierarchical or a matrix structure. In an hierarchical organizational structure (Figure 2.3) we see that the responsibilities are taken at a higher level in the organizational structure than the authorizations, and that there is very little answering for responsibilities by employees to their direct manager. The direct manager himself may be supported by staff

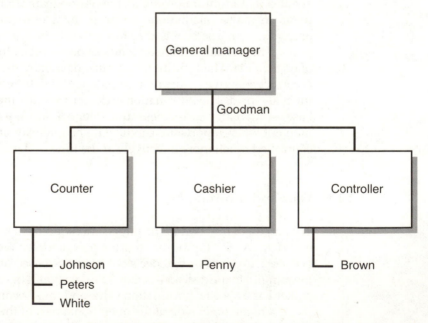

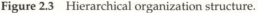

Figure 2.3   Hierarchical organization structure.

departments in organizations that have them, but these staff do not take over the responsibilities from the direct manager.

In a matrix organization the responsibilities are distributed among a larger number of managers. Each manager carries his share of responsibility for one or more areas of the operational activities. These areas should be clearly distinguished from each other in order to prevent conflict.

The distinction between the responsibilities of the different functionaries must be expressed in the organizational control model. Doing this should ensure that questions will be prompted about responsibilities for any similar business process. It is necessary to know when the responsibility rests with the same employee, and if the business processes need to be further split to indicate the sort of responsibility an employee has.

In the organizational control model, each business process in the organization must be assigned to at least one responsible employee. If a responsible employee cannot be named then we must check if the process in question is relevant for the organization. If it is not relevant, then it can be removed from the list of processes.

The way in which the organization's employees use the information system lies, in the information quadrant, on the control process and action axis. On the left-hand side of the axis we see the information system and on the right-hand side the organization's procedural system (Figure 2.4).

The controlling part at the top of the information quadrant indicates on which matters a manager requires information support from the information architecture. The support required can differ greatly from one manager to another because this varies by the way in which a particular manager works. One manager prefers, for example, in-depth statistical analyses and extensive numerical reports, while another manager wants his information presented mainly in the form of simple graphs and figures, and yet other managers only require details.

The strongly-individual and distinct preferences for information make it necessary for the dialogue between the information system and the manager to be as flexible, clear and comprehensible as possible.

The solution for flexibility, clarity and comprehension is often sought in the technique without considering the manager's problem area. Much-used techniques designed to improve the communication between the manager and the information system are, for example, fast-track training courses in SQL given to a manager, or the purchase of a new and better management tool requiring a number of specialists to be trained in its use. A common conclusion, after a short time of using SQL or the management tool, is that it takes too much effort to get information out of the system, or that the information is not completely reliable, causing it to be under-utilized in decision-making by the management.

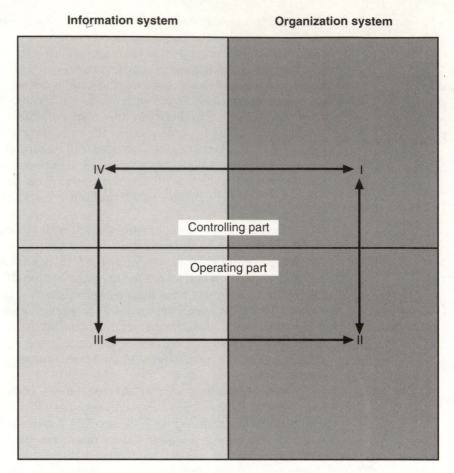

Figure 2.4   The interrelationship between the quadrants.

The underlying cause is not usually that the technical tools are no good, but more that the manager's problem area is not included in the basic structure of the information system. Information systems do not in general have access to the organizational plan and description of the structure in the form of a detailed information architecture on which basis the manager can ask specific questions, and whereby he can rely on the information system without fear of it producing nonsense results.

The condition under which the information architecture can support the information demands of a manager is that the information architecture must be drawn up based on the manager's area of interest, and not just from the viewpoint of the technical possibilities. The manager's area of interest includes, then, gaining and maintaining control of the information regarding, for example, the operational activities carried out by the employees. The basis for control of the stream of information lies in the information architecture, for which the operational activities in the form of actions are the most important building blocks.

An important premise for the information quadrant is that a manager can never get more information for the controlling of activities than the operational actions known to the organization in the information quadrant. Information on objects cannot be obtained from an information system when a number of relevant actions are missing from the information architecture. If a manager desires information from an information system about operational actions which are not included in the information architecture, then he will be disappointed because he cannot get this information. He has to wait until these actions are added to the information architecture. Similarly, an employee must be assigned authorization to perform the action and to input the action data. The effect of not adding the action to the information architecture is that the manager cannot control the organizational execution of the missing action.

In the information quadrant we can check whether or not we have specified sufficient actions to satisfy the information and control requirements of the manager. We do this by walking backwards through the information quadrant. We start with the specific manager and establish which control processes he is responsible for. For each process we define from which objects the necessary information will be requested to enable us to optimally perform a business process. Subsequently, we determine which actions change the object. For each of these actions we check whether this is sufficient to provide the manager with his information requirements. If there are not enough objects and actions defined, then the number of objects and actions must be increased.

If we take another step backwards in the information quadrant, we can see who is authorized to carry out the actions. When the authorized employees answer directly to the manager who has requested the information, the need for horizontal coordination between the managers in the organization is relatively small. When the operational employees also report to another manager, the need for horizontal coordination between managers grows. The coordination of the activities between the various managers leads to an increase in the demand for a substantial provision of information. This then demands a far-reaching standardization of actions. In fact, a correct forming of ideas by responsible managers can only be gained when clarity exists between the actions carried out and their effects.

In summary, this means that the actions which change objects provide the basis upon which managers in an organization can manage and with which information can be recorded in an information system. The actions and objects are modelled in a structure, which becomes the information architecture.

The information quadrant shows, globally, the relation between the information architecture, the information system and the method of working of the organization's procedural system. We can apply the information quadrant in a number of situations such as defining the boundaries of projects with their specific objectives, planning the setting up and filling in of an information architecture, controlling a project to structure an organization's procedural system, and so forth. An information quadrant is helpful in providing an overview of the internal relationship between the parts of the organization's procedural system and those of the information system.

2.5   Example of an information quadrant

Using a simple banking example we explain how an information quadrant is created. The information quadrant uses, as a starting point, a brief textual description of the processes and actions of a bank.

Bank example   The example describes a small bank with a number of branches including the following processes: client recruitment, relations management, cash management, credit control and business planning. The business processes are carried out in the bank within four functions. They are respectively: general manager, controller, cashier and counter assistant.

The general manager of the bank is personally responsible for the business plan. In addition, he takes care of the management of relations with larger clients and personally recruits those individuals and businesses with large amounts of capital. The registration and management of relations with the remaining clients is left to the counter assistants.

The controller is responsible for the financial part of the business plan. He also controls all the credit and the level of cash. The operational control of the cash is left to the cashier. The controller regularly counts the cash in the branches to check that no mistakes have been made. When a branch requires more cash, he arranges this.

The cashier also counts his branch's cash every day. He takes care of the financial processing of clients' cash deposits and withdrawals, while the counter assistants take care of the administrative processing of clients' deposits and withdrawals. In addition, they cater for the registration of clients with the branch, the cancelling of registrations and also the opening and closing of clients' accounts.

The general manager of the bank has no operational tasks. When creating the business plan he assesses the progress of all the branch activities of the preceding five years. He devises the financial part of the business plan together with the controller. Using the general picture of the progress of activities of specific groups of clients, he selects candidate groups who are to be catered for more intensively. For the rest of the clients, he defines the guidelines to be followed by the counter assistants when registering new clients.

Relations management is based on the total picture of all the accounts a client has at all branches. Priorities and points to note are discussed monthly with the controller, who indicates from his credit-control viewpoint which items in the relation file are noteworthy for the general manager.

The counter assistants are periodically given renewed guidelines for their dealings with clients. The information needed by the counter assistant is accessible per client by account for that branch.

The controlling of the cash is done by the cashier who maintains a total overview of the adding-machine tapes and of all cash deposited and withdrawn.

2.6   Summary

The relationship between the organization's procedural system and the information system is represented in an information quadrant (Figure 2.5). The information quadrant gives the information management insight into the mutual influences of the organization's procedural system and the information system, in a simple manner.

The four areas of interest of the information quadrant are:

(1) Controlling processes;
(2) Employees;
(3) Actions;
(4) Objects.

The four resulting quadrants are respectively:

(1) Organizational control model;
(2) Input functions;
(3) Information architecture;
(4) Output functions.

The four quadrants of the information quadrant show the distinction between the controlling part, which is highly variable in nature, and the information architecture in the operational part, which is extremely

Branch	Client	Account	Cash drawer	Processes / Objects / Employees / Actions	General manager	Cashier	Counter assistant	Controller
x	x			Client recruitment	x		x	
x	x	x		Relation management	x		x	
			x	Cash management		x		x
	x	x		Credit control				x
x				Business planning	x			x
x	x			To register			x	
x	x	x		To open			x	
x	x	x	x	To deposit		x	x	
x	x	x	x	To withdraw		x	x	
x			x	To install				x
x			x	To count		x		x
x	x	x		To close			x	
x	x			To de-register			x	

Figure 2.5   The information quadrant for a bank.

stable. The distinction between the regulating and operational parts is synchronous with the distinction between information and data.

- The controlling model covers the responsibilities of the employees of an organization.
- The input functions cover the authorizations of the employees in an organization.
- The information architecture defines the structural relationship of the information system of an organization.
- The output function caters for the information requirements of an organization.

2.7   Questions

(1)   What are the organization system and the information system? Give examples for both kinds of system.

(2)   What are the control system and the executing system? Give examples for both kinds of system.

(3)   Discuss in what ways the stability of information systems is increased by defining its structure upon objects. Make a comparison with the top-down approaches that start with functional decomposition based upon functions of the organizational system.

(4)   Describe the elements of the information quadrant and discuss in what way it can be used as tool for information management.

(5)   Discuss the difference between authorization and responsibility in relation to the distinction between action and function.

3 The KISS method for object orientation

3.1 Introduction

In the KISS method for object orientation we assume that the provision of information serves the purpose of directing the activities of an organization and that the user of the information system completely understands the system.

The relationship between the building blocks of the controlling and operational systems is modelled in the KISS method by the 'KISS paradigm'. The definitions of the building blocks of the KISS paradigm are discussed informally in this chapter, by indicating how the objects themselves possess regulating attributes to a greater or lesser degree.

With the 'communication paradigm' we show what the general principles of communication are. We illustrate the general principles of communication among objects themselves and between objects and the eventual users.

Using the 'subject-communication model' we discuss how we can gain insight into the current IST-situation (Germanistic for the existing IS-situation) of the communication pattern of an organization. We expound on how we can specify a desired SOLL-situation (Germanistic for HAS-TO-BE-situation) using a work-flow analysis. The SOLL-situation functions as the basis for the content of the information system and gives direction to Business Process Redesign.

3.2 Starting points of the KISS method

The KISS method defines the boundaries for the description and modelling of objects and events in the real world. The description serves a second purpose as the basis for the realization and management of the information system and the organization's procedural system.

The two basic premises of the KISS method for modelling the real world are the KISS paradigm and the communication paradigm.

3.2.1   The KISS paradigm: information for the controlling of activities

The first premise of the KISS method is that the provision of information supports the *controlling* of the organizational activities, now and in the future. The idea of controlling must be interpreted in a broad sense because it refers to the operational as well as the more tactical and strategic tasks.

The administration of data without any controlling objective motivates us, according to this first premise, to review the administration's purpose. When the administration has no single purpose then we can decide to do away with the administration.

3.2.2   The communication paradigm: language of the user

The second premise of the KISS method for object orientation is that system specifications and the functionality of the resulting information system must be completely *understandable* to, and able to be *validated* by, the user. We also apply this requirement to the information architecture and the information system, such that both must be presented to the end user in a simple fashion using our daily *spoken and written language*.

The reasons for making use of the daily spoken and written language are:

- Everybody has grasped the spoken and written language at a young age and is trained in its use.

- We use the spoken and written language daily to communicate with each other. A good understanding of the workings of the communication process between people is therefore one of the fundamentals of the KISS method.

- The extent to which the end user is supported by an information system is determined by the extent to which the information system is understood by the end user.

The KISS method builds a direct rapport with the end user by using the vocabulary and grammar rules of our language throughout the entire range of specifying, building and maintaining information systems. And where necessary the grammar rules of our language are further strengthened to become more precise and formal than we ourselves are in our communication with each other.

3.3   The KISS paradigm

In the information quadrant we see a difference between the controlling and the operational system. The controlling system is responsible for the controlling of activities which are conducted by the operational system. The controlling and the operational parts of an organization can be recognized in the information quadrant respectively as the highest and lowest quadrants. The communication takes place via input and output functions. See Figure 3.1.

The controlling system initiates and controls the actions an organization carries out. It includes all of the management processes and functions such as the defining of goals, the setting of norms, the requesting of information, the provision of information and the taking of decisions. In addition, the processes and functions that activate other functions are also included as part of the controlling system.

As a link between the controlling and operational systems we steer the actions by the use of input functions. The input functions are given the values of the action parameters for the execution of an action.

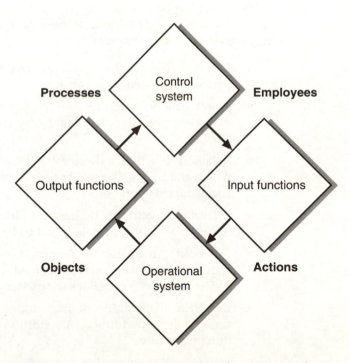

Figure 3.1   The control model in the information quadrant.

It is possible for the input to be provided by the output part of another controlling system that exists outside of the organization itself. The input function then becomes the interface between our own information system and the controlling system outside the organization. The communication between the information systems is realized with messages that can be forms, disks, tapes and such like.

The output functions also form a link between the operational system and the controlling system. Using the output functions we can produce reports of the objects and their values. They allow the encapsulated attributes of the objects to be seen by the controlling system. If the controlling system is intended for one or more end users then the information produced by the output function must be presented in a form that can be read and interpreted by the end user.

The KISS paradigm is the presentation method which forms the foundation of the collection of theories, standards and methods of working of the KISS method.

The relationships between the various parts of the KISS paradigm are represented diagrammatically in a model. The model of the KISS paradigm (Figure 3.2) globally shows how the functions, objects, actions, attributes, inspections, messages, operations, conditions and triggers are related to each other.

The informal definitions of these components, which are covered in more detail in later chapters, are:

- *Function.* The function controls, manages and coordinates the performing of actions on objects.

- *Object.* The object represents the status of a real or conceptual subject or phenomena in reality, by recording the values of the attributes of objects.

- *Action.* The action indicates the manner in which, and under which conditions, the attributes of an object can be changed by encapsulated operations.

- *Attribute.* An attribute defines the features of an object or action. An attribute is encapsulated by the object or action.

- *Operation.* An operation defines how a specific object can be changed when an action is performed. The association between an action and an object defines the existence of operations.

- *Condition.* A condition defines under which circumstances the action may be performed. A condition can have either a static or dynamic nature.

- *Inspection.* With inspections a function can query the attributes of one or more objects.

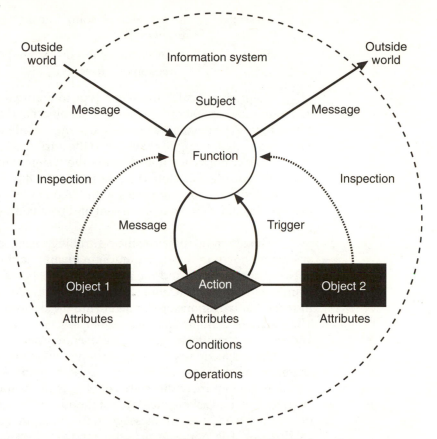

Figure 3.2   The KISS paradigm for object orientation.

Message. A message is a collection of the values of attributes that is sent and must be processed by the receiver.

Trigger. A trigger is a message that is sent from an action to a function. A function can steer other functions or actions with a trigger, if desired. During the execution of an action, certain attributes of an object can cause the trigger to be activated.

The more formal notation conventions for the KISS paradigm are:

Function:	circle
Object type:	rectangle
Action type:	diamond
Operation:	line joining an action type and an object type
Inspection:	arrow with a dotted line in the direction of the inquiring function

Message: arrow with a solid line in the direction of the
                 receiver

Trigger: arrow with a solid line from the action type in the
                 direction of a function

Diagrammatically, the action type in Figure 3.2 indicates that the
conditions and operations are defined per object and encapsulated in the
action types. The details are not visible to the outside world in this figure.
This encapsulation applies likewise to the attributes.

A large encircling line indicates the system boundary. Everything
that falls outside this dotted circle is part of the environment of the
system. A system communicates with the outside world via messages,
inspections and triggers that are sent and received by input and output
functions.

The difference between the controlling system and the operational
system is shown in the KISS paradigm by an imaginary horizontal line
between the function and the action. The function is the singular chief
component of the controlling system. The function is completely and
independently responsible for achieving the desired changes to objects.
The functions communicate with other functions, with the environment
and with the operational system via the sending and receiving of messages.

An inspection is a special message which a function can use to
check on the changes to objects by a sort of feedback, and by which the
function can inquire on the status of objects. An inspection is a message
from the function asking the status of the addressee object. The addressee
object then sends a return message to the function. For inspections to be
carried out it is not relevant whether the object is located inside or
outside the system boundaries. Even objects outside the system under
consideration can be inspected!

The difference between an inspection and a message is that an
inspection is a two-way message whereby a function asks an addressee
object for particular information, and the resultant values are returned to
the function. For a message sent by a function, no return message is sent
with the values of an object. The message does however need to be
processed by the receiver.

Everything underneath the imaginary line belongs to the
operational system. In the operational system the actions and the objects
are the chief components.

The only way in which we are permitted to change the status of an
object is by sending a message from a function to an action. After receiving the message the action will check whether the message meets all the
static and dynamic conditions defined for that action on an object. If the
message does not meet the conditions, the action sends an error message
back to the function.

When all the conditions are met, the associated objects are modified by the encapsulated operations of the action. Each operation defines a strong coupling between the objects and the possible actions to change the objects. The associations between the objects and the actions determine the information architecture of the information system, by way of the strong coupling that they create. For this reason the KISS method is firmly directed to discovering the associations between actions and objects because these define the structure of the information architecture.

The communication between functions and objects is modelled in the KISS paradigm by messages, triggers and inspections. These are weak couplings which do not define any structure of compulsory associations. Because of this, we can relatively easily define new functions based on the information architecture without having to modify the information architecture. Because of the weak coupling we can also remove existing functions from the information architecture without causing far-reaching consequences for the information architecture and the production information systems based on it. The stability of an information system therefore rests entirely on the extent to which we can define the content of the information architecture in a manner that can be validated.

3.4   The organizational control model and the KISS paradigm

As we have discussed, we have made a separation between the controlling and the operational part of the KISS paradigm. The organizational control model describes the manner in which the controlling part is structured and directs the operational part by the use of messages, inspections and triggers. The content of both of these chief functions varies in nature. This can be seen by the modelling of regulating processes using functions in the controlling part of an information system. Functions include all the regulating, coordinating, informing, decision-making and norm-setting types of activities. They cause the appropriate changes to objects in the operational system, by sending addressed messages to the operational system. By definition, the function itself never carries out the change or action, but directs an action to do this via a message. The input and output functions provide the interface between the coordinating and regulating functions and the actions.

3.4.1 Controlling system

An example of a controlling system is a brain. The human brain is a part of the human system that performs many functions. It executes many coordinating tasks such as the gathering of information from the senses about objects in the immediate environment, the coordination of movements and the determination of whether things are good or bad by comparing observations with the 'conscience'. The conscience is defined as the totality of norms and values with which we relate actual and contemplated acts. The input functions can be compared to the senses which observe how changes have taken place. The output functions can be compared to receptors directing muscles to perform actions. The brain would never begin to perform actions on objects independently. Besides the controlling and regulating functions, the brain also records knowledge of the observed objects in our environment. It is this knowledge of objects in the real world that the brain uses to be able to perform functions in the correct way.

3.4.2   Operational system

The operational system performs the actions directed by messages sent from functions. The performing of an action results in a change in the status of objects. This is what happens in reality with actual actions. In an object-oriented model we describe the actions using encapsulated operations that reproduce the rules for changes to objects.

An action may only change the status of objects when all the conditions for the action are met. The conditions for an action can be divided into two sorts. These are *dynamic* and *static* conditions. As well as this, an action has one or more triggers which control a function when one or more value-bounds are exceeded.

To continue with the analogy of the 'human' system, we can regard an action as something we can execute with our hands, legs or mouth. The hands are thus coordinated by the brain by means of our senses to see, hear, feel, smell and potentially also taste how objects change in the environment.

In the example, we have implicitly indicated that with one action we can allow more than one object to interact with other objects. When we, for example, catch a ball with our hands, we see that the action catch changes the status of both hands as well as ball. That is, the ball is caught and the hands have caught the ball. The action catch is therefore the relation and interaction between the limbs and the ball.

With the ball catching we can also distinguish static conditions. One static condition is, for example, that the ball must come down in our immediate environment, because otherwise we are not ready or able to reach it. Another static condition is, for example, that the ball must not be heavier than 10kg, because otherwise it would be too heavy to catch.

With the action we can also specify a trigger: for example, that we must immediately throw the caught ball to a free-standing team member.

The message traffic between the controlling and operational parts and including among other things, the functions, actions and objects, is diagramatically represented in the KISS paradigm for object orientation (Figure 3.2).

3.4.3   Regulated versus self-regulating objects

The distinction in the KISS paradigm between the controlling and operational systems strengthens the concept definition concerning functions, actions and objects. This artificial separation does not mean that a controlling and an operational system must always be seen as two physically disjointed parts of one complete system, or as two completely separate systems. In fact, we can distinguish regulating objects from objects without any regulating or coordinating function. We will further discuss the relationship between these.

In reality, it often happens that the controlling system is viewed as a single independent working function. In an organization, one or more organizational functions are generally carried out by one functionary. The controlling system, or the controlling functionary, therefore becomes totally responsible for the optimal control of actions.

The operational system can be regarded as an independent system when it is distinct from the controlling system. With the controlling system we can give someone authority to perform an action. To be permitted to perform an action, a so-called 'authorization' is needed.

For deep organization structures we generally draw up a complete hierarchy of the employees responsible for the defined functions and the employees authorized to perform the actions. It is desirable that one functionary directs another until the level of performing actions is reached. The controlling between the functionaries takes place by means of the exchange of messages from both sides.

It is advisable for an organization to make and to picture the distinction between performing and directing employees. In fact, as we increase the number of components of the work to be automated, we are confronted with systems in which we can no longer make a strict separation between operational and regulating work. The systems become increasingly more self-regulating. The regulation of the process then occurs within the previously-defined rule-boundaries, which function as the norms for the execution of the process.

We will explain, using the following example of a production company, how the difference between controlling and operational systems can be seen in an organization.

Production company example

In one department of a production company, the production workers work under the supervision of a manager. The production consists of processing pieces of work using processing machines, according to specific instructions.

The pieces of work and the processing machines can be regarded as objects. The type of processing can be regarded as an action.

The production workers are authorized to perform defined processes (actions) on processing machines.

The manager directs the production worker with work-issued coupons, and accepts the work when it is completed.

The manager is thereby responsible for controlling the quality and quantity of the total production of the department.

Discussion of the example

We can define two types of worker in the department. The manager is responsible for the total process for this department and the production workers are authorized to carry out the processing.

We can separate the tasks in the department into those which are responsibility-oriented and those which are authorization-oriented. In particular situations it is sometimes organized so that the manager is responsible for the total process, without even being authorized to work with the production machines.

The message that directs a production worker is the work-issue coupon. The production worker can perform the action on the piece of work using a processing machine when all the conditions of the action are met. For example, one of the most obvious conditions for turning a piece of work on a lathe is that the piece is not too big for the lathe. If the piece is too big then an error signal is sent to the manager who must devise a solution to the problem.

The production worker together with the machine perform the processing on the pieces of work and in combination they can be regarded as a self-regulating system. While he is doing the processing, the production worker must keep an eye on and control the norms of the processing instructions. Any deviation means he must adjust the machine. The messages are sent in a very physical form directly between the machine and the production worker. The production worker can adjust the machine to obtain the desired result. In this manner, there is a continual inspection of the product using, for example, measuring rules on the machine and measurements of the product itself.

When we look at the piece of work or the machine itself, we discover that these are objects that do not provide for any form of control whatsoever. The objects themselves do not have any implicit norms allowing them to control totally independently the actions carried out by them, or carried out on them. All forms of control are done by a controlling system; in our example this is the production worker who keeps an eye on the status of the machine and the piece of work. The piece of work and the production machine become regulated objects (see Figure 3.3).

If we go a step further, we can develop the production machine into a completely self-regulating system, which we call an automaton. To do this we must transfer the control logistics and the way in which the processing instructions are carried out – present·in the production worker as knowledge – to the processing machine. For a new piece of work we then only need to present the processing machine with the new processing instructions in a form readable by the automaton.

When we integrate all the regulating functions into the operational object 'processing machine' we are faced with a 'self-regulating object'. The object has totally absorbed the controlling tasks and functions. The automaton communicates independently with the outside world by means of messages and inspections. See Figure 3.4.

A self-regulating object that independently communicates with other objects is called a subject. A subject represents an identifiable and physical object that behaves in a regulating and coordinating manner. A subject, therefore, is generally responsible for a greater number of functions.

As the objects absorb a greater part of the coordinating and regulating activities, so do they become more autonomous and independent. During modelling, the independence of a subject offers advantages because the exchange of messages leads only to weak relationships which do not influence the structure. In the modelling of subjects it is

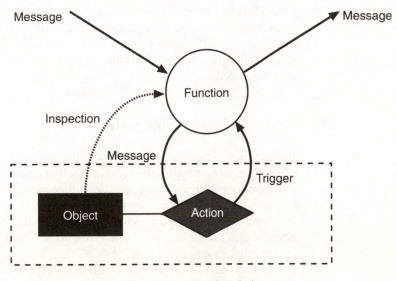

Figure 3.3   Regulated object.

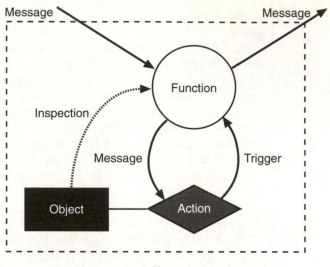

Figure 3.4   Self-regulating object.

important to investigate the way in which the communication from subjects to other subjects and objects is standardized.

One condition for making objects more self-regulating is the inclusion of more knowledge in the object and the specification of the norms within which the object must function. One of the problems confronting us is that not all knowledge and norms can be formalized. In cases where we add more knowledge and business rules to the object, we are creating knowledge and expert systems with all the characteristics of artificial intelligence. Although objects may look intelligent, we must be aware when modelling that most objects are, and will stay, absolutely dumb and regulated!

3.4.4   Norms and knowledge systems

By including knowledge and norms in the description of an object, the object becomes progressively more self-regulating. The object will be able to take more and more decisions independently without consulting the outside world. As a consequence the structure of the information system becomes simpler, with fewer structural relationships between objects. The conditions for intelligent and self-regulating systems will be further discussed.

One condition for an intelligent and self-regulating system is that there must always be input, with norms, to the controlling part, that indicates the rule-boundaries within which the system must carry out its actions and must function. Should a self-regulating system overstep the norms then there has to be a message sent to the outside world to adjust the norms or to adjust the self-regulating system itself, so that it once again falls within the rule-boundaries. The specified norms form, then, the rule-boundaries for the controlling part within which the actions must be directed and upon which decisions can be made.

Even after defining the rules for decisions and boundaries for the objects we still need to define to whom a completely self-regulating system is responsible. The responsible functionary for a self-regulating system is, of course, the person who defines the norms for the execution of actions.

Self-regulating objects occur frequently in nature. 'Human' and 'animal' self-regulating objects can themselves control both the execution and the direction of the performing of actions. With the use of technology we compose mostly self-regulating objects by utilizing measurement and control systems with both simple and complex feedback mechanisms. Examples are heating systems with thermostat controls and automatic taps.

In administrative environments, on the contrary, the amount of direct influence of functionaries on the way in which actions are carried out on administrative objects is generally greater. The decisions are usually made directly by the functionary who is responsible for the correct execution of a function. The objects of administrative systems are more in the nature of regulating objects directed externally.

In reality, over the course of time, the number of self-regulating objects, even in administrative systems, has been increased by the introduction of more decision-rules and greater knowledge of the problem area. This expresses itself in the more frequent use of knowledge and expert systems within administrative environments. Here too, there will be a far-reaching automation of the provision of information, whereby the proportion of self-regulating objects with their own know-how for the direction of their activities in the information system will further increase. As such, artificial intelligence can best be integrated within the development of object-oriented information systems. In the KISS paradigm artificial intelligence and expert systems have to be seen as a rule extension that is added to objects that are already specified for the information system.

3.5 The communication paradigm

In the discussion of the KISS paradigm we saw that objects communicate with each other by sending and receiving messages, inspections and triggers. In the discussion on self-regulating objects we saw that communication structures are simplified by making use of more self-regulating objects, which we term subjects.

Before we continue with the setting up of subject-communication models that describe how the subjects of an organization communicate with each other, we discuss a number of self-evident aspects of the communication process. In the second instance we describe how we can chart the visible information streams in the IST-situation (existing situation) of an organization with a subject-communication model, and then how we can further improve and optimize them, with a work-flow analysis, to attain the desired SOLL-situation (has-to-be situation). The possible Business Process Redesign project is fed with the found information.

3.5.1   What is communication?

We use the word 'communication' in many situations without being conscious of the way the communication process itself works. Communication with others is seen as something so basic that we don't realize the great number of agreements we must have made before we can actually communicate with others. It is important for communication that we possess a certain level of knowledge about the subjects to be discussed.

To explain the further details of the various aspects of communication, we divide the total communication process into a number of sequential stages (Figure 3.5):

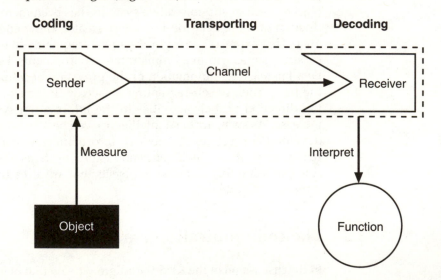

Figure 3.5   The communication process.

- Measuring;

- Coding;

- Sending;

- Transporting;

- Receiving;

- Decoding;

- Interpreting.

A condition for communication is that there is a sender and a receiver. In the simplest form, the sender codes the measured values of the things he wants to communicate in symbols that can be sent by a transport medium. The symbols are then sent in coded form over a channel or transport medium. The signal sent may be subjected to a number of disturbances during transportation.

When the signal is to be processed and interpreted at the place of destination by the receiver, for example when a decision must be made for a function/action to be performed, then the receiver decodes the signal into an understandable form.

The communication process is thereby defined as all the activities necessary for the exchange of coded messages between a sender and a receiver by means of a transport medium.

One example of a communication process between two people is a conversation. Both take turns at being the sender and receiver. The sender is the person who talks about particular things to the other person. The other person is then the receiver. He receives the expression with his hearing and interprets what he receives. At times the message can be distorted, for example, by background noise or because the distance between the two people is too great.

For a conversation, the transport medium is 'air', which transmits the soundwaves of the conversation. In the example we assumed that both people speak English. The message is coded, therefore, into the English spoken language and decoding happens vice versa. If the sender and receiver each speak a different language, the communication process would be much more difficult. A solution could be, for example, to use a translator who translates the spoken word from one language to another language.

It is always true for the communication process that we must create the message before we can send it as information. The first step in communication is that we must find out what the attributes and characteristics of an object are by measuring them. The measuring process specifies the values of the object's attributes.

It is necessary that we make *agreements* for the 'measuring, coding, transporting, decoding and processing', to ensure that we achieve the desired result from the communication. The three important aspects of communication, for which we must make agreements, are:

Syntax: the correctness and sequence of the symbols.

Semantics: the correctness of the meaning.

Pragmatics: the correctness of the intended actions.

The communication process between the information analyst and a programmer is used to illustrate these three aspects. For example, an information analyst has thought up a particular information system that he wants realized. So, he makes a design drawing of his ideas, according to previously-defined agreements. In this way, he has recorded his design and coded it in the form of a drawing. The paper with the drawing on it is the transport medium and this is sent to the programmer.

In order to have a good communication process the receiver (the programmer) must:

- Be able to read the symbols used. This is the syntax aspect. The syntax is only concerned with symbols and series of symbols.
- Know what is meant by the symbols. This is the semantic aspect. The semantics interrogates the meaning of symbol series.
- Finally create a program that conforms to the received design. This is the pragmatic aspect. The pragmatics deals with the effectiveness of the communication and checks whether the intended actions are in fact carried out.

3.5.2   Communication and syntax

The sender and the receiver are an important part of the control of the correctness of the syntax in the communication process. The sender and the receiver ensure that the data is coded and decoded by input and output functions. They take care of the input and output to and from the information system. In Figure 3.6 we have noted the symbols for the sender and the receiver.

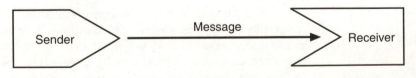

Figure 3.6   Symbols of communication for sender and receiver.

The tasks of the sender and receiver are respectively to code and decode the data, by means of output and input functions, and also to check the data for correctness of syntax. This means that a syntactically-faulty input will be detected by the receiver and reported, whereby a subsequent request will be sent to the sender for the message to be sent again. An example of a syntactically-faulty input which most administrative information systems check is the input of letters for a value which may only be numeric.

In general, the sender and receiver in an organizational communication process are not explicitly defined because they are relatively self-evident. This is because the subject implicitly coordinates and performs the sending and receiving of messages: a subject sends and receives messages to and from another subject. A subject inquires on the information system by means of output functions, and records data in the information system by means of input functions. This is how the subject encapsulates the sending and receiving of messages.

The input function must code the message correctly. This also holds true in general for an information system, so that data input, for example, into a screen, are directly checked for syntax, range and type. This similarly holds true for output functions.

The details of the sender and receiver are important when modelling information systems in situations where the communication protocol is important. This may be so for the specification of distributed data processing, for client/server architectures and for the exchange of data between different kinds of system. In this last case we can, for example, think of data exchange between administrative information systems and technical production installations. Technical production installations generally have to do with analogue measurements which must be converted by an AD-converter (Analogue/Digital) to digital values before they can be accepted by an administrative information system. Then they are frequently converted back with a DA-converter (Digital/Analogue) to an analogue control-signal for the regulating process.

3.6   The subject-communication model

The most visual form of communication in an organization is when subjects send messages to other subjects. This communication is, in general, much easier to see than the internal communication of a subject to actions which are directed by messages to modify the status of one or more objects.

The communication between subjects, such as organizations, departments, people and systems, can take on many manifestations. We can think here of written text on paper, still and moving images on a television screen or a slide projector, a conversation between people, a report from a text processor, a file exchange between computer systems, a traffic light in traffic.

Each form of communication has a specific impact on the receiver of the message, according to the manner in which the receiver receives the message and by the semantic content of the message. It is important for the semantic content that the receiver understands what the message means.

3.6.1 Definition of subject-communication model

The communication process between organizations, departments, people and systems is modelled by a so-called subject-communication model. In the subject-communication model the organizations, departments, people and systems are represented as subjects that send and/or receive messages.

The subjects have a strongly regulating and coordinating function and form a part of the controlling part of the KISS paradigm.

A frequently-occurring manifestation of a subject is the functionary responsible for the execution of one or more controlling functions. By an extreme application of automated computer systems, the computer systems themselves become subjects because they independently receive, process and send messages.

In the subject-communication model the symbol for a subject is the same circle we use in the KISS paradigm to represent a function.

From an organizational viewpoint it is necessary in the first instance to know how the information flows between the various functionaries. When we analyze and optimize the information flow in depth, it becomes increasingly clear that a regrouping of organizational functions among functionaries comes down to an organizational clustering of functions with their accompanying responsibilities. The content of the underlying actions does not in general change with a regrouping of functions.

Definition of a subject

A 'subject' is an object that is responsible for regulating and coordinating functions. A subject is identifiable in the real world and has a frame of reference with norms and values with which it interprets, sends and receives messages from other subjects. A subject has a certain level of knowledge with which, to a greater or lesser extent, it can independently regulate and control processes.

The message itself is given a symbol in the subject-communication model representing an information-carrier. When the information-carrier is, for example, a form, we use a form symbol to represent it. If the information-carrier is a tape or disk then we use a tape symbol or disk symbol respectively. For information-carriers with no special symbol, we use the symbol of a standing rectangle. See Figure 3.7.

The subject-communication model indicates which subject sends a message to which other subject. In addition, the message itself is described and represented in the subject-communication model.

The subject-communication model makes visible the way in which the sending of messages takes place in an organization. We use the subject-communication model to gain insight into the current way of working of the organization. The current way of working is indicated by the IST-situation. In a later phase we use the subject-communication model during the work-flow analysis to improve the communication patterns and the organizational way of working. The new situation is indicated as the desired situation, or the SOLL-situation. By moving from an existing situation to a new desired situation we must take account of the process of change which must be guided with the appropriate care. This is Business Process Redesign.

We now look at how we set up the subject-communication model based on the description of an ordering process. The guideline for this description is the ordering process for a large organization. The ordering process is recorded in the procedures and directives of the administrative organization.

Description of the ordering process   In a large organization the ordering of items is the concern of the department head, the administrator and the manager. To facilitate the delivery of items the department head orders items with an order form. He sends

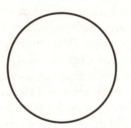

Subject type   Message type   Form

Diskette   Tape

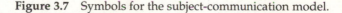
Figure 3.7   Symbols for the subject-communication model.

the order form to the administrator who checks that the value of the order is not above, say, $250, and that there is sufficient remaining budget. If these checks are passed then the administrator sends the order form to the supplier. If the value of the order exceeds $250, then the administrator sends the order form to the manager to be signed. After it has been signed it is sent by the administrator to the supplier.

The supplier delivers the ordered items to the department head and sends the bill to the administrator. The department head checks that the items delivered match those on the delivery docket and sends the delivery docket to the administrator. He sends the received bill to the department head for checking and approval. It is the job of the department head to check the prices. After the department head has approved it, the bill is paid by the administrator by transferring the billed amount into the supplier's bank account.

The above-described way of working is sometimes long-winded. For efficiency, it is desirable that this way of working be improved before a start is made on automation. With a work-flow analysis we can discover how to improve the ordering process.

3.7   Work-flow analysis

The purpose of carrying out a work-flow analysis is to ensure that the organization works more effectively and efficiently. The work-flow analysis is used in organizations who wish to evaluate their communication patterns, before moving on to setting up an information architecture and implementing information systems. The idea behind a work-flow analysis is that information systems can only function optimally when they closely fit in with the organization structure and the manner of communication. Besides this the work-flow analysis provides a direct insight into the way of working of an organization.

In order to conduct a work-flow analysis we add quantitative information about the sending, processing and receiving of information to the subject-communication model, step by step. Based on the quantitative data of the information flows in the subject-communication model, an analysis can be made of the effectiveness of the organization's way of working in the IST-situation. Eventually we can fill in the SOLL-situation with the information flows based on the results of the analysis, in order to allow the organization to work more effectively and efficiently.

We describe the steps of the work-flow analysis globally first and then we use them in the ordering process example, for which we have already created a subject-communication model (Figure 3.8).

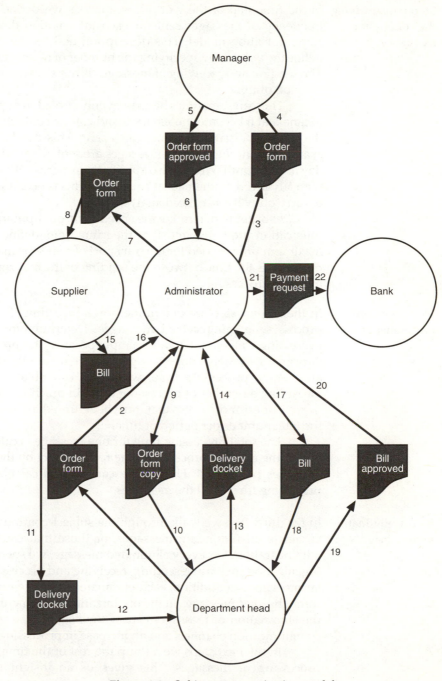

Figure 3.8 Subject-communication model.

Step 1: quantifying the volume and frequency

In the first step of the work-flow analysis we define the volume and frequency of messages sent for each information flow in the subject-communication model. This description defines the IST-situation. We define the volume by specifying the number of messages per time period. The sending and receiving of messages is not always evenly spread over a period of time.

This can sometimes be so unevenly spread over particular periods of time that it becomes necessary to indicate not only the volume but also the frequency pattern of messages sent. This can be done easily, for example, by noting that the messages are sent every Friday or on the last day of the month. We can also specify the progress of message frequency with advanced mathematical equations. This is necessary when we wish to carry out very advanced analyses.

In order to determine the speed of throughput in the subject-communication model we must, at the same time, define the average and maximum time needed for the transport of a specific message. The transport time is the time between the sending of the message and the start of message processing.

Step 2: determine processing time

In the second step we determine how much time it takes a subject to process sent and received messages. Determination of the message processing time is not always simple because the processing time can vary greatly. When it does vary greatly, we try as often as possible to use an average processing time, which we can obtain by, for example, measuring a number of processing times in practice.

For error messages that must be returned to the sender we specify the total number per period of time.

The total processing time for one message is calculated by multiplying the average processing time for a subject by the total number of messages per period. Finally, we can make a calculation of the total processing time of all the messages.

Step 3: eliminating redundancy

In the third step we walk through the subject-communication model to eliminate all redundant messages, or those that cause duplication of administration. For every eliminated message, we spend less time in the organization preparing, sending, receiving and processing these particular messages. In addition, each eliminated message causes the speed of throughput of messages in the organization to be increased. In this way, the elimination of messages causes time-saving, a reduced burden on communication channels and an increase in processing speed.

In the next steps we add up the rest of the time necessary for the processing of messages. This gives us an insight into the possible time savings.

Step 4: evaluating responsibilities and authorizations   In the fourth step we evaluate the entire subject-communication model. We investigate whether all the organizational responsibilities and authorizations are still correctly placed, even after the removal of messages. If this is not the case, then we must modify the allocation of responsibilities and authorizations, and possibly add new information flows to the subject-communication model. These new messages have by preference a shorter total processing time and a faster elapsed-time than the messages that have been removed. By naming new forms of communication in the subject-communication model we introduce, by choice, messages with a lower frequency than the removed messages.

Step 5: Creating subject-communication models for the SOLL-situation   In the fifth step of the work-flow analysis we calculate the total processing time for the revised subject-communication model (Figure 3.9). We compare the advantages of the new model with the existing situation. If there are sufficient reasons to move over to the new model, then a change process is initiated for the introduction of the new communication-form in the SOLL-situation.

For the implementation, it is necessary to describe clearly the organizational procedures. With changes in responsibilities and authorizations, the necessary thought must be given to the consequences this may have for the individual employee.

The five steps of the work-flow analysis are used to determine possible bottlenecks in the organization's information flow. Using the work-flow analysis we can determine the quality and quantity that would be produced by removing these bottlenecks.

We will now discuss how the work-flow analysis is used, using the example for which we have already created the subject-communication model, that is, the ordering of items. There are a number of problems signalled throughout the organization, in the area of information provision. The problems signalled are:

- The period of time between the department head's orders of items and their delivery by the supplier is far too long.
- The supplier complains that it takes too long to pay the bill.
- Not all the orders are processed by the administration department because extremely urgent orders are placed directly with the supplier without being seen by administration.
- The department head has no view over the total number of open orders with the suppliers.
- The responsibility for ordering items lies implicitly with the administration. The department head feels no responsibility whatsoever for high expenses.

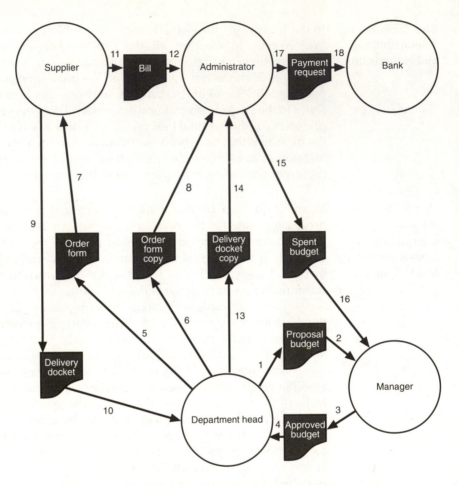

Figure 3.9   Subject-communication model: the SOLL-situation.

Step 1: quantifying the volume and frequency   An overview of the quantity of messages (per year) that are processed by the organization:

(1) Department head sends order form to administration   300
(2) Administration sends order form to manager   100
(3) Manager sends order form to administration   100
(4) Administration sends order form to supplier   300
(5) Administration sends order form to department head   300
(6) Supplier sends delivery docket to department head   300
(7) Department head sends delivery docket to administration   300

(8) Supplier sends bill to administration		250
(9) Administration sends bill to department head		250
(10) Department head sends bill to administration		250
(11) Administration sends payment request to the bank		250

For the calculation we assume that the messages are spread evenly throughout the year.

Step 2: determine processing time   The processing time for sending, processing and receiving a message is given (in minutes) in the following list, by subject.

(1) Department head	to write order form	10
(2) Administration	to check order form	8
(3) Manager	to approve form	4
(4) Department head	to administer order form	3
(5) Department head	to check item delivery docket	5
(6) Department head	to write receipt	5
(7) Administration	to administer delivery docket	3
(8) Administration	to administer bill	5
(9) Administration	to write payment request	3
(10) Department head	to check bill	5
(11) Administration	to book payment	5

The total time needed for the administration and checking, can be calculated by multiplying the volumes per line by the average processing time of a message (in minutes).

(1) To write order form	$300 \times 10 =$	3000
(2) To check order form	$300 \times 8 =$	2400
(3) To approve order form	$100 \times 4 =$	400
(4) To administer order form	$300 \times 3 =$	900
(5) To check item delivery docket	$300 \times 5 =$	1500
(6) To write delivery receipt	$300 \times 5 =$	1500
(7) To administer delivery docket	$300 \times 3 =$	900
(8) To administer bill	$250 \times 5 =$	1250
(9) To write payment request	$250 \times 3 =$	750
(10) To check bill	$250 \times 5 =$	1250
(11) To book payment	$250 \times 5 =$	1250

total 15 100 (250 hours)

Step 3: eliminating redundancy

In the third step we eliminate all messages occurring more than once in the order process.

The first message to be omitted is the order form, which is sent from the department head to a number of different functionaries in the organization. When a department head receives approval to send his order form direct to the supplier, messages 2, 3, 4 and 5 become redundant. The saving in processing time is: 2400 + 400 + 900 + 1500 = 5200 minutes. Whether the messages can in fact be eliminated without undesirable consequences will be looked at in the next step.

Message 7, sending the delivery docket from the department head to the administrator, can be omitted if we require the department head to administer independently the delivery dockets when items are delivered. The saving in processing time: 900 minutes.

Messages 9 and 10 are not required if the department head completely and independently administers and pays the bills. The tasks for the administration, checking and paying of bills, are then handed over from the administrator to the department head. Saving in processing time: 750 + 1250 = 2000 minutes.

The total saving in processing time then becomes: 5200 + 900 + 2000 = 8100 minutes, or 135 hours. There remains 7000 minutes, or 115 hours, of processing time.

Step 4: evaluating responsibilities and authorizations

In the fourth step we check whether all the responsibilities and authorizations for the organization are correctly defined.

The result of eliminating messages is that the department head becomes authorized both to order items as well as to pay the bills. This can lead to undesirable situations from a fraud point of view, because no single check takes place. To include checkpoints we introduce a number of organizational measures. We do this to make a separation between the processing of bills by the administrator and the ordering by the department head. To keep the administrator informed of orders and deliveries the department head sends a copy of the order form and delivery docket with the actual delivered quantities noted on it, to the administrator. The messages resulting from this are:

(1) Administrator sends the request for payment to the bank;

(2) Department head orders directly from the supplier;

(3) Administrator receives the bills from the supplier;

(4) Supplier delivers the goods directly to the department head;

(5) Department head sends a copy of the order form to the administrator;

(6) Department head sends a copy of the delivery docket to the administrator.

By making a separation between ordering and paying, we end up with two extra messages between the department head and the administrator. These are the copy of the order form and the copy of the delivery docket, respectively, which are sent by the department head to the administrator.

To process the copy of the order form and deliver docket takes on average 3 minutes. There are 300 copies of order forms and delivery dockets processed per year. The extra time for the processing is: 900 + 900 = 1800 minutes. The total processing time then becomes: 7000 + 1800 = 8800 minutes, or 145 hours. In the new situation the administrator no longer checks that every order does not exceed the budget, so we must define a separate budget procedure to check on expenditures.

In the IST-situation an important part-responsibility for expenditures lies with the administrator. He decides, based on the available budget, whether or not an order can be sent to the supplier. Another part of the responsibility lies with the manager who makes decisions on amounts above $250. Therefore, the department head has no responsibility to check on the level of expenditure.

In the IST-situation this leads to undesirable situations because eventually it is the department head who can best judge if particular orders are in fact necessary or not. Therefore, it is suggested that the department head be given total responsibility for the orders. To achieve this, the department head proposes a monthly budget, which he discusses with the manager. After it has been approved by the manager the department head can use the monthly budget to order items. All orders are subtracted from the remaining monthly budget, by the department head. The manager himself receives a periodic overview, from the administrator, of financial budget information with respect to orders and payments. This is used as a basis for regular meetings with the department head.

Step 5: creating subject-communication models for the SOLL-situation

The way of working in the above-described SOLL-situation has the advantage that the controlling of activities lies much closer to their execution. This makes the decision phase shorter and causes the communication channels in the organization to be less burdened by operational information. We expect the processing speed of information to be improved structurally in the SOLL-situation.

The time needed to formulate and approve the budgets still needs to be calculated (in minutes) to be able to show the total time saving in the SOLL-situation.

(7) To formulate monthly budget by department head   500
(8) To approve of budget by manager   100
(9) To report on spent budget by administrator   200

Total extra 800 minutes

The total processing time for the SOLL-situation becomes: 8800 + 800 = 9600 minutes, or 160 hours. This is 90 hours less than the IST-situation where the processing time was 250 hours.

Summarized here are the results of the proposed SOLL-situation:

(1) A saving of 36% on the total processing time;

(2) A shorter elapsed time for decisions;

(3) Better budget control by a simplification of responsibilities;

(4) Reduced load on the communication channels;

(5) Smaller chance of errors which need to be corrected later.

Seen absolutely, the saving of 90 hours does not appear so big for a department head, but for an organization's manager who directs five department heads this is a total saving of 450 hours. There is, thus, almost a quarter of a human-year used to execute a sub-optimal administration.

The decision to implement the proposed SOLL-situation must be made in conjunction with the creation of a plan to implement the new procedures and way of working in the organization. As for any change, the implementation of a new way of working is coupled with the overcoming of resistance and training of employees so that they can carry out the activities in the desired manner.

The implementation of an automated information system to support the new situation will always need to occur together with the streamlining of the way of working of the organization itself, according to the desired SOLL-situation. A frequent problem that occurs when this is overlooked is that the organization does not use, or only partly uses, the new information system.

To gain an overview of both the organization's procedural system and the information system we chart the new responsibilities, authorizations, functions and actions in the information quadrant. Using the information quadrant we can direct the further modelling and realization processes for the information architecture and the individual information systems.

3.8 Summary

In this chapter on the KISS method we have seen how two premises lay the foundation:

(1) The KISS paradigm;

(2) The communication paradigm.

The KISS paradigm describes the relationship between the parts of the information provision needed to control an organization's activities. The parts making up the KISS paradigm are:

- Function;
- Object type;
- Action type;
- Attribute type;
- Operation;
- Condition;
- Message;
- Inspection;
- Trigger.

We indicated how the KISS paradigm can be fitted into the information quadrant. By a further detailing of the rule possibilities of objects, we proposed a definition for the 'subject'. It was stated that a subject is a self-regulating object that communicates autonomously with other objects.

The communication paradigm provides a general base for the communication between people, objects, subjects and so on. The subject communication module specifies the visual communication between the subjects in an organization in more detail. A condition for each communication is that a number of agreements must be made. The common agreements for communication processes lie in the areas of:

- Syntax;
- Semantics;
- Pragmatics.

Because the current situation, the IST-situation, of the communication processes is not optimal, we define the desired situation, called the SOLL-situation, by a work-flow analysis. With the work-flow analysis we can define the quantitative and qualitative advantages of the new way of working.

3.9 Questions

(1) Describe the premises of the KISS method in your own words and discuss its importance.

(2) Describe the analogy between the information quadrant and the KISS paradigm.

(3)   Describe how the process of a thermostat valve on a radiator that heats a living room is described using the concepts of the KISS paradigm.

(4)   What is the difference between a controlled and a self-regulating object? Give examples of these.

(5)   What is communication, its components and the reason for the existence of formal and informal communication in organizations?

(6)   Discuss the concept of subject related to the concepts of function, action and inspection.

(7)   Describe the techniques of the subject-communication model and discuss how it must be used for a work-flow analysis.

(8)   Discuss the goals of performing a work-flow analysis and business process redesign.

(9)   Describe the relationship between the subject-communication model and the technical information architecture, such as a client/server environment.

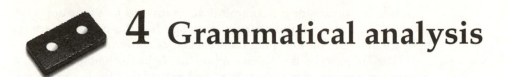

4 Grammatical analysis

4.1 Introduction

In this chapter we discuss the basic concepts of our natural language. We need to look at the grammatical terms of our natural language because they form the basis of the communication process between people. The use of grammar rules places us in a position to understand each other. The grammar rules of our natural language are used in the KISS method for the communication process between designers, users and the information system itself. The method of modelling of the KISS method is therefore strongly based on the general grammatical principles that we use daily. In subsequent chapters this knowledge of grammar rules is indispensable for the creation of correct models.

4.2 Natural language for communication

The word communication is often used by computing specialists in direct reference to the technical infrastructure of networks and protocols that, from a technical perspective, are necessary for the sending, transporting and receiving of information. This gives meaning to the concept of communication from a restricted technical point of view.

Within the total subject area of the automated provision of information we also use the term communication but in a much broader sense. In this way we can view the reading and writing of a book, the watching of a play and talking with others as communication processes.

A communication process varies from the observation of colours and smells to the sending of electronic messages. This can be structured, unstructured, formal or informal by nature. The only characteristic of communication is that the attributes of particular things are observable and that after they are coded, sent, received and decoded they can still be processed and interpreted.

It is important for the communication process that a meaningful message is transferred and that the message has the intended effect. These are the semantic and pragmatic aspects of communication.

The premise of the KISS method for object orientation is that information systems must always be understandable for the end user and that information systems must communicate with their end users in their spoken and written languages. This means that the information system must be based on the concepts of our spoken and written languages. To lay the foundation for the formulation of understandable information architectures and information systems we now discuss the principles of our spoken and written languages.

The strength of our natural language is that for generations we have been able to express ourselves in an understandable way. After we have looked at the most important principles of our language, we will use these integrally in the creation of object-oriented information architectures.

The most common form of communication used by everybody daily is the language we speak, read and write.

Everybody who can use their voice normally was spoon-fed the natural spoken language as a baby. Slowly but surely the baby learns the spoken language by imitating his parents, family and anyone with whom he comes into contact. His first words are usually sounds such as 'mama' and 'dada'. Gradually the toddler comes to understand what everyone is telling him, and he says his first short sentences using the words he has absorbed. Slowly but surely he begins to learn the rules of the natural language.

How we learnt our language is something we need not worry about, because it is something as obvious as growing up and becoming adult. In learning the language it was essential that we took over the many agreed conventions which allow us to understand each other. It is precisely these conventions that enable us to communicate with others in a simple way.

4.2.1   The language of gestures

The making of agreements about the use of a language was not a simple process. It took many centuries before there was any development and use of formal language rules.

In the history of mankind one of the first forms of formal communication was undoubtedly the language of gestures, also called the non-verbal language. The characteristic of the language of gestures is that the communication takes place in a strongly visual manner by the use of poses and facial expressions. Communicating with the language of gestures also requires that the other person can understand what is meant, based on consciously or unconsciously agreed conventions. A faulty interpretation of the meaning of gestures could, certainly in prehistoric times, have dramatic consequences. We could, for example, imagine a Neanderthal person showing aggression to another Neanderthal person because he felt threatened at the moment the other wished to shake his hand.

Non-verbal language is still an important way to communicate in our everyday associations, for example, to display our mood. So we laugh when we are happy, we cry when we are emotionally touched by joyful or less joyful events, we look surprised when we witness unbelievable or unrealistic situations. However, the language of gestures appeared in the course of time not to be sufficient for all the communication requirements, thus stimulating the development of spoken language.

4.2.2   The spoken language

After a long period of development mankind began to make use of a spoken language by using the voice to produce groups of sounds, in a formalized manner. Within races and groups, agreements were made for the use of particular groups of sounds to identify living beings, things and events.

In the beginning the spoken language was very primitive and the number of words was restricted to those things strictly necessary for survival. In the course of time the vocabulary of the spoken language was developed and became more uniform, within races and between races, by means of contact, wars and barter trade. The spoken language eventually formed the basis for the written language.

4.2.3   The written language

Some time after the development of the spoken language, man learnt to express himself with not only the gesture and spoken languages but also with a written language.

The first written languages pictured the objects in the real world by using figures and special characters, the so-called ideograms. An ideogram is a more or less true to life picture of an object or thing in reality, such as a person, an animal, or a boat. Originally these ideograms were very true to life, but because the drawing of an ideogram required much skill and took much time, they were simplified in the course of time to become more practical in use. The ideograms became more and more abstract and less realistic during the centuries and evolved to a script using established characters and conventions.

We classify the scripts we know of into three categories:

- Ideographic script;
- Alphabetic script;
- Syllable script.

Ideographic script The oldest ideographic script is the cuneiform script of the Sumerians. The information-carriers for the cuneiform script were clay tablets which were baked after they had wedge-shaped characters scratched onto them. This is the oldest administration system we know of, which the Sumerians used around 4000 BC for their inventory administration of the production and consumption of agricultural products.

A less ancient ideographic script is the hieroglyphic script of the ancient Egyptians. The hieroglyphic script goes back to around 3200 BC. It was mainly used by high priests for religious purposes, for example, in the pyramids and tomb graves.

Another equally ancient script of the Egyptians is the hieratic script that was written mainly on to papyrus leaves. The hieratic script was used primarily for trade purposes such as the registration of payments, inventory calculation and the writing of letters. The main feature of this script is that there was much less frill around the ideograms than with the hieroglyphic script. The reason for this can be found in its use for trade purposes where frills were seen as unnecessary baggage. The hieratic script is therefore a simplification of the hieroglyphic script.

The Chinese script is an ideographic script that is still in daily use. It originates from around 2000 BC. The Chinese script contains more than 50 000 characters; this is because it has a different character for every object or concept. It should be noted that the Chinese written language is uniform for the whole of China, while the spoken languages of the various provinces of China are completely different in nature. This means that someone from one province cannot understand the spoken word of someone from another province.

Modern forms of ideographic script are the 'icons' used by many graphical and windows-type computer programs, the 'pictograms', for example, at stations and airports and the 'graffiti' sprayed, among other places, on trains in New York, as a sign of the artist. The use of 'icons' in computer programs can be regarded as a rediscovery of ideographic script. To be able to use and interpret the icons in the proper way there must be agreement on what they mean.

Alphabetic script In the course of the centuries we have seen further simplification of the ideograms used in written language through the integration of the written language with the spoken language. No longer was a separate symbol defined for each object or concept: a different character was developed for each sound used.

In a conversation, people can differentiate between 20 and 35 different sounds. Therefore, the spoken language defined in general between 20 and 35 symbols for the sounds we can produce. This is the reason that the alphabetic script uses a different symbol for each sound and no longer has a different symbol for each object. In this way, the extremely large number of ideograms in the ideographic script was reduced in one blow to approximately 26 phonetic characters, or letters.

We compose words by placing the letters of the alphabet in the order of the sounds made for an identifiable object. Each word is thus a sequence of letters, each representing a sound in the spoken language. The integration of the spoken and written language has been made by the use of the alphabet, both simple and powerful for its function as a building block in the communication process.

Syllable script   The Japanese script lies somewhere between an ideographic and an alphabetic script. The Japanese script is based on syllables requiring far fewer characters than an ideographic script, but more than an alphabetic script. The Japanese script has about 56 different characters, which were taken over from the Chinese script in the eighth century.

In summary this means that the first scripts were developed by representing objects, observed in reality, which were as true-to-life as possible. The oldest prehistoric drawings show non-standardized pictures of deer, mammoths and hunters. Later pictures in the period of the ancient Egyptians tell stories using standardized figures of real world objects, of the lives of Pharaohs and of battles fought. In modern scripts the use of abstract representations of objects is replaced by the spoken groups of sounds which represent the object. The alphabetic scripts are therefore more 'communication-oriented' than the ideographic scripts, which are more 'representation-oriented'. However, before we can use letters and words for the communication process, we must make a number of agreements on the meanings we should give to the words.

4.2.4   Grammar and semantics

For correct communication we need to know how to interpret the various words in a sentence. While we now know how to form individual words in a modern language, we do not yet know, for example, how we can put our feelings on paper or how we can describe events in reality in an understandable manner. To make this possible we divide the natural language into:

- Vocabulary;
- Grammar.

The vocabulary consists of all the words of a natural language. It includes all the ideas for objects and phenomena that can be observed in reality and which can be differentiated by the users of the language. For daily use, the average English person has a vocabulary of 1200 to 1400 words. The syntax of each word originated from the sequence of spoken sounds.

The grammar of a natural language includes all the rules and conventions used to create a significant meaning, also known as semantics, for the various words used in our communication.

It is precisely all these grammatical laws and rules which ensure that we can, with a restricted vocabulary of 1200 to 1400 words in daily use, clearly and correctly indicate to others what we mean. This is because some grammar rules reuse words by forming new words. An example is the combination of 'boat with sails' into the word 'sailboat'.

To define the semantics of the words in our communication we will look at a number of grammar rules required to lay the foundation from which we create the information architecture. We deal with the grammar rules by looking at structured sentences. We use these structured sentences to perform a grammatical analysis. The structured sentences are composed from a textual description of reality relevant to the provision of information.

4.3   Structured sentences

In the first instance we can describe things in the real world without taking account of any restrictions in the area of modelling information architectures and information systems. This description is written in our natural language based on the actions an end user performs and observes in his work environment.

In the second instance, in order to simplify and structure this textual description of reality, we rewrite the text as structured sentences. A structured sentence has a main structure and an additional number of parts, which add further detail to the main structure.

The most important rules for the grammatical analysis of structured sentences are explained using the main structure of a sentence. Then we discuss how the characteristics of the parts of the main structure are detailed using grammar rules. Finally we look at a number of extra grammar rules that are frequently used when creating an information architecture.

4.3.1   The main structure of a sentence

A 'sentence' is a logical whole in which words are placed in a particular order to communicate something meaningful. A sentence is therefore also a linear sequence of words, the foundation of which is formed by a number of grammar rules and conventions which indicate the semantics of the structured sentence.

The main structure of a structured sentence after dissection is: subject, predicate, direct object, preposition and indirect object. A structured sentence is always in the active form. The passive form is never used for a structured sentence. The active form demonstrates an actual change by means of the action carried out by the preposition on the direct object.

An example of an active sentence is: 'John throws the ball at the window.'

Seen grammatically we can convert each active form into a passive form, whereby the direct object is placed where the subject was, although in reality it does not take the place of the subject. In our example the passive sentence becomes: 'The ball is thrown by John at the window.' But as stated, we do not use the passive form when creating structured sentences.

The subject

The subject in the active structured sentence is equal to the person, the organization, the animal or thing that the action of the preposition carries out on the direct object. The subject in the structured sentence has control of initiating and executing a specific action. The subject of the sentence is, speaking in terms of the KISS paradigm, the controlling part of the structured sentence and exactly matches the subject we have discussed in previous chapters.

The predicate

The predicate of the active structured sentence tells us exactly which action, precisely at this moment in time, is taking place. In the active sentence of the example, 'throws' is the conjugation of the verb 'to throw'; it indicates that the action is happening now. By conjugating the verb 'to throw' in a different way we can also indicate in our language the situation for another moment in time. For example we can conjugate the verb to indicate a future action or an action that has already taken place. Common conjugations of the verb are:

imperfect present tense:	John throws the ball at the window.
imperfect past tense:	John threw the ball at the window.
perfect past tense:	John has thrown the ball at the window.
imperfect future tense:	John will throw the ball at the window.
perfect future tense:	John will have thrown the ball at the window.

By the conjugation of the verb we can bring the time dimension into the language in a simple manner and so increase the semantic content of a sentence while retaining the same vocabulary. With the technique of conjugation and using general grammar rules we can easily indicate the present, past and future with one verb.

The direct object   The direct object in an active sentence is the thing or object upon which the action is carried out by the predicate. In our example sentence the direct object is the ball which is thrown by John. We implicitly know that the state of the ball changes by the execution of the action. If we were to change the active sentence to a passive sentence then the direct object would become the subject thus giving wrong results. We therefore have to set up active sentences.

The preposition   A preposition is often used to indicate a direction, place, location and so forth. In our example sentence the preposition indicates the direction. Prepositions can also be used in many other structures. An important structure, used in the analysis of a problem area, is the 'attributive adjunct' that indicates a kind of posession or existence dependency.

Attributive adjunct   Besides indicating a place or direction the 'of' positioned between two substantive nouns is often used in our language as an attributive adjunct. With an attributive adjunct we can distinguish between an owner or possessor and a possession.

We can explain this indication of possession by expanding the example sentence with an attributive adjunct: 'John throws the ball of Pete at the window.' In this sentence Pete is the possessor of the ball and 'the ball of Pete' is the attributive adjunct. In English, possession is normally shown by expanding the possessor with an apostrophe 's': 'Pete's ball', or by using the verb 'to have': 'Pete has a ball' or 'is' combined with apostrophe 's': 'The ball is Pete's'.

The indirect object   The indirect object indicates an object which interacts directly with the direct object according to the direction, the place or the relation defined by the preposition. An example of a sentence with the indirect object 'Kevin' is: 'John throws the ball to Kevin.'

4.4   Grammar and the KISS paradigm

The basic starting point of the KISS method for object orientation is the natural language. The natural language is used in the KISS method for describing the semantics of objects in the real world as well as the changes which happen to them and the associated communication processes.

The first step to be taken in order to use the natural language for the setting up of an information architecture is the representation of the grammatical concepts within the KISS paradigm for object orientation. We do this by taking the relevant events that happen in the real world and that can be described by active structured sentences, and including them in the structure of the KISS paradigm.

Active structured sentence

We indicate by an active structured sentence how one subject carries out an action on another person or another object. The subject is the person or thing that carries out the act.

The direct object is the person or thing that undergoes the act.

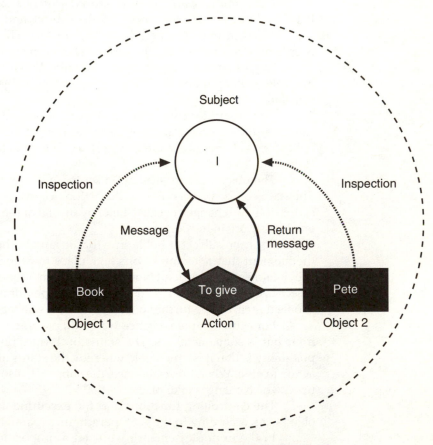

Figure 4.1   Paradigm of the KISS method

There are a number of rules necessary in order for us to be able to represent the most important grammatical concepts in the KISS paradigm:

(1) The subject of an active structured sentence is the *subject*. The subject has the task of correctly controlling and executing the action. This means that the subject implicitly includes all the controlling activities of a function. A subject is an object with controlling tasks. Whether or not we will also view the subject as an object in the information system is dependent on the environment.

(2) The direct object and the indirect object become the *objects* upon which and by which actions take place.

(3) The active verb in the structured sentence becomes the *action* with which objects are changed.

An example of an active structured sentence is: 'I give the book to Pete.' In the structured sentence 'I' is the subject, and therefore becomes the 'subject' in the KISS paradigm (Figure 4.1). The subject 'I' totally coordinates and carries out the action. The norms to which the function 'the giving of a book' must conform lie entirely with the subject in this example, making it possible for us to regard the subject as a controlling function.

The predicate 'give' is in the 'imperfect present tense' which indicates that the action is taking place and is not yet finished. The name of the action is always in the infinitive form of the verb. In our example this is the verb 'to give'.

The objects in our structured sentence are then 'book' and 'Pete' The status of 'book' becomes by the action 'to give', a 'given book'. The status of 'Pete' changes because Pete, by means of the action to give, has one book more in his possession.

For each subject it holds true that it can also become an object at the moment that relevant actions take place to change its status. In the previous section we dealt with how we can identify self-regulating objects. A subject is always an object that, depending on the size of the problem area, can be further developed into a self-regulating object.

For our example sentence we could assume that the book is not mine but is someone else's. The status of 'I' does not change. Another possibility is that it is 'my' book, whereby the status of 'I' changes by the action to give. When this is the case, the subject 'I' also becomes an object upon which changes take place.

The controlling functions and the executing actions that change objects are, according to the KISS paradigm, separately modelled.

In the example sentence we used a preposition in combination with an indirect object. In the KISS paradigm model we place the name of the preposition beside the association between the action and the object.

Between the action 'to give' and the object 'Pete' we place the preposition 'to' beside the association line. When the preposition defines the direction for the execution of the operations, it can therefore indicate the direction in which the operations of the action must be carried out.

Between the subject 'I' and the action 'to give' is an arrow which shows that the function of the subject initiates the action with a message. Before the function can initiate the action, the subject must inspect whether the 'book' in fact exists, and that 'Pete' is present.

When we send a message from the function of the subject to the action to execute this action, we can also send a return-message to the function with the results of the action. This return-message can also be an error message indicating that the action could not be carried out, whereby other possible actions must be investigated. In this last case, we speak of a trigger because we must define specifically what the other activities are that need to be investigated.

4.5   Encapsulation in the natural language

Adjectives are used in our language to represent details of the subject, direct object and indirect object. 'Adverbs' are used for the details of the predicate. For this detailing we make a distinction between the roles played in the sentence by the subject, direct object and indirect object. In the case of the adjective we regard the subject, direct object and indirect object all as substantive nouns.

4.5.1   The adjective

Adjectives are descriptive words such as small, large, big, fat, heavy, grey, red. An adjective always illustrates the attributes of the substantive noun with which it is associated.

By adding adjectives to our example sentence we get: 'I give the large, fat and expensive book to mad old Pete.'

In normal communication processes we do not usually speak in great detail of the attributes and details of substantive nouns. This generally disrupts the communication process too much, because the main message is then bogged down in detail. It should be noted that the structure of the main sentence must not be modified by the use of adjectives and adverbs.

Another point which plays an important role in the communication process is the level of knowledge of the receiver. In the communication process between people it is presumed that a great number of issues are clear to the receiver and therefore require no extra explanation. We accept, for example, that fire is hot, water is colourless, stone is hard. In this way, we can suppress those attributes of which we assume the other person has the same knowledge and perception.

4.5.2   The adverbs

Adverbs define the attributes of the verb and in some cases also the attributes of the adjective. An adverb in an active structured sentence says something about the way in which the action takes place.

By adding an adverb the example sentence becomes: 'I give the book now quickly to Pete.' The adverbs 'now' and 'quickly' both say something about the way in which the book is given to Pete.

Adverbs can be divided into a number of categories. The most important categories of adverbs are:

place:	here, there, somewhere, far, close by
time:	now, yesterday, today, tomorrow
quality:	good, easy, bad
quantity:	little, much, often
intensity:	extreme, very, strong
certainty:	maybe, certain, unsafe

Adverbs give answers to questions that are asked about the execution of an action. The adverb also provides information about the way changes take place, seen in the dimension of time.

4.5.3   Properties and attributes

In our natural language we have the tendency, when communicating, to encapsulate a large portion of the details. This is because we assume that the receiver is in possession of a certain level of knowledge of the things being discussed, which he uses as a reference. When we do decide to go into more detail about objects and their actions, we can add them to the structured sentence within the existing sentence structures. As we have seen, we do this by specifying the values of object and action attributes using adjectives, adverbs and clauses.

The adjective gives further detail on the properties of the subject, direct object or indirect object, which in turn become objects. An adjective implicitly indicates therefore, the attributes of an object. An adverb gives further detail on the attributes of an action.

Combining the example sentences gives the following sentence: 'I give the large, fat and expensive book now quickly to mad, old Pete.'

We can see that the structured sentence does in fact, become less fluent to read and takes more time to be entirely understood by us.

The attributes of the objects and the action in this sentence are:

Object/Action	Attribute values
book	large, fat, expensive
Pete	mad, old
to give	now, quickly

The adjectives and adverbs give the attribute-values of the object and action attributes. The general description to which is referred has not yet been named. So we can presume that the attribute 'large' has to do with 'the size', 'fat' to do with 'the fatness' and 'expensive' to do with 'the value'.

The generic description, to which objects and actions are referred, is often given by making the adjective or adverb independent, thereby creating a substantive noun. The substantiation becomes the reference-object. To give emphasis to the reference-object we place the word 'the' in front of it. Then we combine it with the name of an object or action in order to arrive at a description for the attribute-type.

In the information architecture, the attribute-type is the more generic description of the measured and communicated property of an object. The values of the attribute-type are called attributes.

Definition attribute type
An 'attribute type' is the general description of a property of an object or action.

By further consideration of the objects 'Pete' and 'book' we can discern that they too are occurrences of a more generic group of objects. The generic object that describes how individual objects carry out an action is called the object type. The object 'Pete' is one of the object occurrences of the object type 'person'. The object 'book' is one of the object occurrences of the object type 'gift'.

Definition object type
An 'object type' is a group of objects with identical properties which we can change in an identical manner with actions.

To be able to record the name of Pete along with his height in the object type 'Person', we define the attribute types 'Person-name' and 'Person-height'. In the object type 'gift' we include the attribute type 'gift description'. See Figure 4.2.

It is absolutely necessary for an object type to minimally define the

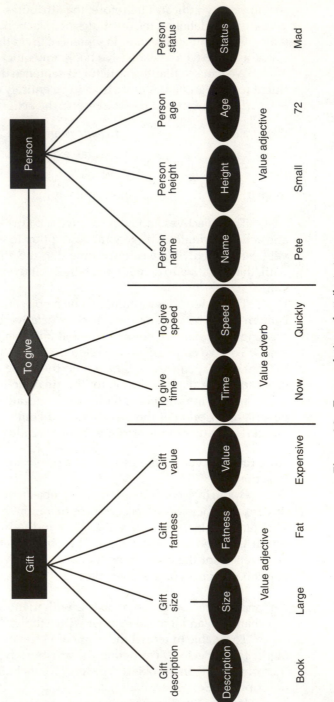

Figure 4.2 Encapsulation of attribute types.

identifying properties of each individual object, because this is the only way to distinguish one object from another. The identifying properties may also be recorded by means of an identification number.

For each attribute type we can define its values with a domain, by way of a predefined method. So we can, for example, select the value of the fatness of the book from the domain 'thin', 'normal' and 'fat'. We can also define the fatness of the book in millimetres. When we agree to measure the fatness in whole numbers with a maximum of three positions, then we can record the value as a numeric number with three positions (N,3). The value type indicates the way in which the numbers are recorded.

The unit with which we measure, for example, the 'fatness', must be added separately to the measured value. We can do this by recording how the values of the size of the attribute type are measured. A value can be measured for example in cm, m, $, days, months. The unit with which we represent the measurement is very important. The receiver of the data must be able to interpret the received values correctly.

Object type	Value	Attribute type	Representation unit	
gift	book	gift description	C,30	alphabet
	large	gift size	N,5.2	cm^2
	fat	gift fatness	N,3	mm
	expensive	gift value	N,5.2	$
person	Pete	person name	C,30	alphabet
	small	person height	N,3.2	cm
	old	person age	N,3	years
	mad	person status	C,30	alphabet

Action	Value	Attribute type		
to give	now	to give time	N,6	day
	quickly	to give speed	C,15	alphabet

Diagrammatically, we place attribute types on the line segment between the object type or the action type and the reference object to which we relate the object by the measurement of the attribute type. The reference object is represented by a small ellipse.

The values of the properties defined in the example are not yet sufficiently generic in the sense that they often suggest particularly relative values. The values for the attribute types used here are not completely objectively measurable. To make them objectively measurable we must further develop the way in which they are measured, for example, by using a reference scale.

The property 'large' is relative in the sense that the same object can be 'large' in the view of one person and 'small' in the view of another. The same counts for fat, expensive, old, mad and quickly.

To be able to compare properties of objects in a fast and easy manner, we use measuring scales and standardized measuring units.

Attribute types that express a size, time, height, and such like can be represented in a simple way with numbers. It is however, more difficult to find reference scales for attribute types which indicate the more personal experience of individuals with values such as, 'mad', 'dusty', 'nice'. We look at how to go about solving this problem in Chapter 7.

4.6   Special grammatical concepts

With the above concepts forming the foundation of the simple structured sentence, we have a large amount of information to enable us to carry out a grammatical analysis and create part of the information architecture. But for a complete picture we are missing a number of other grammatical concepts such as the plural form, the nominal predicate, reflexive verbs, the gerund (the independently used infinitive mood of the verb), the clause, the question and the command form. We discuss these concepts and indicate how we distinguish them in Section 4.7. We will look to a limited extent at the application of the grammatical concepts in setting up the information architecture. Chapters 5, 8 and 10 deal with the grammatical principles.

4.6.1   The plural form

The plural form is generally shown in the English language by expanding the substantive noun with an 's'. There are a great number of exceptions to this rule owing to irregularities in the language. The example sentence can be pluralized as follows: 'John and Pete throw the balls at the windows.'

Using the plural form we indicate in the structured sentence that an action has a bearing on one or more substantive nouns. In this way John can throw one ball many times at the windows. Also John can throw once and Pete can throw once many balls at the windows, and so on. The further specification of who, how, when and how many can be further specified later with the plural form.

The plural form is important for the information architecture because it shows whether an action can be performed one or more times on one or more objects.

4.6.2   The nominal predicate

The nominal predicate points to an equality between two nouns. We use this in our language in many situations.
Examples of nominal predicates are:

- A tree is vegetation.
- A window is a building element.
- John is a basketballer.
- Pete is a basketballer.

The nominal predicate in the first example shows that a tree belongs to the category vegetation. A tree is green and grows. Vegetation is the general definition of the group of living things that are green and grow.
The equivalence relationship can be given in singular form by 'is a' and in plural form by 'are'. Not every equivalence relationship that holds true in singular form holds true in the plural. This is explained by writing the above sentences in plural form:

- Trees are vegetation.
- Windows are building elements.
- Johns are basketballers.
- Petes are basketballers.

In the first sentence we see that 'vegetation' indicates a group of things that are green and grow. It is therefore not necessary to write the word in plural. The second sentence is generally true while the third and fourth sentences are rubbish. The reason for this is that John and Pete are individual people who cannot be isolated as a 'John' or a 'Pete' from the groups of 'Johns' or 'Petes'.
By using the plural form 'are' for the equivalence relationship we can find out whether we are dealing with unique objects or with groups of unique objects.

4.6.3   Intransitive verbs and reflexive verbs

An intransitive verb represents the status of something in reality without requiring a direct object. Examples of intransitive verbs are: 'it rains', 'he walks'.
Intransitive verbs indicate the status or perhaps also the situation of an object that is not included in the sentence. We must always be

aware of the beginning, where we can say that the object has a particular status, and of the end, where the object no longer has that status.

Examples of the use of reflexive verbs are: 'I see myself in the mirror', 'he wounded himself'.

The verb shows here that the subject initiating the action is itself also included in the action. Reflexive verbs indicate that the action can only be modelled for one object. The action will then only be associated with one object.

4.6.4 The gerund

A gerund is a substantive noun that is derived from the infinitive form of a verb by suffixing this initially with '-ing'. Examples are:

Verb	Gerund
to insure	the insuring
to expand	the expanding
to store	the storing
to pay	the paying
to end	the ending

The reason for introducing a gerund is that we cannot include two or more active verbs in one structured sentence without making use of the adjunctive word 'and'. To indicate a sequence in the order of actions, we therefore substantiate the verb of the first action to a gerund. For example: 'We pay the insuring for the car.'

In everyday English however it has become common to replace the -ing suffix with a number of other suffices such as -ance, -age, -ment and so on. The commonly-used form of the above examples therefore becomes:

Verb	Gerund
to insure	the insurance
to expand	the expansion
to store	the storage
to pay	the payment
to end	the end

And the example sentence becomes: 'We pay the insurance for the car.' This sentence shows implicitly that we first insure the car and then pay the insurance premium.

4.6.5   The clause

When parts of a sentence need extra explanation that cannot be included in the main sentence, then we add the explanation as a sentence section within the main sentence. This is called a clause. A clause functions as a further enlightening of the main sentence. It is important to check which part of the main sentence has to do with the extra specification in the clause. For example: 'John, who is small and naughty, throws a ball at the window.'

The clause construct is used to separate the properties of objects and actions. The clause hereby defines the attributes.

4.6.6   The question

When someone wants to ask someone else something he can make this clear by means of a question. A question generally concerns the status of a person, animals or things in reality. A question is indicated by a question mark at the end of the sentence. For example: 'Is John older than 18 years?'.

A question is usually used to gain more information in order to form an opinion or make a decision. In the KISS paradigm questions are equivalent to inspections of objects.

4.6.7   The command form

A short sentence demanding something to be done is a command; this is pointed out with the 'command form'. A sentence in the command form can be ended with an explanation mark. For example: 'Throw!', 'Stand still!'. A command can also be formed using the auxiliary verb 'must'. For example: 'John, you must throw!', 'Pete, you must stand still!'. We interpret the second form as weaker than the first, but both forms indicate that there is a need for something to be done.

In the KISS paradigm the command form is the message from a function to an action to cause the action to be performed. There is no way for the action to prevent this, unless the conditions are not met.

4.7   Grammatical analysis

While describing the grammatical principles we illustrated to a greater or lesser extent how these principles can be used when creating an information architecture and an information system. The steps for carrying out a grammatical analysis were left out of the discussion of the grammatical principles. To carry out a grammatical analysis we make a distinction between a number of activities which are performed in phases. We start with a textual description of the activities an organization carries out. Then we produce, by grammatical analysis, a definition and description of the objects, actions, functions and subjects that are relevant for the information system, in steps. Finally we summarize the results in an information quadrant.

For the grammatical analysis we do not immediately analyse the encapsulated details of objects and actions. These are targeted later in the modelling process. The objective of the grammatical analysis itself is to provide a basis for the definition of the main structure of the automated provision of information. The grammatical analysis aims to fully chart the organizational way of working and control structures with the associated responsibilities and authorizations. These are amplified in a work-flow analysis.

4.7.1   The starting point: the textual description

A textual description of the relevant activities is the starting point of an object-oriented information analysis. We describe the activities in normal English without taking into account any of the subsequent phases.

Before we start the textual description we must define the scope. The scope is defined by specifying which of the activities carried out by employees must be described. The determination of the boundaries of the project takes place by defining, in the information quadrant, the employees and activities for which a textual description must be made.

The style of the textual description preferably is narrative. The description must explain 'what' an employee does. 'What' an employee does must be described as fully as possible with activities that actually happen, with nothing left out.

Because it is the employee who knows most about his activities, he can in most cases write his own textual description. The advantage of this is that we obtain, for the grammatical analysis, a description of the way of working incorporating the concepts used by the employee himself. Continuing to use these concepts produces an information system that very closely matches the world experience and daily terminology of the end user.

We generally carry out a grammatical analysis on the textual description of the activities of many employees. This is sometimes further illustrated with descriptions of work regulations, procedures, function descriptions and such like. The eventual aim of the textual description is to provide an insight into 'who or what performs which activities in the organization on what objects'. The textual description is therefore continued until we have sufficient material to allow us to carry out a grammatical analysis.

4.7.2 The steps of the grammatical analysis

For the grammatical analysis we define a number of steps using important lists. Initially the lists serve the purpose of aiding the specification of the content of the textual description. After the textual descriptions have been dissected, the lists are used for further analysis.

1. *List of structured sentences* The list of structured sentences is created by working through the whole textual description, adding to the list all the active sentences, and those which, in one way or another, can be made active. Using these structured sentences we can make lists of candidate objects, actions and subjects. The structured sentences do not need to be restricted to subject, predicate, direct object, preposition, indirect object, but can also be expanded to include attributive adjuncts and nominal predicates.

2. *List of candidate objects*

3. *List of candidate actions*

4. *List of candidate subjects*

We include all substantive nouns as candidate objects, all predicates as candidate actions and all subjects as candidate subjects in the lists.

It is often useful in the list of candidate actions to indicate the objects upon which they act. This gives a better overview of the meaning and context of the actions.

Before we can make a definite list of objects, actions and subjects we must interpret and validate the lists, which have been created in a somewhat mechanical fashion. It can for example occur that synonyms and homonyms have been used in the lists of objects, actions and subjects. To gain a good picture of the actual size of a list, we check all candidate objects, actions and subjects for synonyms and homonyms.

When we come across synonyms in the list we must decide which concept we will continue to use. The synonym itself is entered on another list. When we come across homonyms (the same word used for two different meanings) in the list, we must separate the two different ideas by giving them, for our purpose, new unique names.

5. *List of synonyms and homonyms* Synonyms are often confused with the objects in a nominal predicate. The difference between a synonym and a nominal predicate is that a synonym, which in a nominal predicate is on the left-hand side of an ISA, can be swapped with the synonym standing to the right of the ISA. This is not possible with objects. To be able to make the correct groupings in the textual description we create, in addition to the list of synonyms, a separate list for nominal predicates.

6. *List of nominal predicates, sentences with ISA*

We can also include in the list of candidate objects those which are derived as a gerund from a verb. For all the gerunds included in the list of candidate objects, we make a list containing both the action underlying the gerund, as well as the gerund itself. The actions from which the gerunds were created are added to the list of candidate actions.

7. *List of gerunds*
8. *List of attributive adjuncts*

In the structured sentences attributive adjuncts can also be included to indicate that something is 'of' something or someone else or belongs to them. The structure of possession among objects can thus be defined. The list of attributive adjuncts is therefore added to the object list.

4.7.3 Conversion of candidate lists into definite lists

After we have created the lists resulting from the dissection of the structured sentences, we move on to defining definitive lists of actions, objects and subjects which we then further model within the information architecture. To be able to create these lists we must make a number of decisions. We draw up the lists in such a way that the defined objects, actions and subjects fall within the scope of the project. In addition, the lists must give insight into the meaning and definitions of the concepts and ideas employed.

The definitive list of objects, actions, gerunds and subjects consists of more data than the candidate list. In the definitive list we also take up precisely as much information as is needed to conduct the modelling process.

When an object undergoes a number of relevant actions, we convert the candidate object into an object that will be later further modelled. If we cannot find actions for a candidate object then by definition we do not place it on the definitive object list. We show by an attributive adjunct where an object belongs and we show with an equivalence relationship (ISA) to what it is equal.

List of objects:

Per object:

(1) Name of the object

(2) Synonym object

(3) Brief description of the object

(4) Actions performed on the object

(5) Equivalence relationship with other object (ISA)

(6) Possession of another object according to the attributive adjunct

A candidate action becomes an action only when it causes a change to one or more objects at one moment in time. If this is not the case then we can further investigate if it has a managing, controlling or calculating nature. If so, then we place the candidate action on the list of functions.

List of actions:

Per action:

(1) Name of the action

(2) Synonym action

(3) Objects upon which it acts

(4) Per object a brief description of the change

(5) Possible derived gerunds

(6) Subjects authorized to perform the action

List of functions:

Per function:

(1) Name of the function

(2) Brief description of the function

(3) Subject responsible for the function

(4) Objects to be inspected by the function

The list of gerunds is made by analysing the relevance of the derived actions.

List of gerunds:

Per gerund:

(1) Name of the gerund

(2) Name of the derived action

(3) Description of the changes of initiating actions

The list of subjects is made by checking through the list of relevant actions and functions for subjects that are responsible or authorized for them.

List of subjects:

Per subject:

(1) Name of the subject

(2) Synonym subject

(3) Actions the subject is authorized to perform

(4) Functions for which the subject is responsible

4.8   Example of a grammatical analysis

Using the example of the order process we will explain how a grammatical analysis can be carried out. The description has previously been used to create a subject-communication model. We repeat the description here.

Description of the ordering process

In a large organization the ordering of items is the concern of the department head, the administrator and the manager. To facilitate the delivery of items the department head orders items with an order form. He sends the order form to the administrator who checks that the value of the order is not above, say, $250, and that there is sufficient remaining budget. If these checks are passed then the administrator sends the order form to the supplier. If the value of the order exceeds $250, then the administrator sends the order form to the manager to be signed. After it has been signed it is sent by the administrator to the supplier.

The supplier delivers the ordered items to the department head and sends the bill to the administrator. The department head checks that the items delivered match those on the delivery docket and sends the delivery docket to the administrator. He sends the received bill to the department head for checking and approval. It is the job of the department head to check the prices. After the department head has approved it, the bill is paid by the administrator by transferring the billed amount into the supplier's bank account.

4.8.1   Structured sentences

The first step of the grammatical analysis is the writing of structured sentences:

Subject	Action	Object	Preposition	Object
Department head	to order	item	with	order form
Department head	to send through	order form	to	administrator
Administrator	to check	value	of	order
Administrator	to check	budget	of	department

Administrator	to send through	order form	to		supplier
Administrator	to send through	order form	to		manager
Manager	to sign	order form			
Supplier	to deliver	item			
Administrator	to receive	bill		from	delivery
Department head	to check	item		on	delivery docket
Department head	to send through	delivery docket	to		administrator
Administrator	to send through	bill	to		department head
Department head	to check	bill		from	supplier
Department head	to approve	bill		from	supplier
Administrator	to pay	bill		from	supplier
Administrator	to transfer	billed amount	to		bank account

4.8.2   Candidate objects

We differentiate the following candidate objects:

item	supplier
order from	bill
value	delivery
order	delivery docket
budget	bill amount
department	bank account

4.8.3   Candidate actions

We differentiate the following candidate actions:

to order	to receive
to send through	to check
to check	to approve
to sign	to pay
to deliver	to transfer

4.8.4   Candidate subjects

We differentiate the following candidate subjects:

department head
administrator
manager
supplier

4.8.5   Synonyms

We differentiate the following synonyms or similar concepts:

order form	order
delivery docket	delivery
to sign	to check
to pay	to transfer

We will subsequently use the concepts in the right-hand column.

4.8.6   Nominal predicates

We can differentiate the following nominal predicates:

An order form	is a document
A delivery docket	is a document
A bill	is a document

4.8.7   Gerunds

We have made the following list of gerunds:

order	to order
delivery	to deliver

4.8.8   Attributive adjuncts

We have created this list of attributive adjuncts:

order value
department budget

delivery bill
supplier's bill
delivery from supplier
supplier's bank account

Review of the list of candidate objects	item	relevant object that undergoes actions
	order form	synonym of order
	value	no actions therefore no object
	order	relevant object that undergoes actions
	budget`	no actions therefore no object
	department	outside scope of project
	supplier	relevant object that undergoes actions
	bill	relevant object that undergoes actions
	delivery	relevant object that undergoes actions
	delivery docket	synonym of delivery
	bill amount	no actions therefore no object
	bank account	no relevant actions therefore no object
Review of the list of candidate actions	to order	action
	to send through	function
	to check	function
	to sign	synonym of check
	to deliver	action
	to receive	action
	to check	action
	to approve	function
	to pay	synonym of transfer
	to transfer	action
Review of the list of candidate subjects	department head	relevant
	administrator	relevant
	manager	relevant
	supplier	relevant

Note that 'bank', to which we transfer the money, is missing from the list of subjects. We therefore add 'bank' to the list of subjects.

We can now create a list from which we can start to model, based on the candidate lists and their reviews.

List of objects

Item:	An item is ordered from a supplier after which it is delivered.
	After delivery the items are checked.
action:	to order
	to deliver
	to check
Order	synonym: order form
	With an order we order a number of items from a supplier.
action:	to order
Supplier	From the supplier we order items which are thereafter delivered.
	From the supplier we receive a bill and we transfer money to his bank account.
action:	to order
	to deliver
	to check
	to receive
	to transfer
Bill	A bill is received from the supplier. For a bill we transfer money.
action:	to receive
	to transfer
Delivery	synonym: delivery docket
	A delivery is the delivering of a number of items by the supplier.
	After delivery of the items we transfer money to the supplier.
action:	to deliver
	to transfer
	to check
	to receive

List of actions

To order		the ordering of items from a supplier
	object:	supplier
		item
		order

To deliver	the delivery of items by a supplier
object:	supplier
	item
	delivery

To receive	the receipt of a bill from the supplier
object:	supplier
	bill
	delivery

To check	the checking of items delivered by the supplier
object:	supplier
	item
	delivery

To transfer	synonym: pay
	the transferring of money by bank to pay for the bill
object:	supplier
	bill
	delivery

List of functions   From the list of actions we can specify a number of managing and controlling activities. In addition, it is necessary that each action be directed by at least one function, which controls it. We suggest the following functions, based partly on organizational functions, as an initial list:

Inventory control	Management of the inventory by the department head
Budget control	Control of the available budget
General management	Management activities of a business unit
Logistic control	The control over orders, deliveries and associated control activities
Financial management	Control of all incomes and expenditures

List of subjects   Department head
Administrator
Manager
Supplier
Bank

Supplier and bank are subjects external to the organization. The remaining subjects are internal subjects in the organization. Supplier appears both as object and as subject. A supplier can be regarded as a self-regulating object that does in fact direct actions with functions, needing to record data.

List of existence-dependencies

By reviewing all the attributive adjuncts we can obtain an overview of the development of existence-dependencies. To be able to represent this in an existence hierarchy we place as many 'of-associations' in one line as possible.

ordering	of	item	of	supplier
billing	of	delivery	of	supplier
delivering	of	item	of	supplier

Setting up the information quadrant

Before we can set up the information quadrant, we may want to add things that we overlooked the first time to the lists. When we have completed the lists containing the descriptions of the main components,

Item	Order	Supplier	Bill	Delivery		Department head	Administrator	Manager
x	x	x		x	Inventory control	x		
	x		x		Budget control		x	x
		x			General management			x
x	x	x		x	Logistic control	x		
	x		x		Financial management		x	x
					Processes / Objects — Employees / Actions			
x	x	x			To order	x	x	
x		x		x	To deliver	x		
		x	x	x	To receive		x	
x		x		x	To check	x		
		x	x		To transfer		x	

Figure 4.3   Information quadrant for the ordering process.

then we can set up the information quadrant. We include the gerunds both as object and as action.

The relationships in the four quadrants are indicated in the structured sentences that we used for the grammatical analysis. We add new structured sentences to the list when we see that they can be formed from the quadrants and are not already present. In this way we have a simple method for the validation of the results from the grammatical analysis.

In addition, we obtain from the information quadrant an overview of the most important components which will later be further modelled into an information system and into an information architecture. With the grammatical analysis we have laid the basis for more detailed modelling.

We will set up an information quadrant, as the example, in which we show the relationships between the objects, actions, internal subjects and functions.

In the information quadrant (Figure 4.3) we see that the supplier is, in one way or another, included in every action. This is caused mainly by the structure of the attributive adjunct contained in the text, making almost everything reliant on the supplier.

We can add things at a later stage to the information quadrant when we further review and consider its contents, and conclude that actions, objects, subjects or functions are missing.

4.9 Summary

In this chapter we have discussed the basic grammar elements of our natural language. The grammar rules are used to perform an analysis of the textual description of a real world situation. The textual description is first translated into active structured sentences. Using these we carry out a grammatical analysis that results in an overview of candidate objects, actions, subjects, synonyms, homonyms, nominal predicates and attributive adjuncts. The grammatical analysis is carried out using the generally-known grammatical conventions of our natural language. The grammatical analysis provides us with the building blocks that we can fit into the information quadrant and the KISS paradigm during further modelling of the information architecture.

4.10 Questions

(1)   Discuss the conditions necessary for communication between persons.

(2)   Describe in what ways 'grammar' has a relationship with 'semantics'.

(3)   What is the age of natural language? Give examples of different types of communication.

(4)   Discuss the relationship between natural language and object orientation. For how long has object orientation been used in the natural language? Give examples.

(5)   Discuss the concepts of our natural language and relate them to the KISS paradigm.

(6)   How do we apply encapsulation in our language, hiding information? When do we communicate with others using encapsulation of details of objects and actions?

(7)   Describe the steps of the grammatical analysis.

5 Information architecture

5.1 Introduction

The importance of the information architecture is that it gives us a stable foundation for the information system of an organization. The information architecture has two major model types: the KISS model and the object-interaction model. By specifying these models we will find the reason for a 'real world object' from our grammatical analysis becoming a relevant 'analysis and design object'.

We define the main structure of an information system with an information architecture. We create the information architecture by looking, on one hand, at the behaviour of objects, and on the other, at the structural relationship between objects.

We specify the behaviour of objects of the object types by means of KISS models. An object type describes in a general manner the possible life of an object by specifying the order in which actions are executed by means of iterations, selections and sequences.

The structural relationship between object types is found by allowing the various object types in the object-interaction model to interact with each other on the basis of their common actions.

We define the generic description of the behaviour of objects with an object type. Additionally, we generically name objects with the same attribute values by a 'class'. The 'class level' serves to group similar objects into a 'specialization', 'category' or 'object class'.

We then discuss the attributes of the associations between the various figures in the object-interaction model. The attributes discussed are 'degree', 'cardinality', 'plurality' and 'prepositions'.

Finally we apply these concepts to an example.

5.2   Object, object type and object class

In the previous chapters we learnt about the chief concepts 'object', 'object type' and 'object class', in an informal way. We have used the various concepts in a more or less intuitive way without defining them precisely for the creation of an information architecture. To gain a correct understanding of the chief components used in the KISS method for object orientation, it is important to spend some more time on the definitions of 'object', object type' and 'object class'.

One of the most important features of object orientation is that we can look at the real world through 'object glasses'. We see the phenomena of the real world from the viewpoint of the changes happening to one or more objects. The concept 'object' hereby forms the basis of object orientation.

Definition of an object

An object is a visible and identifiable thing or notion in the real world that encapsulates its characteristics from the outside world. An object can be real or conceptual and can have a relevant behaviour which illustrates its changes.

An object is represented by a solid ellipse (Figure 5.1).

An object hides its characteristics and behaviour from the outside world. This means that we can assume that an object reacts in a particular way to actions carried out by it or on it. The way in which an object reacts is hidden inside the object itself.

An object is always identifiable by its name or identifier.

Objects can be found all around us. Examples of objects with their specific behaviour and characteristics are:

- Cow Bertha III standing in the pasture next to our house wakes us in the morning with her mooing. Bertha III lets us know that she is ready to be milked. Bertha III has just given birth to her first calf. An important characteristic of Bertha III is that she produces more than 10 000 litres of milk each year, which is a lot.

- Our television set in the living room. We can turn the television on and off and we can select programmes. The TV set can break down and be repaired again, or not. A characteristic of our TV is that it has 25 channels.

Figure 5.1   Object.

- Order 5678, sent yesterday, can be delivered in parts, can be paid for and can be cancelled. The order has a value of $10 000.

Each object is concrete and has specific values which are inseparably bound to the object. An object is identified by an identifier or a unique name and by a number of specific characteristics of the object itself.

If we wish to specify an information system in a general manner, then modelling with identifiable objects is usually not appropriate. If we were to do this, the extreme amount of detail of the relevant objects would quickly cause a problem. The solution is to specify the attributes of objects more generically on a higher level of abstraction.

The generic description of objects takes place in two complementary ways. The two levels of generic description of the characteristics of objects are:

(1) Type level;

(2) Class level.

The 'type level' describes the behaviour of objects and their dynamic relationship in a generic manner. The type level gives a general description of the changes that can be executed on, or by, objects.

The 'class level' indicates how we can group objects in a logical manner based on their common characteristics.

For both the type level and the class level we can distinguish three manifestations, which we look at step by step.

5.2.1   Type level

At the type level we describe, generally, the behaviour of an individual object. The three manifestations arise from the fact that an object type can be dependent on zero, one or more other object types. We call these the 'parent'. The three manifestations are:

Type level	Dependent on
(1) Object type	0 parents
(2) Weak object type	1 parent
(3) Gerund	2 or more parents

The difference between these concepts is determined by the extent to which they are directly existence-dependent on other object types which are their parents.

The three type-concepts are symbolized by a solid rectangle (Figure 5.2). The weak object type has an extra smaller rectangle in the object type rectangle to symbolize the life of the existence-dependent object type within the life of the parent object type. The gerund has an extra diamond in the rectangle because it is derived from an action type, which will be discussed later.

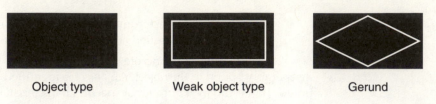

Object type   Weak object type   Gerund

Figure 5.2   Symbols for the type level.

Definition of type level objects

Individual objects with the same behaviour and the same type of attributes are described generally on a type level. Each individual object with the same dynamic behaviour is fitted into the general description at type level. The general behaviour of objects is recorded, in the KISS model, with a description of the order in which an object can undergo actions. For example, Persons with the names Janssen, Peters, Kristen, van Lieshout, Laane, van den Broeck and van Dongen have exactly the same sorts of attributes and behaviour. We represent them generically with a rectangle for the object type with the name Person. We must keep in mind that all the objects inside the rectangle are instances of the object type Person (Figure 5.3).

To be able to describe objects as object type, weak object type or gerund, we must determine if the objects undergo actions which are relevant to us. For a person we can think of, for example, 'to register' in a citizens' register, 'to commence work' for an employer and 'to purchase' a car.

In the course of this chapter we indicate how we can model the time sequence according to which the actions may be carried out by the objects of an object type.

Definition of an action type:

An action type is the general description of the changes to attributes of one or more objects of object types at one moment in time. The action of an action type takes place in a time interval tending to zero; or said differently: the action of an action type is a change happening in an extremely short time period.

The action type is shown in the model by a diamond (Figure 5.4). The action type itself encapsulates the way in which the change takes place on an object and under which conditions the changes are permitted to take place.

5.2.2   Class level

A class is the result of classifying objects based on their identical attributes. The grouping criteria for a class are not limited to the actions and general behaviour of object types but can also be defined by the values of attributes of objects.

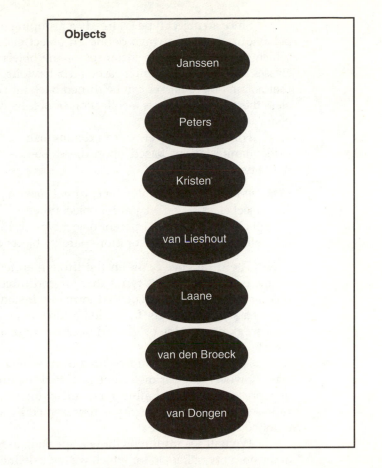

Figure 5.3   Object type Person.

When we group objects into classes there is no restriction on the number of attributes used as the basis for grouping. The only condition for the grouping is that one object may only belong to one class for a measurement scale and that the class grouping is meaningful for the problem area.

Figure 5.4   Symbol for an action type.

Since an object type is already a grouping of objects with common behaviour, we can always define an object class for each object type which then contains the instances of the object type. Because not all classes arise from a grouping based on behaviour, it is also true in reverse that not all object classes can be turned back into object types. An object class therefore represents a collection of objects with the same group of characteristics.

For the class level we can distinguish, just as for the type level, three manifestations based upon the existence dependency on parent object types. They are:

Class level	Number of parent object types
(1) Object class	0 parent object types
(2) Specialization	1 parent object type (is the generalization)
(3) Category	2 or more parent object types

The difference between the three manifestations is determined by the number of object types that are indicated as parents. A parent object type is the object type that in reality instantiates and changes the data of a group of objects. In the definition we can also replace object type with weak object type or gerund because these are specific roles of the object type.

An object class is represented by a rectangle in the same way as a type; however, the perimeter line is dotted (Figure 5.5). A specialization is represented by a double rectangle with dotted lines in order to represent a subset. A category is represented by a dotted rectangle with a dotted diamond inside it.

We will see intuitively how a specialization arises when we look at the object type Person for which we have defined a group Persons. We can also call this group the object class Persons.

Within the object class Persons there are five persons fulfilling the role of Employee. These five employees are placed in the rectangle with the dotted line inside the rectangle of the object class Persons (Figure 5.6). The two other persons are not employees. The general characteristics of the object class Persons also hold true for the specialized object class Employees. It thus becomes the specialization Employees.

Object class   Specialization   Category

Figure 5.5   Symbols for class level.

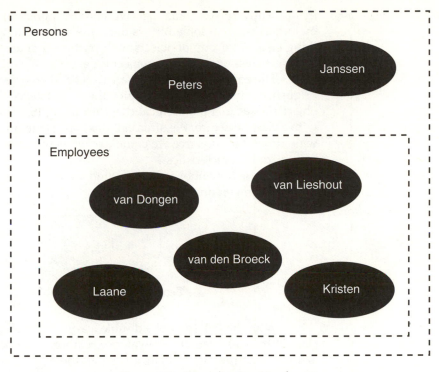

Figure 5.6   Specialization Employees.

In the example of Employees we see that the action type 'To hire' of the object type Person has implicitly been used as the grouping criterion for the specialization Employees. The general data for person remain valid for the formed specializations. The general data for person, such as 'name', 'first name', 'date of birth' are instantiated and changed by the object type Person.

We can note that the specializations fall completely inside the boundaries of the parent object type Person and associated object class Persons, also known as the generalization. This is why we represent a specialization symbolically with a rectangle inside another rectangle. A specialization has the characteristics of the class level, which is why we give the figure dotted lines. No objects are instantiated from a specialization, because they are already instantiated from the object type that is the parent.

When naming the class level we try to keep in mind that a class represents a group of objects. This means that we give object classes, specializations and categories names which match groups of objects. This is usually in the plural form.

Classifying symbol In our daily spoken language we classify things in our environment by indicating that 'something is the same as something else'. The 'something else' is a group of objects with particular characteristics that form an object class or perhaps an object type.

The equivalence between an object and an object class is shown in English by ISA. When we depict the equivalence structure between object classes in a hierarchical diagram using ISA symbols, we end up with a class structure. We often call this class structure a class tree. As we walk down the class tree we come to classes with less generic and more specialized characteristics.

The ISA symbol is represented by a rounded rectangle with a dotted perimeter line (Figure 5.7).

Figure 5.7   The ISA symbol.

With the ISA symbol a double arrow indicates from which object class in the class tree the equivalence-relation must be read. The double arrow going from the specialized classes indicates in which direction the more generic classes are to be found.

In a simplified class tree we can replace the ISA symbols with a dotted arrow showing the direction of the more generic object classes. The setting up of a class tree is illustrated by the use of an example (see Section 5.2.3).

5.2.3   Class tree

Cow Bertha III is an object of the object type milking cow. Each milking cow moos, is milked and can bear calves. Bertha III has just given birth to her first calf and suckles it herself. The calf can be a steer-calf or a cow-calf. Steers and cows are beef cattle. Beef cattle are mammals.

When we classify the example of Bertha III with her biological characteristics we get:

- Bertha III is a Milking cow.
- Calf I is a Calf.
- Milking cows are Cows.
- Calves are Steers or Cows.
- Cows are Beef cattle.

- Steers are Beef cattle.
- Beef cattle are Mammals.

In the sentences above we see that we can only use the singular form 'is a' for Bertha III. The sentence 'Bertha III are Milking cows' is not possible. This emphasizes, conforming to the grammatical rules, that we are talking about a specific object. Because we can differentiate relevant actions for Bertha III and Calf I, we name the object types respectively Milking cow and Calf.

The equivalence-relation used in the sentences can be shown by a dotted arrow. The example of Bertha III then becomes:

- Bertha III   ············>>   Milking cow
- Calf I   ············>>   Calf
- Milking cows   ············>>   Cows
- Calves   ············>>   Steers/Cows
- Cows   ············>>   Beef cattle
- Steers   ············>>   Beef cattle
- Beef cattle   ············>>   Mammals

The 'or' situation is indicated in the equivalence-relation with a '/' symbol.

In Figure 5.8 we have drawn the class tree to show Bertha III and Calf I as objects. Above them are drawn the object types Milking cow and Calf. Above the object types are drawn the object classes Cows, Steers, Beef cattle and Mammals.

For the object types Milking cow and Calf we assume in the diagram that they can be converted to the object classes Milking cow and Calves.

The general principle we use when drawing the class tree is that groups of objects with more generic characteristics are placed at a higher level. Thus Mammals are a more generic object class than Beef cattle. Besides Beef cattle there are also, for example, Whales, Elephants, Mice, Cats and Dogs, which are mammals. The grouping criteria for mammals are that the female animals bear their babies live and suckle them with special glands which produce milk. These attributes are not present in the object classes Fish, Insects and Birds.

Should we wish to generically describe 'to bear' and 'to suckle' Calf I by Bertha III, we must do this at the type level for the object types Milking cow and Calf and not for the object classes (Figure 5.9).

When classifying objects to an object class there is no superiority implied, where one object class is better than another object class. We are only making use of a different grouping criterion.

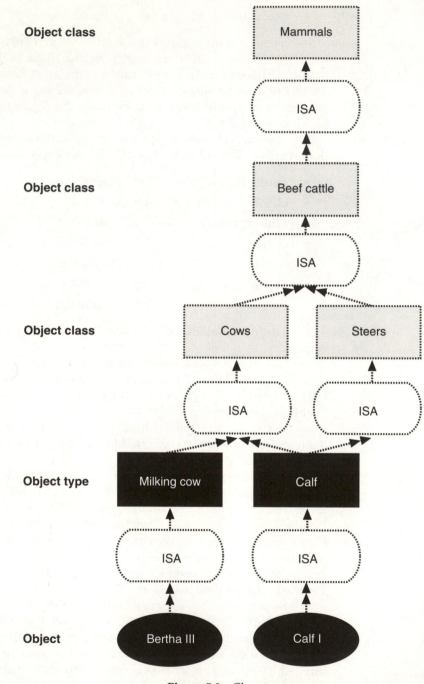

Figure 5.8   Class tree.

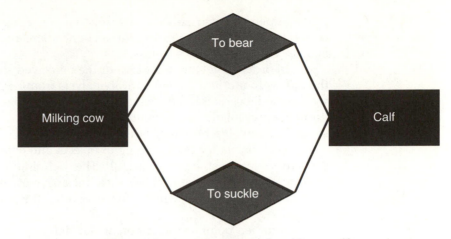

Figure 5.9 A cow bearing and suckling a calf.

5.2.4 The class tree related to superclasses and subclasses

We can expand the example of Bertha III with a random number of object classes. And so we can extend the class tree with the object classes Vertebrate animal, Animal, Living being. Each extension embraces a wider group of objects. At the level of object-oriented languages we very often make use of the concepts superclass and subclass for implementing inheritance structures.

Definition of superclass and subclass

In object-oriented languages we call the class which embraces a larger group of objects the superclass. The class which consists of objects that fall inside the superclass is called the subclass.

The relatively limited concepts of superclass and subclass of object-oriented languages must not be confused with the concepts of object class, specialization and gerund, or parent and child associations between the type level and class level as previously discussed. For example, an object class itself is not dependent on the existence of another group of objects but it can still be a subclass. The significance of this is that an object class can be taken out of the class tree without consequence, even if it is implemented in an object-oriented language as a subclass. This is simply demonstrated by taking the object class Beef cattle out of the class tree, and noting that the rest of the class tree remains valid.

For implementing the superclasses in an object-oriented language we have to define the more generic attributes of objects in the superclass and the specialized object characteristics in the subclass. By the implicit inheritance mechanism of object-oriented languages the characteristics of the superclass become available at the level of the subclass.

Superclass and subclass are relative concepts. In this way an object class seen from one viewpoint can be a superclass, while seen from another viewpoint it is a subclass.

In order to get an initial idea of the perceived structure between the objects found in the grammatical analysis from nominal predicates, we can model class trees. We have to keep in mind that these class trees do not represent the implementation structure of a class inheritance structure in an object-oriented language.

The criteria for the grouping of objects into object classes is that the grouping must be meaningful. The defining of object classes provides insight into the problem area but does not yet give rise to an information system in which, for example, the change rules are embedded.

Another point for attention when defining object classes and setting up the class tree is that we do not yet know where the exact boundaries of the area of interest lie. We can, in fact, always regroup the object classes into new object classes, which include or replace the original object classes. In this way we can continually change and expand the class structure to more general and specific characteristics without this resulting in a firm and stable basis which can serve as the information architecture.

For a sound basis for the information architecture we must have rules, and these will be further elaborated at a later stage. We show how we can achieve this by modelling the behaviour and interrelationships of the objects.

We can however perform a number of tests on the class tree before we move on to modelling the dynamic behaviour of objects.

Test for transitivity. First test the class structure for transitivity. We do this by checking if all the equivalence-relations remain valid when they are made transitive. Transitive means that the equivalence-relation still holds true when one or more intermediate object classes are skipped. If this is not possible then the class structure must be further investigated and modified.

In our example, Bertha III belongs to the object classes Milking cows, Cows, Beef Cattle and Mammals. The example therefore passes the test for transivity.

Test for plurality. When we cannot relate the object classes of the class structure to each other in the plural form, then we must further investigate the particular object class to see whether it must be regarded as an object or object attribute. The equivalence relation should be in plural form in order to talk at the class level.

Test for relevance. The test for relevance is relatively subjective but does indicate where the points of consideration lie for further analysis. To specify what the relevance of the defined class structure is, we need to look at a number of aspects of the problem area that have not yet been modelled. To determine the relevance we must validate the class tree against the dynamic behaviour of objects. The validation of the class tree takes place by creating the specifications of the object types. After we have specified these, we can fully validate the class structure and specify a definitive class structure.

5.3 Modelling the object type

In the KISS method for object orientation the modelling of dynamic behaviour plays an extremely important role. Modelling takes place in a generic manner without looking further at the behaviour of each individual object. Before starting to model the dynamic behaviour, we indicate for each object what its specific actions are and how we can describe the behaviour of objects with their actions in a simple way. Since we do not wish to describe the behaviour for each individual object, we make a description for a group of objects with the same behaviour on a so-called 'meta-level'.

The possible progress of the status of an object is recorded by the object type, weak object type or gerund. The difference between these three forms is determined by the way in which the object types are dependent on each other. So a weak object type is dependent on the existence of one other object type and a gerund is dependent on the existence of two or more object types.

The object type is shown graphically by a rectangle, the weak object type by a double rectangle and the gerund by a rectangle containing a diamond (Figure 5.10).

In the KISS method we define the dynamic behaviour of objects in a generic way with a KISS model for an object type, a weak object type or a gerund.

The KISS model describes the life of an object from the moment of its birth, to and including, the end of its life. The KISS model records the order of the action types within which the actions relevant to us can be executed. The action types themselves give a general description of the actions that can be executed in the real world on the object.

Object type

Weak object type

Gerund

Figure 5.10   Manifestations of the object type.

We make a KISS model using the description of the order of actions which can be carried out by an object. An example of a textual description of the relevant behaviour of a customer is:

> The first action of a warehouse customer is 'to register'. After he has been registered, the customer can 'order', 'pay' and 'collect' many times. A customer ceases to exist when the warehouse 'de-registers' him and so he can no longer 'order', 'pay' and 'collect'.

To make the KISS model we view reality from an activity viewpoint. Before we move on to creating the KISS model we write the rules for the order in which the relevant action types can change the object type in textual form. The behaviour of the object type is then modelled for an object type, a weak object type or a gerund by recording the time sequence of the execution of the actions in a KISS model with a combination of coordination symbols and action types.

5.3.1   The KISS model

A KISS model describes in a generic manner both the status and the behaviour of single objects. The KISS model is created for the:

- Object type;
- Weak object type;
- Gerund.

The method of creating the KISS model is identical for the object type, weak object type and gerund.

The behaviour of objects is modelled with coordination symbols by describing the relationship between action types. The coordination symbols used in the KISS model to record the dynamic constraints between the action types, based on the ordering rules, are:

- Iteration;
- Selection;
- Sequence;
- Parallel iteration.

A KISS model shows, by the combination of coordination symbols, the sequence in which the actions are allowed to be executed by an object of an object type. In this way the KISS models show graphically the dynamic constraints of the object type.

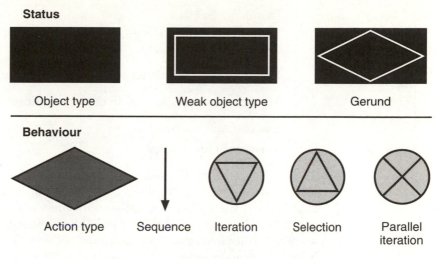

Figure 5.11   Building blocks of KISS models.

The conventions for the various coordination symbols of the KISS model differ from each other. In this section we look at how to use these coordination symbols in order to be able to compose a KISS model correctly. The building blocks of a KISS model are shown in Figure 5.11.

5.3.2   Sequence rules for the composition of KISS models

Before we go any further, we take a step back and look at the textual description of the real world and the grammatical analysis. One of the aims of the grammatical analysis was to produce a list of candidate objects and candidate actions.

Using the list of candidate actions we investigate the ordering rules for the execution of the actions on or by an object. The purpose of defining ordering rules is that they indicate, in a simple way, what the structure of sequence, selection and iteration is for the execution of actions on an object.

The ordering rules for a sequence on an object are defined by using the general sentence structure:

Sequence:

First action 1, **then** action 2, **then** action 3, and so on.

In the ordering rule sentences we can also include the iteration of actions and selection between actions.

Iteration:

First action 1, then iteratively action 2.

Selection:

First action 1, **then either** action 2 **or** action 3 **or** action 4.

The first and last action of an object is indicated by:

Instantiation: action 1

Termination: action 9

When we have defined the ordering rules then we can create the KISS model by working through all the ordering rules. Whilst creating KISS models we will be regularly confronted with indistinctness and questions. Often there is nothing to be done other than to ask the end users to further investigate and take stock of how the way of working is in reality. Working interactively with the end user ensures eventually that the definitive KISS models match closely the way of working of the organization.

Instantiation of an object

Each object begins its 'life' at a particular point in time which is important for us or our information system. So, for example, Mr Peters begins his active life as a client of the warehouse Fastsales Ltd after he was registered on 15 January 1994. Mrs Johnson begins her active life after she is registered with the warehouse Fastsales Ltd on 16 January 1994.

To create a generic model describing the lives of clients, we can consider the individual named persons to gain the necessary insight into the ordering of the actions. This description is actually too detailed to serve as a general model.

The behaviour of objects is more generically described with models which are based on the description of the general behaviour of objects with the sequence of execution of the actions. Before we can actually create a complete model we must explain its conventions. So first we will discuss how an object is instantiated.

To represent the object type, the model starts with a rectangle for the object type containing its name. The object type is always placed at the top of the model. Beginning with this object type, the model continues below the object type with either an initiating action type or a coordination symbol that allows the life of a specific object to be started. This is indicated in the model by a vertical arrow (sequence) to the first action type (see Figure 5.12).

After an action has been carried out on the first action type in the model, we can state that a new 'object-instantiation' of the object type has been created. This can also be called an 'occurrence' of an object type.

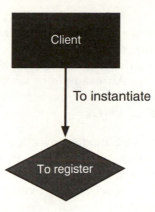

Figure 5.12   The instantiation of a new object from the object type Client.

The object type and the action type are connected with an arrow which indicates the direction in which the model should be read. The instantiating action ensures that the object acquires an identifier and that a number of attribute types are given initial values. The attributes hereby also define the status of the instantiated object.

Similarly to the object type, the models for the weak object type and gerund start with a double rectangle or rectangle containing a diamond, respectively. The attributes of the model generally also hold true for the weak object type and the gerund which allows us to limit the discussion of the model to a discussion of the object type.

Sequence   We model a sequence in the KISS model when we wish to show a compulsory time succession of action types. A sequence is shown in the model by an arrow that indicates the reading direction (Figure 5.13).

A sequence can only exist in combination with an action or a coordination symbol such as the iteration or selection symbol. A sequence has its own identifier and also contains the position which it occupies in the model.

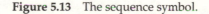

Figure 5.13   The sequence symbol.

A sequence of action types is shown in the model by placing the action types in a line underneath each other and connecting them with downward pointing arrows (Figure 5.14). A sequential path is shown in the model by reading the path of action types from top to bottom.

An example of an object type that consists of one sequential path is a client who is registered, places one order and is subsequently de-registered.

Selection

In a KISS model we include a selection symbol when we can carry out a number of alternative action types for the object in the real world, and between which we must make an explicit choice.

A selection between two or more action types is indicated in the model by the selection symbol: a circle containing a triangle (Figure 5.15). The entrance to the selection symbol is at the top or on the left-hand side. Underneath the selection symbol are two or more paths, each

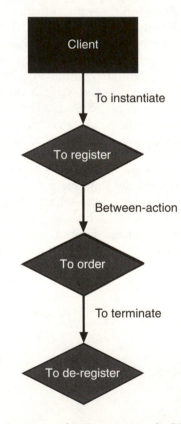

Figure 5.14   Sequence of action types in the KISS model.

Figure 5.15   The selection symbol.

containing a sequence of one or more action types (Figure 5.16). We are compelled to choose between one path or another and we must follow this path to its end.

After the action types of the chosen path have been followed, we must always go back to the selection symbol and continue with the alternative which begins to the right of the selection symbol. This alternative can be a new action type or another coordination symbol. A selection symbol is not necessarily always followed by an action type or another coordination symbol. A KISS model can end in one of the paths under the selection symbol.

When no new action type or new coordination symbol starts to the right of a selection symbol, then we must search for a possible iteration symbol higher in the KISS model, before we entered the selection symbol. We can decide, based on this higher-positioned iteration symbol, what the possible subsequent iterated action types might be. In this manner we see that selections in the model are embedded in iterations by higher-positioned iteration symbols. The iteration loops are not pictured with separate lines. These imaginary lines are actually implicitly specified with the conventions for the iteration symbols, which are discussed in a separate paragraph.

Each selection symbol used in a KISS model is given its own identifier. We may also give the selection symbol a name to make the model more readable.

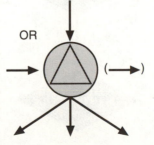

Figure 5.16   Rules for drawing the selection symbol.

In Figure 5.17 we look at a KISS model for the object type Item. First we give a short textual description of the ordering rules.

- Instantiation: order;
- First order, then either pack or cancel;
- First pack, then deliver;
- Termination: either deliver or cancel.

The model shows that we can only 'deliver' when we have 'packed' the item. A possible subsequence for the selection takes place when either the packed item is 'delivered' or is 'cancelled'.

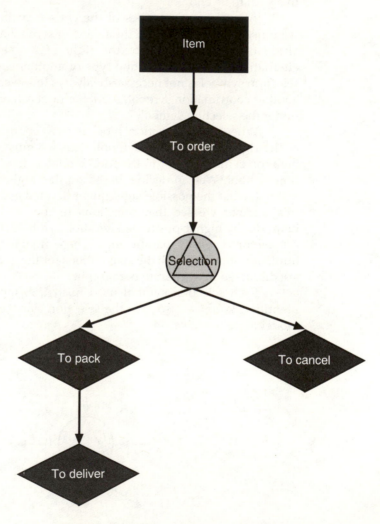

Figure 5.17   KISS model with a selection symbol.

Figure 5.18   The iteration symbol.

At the exit on the right of the selection symbol there are no subsequent action types defined. This makes 'To deliver' and 'To cancel' the action types that can terminate the life of the item.

It should be noted that Figure 5.17 does not yet provide a complete description of the life of an item. The life of an item does not usually begin with 'to order', but with, for example, 'to include' the item in an assortment. The KISS model in Figure 5.17 must now be expanded by other action types.

Iteration

In a KISS model an iteration of action types is modelled when the same action-structure can be carried out by an object many times, in the real world. An iteration is shown in the KISS model by a small circle containing a triangle with a corner pointing down (Figure 5.18).

The conventions of the iteration symbol appear similar to those of the selection symbol. The difference between them is that for an iteration symbol there is only one path leading from under the iteration symbol, which can be followed zero, one or more times.

We can enter an iteration symbol from the top and from the left-hand side (Figure 5.19). Under the iteration symbol there must be only one path commencing with an action type or a selection symbol. When, for example, we can iteratively make a choice between many paths, we place a selection symbol underneath the iteration symbol. For all the action types placed under the selection symbol, the rules for the selection symbol apply.

When a path leading from under the iteration symbol has been followed completely, we must return to the iteration symbol to see if the iteration must be executed one more time, or if we should take the exit on

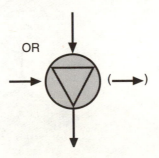

Figure 5.19   Rules for drawing the iteration symbol.

the right-hand side of the iteration. The exit on the right-hand side of the iteration symbol can begin with an action type or with another coordination symbol.

An example of an iteration is a client who, after being 'registered', 'orders' many times in a row before he is de-registered. The action type 'To order' is then placed under an iteration symbol (Figure 5.20). The loop back to the next higher iteration symbol is not depicted in a KISS model.

After we have executed one or more action types, we can place another iteration symbol under an iteration symbol. The iterations are then placed under each other and form iteration loops nested within each other. One iteration falls inside the other iteration. We call this a vertical iteration.

Horizontal iteration When we terminate an iteration with a subsequent iteration, we end up with a succession of possible iterations for an object type, viewed in time. We also call this a horizontal iteration structure. The iterations are now not nested but follow each other in time sequence.

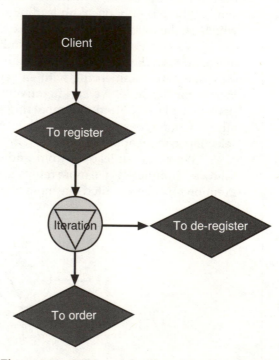

Figure 5.20　KISS model with an iteration symbol.

The ordering rules provided by a KISS model with a horizontal iteration for the object type 'order' are:

- Instantiation: to receive;
- First receive order, then iteratively order items;
- First order all items, then iteratively deliver items;
- First iteratively deliver all items, then finish off order;
- Termination: to finish off.

The resulting model (Figure 5.21) shows two iteration symbols standing next to each other. With this model we indicate that all the items are ordered and only then delivered. After the delivery of an item has taken place, it is no longer possible to order more items on this order.

To improve the readability we can place a name inside the iteration symbol. The first iteration symbol can be given, for example, the name 'iteration order line' and the second iteration symbol the name 'iteration delivery line'.

With the iteration symbol we can also define iteration conditions. We then indicate the maximum and minimum number of iterations that must be executed and how many we expect to be executed on average. The iteration conditions are defined in a separate iteration specification.

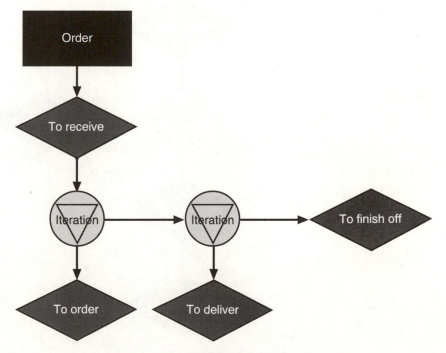

Figure 5.21   Horizontal iteration in a KISS model.

Iteration with a sequence

We may draw a sequence of two or more action types underneath an iteration symbol. An example of this is a client who is registered. After he has been registered, we can iteratively receive an order that is subsequently delivered.

The ordering rules for the client are:

- Instantiation: to register;
- First register, then iteratively receive and deliver;
- First receive, then deliver.

In Figure 5.22 there is a structure in which 'To receive' and 'To deliver' are placed sequentially behind each other.

The KISS model with a sequence of action types underneath the iteration symbol indicates that the order must be delivered before a new

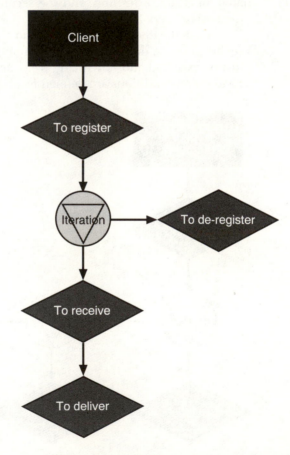

Figure 5.22 KISS model for Client.

order can be received from the client. When we illustrate the course of receiving and delivering orders in a figure that indicates for a time period how many orders are received (Figure 5.23), we can follow the progress of orders sequentially received one after the other from one client. We can also discern that there is at most one outstanding order. The figure shows that for an iteration symbol we must completely follow a path of sequential actions before we can repeat the execution of the first action of the path.

The weak object type

The structure of an iteration and a sequence of action types is not sufficient when we can receive several new orders from a client before we have delivered the previous order. A solution is to be found by defining a new object type Order that is existence-dependent on the object type Client. The object type Order becomes weak by its existence dependence with respect to Client. The object type Client is called the parent or the strong object type.

When we have defined the weak object type Order by a sequence of To receive and To deliver, we can remove the action type To deliver from the KISS model of the strong object type Client and place To deliver in the KISS model of the weak object type Order. In the model we indicate the weak object type by a double rectangle.

In order to guarantee that orders can be received in parallel, we must allow a synchronization to take place between the various object types based on the common action type 'To receive' that is included in the KISS models for both Client and Order (Figure 5.24). Since the model for Client no longer has a sequence of action types under the iteration symbol, we can now allow more orders to be open concurrently for one client.

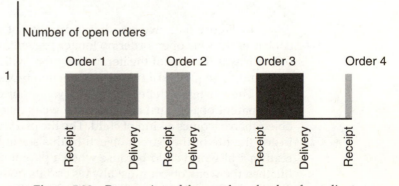

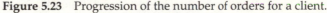

Figure 5.23 Progression of the number of orders for a client.

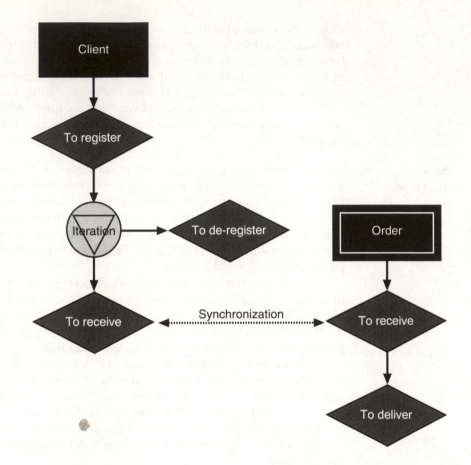

Figure 5.24 Synchronization of the weak object type Order with its parent object type Client.

In Figure 5.25, we see that a number of open orders can exist concurrently. One open order no longer prevents the receiving of a new order, as was the case of the iteration symbol with a path leading from it containing a sequence of two or more action types.

The existence dependence of a weak object type says implicitly that a parent object must exist before a weak object can exist. The weak object then becomes a kind of child. The life of a weak object falls entirely inside the life of the parent object. In this sense the weak object is not really a real-world child because when a parent object wishes to end its life then the weak object must always end its own life first. Parent–child relationships in real life do not usually work this way.

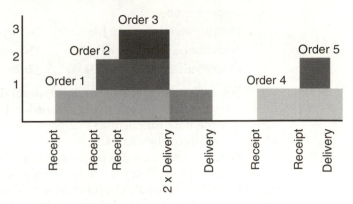

Number of open orders

Figure 5.25   Progress of the number of open orders.

Rule for creating a weak object type

The general rule for creating a weak object type is that a weak object type comes into being when, following an iteration symbol, there are two or more action types depicted in sequence that do not have to be executed after each other in a sequence of action types.

Rule for recognizing a weak object type in the textual description

During the grammatical analysis we had already discovered an existence dependence between objects distinguished by the 'attributive adjunct'. We can test our example for the attributive adjunct by defining 'the order of the customer'. By distinguishing the attributive adjunct we have already gained insight into structures with existence-dependent weak object types.

Normalization by weak object types

A side-effect from the naming of weak object types is that an implicit normalization of the data structures of the objects occurs. The benefit of this manner of working is that the functional dependence of a weak object type is visible in an extremely explicit way.

We explain the implicit normalization in the example below.

Action:	to register customer 2345
Date of registration:	29 May 1990
Name of client:	Jansen
First names:	Gerard Willem
City or town:	Amsterdam
Postal address:	Klaverstraat 234
Client number:	2345

Action: to receiver order from customer 2345

Order number:	1	2	3
Date received:	6 June	20 June	7 July
Number of items:	100	150	50
Order value:	$1234.00	$2678.00	$3456.00

For each action 'to receive' the general data for the client remain valid and the data for receiving an order form a repeating group. Removing the data for client 2345 means that we no longer know from whom we received the orders.

When a weak object type is existence-dependent on two or more parent object types, then we are no longer dealing with a weak object type, but with a 'gerund'. The difference between an object type, a weak object type and a gerund is determined by the number of object types on which it has a direct hierarchical line of existence dependence.

Type level	*Dependent on*
(1) Object type	No single object type
(2) Weak object type	One object type
(3) Gerund	Two or more object types

Parallel iteration

An alternative way to execute a sequence of action types iteratively in a KISS model, without being blocked on any path by a sequence of action types, is to make use of parallel iterations.

A parallel iteration is indicated by a small circle containing a diagonal cross (Figure 5.26).

The parallel iteration ensures that the progress of the life of weak object types can be represented in one large KISS model without having to model the weak object type explicitly. This way of representation is especially useful when we want to represent the total behavioural structure of objects in one diagram. The result is that the object can be visualized as one big process with many dependent processes. The disadvantage of using parallel iterations is that we do not explicitly define the weak object types. Because of this aspect it is preferable to avoid the use of the parallel iteration. In some application areas such as real-time processing, though, parallel iteration is a powerful tool for representing the total process structure of an object type in one KISS model.

Figure 5.26 Symbol for parallel iteration.

The parallel iteration is used in the real-time environment to model threads of actions that can be active concurrently next to each other. As such, the parallel iteration models implicitly the concurrent behaviour of objects, seen as threads.

The drawing convention for the parallel iteration specifies that there may be one or more subsequent paths leading from under the parallel iteration to underlying action types. At the end of each arrow a new action type begins with its possible subsequent actions (Figure 5.27).

Between the paths there is no exclusion such as we have for the combination of a selection symbol and an iteration symbol. The parallel iteration has the option of allowing objects of many weak object types to exist side by side.

The entrance to the parallel iteration is at the top or at the left-hand side. The definite exit is on the right-hand side. This can optionally be used although it is preferable to have a terminating action type after each parallel iteration. The parallel iteration has its own identifier, and optionally a name, in the KISS model.

It holds true for a parallel iteration that for each action type under the symbol we define the maxima and minima for the iterative execution of the specific action type. Besides this we can also specify maximum and minimum constraints for the simultaneous execution of parallel paths.

Parallel iteration places us in a state of being able to follow many paths with sequences of action types next to each other. The maximum number of paths that can be simultaneously followed commencing from under a parallel iteration symbol is greater than or equal to 1. Figure 5.28 shows a model with parallel iteration for one path.

A parallel iteration is not limited to following only one type of path. Many different paths may start from under a parallel iteration (Figure 5.29). This makes a parallel iteration a unique combination of iteration and selection symbols that results in loosening up the rules for the sequential execution of the paths that otherwise apply to the iteration

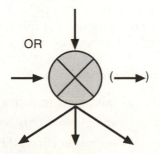

Figure 5.27 Rules for drawing a parallel iteration.

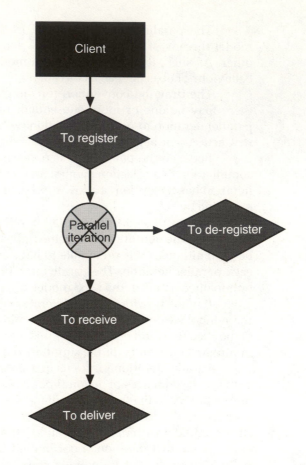

Figure 5.28   KISS model with parallel iteration for one path.

and selection symbols. Every path that is instantiated has to keep track of its own state. We have to administer the threads of every instantiated path.

The capability of a parallel iteration to execute the paths simultaneously cannot always be modelled by a combination of iteration and selection symbols. For this we need weak object types that are synchronized on the basis of common action types.

An example of ordering rules produced by a KISS model with a parallel iteration is:

Instantiation: to register

First register client, then iteratively receive order

First register client, then iteratively visit by sales representative

First register client, then iteratively make up bill

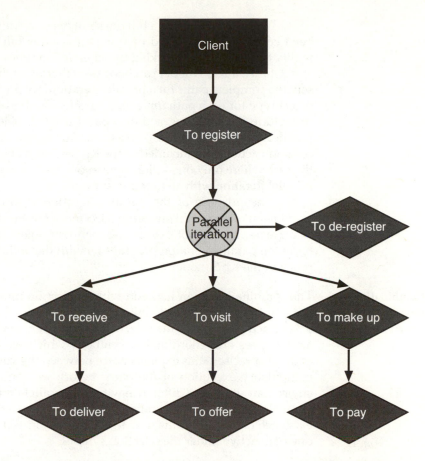

Figure 5.29   KISS model with parallel iteration for more than one path.

First receive, then deliver

First visit, then offer

First make up bill, then pay

Receive, visit and make up bill do not lock each other out.

First register client, then deregister client

Termination: to de-register

The action types 'To receive', 'To visit' and 'To make up bill' do not lock each other out and can be executed in parallel for as long as desired until the customer is de-registered.

The receiving of orders means that new orders are instantiated for one client. This takes place simultaneously with the instantiation of new bills and offers for the client.

The instantiation of a bill does not need to wait until a receipt has been completely processed or until a previous bill has been paid. In reality there is also no blocking by other action types.

Since a KISS model can become rather extensive when we represent the complete paths for a parallel iteration, we prefer to define a weak object type for each path under the parallel iteration. It is then sufficient to include the initiating action type of a weak object type under the parallel iteration (Figure 5.30). A synchronization then takes place on the common action type included in the KISS models of both object types. In the case where only one action type in one path remains, we replace the parallel iteration with an iteration symbol.

The purpose of the parallel iteration is, on the one hand, to provide an overview in one large KISS model of the dynamic behaviour of a greater number of existence-dependent object types. On the other hand the parallel iteration provides us with the ability to model concurrency in the KISS model.

Combination of the iteration and selection symbol The combination of an iteration with a selection underneath it gives us the ability to indicate a definite choice between various paths (Figure 5.31). Each path under the selection symbol can consist of a number of action types and coordination symbols, which we must follow to its end. It is precisely this explicit choice between the various paths and the compulsory execution of the paths before we can again make a new choice that shows the difference with the parallel iteration.

With a selection symbol there is no suggestion of the parallel existence of various paths next to each other; in fact there may only be one path active under the selection symbol.

5.3.3   Multiple use of action types in a KISS model

In a KISS model the same action type can be found in multiple locations (Figure 5.32). The content of this action type is identical in the different locations. However, these action types are used in the various places in the model and they differ from each other.

An example of an action type that is included many times is where we can order items for one order in a proposal or we can order the items for an order and at the same time reserve them. The difference between the two ways of working is that for an order, items are reserved, but for the proposal there is no definite reserving of items. In the example it holds true that when items are ordered once for an order and reserved, then it is no longer possible to use this order for a proposal where only the action type 'to order' can be executed.

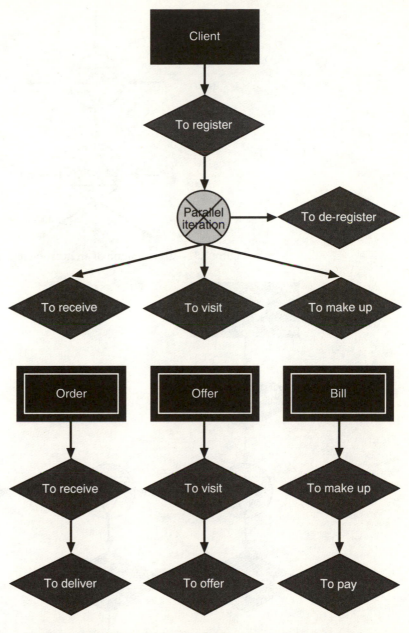

Figure 5.30   KISS model for parallel iteration and weak object types.

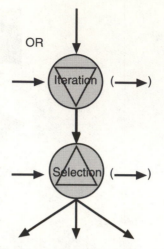

Figure 5.31   Combination of an iteration and a selection.

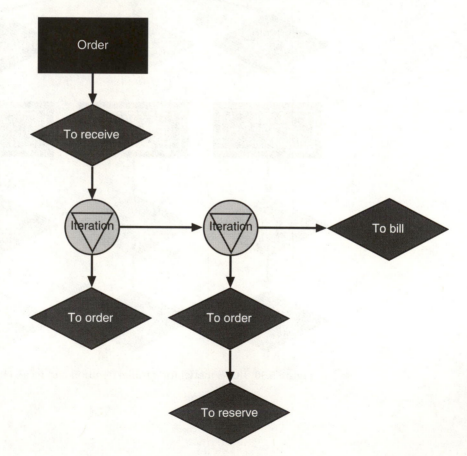

Figure 5.32   Multiple use of one action.

5.4   The object-interaction model

When we compare a KISS model to our natural language, the KISS model can be compared to the 'singular form'. The behaviour of objects is specified with a KISS model in a generic manner for one object-instantiation of an object type.

With an object-interaction model we illustrate how one or more objects of an object type interact with the objects of another object type by means of common action types. With an object-interaction model we can represent the 'plural form' of our natural language. We do this by creating the object-interaction model at 'type level' using the interaction between the defined KISS models. The building blocks of an object-interaction model are shown in Figure 5.33.

We create an object-interaction model by allowing the common action types of various KISS models to be the 'linking pin' that takes care of the interaction between the object types. The common action types ensure that synchronization takes place between the autonomous KISS models. The object-interaction model uses the action types to define the structural relationship between the object types, weak object types and gerunds, which is formed by their individual behaviour.

After the interaction between the autonomous KISS models has been modelled, we can also represent the grouping of objects into object types with identical attributes in an object-interaction model. The grouping of objects into various classes is done by using an 'ISA symbol'. The ISA symbol indicates an equivalence relationship.

We can distinguish between three forms of grouping: object class, specialization and category. To be able to clearly differentiate the classification of objects from the object types, we draw the figures of object class, specialization and category with dotted lines. All the ISA association lines are also dotted to differentiate them from the association lines of the interactions.

In the object-interaction model we can add an additional differentiating factor between 'type level' and 'class level' by the use of names. The names for the object type, weak object type and gerund are always singular. We can give names to the object class, the specialization and the category which are in the plural form or we can give a name which specifies a group of objects such as 'fruit', or 'vegetation'. Giving a name in the plural form is always easy since the class level always defines a group of many objects. In some situations it is an exaggeration to use the plural form, in which case we go back to the singular form combined with the semantics of the symbols used in order to indicate the class level.

Type level and class level have a strong relationship with each other and cannot be viewed separately from each other. So, for example, there is an automatic grouping of objects into a classification when the

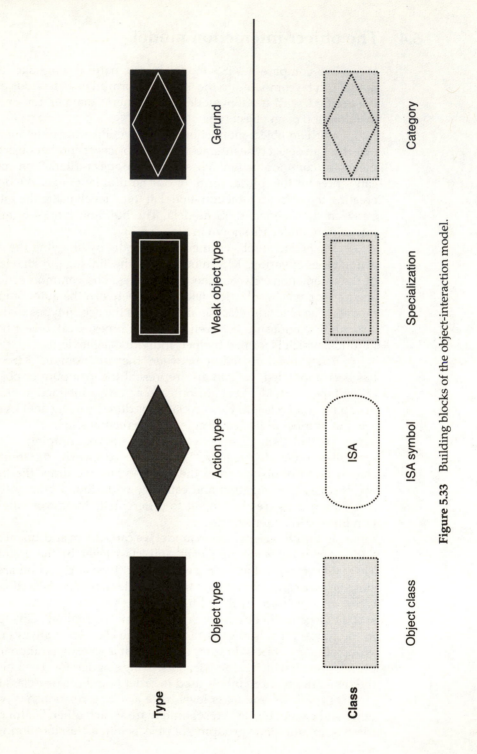

Type

Object type Action type Weak object type Gerund

Class

Object class ISA symbol Specialization Category

ISA

Figure 5.33 Building blocks of the object-interaction model.

objects of an object type undergo an identical action. The common grouping element for the class is the undergoing of the action. In this way both the specialization and the category come into existence.

With the manipulation of the object-interaction model we first look at the aspects which have to do with the synchronization of object types. Then we expand the object-interaction model with the aspects that have to do with the grouping of objects into various classifications. Finally we discuss the characteristics of the associations in the object-interaction model, such as connectivity, totality, cardinality, plurality, prepositions and concurrency.

Definition of interaction

In an object-interaction model we speak of an interaction when, at one moment in time, objects of two or more different object types undergo change by an action of the same action type.

An example of an interaction between object types is the ordering of items by a client (Figure 5.34).

To gain insight into the interrelationships of the object types in the structured sentences we can create an initial object-interaction model using the list of candidate objects and candidate actions from the grammatical analysis. The active verbs become the action types and the direct and indirect objects become the object types upon which the actions are carried out. The initial object-interaction model consists of only object types and action types that may be further expanded with ISA symbols to represent the classifications that have been determined.

The advantage of creating an initial object-interaction model at an early stage is that it allows us to gain an insight into the two-dimensional relationship between the single-dimensional sentence structures of the textual description. Using the initial object-interaction model we can move on to the creation of KISS models in a structured manner, which in their turn verify the initial object-interaction model and lead to the definitive object-interaction model. It is necessary for the definitive object-interaction model that the initial object-interaction model is enlarged to include some extra concepts.

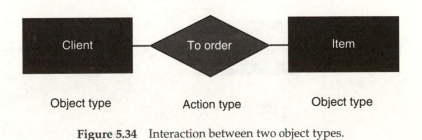

Figure 5.34 Interaction between two object types.

5.4.1   Weak object type

During the discussion of KISS models we have seen how a weak object type comes into existence. We have also seen that a weak object type is an object type that is existence-dependent on one other object type which we refer to as the parent or the strong object type. The weak object type is shown with a double rectangle.

There can be many action types associated with a weak object type. It is therefore important to know which action type instantiates the weak object type. In the object-interaction model we show this by drawing a double arrow in the direction of the instantiating action type (Figure 5.35).

A weak object type can be recognized in the textual description of the problem area when it is indicated in an attributive adjunct as a possession. The indication of possession in our spoken language specifies the existence dependence with respect to another object type. In our language we use the verb 'to have' or the preposition 'of' in an attributive adjunct. In the latter case the substantive noun standing to the right of the preposition 'of' in the sentence is the owner, and the substantive noun to the left is the possession.

To verify if a weak object type also has a relevant behaviour, we must always indicate the relevant action types that instantiate and change the weak object type. When we cannot find any actions in the structured sentences, then the substantive noun does not become a weak object type but an attribute type of the object type.

The modelling of object-interaction models with weak object types has the advantage of a reduction of data definitions by the single recording of data, resulting in an implicit normalization of the data collection. For this it is, however, necessary that the existence dependencies between the weak object types and the strong parent object types are defined.

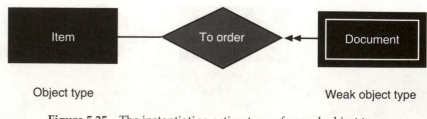

Object type   Weak object type

Figure 5.35   The instantiating action type of a weak object type.

5.4.2   Gerund

A gerund is a concept in the grammar of the natural language. A gerund is the substantiated form of the infinitive form of a verb. This substantiation occurs, for example, by adding the suffix '-ing' to the infinitive form. For example, the verb 'to insure' leads to the gerund 'the insuring'. The verb 'to pay' leads to the gerund 'the paying'.

In our natural language we make use of a gerund because we cannot combine two active verbs in one active structured sentence without using a conjunction. We cannot for example say: 'We pay insure our car to the company.'

In these situations we must always substantiate one verb into a gerund. In English, however, it has become more customary to replace 'insuring' with the word 'insurance'. 'Paying' becomes 'payment'. In practice therefore, the infinitive form of the verb is turned into a gerund by the addition of such suffixes as '-ance', '-ment', '-ion' and so on. After we have applied the rule strictly we obtain the following sentences: 'We pay the car insuring to the company.' 'We insure the paying of the car to the company.'

In practice these sentences become: 'We pay the car insurance to the company' and 'We insure the payment of the car to the company.'

It should be noted that technically-speaking, following grammatical rules, the '-ing' form of the verb is still the gerund, but that other forms are in current use in the English language.

These two sentences are, semantically, completely different. This is because the use of a gerund adds an implicit existence dependence to the structured sentence. In this way the car in the first sentence must be insured before we can pay the insurance. In the second sentence the payment of the car must exist before we can insure the payment.

The common element of the above two sentences is that the gerunds are dependent on the existence of both the car and the company that insures the car. As well as this, a follow-up action takes place in both sentences, based on the result of an action which takes place that is substantiated to a gerund.

In an object-interaction model an action type is shown by a diamond and an object type by a rectangle. Because the gerund has both the attributes of an action type and of an object type hidden inside it, we show this with a rectangle containing the action type symbol (Figure 5.36). The initiating action type for the gerund is thus the initial action type that is substantiated. In the KISS model for the gerund the initiating action type is also then the first action type drawn under the gerund symbol.

In an object-interaction model there is always at least one action type associated as a consequence of the gerund, because otherwise there are no grounds for the existence of the gerund!

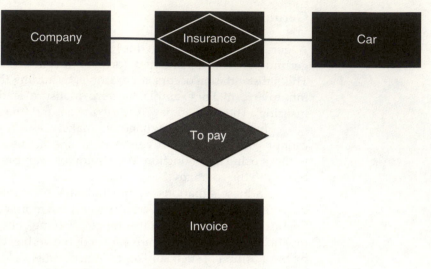

Figure 5.36   Gerund.

When setting up an object-interaction model it is not intended that the gerund *per se* be given a name ending in -ing. For the substantiation of, for example, the action type 'insert' we use the substantive noun 'insertion' and not 'inserting'. We choose insertion because this is much more natural to our ear.

We do not need to indicate the initiating action type with a double arrow on the association line for the gerund as we do for the weak object type. This is because the initiating action type is encapsulated in the gerund and thus there can be no action types located between the gerund and its parent object types.

An alternative representation is to draw both the gerund and its instantiating action type. In this case, we must draw a double arrow linking directly to the action type.

5.4.3   Classification of objects

The principles of the object-interaction model discussed so far have to do with the way the individual object types interact. We have also seen how a weak object type and a gerund are represented in the object-interaction model. We have used the relationship between objects as a base for this as they are formed by the interaction of autonomous object types.

In the introduction we saw that there was another form that represents the relationship between objects. The second form was achieved by the grouping of objects into classes. The division was made on the basis of commonality of the attributes of the various objects. Based on these common attributes we can divide the objects into classes.

The classification is shown in the object-interaction model by an ISA symbol. There can be three class types inside the object-interaction model: specialization, category and object class.

In an object-interaction model we can adopt the class level by adding an ISA symbol in combination with the specific classification-type. There are a number of rules about including a specialization or a category, which are discussed below in detail.

5.4.4   Specialization

A specialization always occurs in combination with a generalization. The generalization gives a description of the generic characteristics of objects. A specialization classifies objects based on local characteristics for which the general characteristics of the generalization hold. The generalization is the parent of a specialization. The objects of a specialization belong to a broader class of objects.

The specialization itself has all the characteristics of the class level and has no single attribute of an object type. This is why we do not create a KISS model for a specialization. A specialization itself undergoes no actions of an action type. The action is always executed on the generic object type, that is, a generalization. The specialization groups the object instantiations that have undergone a specific action of an action type. Concurring with this, the highest generalization in the hierarchy will always be an object type, for which we must specify a KISS model that includes the action type that created the specializations.

A specialization is represented in an object-interaction model by a double rectangle with dotted lines (Figure 5.37).

Specializations are always modelled in combination with an ISA symbol. The ISA symbol is directly associated with the generalization, which is the parent. The specialization is the child, just as in weak object types.

The reading direction from the specialization to the generalization is shown by a double arrow on the line segment between the specialization and the ISA symbol. The line segments connected to the ISA symbol are always dotted. The generalization is indicated with a single arrow.

The purpose of a specialization for modelling is that by using it we can incorporate the general current concepts of an organization into an object-interaction model in a simple manner. Also, the objects of a specialization inherit the general attributes of the generalization. By taking them over from the generalization and individually specifying them, we can use them in the translation to physical data storage structures.

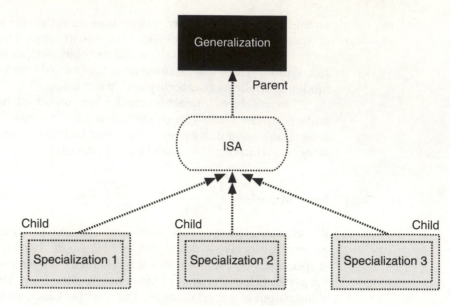

Figure 5.37   Specialization.

One of the most common applications of a specialization is the modelling of role processes. Role processes are explained below, using the example of a housing association.

The housing association

The housing association has 100 houses, 80 tenants, 350 occupants and 400 people on record. All the houses are rented out. All the occupants are registered on file. The administrator begins to build a model of this situation with an object-interaction model.

The first equivalency rules he formulates are:

- An occupant is a person.
- A tenant is a person.
- A person is not always a tenant.
- A person is not always an occupant.

These four equivalency rules indicate that a person is the generalization and that a tenant and an occupant are specializations.

The specializations come into being when the persons carry out a specific action, in our case to rent and to occupy. We incorporate the tenants and occupants into a separate class and we include and change the common attributes of person in the generalization.

In the example we see that the same person can be both tenant and occupant and that he does not have to exist as a specialization. The specializations do not exclude each other in the proposed object-interaction model.

The distinguishing feature of the specialization is that the division of the objects into classes is based on action types. This automatically leads to the fact that a specialization in the object-interaction model corresponds to a role process of an object type. The object type itself is then the generalization. The specialization represents the state of an object undertaking an action. See Figure 5.38.

The method of naming a specialization is shown below, using the example of a contract.

The contract   A contract is written for a client. In a contract we can propose/order/ deliver items. Ordering always takes place after proposing, and delivery always takes place after ordering. When the contract for the ordering of

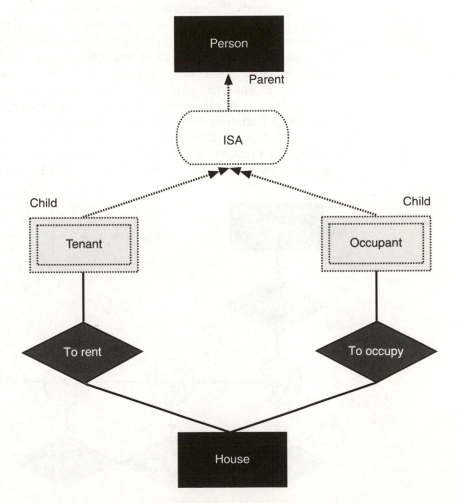

Figure 5.38   Example of role processes Tenant and Occupant.

items has been used, it can no longer be used for proposing. When the contract has been used for delivery, it can no longer be used for ordering. Finally, the contract is used for invoicing.

In the KISS model we see that the iterations are not placed underneath each other but are in line horizontally (Figure 5.39). Therefore, we do not have a hierarchy with existence dependence between proposing, ordering and delivering, which would have required a definition of weak object types.

The contract must be written before we can iteratively execute the action types. The action types must be executed one after the other in time sequence and they can only be executed when the contract has been written.

To clarify the status of the contract we can place names above the action types: 'proposal', 'order form' and 'delivery docket'. We do not create weak object types for 'proposal', 'order form' or 'delivery docket' because there is no sequence of multiple action types inside the iterations. 'Proposal', 'order form' and 'delivery docket' are just different states of 'contract'. The creation of a weak object type purely to guard the status is superfluous. We can, however, name specializations, which are incorporated as dotted figures in the object-interaction model (Figure 5.40).

We use an ISA symbol to represent the specializations. This is because Proposal, Order form and Delivery docket have only one generalization, Contract, that is common to all three specializations.

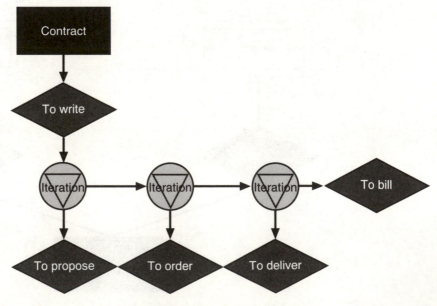

Figure 5.39   KISS model for a Contract.

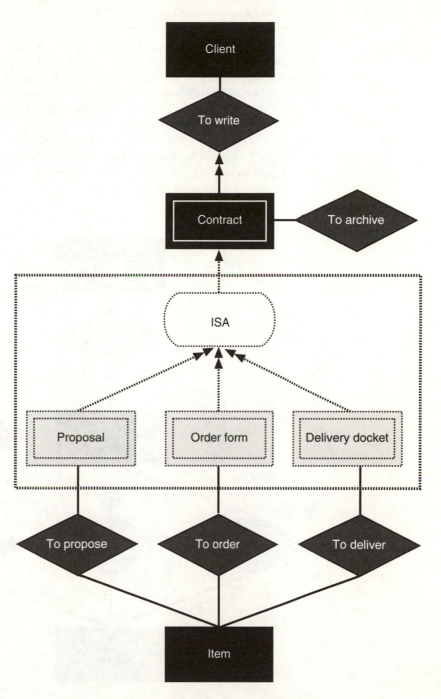

Figure 5.40 The role processes for Contract.

We have observed in Figure 5.39 that the contract has completely independent behaviour, with the iterated action types included in it. The three specializations issuing from it do not have their own KISS model. All three do, however, represent a group of objects of the object type Contract. Just as for the weak object type, the rule holds true here that the specialization is existence-dependent on the generalization. We show this (Figure 5.40) by a double arrow on the line segment between the specialization and the ISA symbol, and a single arrow for the generalization.

We can now indicate the three role processes of Contract by specialization symbols. Role processes are formed by the grouping of objects that have undergone the same actions. This is why it is relevant to show them in the object-interaction model.

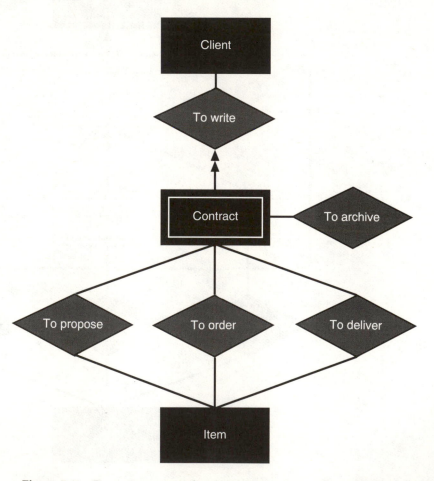

Figure 5.41   Removing a specialization from an object-interaction model.

The role process, represented by a specialization, will become an existence-dependent group of objects. The specialization will make use of the characteristics maintained at the generic level with the action types that apply to the generalization, also known as the parent object type.

The specialization can be removed from the object-interaction model without further consequence for the iteration structure. We see then that the solid line from the action type links directly to the parent object type (Figure 5.41).

The consequence of removing specializations is that we can no longer determine a logical name for a group of objects that have undergone a specific action.

The purpose of modelling specializations is to be able to implement them as autonomous files at a later stage. There must be integrity between the generalization and the specialization, conforming to the given definitions of the specialization. This means that a generalization, in principle, is the leader in the whole process of instantiating and changing objects. This is also the case for distributed and client/server implementations. The generalization takes care of the 'distribution integrity' of the objects.

5.4.5 Metamorphism

In the real world we can easily identify objects whose appearance undergoes change during their life time. The example of a butterfly is described below.

The life of a butterfly starts with the fertilization of an egg. The female lays many eggs. From these hatch tiny larvae called caterpillars. At this point they are pests, eating the food plants of man. The female always lays her eggs on the type of plant that the caterpillars will use for food. After several skin sheddings the full grown caterpillar is ready to turn into a pupa. At this stage the butterfly spins a button of silk, called a cocoon. It then clings to the cocoon by a sharp spine at the end of the body and moults for the last time. As the old caterpillar skin peels off, a naked pupa called a chrysalis appears in the cocoon. It is an 'insect in the making', encased in a tough, flexible shell. Then the caterpillar moults for the last time. Marvellous changes take place in the cocoon. Most of the organs of the caterpillar break down, turning into semi-liquid. The wings, legs and other parts of the adult butterfly are formed from this material. After the pupa has freed itself, it is wet and its wings are soft and limp. It slowly pumps blood into the wings. Gradually the wings expand and harden. In a few hours the adult butterfly is ready to fly and seek a mate.

This decribes the life of one butterfly. As such, a butterfly can be seen as an object that undergoes several metamorphoses. It would be incorrect to describe the life of the butterfly using several object instantiations because although the appearance of the object changes, it remains the same object during its lifetime. As such, we can specify the life of a butterfly in one KISS model (Figure 5.42).

In this figure we have not represented the different states of the caterpillar. The states of the butterfly are represented in Figure 5.43 by specializations of the object type 'butterfly'. The metamorphic states of the butterfly are respectively 'egg', 'caterpillar', 'pupa', and 'adult'. Distinct action types take care of the metamorphic transition.

We see that the object type 'butterfly' is instantiated by the action type 'to fertilize' through the specialization 'egg'. The fertilization is done by an another adult butterfly. The action types that change the visual state of the butterfly are placed between the specializations.

It can be seen easily that the specializations are not object types in themselves, but only states in the life of the butterfly. The metamorphic behaviour of the butterfly makes it difficult to see this at first sight. It is only the KISS model that can give the answer to the question: 'what is an object type?'.

The example of the butterfly is different from the example in which the person can rent and occupy a house, in that the butterfly can only be in one distinct specialization whereas the person can be in both roles concurrently. This is specified explicity in the respective KISS models.

Definition of metamorphism

Metamorphism is the attribute of one single object showing different behaviour/characteristics in distinct parts of its life. The metamorphic states can be represented explicity in the object-interaction model by specializations.

In addition to modelling metamorphism by a specialization we describe in Section 5.4.6 how polymorphism is modelled by the category.

5.4.6   Category

With the generalization/specialization structure we have seen how we can reuse the attribute types, specified generically for the generalization, in the specialization. The specialization is thus a group of objects which directly incorporates the changes that take place on an object at a generic level.

As well as incorporating and reusing the defined object attributes with attribute types, we are also acquainted with the reuse of the same action type by various object types. Reuse of action types is modelled by a so-called category. A category indicates that we can change the objects

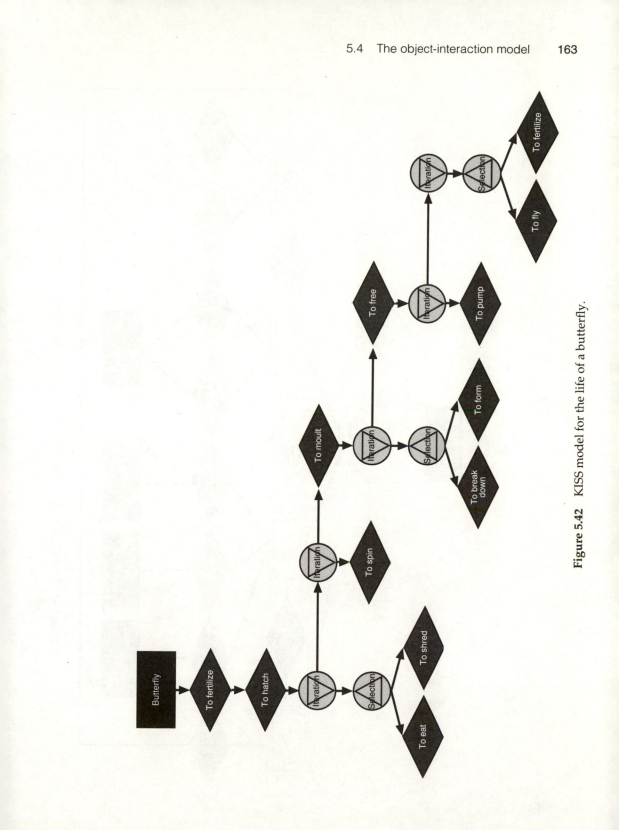

Figure 5.42   KISS model for the life of a butterfly.

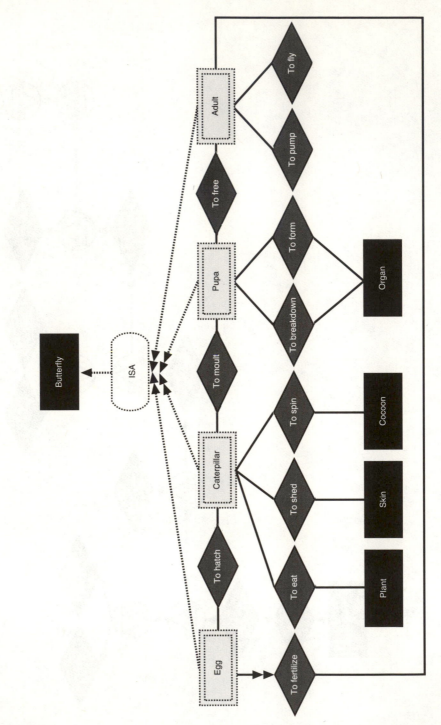

Figure 5.43   Object-interaction model for metamorphic object type Butterfly.

of different object types with the same action type without the requirement that the changes take place simultaneously on all object types. A
category functions as a 'switching element' between object types.

How and when we include a category in the object-interaction
model is discussed below using the example of 'fruit'. Here we set up an
object-interaction model in which an action type is used by different
object types that are more or less mutually exclusive.

Example of a category of 'edible fruit'

An example of a category is a person who can eat a banana, an apple and
an orange. By allowing the KISS models for person, banana, apple and
orange to interact with each other, all of which include the action type 'To
eat', we end up with an object-interaction model with an action type that
has four association lines to, respectively, the object types person,
banana, apple and orange (Figure 5.44). We now have a problem because
the four association lines tell us that all four object types interact with
each other at the same time. This is not true in reality because we cannot
eat the banana, apple and orange at the same time.

A solution to this problem can be found in the use of a category.
We give the category the name Fruit because this is the common characteristic of all three object types. The category Edible fruit is a class
we associate with the action type 'To eat'. Apple, banana and orange
are in turn connected to the category fruit, with separate ISA symbols
(Figure 5.45).

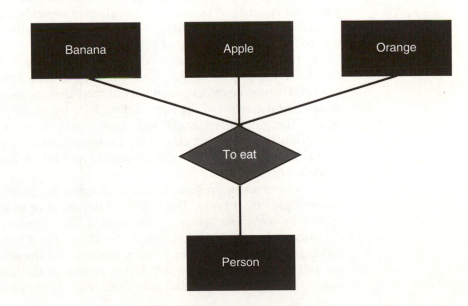

Figure 5.44   Object-interaction model.

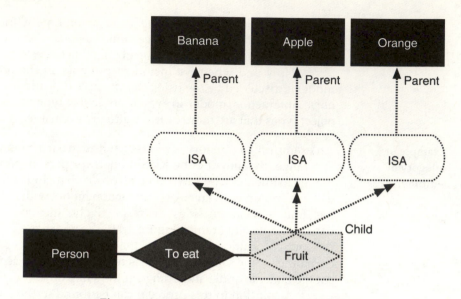

Figure 5.45   Example of the category Edible fruit.

Definition of a category

A category is a class that enables the reuse of action types by different object types. The category does not have a KISS model or attributes that a parent object type does not have. The KISS models and attribute types are in fact entirely specified by the parent object types. The category is named using the grouping characteristic that indicates whether or not particular actions can be executed by different object types. The name of the category is therefore often derived from an adjective that indicates the characteristic of the related object types.

The symbol that is used to represent a category is identical to that used for a gerund except that it uses dotted lines. The dotted diamond inside the category symbol indicates that the category has come to exist by the reuse of the same action type by many different object types. The dotted rectangle indicates that we can also represent the attributes of an object class with a category, owing to the fact that a category groups objects of different object types on the basis of identical action types.

By means of an ISA symbol a category is existence-dependent on multiple object types. The existence dependence of the category is shown by a double arrow on the dotted line segment between the category and the ISA symbol. The arrow shows the direction of the ISA symbol. The existence dependence arises because the action types that are related to the category are incorporated in the individual KISS models of the object types that are associated with the category.

5.4.7 Integration of the class tree in the object-interaction model

When modelling a category we can evaluate the object classes we named in Section 5.2.3 in a class tree, in steps, in order to incorporate them into the object-interaction model.

We explain this by enlarging the scope of the example of Bertha III, which we discussed in Section 5.2.3. We included the object classes Mammals, Beef cattle, Cows and Steers in the class tree. We will expand the example to include Pigs and Horses. We see that we can still use Mammals as the object class and that beside the subclass Beef cattle we must add the subclasses Pigs and Horses.

When creating the object-interaction model we must first determine for which object types we will create KISS models. In our example (Figure 5.46) we choose the object types Beef cattle, Pig and Horse because they exhibit differing behaviour, which is modelled in their KISS models. We can ride horses, milk the cows and fatten the pigs. We specify the common action types 'To bear' and 'To suckle' babies which are identical for the object types. We model the reuse of the action type with the categories Female and Young.

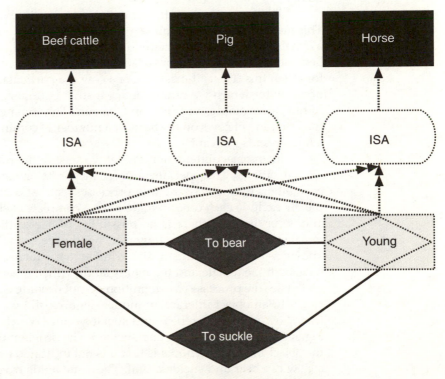

Figure 5.46 Two categories.

Table 5.1 Permitted interactions between object types.

Action type	Female		
To bear	Beef cattle	Pig	Horse
Young			
Beef cattle	x		
Pig		x	
Horse			x

Owing to the fact that female beef cattle cannot bear a young pig or a young horse, we must define explicitly the restrictions that apply to the reuse of action types by the categories, in a separate table for the object-interaction model (Table 5.1).

In natural language the female and young beef cattle, pigs and horses each have their own name. So we indicate the female animals with the names Cow, Sow and Mare and the young animals Calf, Piglet and Foal.

The two concepts do not entirely mutually exclude each other. This means that a female calf can also be called a cow, just as we can call a female foal a mare. A strict dividing line cannot be drawn. This is partly because each mature cow has at some time been a calf, even though it has forgotten this. The calf-existence of a cow is a particular phase in the life of a cow for which we cannot define a strict boundary. Other phases of life are, for example, 'yearling' and 'barren'. These come into existence by the grouping of cows on the basis of a number of common attributes that a farmer finds relevant.

In an object-interaction model we specify the role processes with specializations. The specializations can partly or completely exclude each other. In this way the role processes 'calf' and 'cow' do not completely exclude each other. We do have a complete exclusion with 'cow' and 'steer' because there is no possibility of beef cattle changing from female to male. In nature, however, we do see sexual ambiguity, also known as hermaphroditism, occurring in many forms. Hermaphrodites have both the female and the male glands, which means that the female and male role processes by definition do not exclude each other.

In an object-interaction model (Figure 5.47) we see that either a Cow, Sow or Mare can bear and suckle young. We also see that a Calf, Piglet and Foal can be born and suckled. The problem that we have with the object-interaction model is that it is not indicated explicitly that only a Cow can bear and suckle a Calf. The same holds true for a Sow and a Piglet, and a Mare and a Foal.

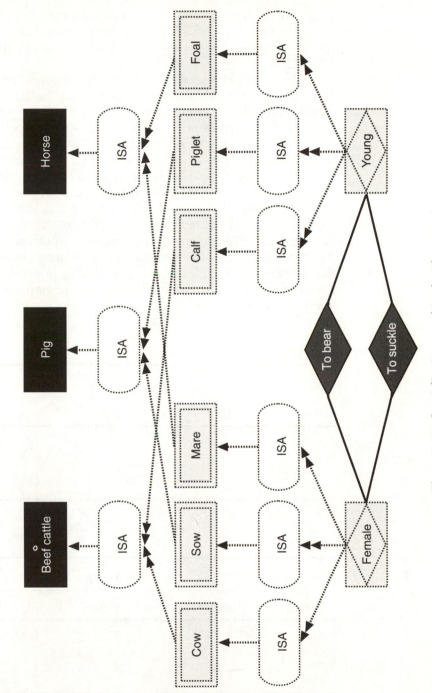

Figure 5.47 Specializations combined with categories.

To make the relationship explicit, we draw up two tables for the action types 'To bear' and 'To suckle' with the columns 'female' and 'young'. In the tables we show what the permitted combinations of the specializations of object types are for iterations among them (see Tables 5.2 and 5.3).

In the object-interaction model, the 'category' models the reuse of action types in an explicit manner. This is the consequence of including the action types in the singular form in the object-interaction model with the appropriate degree. The action types related to the category are reusable by all object types that are directly or indirectly related to the category as parent object types, by means of ISA symbols.

The action types associated with the category change the attributes of all the object types directly or indirectly related to the category. When we execute the same action on a group of objects with apparently totally different attributes, then it would seem that we have a strongly varying, also called polymorphic, behaviour of objects in the category. Applying this to the object-oriented programming environment we see that the category provides us with a modelling principle for defining, in a well-founded manner, where and how polymorphism occurs in the information architecture.

Table 5.2

Action type		Young	
To bear	Calf	Piglet	Foal
Female			
Cow	x		
Sow		x	
Mare			x

Table 5.3

Action type		Young	
To suckle	Calf	Piglet	Foal
Female			
Cow	x		
Sow		x	
Mare			x

Definition of polymorphism

Polymorphism is the attribute where the objects in a group display different behaviour on execution of the same action. Polymorphism is modelled explicitly with a category.

The interpretation of polymorphism, when it is modelled by a category, is that the category functions as a link that allows the various object types to reuse one or more action types. The reaction of the group of objects can be very diverse, so that the result of the execution of the action can have very different manifestations. The category gives a structural form for the object-interaction model of the reuse of the specifications of the action type.

In action types related to a category, we must define how the reuse by the various object types takes place. We do this, for example, by making a matrix in which the permitted options are indicated. In a category we specify in detail how a common action type acts on each individual object type. We also specify the concurrency of the execution of the action type on the various object types.

During the grammatical analysis of structured sentences, a category is often recognizable when a predicate (verb) is used in relation to a choice between objects or a combination of many objects. In a structured sentence the choice is indicated by: 'or/or', 'and/or' and 'and/and'. The categories we have considered have described situations where only one parent object type with one action type interacts with the category. In daily practical situations it is possible for there to be more than one. We illustrate this below, using the example of making jam.

Example of 'making jam'

An example in which different object types combine to carry out one action type by means of a category is to be found in the making of two sorts of jam using different ingredients. The jams have the following ingredients:

Plum jam	*Cherry jam*
Plums	Cherries
Sugar	Apples
Setting agent	Sugar
	Setting agent

The two sorts of jam that we can make are plum and cherry. In both sorts, sugar and setting agent are used. In an object-interaction model (Figure 5.48) we show this by including a category 'ingredient' that reuses the action type 'To cook' for the combination of ingredients for the two different sorts of jam.

Each jam has its own ISA symbol for the category, because each has its own composition of different object types whereby each object type combined with another object type at one moment in time interacts with the action type.

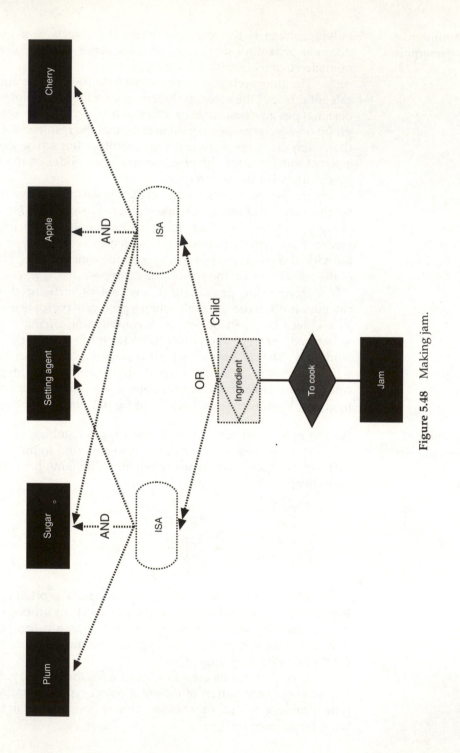

Figure 5.48 Making jam.

The premise for the object types in the example is that the different ingredients each have their own set of action types, which justify the inclusion of the object types in the object-interaction model. The relevant action types we can distinguish are, for example, the picking of fruit, the peeling of apples, the pit-removal of plums and cherries, and the dissolving of sugar.

In many situations it is no longer practical to allow all the possible combinations in which the object types by means of one action type can interact with each other to be modelled in an object-interaction model. In these cases it is sufficient to connect the individual parent object type with only one ISA symbol. In addition to this we create a matrix in which we note the possible combinations of the object types that can undergo a common action. We can expand the matrix with new combinations and add specific names for these combinations.

Table 5.4

	1	2	3	4
Plums		x		
Apples	x		x	
Cherries	x			x
Sugar	x	x	x	x
Setting agent	x	x		x
Cherry jam	x			
Plum jam		x		
Apple sauce			x	
Apple syrup			x	
Plain cherry jam				x

In Table 5.4 we see that both apple sauce and apple syrup are made from apples and sugar. The difference between apple sauce and apple syrup is determined by the method of cooking.

The time sequence in which an action type may be executed for an object type is always modelled for the object type itself. For this we also include in the KISS model all the action types that are connected to a category in the object-interaction model. The object types themselves are always parent to the defined category. Should the object type or a particular action type be cancelled or removed then we must check that the category still has grounds to exist. It is a requirement of a category that there are at least two existing parent object types.

In the above example the category is used to represent an assembly situation. The cooking of different products is similar to assembling a car from parts. If different parts have different behaviour, they will also have different KISS models. In this case we need to make use of the category in order to assemble the individual parts.

We can also use the category as a basis for decision-oriented questions. An example is the determination of the result of crossing donkeys with horses. The result is a mule or a hinny. The difference in serviceability between a mule and a hinny is that a mule is best used as a pack animal and draught animal while a hinny is only good as a pack animal. A hinny is smaller than a mule. A mule differs from a horse by the shape of the head, the long ears and short-haired tail.

We get a mule-young by crossing a donkey-stallion with a horse-mare, while we get a hinny-young by crossing a horse-stallion with a donkey-mare. The mule-stallions and hinny-stallions are infertile. The mule-mares and hinny-mares are fertile and can be fertilized by horse and donkey stallions (Table 5.5). Figure 5.49 shows the object-interaction model for 'To fertilize' and 'To bear'.

Table 5.5   The result of stallions fertilizing mares.

To fertilize	Mare			
	Donkey	Horse mare	Hinny	Mule
Stallion				
Donkey	Donkey	Mule	Hinny	Hinny
Horse stallion	Hinny	Horse	Hinny	Mule
Young				
Hinny	–	–	–	–
Mule	–	–	–	–

Table 5.6   Decision table for fertilization.

To fertilize	1	2	3	4	5	6	7	8
Donkey mare by a donkey stallion	x							
Donkey mare by a horse stallion		x						
Horse mare by a donkey stallion			x					
Horse mare by a horse stallion				x				
Hinny mare by a donkey stallion					x			
Hinny mare by a horse stallion						x		
Mule mare by a donkey stallion							x	
Mule mare by a horse stallion								x
To bear donkey young	x							
To bear horse young				x				
To bear hinny young		x			x	x	x	
To bear mule young			x					x

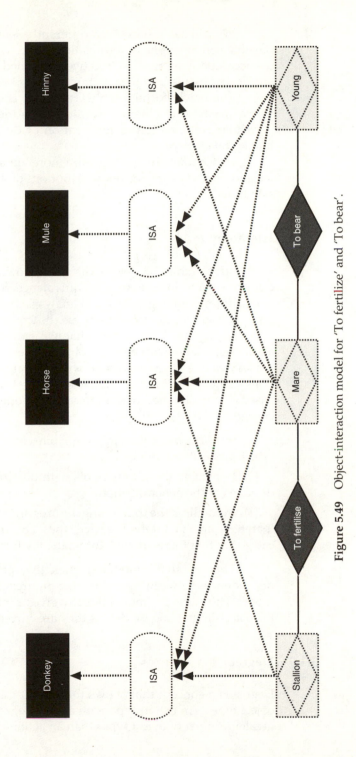

Figure 5.49 Object-interaction model for 'To fertilize' and 'To bear'.

We can set Table 5.5 up differently. We place the distribution of possible combinations of fertilization of the mares by the stallions, with the accompanying results, into two combined tables. The combinations are viewed by reading the columns from top to bottom.

The newly-formed table (Table 5.6) is called a decision table, in which we indicate what the result is from the action 'To bear' when a particular combination of fertilization of donkeys, horses, mules and hinnies takes place.

In Chapter 10 we go into more detail about the underlying techniques and further application options of the decision table and decision functions.

5.4.8   Hierarchy model

At the start of this chapter we discussed how to set up a class tree. The class tree gave insight in the equivalence relationships between the objects found in the grammatical analysis. The equivalence relationship is based upon the nominal predicate (ISA relationships).

In Section 5.4 we saw that we can also define an important additional relationship between objects, like existence dependence. With the knowledge we now have of weak object types, gerunds, specializations and categories, it is relatively simple to create a hierarchy model based on the obtained object-interaction model. The hierarchy model is created by:

(1) Suppressing and removing from view all action types from the object-interaction model;

(2) Replacing the ISA symbols with dotted arrows that point in the direction of the generalization;

(3) Modelling the remaining figures in a hierarchy such that the 'parents' are positioned above the 'children'. Any gerunds and categories that there are will automatically form a network structure.

The hierarchy model defines the structure of the existence-dependence between the different figures of the object-interaction model. The hierarchy model thereby gives a relatively quick insight into the object-interaction models as they are currently set up.

5.4.9   Degree

Degree is a concept that shows the impact that one action type has on object types. An action type with a high degree will effect changes in a greater number of object types than an action type with a low degree.

Definition of degree

The degree of an action type is equal to the number of 'strong' object types that are associated with the action type.

The degree of an action type can be unary, binary, ternary or *n*-ary. The higher the degree of an action type the greater the influence of the execution of the action on the object-interaction model. In the example in Figure 5.50 the action type 'to see' only impacts Person, while 'To insure' impacts Person in addition to Car and Agent.

In the example we see how unary action types are represented. In reality we frequently come across unary action types. The reflexive verbs in our natural language are often unary. For example, 'I see myself', 'the car falls to pieces', and so on.

The actual degree is not found for weak object types and gerunds in an object-interaction model by counting the number of association lines to the action type, but is derived by following the existence dependencies. When deriving the degree of an action type we must take account of the implicit dependencies of the weak object types and gerunds.

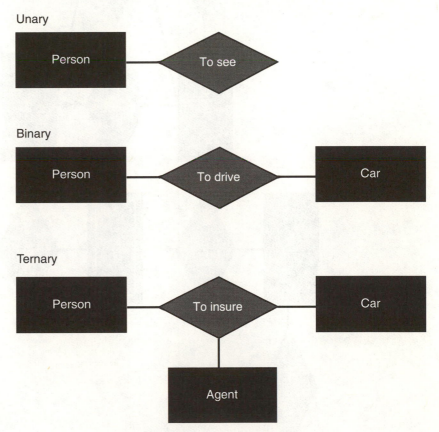

Figure 5.50   The degree of an action type.

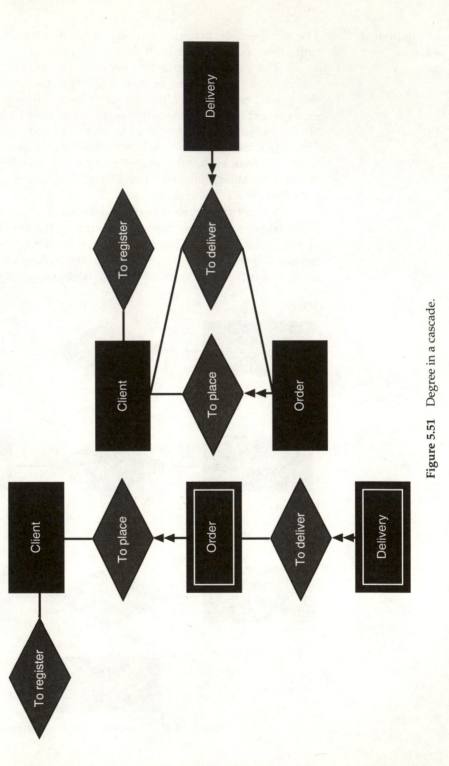

Figure 5.51 Degree in a cascade.

The degree of an action type is, for weak object types and gerunds, 'hidden' in the object-interaction model. To make the degree clear and visible we must directly connect the action types that are associated with weak object types to all the parent object types of the weak object types and gerunds, and then by counting the total number of association lines an action type has with strong object types, we get the degree of the action type.

By using the example of a cascade with three object types, of which two are weak, we explain the determination of the actual degree (Figure 5.51). The first step is to take the action types that are associated with the weak object types, and connect them with the object types upon which the weak object types are dependent. When we have done this we count the number of association lines of one action type. We see that the action type related to the weakest object type has the highest degree. In Figure 5.51 this is Degree 3.

Owing to the existence dependencies, we must always take account of the implicit relations with stronger parent object types in the cascade when determining the actual degree.

For a gerund with two parent object types the degree is always equal to 3. The action type that instantiates the gerund is associated with the two parent object types and the gerund itself.

The consequence of the direct associations for the determination of the degree is that by using them we can indicate immediately upon which object types an action type can possibly bring about changes. This also means that the action type in Figure 5.52 that appears to be unary for the weak object type 'delivery' does in fact have Degree 3. The particular action type can therefore effect changes on the data of Delivery, Order and Client.

The implicit associations of the action type 'To pay' will result in Degree 4 after the gerund is despecialized into object types and action types that can be existence-dependent on other object types. This is indicated by a double arrowhead (Figure 5.52).

5.4.10   Cardinality

Cardinality is a concept that is often used in the design of database systems. Cardinality indicates how the object collections of one or more object types are related to each other. With this we can determine the appearance of the data structure for the recording of information.

The cardinality consists of two components:

(1) Connectivity;
(2) Totality.

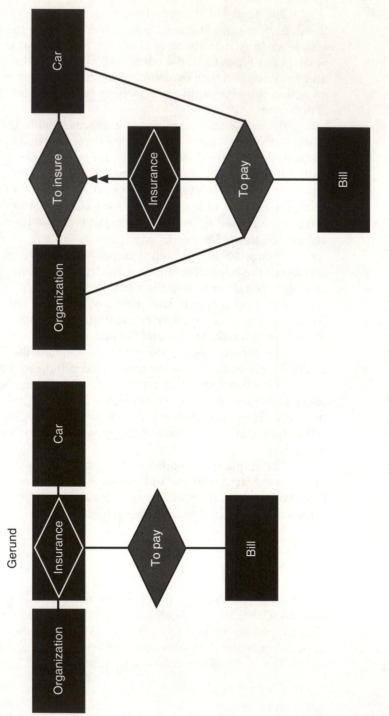

Figure 5.52   Despecialization of a gerund.

The connectivity is also called the upper boundary of the cardinality, while the totality is equal to the lower boundary of the cardinality.

In the discussion of the components of the cardinality we indicate how the cardinality is defined for the object-interaction model. The difference between an object-interaction model and a logical or physical data model is that in an object-interaction model we explicitly name the action types, in contrast to the logical and physical data model. The cardinality is specified in the object-interaction model for the association with the action type.

Connectivity

The upper boundary of the cardinality is also known as the connectivity.

Definition of connectivity

The connectivity indicates how often an action of an action type can be executed on a particular object of the object type.

The connectivity is included in the object-interaction model on the association line between the action type and the object type and is positioned immediately next to the action type.

When we further consider the concept of connectivity in relation to the KISS models, it becomes clear that we have already specified implicitly the connectivity in the KISS models. The connectivity becomes 'n' when an action type is situated under an iteration symbol or parallel iteration symbol. The connectivity is equal to '1' for all the other action types. Thus connectivity is defined as the number of times that an action can be carried out on the same object.

The connectivities in an object-interaction model derive directly from the combination symbols in the KISS models. Where an iteration of actions takes place, the association line in the object-interaction model for an action type with an object type will have a connectivity of 'n'.

We use connectivity as the starting point for the creation of a logical data structure and for the definition of the technical structure of the database. When we set up a logical and technical structure for the picture representing the real world, we must decide whether all the structures will be entirely implemented or whether a less ideal picture would suffice.

The connectivity in the KISS method is virtually identical to the connectivity of the extended entity relationship method. In comparison to the extended entity relationship method the KISS method is supplementary because connectivity is also defined for singular action types that are only connected to one object type in the object-interaction model. The focus of the extended entity relationship method is restricted and directed purely to the creation of the structure of a conceptual database diagram. Care must be taken with the positioning of the connectivity if we are accustomed to the entity relationship method.

Figure 5.53

This is because the connectivity is specified in a way that results in reversing the position of the connectivity in relation to the relationship or action type symbol.

In the object-interaction model we place the connectivity by the side of the association line by the action type. We do this by checking how often the action can be executed on the object type. An immediate validation of the included connectivity with the iteration symbols in the KISS model must take place in the second instance.

The connectivity is shown with letters.

Example of connectivity '1' to 'n'

A contract can only be made once for one client. For a client we can make multiple contracts.

In Figure 5.53 we see that the connectivity is defined for both the object type as well as the weak object type. We define the connectivity for the gerund by checking how often the associated object types can execute the initiating action on the gerund.

Example of connectivity 'n' to 'n'

With a contract we can order an item many times and an item can be ordered many times (Figure 5.54).

5.4.11 Totality

Totality indicates whether or not an action of an action type must be executed by an object. The possible values for totality are '0', '1' or higher. When the execution of the action is optional, that is, not compulsory, the value of the totality becomes '0'. When the execution of the action is compulsory, the value of the totality becomes '1'.

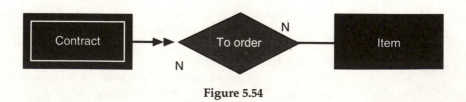

Figure 5.54

Figure 5.55

An example in which the totality is '1' is the instantiating action type of an object type. For the lower boundary it may be a requirement that an action type be executed more than once. In this case the totality has a value higher than '1'.

The totality is shown in an object-interaction model together with the connectivity alongside the association line of the action type. The combination of the totality (lower boundary) and the connectivity (upper boundary) is called the cardinality. The cardinality is made up of two values separated by a colon. The first value of the cardinality (in front of the colon) is the totality and the second value (after the colon) is the connectivity.

In Figure 5.55 we see that the connectivity for contract is '1' because the contract can only be made once. The totality is also '1' because it is the instantiating action type. For a client we can make many contracts although the execution of this action is not compulsory.

Figure 5.56 shows that one item can be ordered many times with a contract. To give the contract relevance at least one item must be ordered. An item can be ordered multiple times, but 'To order' is not a compulsory action type.

5.4.12 Plurality

In the introduction to the object-interaction model we indicated that we represented the 'plural form' of our natural language with it. To represent the plural form explicitly in the object-interaction model we utilize the concept of plurality.

Definition of plurality

Plurality defines how many objects of one object type are involved in the action at one moment in time.

Figure 5.56

In reality one action can take place on more than one object of an object type at one moment in time. To show this in the object-interaction model we place the plurality beside the association line, between an action type and an object type. The plurality is positioned by the association line directly beside the object type.

The plurality has a minimum lower bound of 1. The highest value for the plurality is infinite. In some cases we can specify the values for the plurality very precisely. In this way we give the range of values for which the plurality is valid.

An example of an action type with a plurality of '1' is a car that crashes. We have not specified what the car crashes into. The action type therefore stays singular.

Figure 5.57 shows where the plurality is included in the object-interaction model. In addition, we have clarified the example by showing how many objects of the object type 'car' interact with the action type.

The figures with association lines between the ellipse and the action type are not object-interaction models although we have included them in order to provide a greater clarification and understanding of the concepts of plurality.

When two cars crash into each other the plurality becomes '2'. The structure of the object-interaction model does not change in relation to the previous object-interaction model, but the value of the plurality changes (Figure 5.58).

A recursive relationship in the entity relationship method is equivalent in the KISS method to a unary action type with a plurality of '2'. A recursive action type is the execution of one action on two objects of one object type.

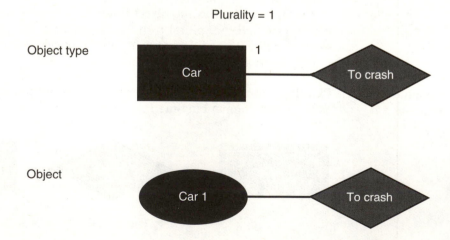

Figure 5.57   Plurality of 1 for a unary action type.

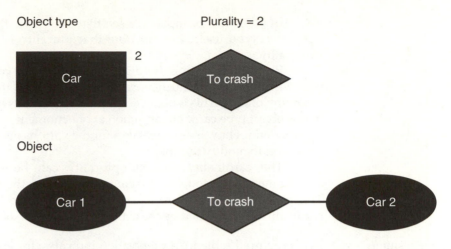

Figure 5.58   Plurality of 2 for a unary action type.

When three cars crash into each other at one point in time, we are still dealing with a unary action type. Meanwhile the plurality has become '3'. When we represent this in an object-interaction model, we see that the structure has remained identical but the plurality has been increased to '3' (Figure 5.59).

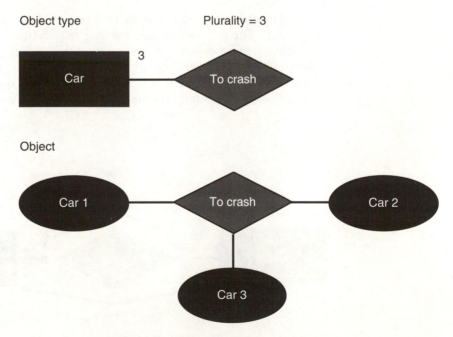

Figure 5.59   Plurality of 3 for a unary action type.

In all of the examples we see that we define the plurality from the action type itself. We can note that plurality is not the same as cardinality.

Plurality is a strongly-functional concept, in contrast to cardinality which is directed much more to the definition of the structure of the recording of data. This is because the plurality defines how many objects of one object type carry out an action at one moment in time. The plurality also defines how many messages for the various objects can be sent to the action to modify the objects.

The cardinality and the plurality can be illustrated in an object-interaction model by placing them beside the association lines. The plurality is then positioned next to the object type while the cardinality is positioned by the action type (Figure 5.60).

Preposition alongside the association line

In a structured sentence a preposition indicates, for example, the place, time or direction. The reason for using the preposition is that it provides clarification on the way in which the action is related to the indirect object. The relationship can be strongly bound to place and time.

To improve the readability of the object-interaction model we place one or more prepositions beside the association between the action type and the object type that we derived from the indirect object (Figure 5.61). We may need more prepositions when the plurality is greater than '1'.

It should be noted that a preposition specifically belongs to one object. 'The car crashes into another car' indicates that more than one object of one object type interacts with another. The preposition determines the way in which the interaction occurs, for example the preposition in our example provides clarity into the question of blame. This can be very relevant information for an insurance company.

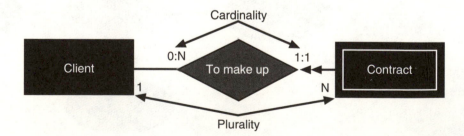

Figure 5.60   Positioning the plurality and cardinality.

Figure 5.61 Objects with a preposition.

5.4.13 Hierarchy model

The hierarchy model represents the existence-dependency between object types, weak object types, gerunds, object-classes, specializations and categories. We get a hierarchy model when we take out all action types and ISA symbols from an object-interaction model and replace them by so-called hierarchy-relations. A hierarchy-relation is represented by a dotted arrow with a double head pointing in the direction of the parent.

The main purpose of the hierarchy model is to get a better and clearer insight into the information architecture. The price we pay is that the semantics of the action types are left out of the model. The hierarchy model has to be seen as an abstract from the object-interaction model. It cannot replace the object-interaction model.

The second purpose of the hierarchy model is to calculate the static load of the information architecture. This is done by adding an 'occurrence number' to every object type with its 'growth rate'. In addition to these attributes we add the 'fertility index' to the hierarchy relation. A fertility index of 10% says that only 1 out of 10 parent-objects has a child. A fertility index of 2000% states that a parent-object has, on average, 20 child-objects.

An example of the hierarchy model is described in Chapter 6.

5.5 Summary

In this chapter we have specified two levels of modelling:

(1) Type level;
(2) Class level.

At the type level we have shown how we can use the KISS models to model the behaviour of objects. In the second instance we can model the structural relationship between the object types in the object-interaction model, by allowing the autonomous object types to interact with each other on the basis of their common action types.

With the class level we model the autonomous groups of objects that have a common attribute and state. The grouping criteria can originate either from an action type (specialization and category) or from common attributes (object type). The class level is incorporated into the object-interaction model with ISA symbols.

In this chapter we briefly discussed how to create the hierarchy model. The hierarchy model comes into existence by tracing the existence dependencies between the figures of the object-interaction model.

The degree of an action type is determined by checking the number of associations an action type directly and indirectly has with strong object types. The degree of an action type shows what the impact of carrying out the action type is on the information system. An action type with a high degree has a much greater impact than one with a low degree.

The associations in the object-interaction model can consist of the following:

(1) Cardinality

   (a) connectivity or upper boundary

   (b) totality or lower boundary;

(2) Plurality.

The cardinality is defined as the number of times that an action of an action type can be executed by an object. The plurality indicates how many objects of one object type can be involved with the action, at one moment in time.

In summary, we have been able to determine the structure of the information architecture by the use of KISS models, the object-interaction model and the hierarchy model. The hierarchy model describes the existence dependency between objects. Further details of the information architecture are exemplified by specifying the encapsulated attribute-types, operations and conditions, and by filling in the information architecture with functions. In both cases a further verification of the information architecture occurs.

5.6   Questions

(1)   Describe the concepts of object, object type and object class. Discuss also the different kinds of type level and class level.

(2)   Describe the relationship between grammatical concepts and the modelling concepts of the KISS method.

(3)   Describe the way of modelling a KISS model with its control symbols.

(4)   What is represented in the object-interaction model in addition to the KISS model, and what makes the KISS model necessary?

(5)   Discuss the application and benefits of the specialization and the category.

(6)   What is the distinction between inheritance and existence-dependency? Does inheritance determine existence dependency or is inheritance dependent upon existence dependency?

(7)   What are horizontal iteration, vertical iteration, sequential iteration and parallel iteration?

(8)   When will we create a weak object type and when a gerund?

(9)   Discuss the relationship between the cardinality and the structure of the KISS model.

(10)   Discuss the use of the concept 'plurality'.

(11)   What is 'polymorphism'? Describe how we model it.

(12)   In many other object-oriented methodologies the assemblage concept is used. Discuss why this is not an explicit concept of the KISS method and how it is implemented in the KISS method.

(13)   Discuss the use and benefit of the hierarchy model.

6 Bank example

6.1 Introduction

Using a bank as a simple example we look at the way in which a grammatical analysis is carried out on the textual description of the bank. We create an initial object-interaction model, after which we move to the specification of KISS models for each object type in the initial object-interaction model. Finally we show how to use concepts such as specialization and category in the definitive object-interaction model.

6.2 Description of the bank

A large international banking organization has opened a new branch. The branch can register clients wishing to open one or more accounts. A client can deposit cash into an account and can withdraw cash from the account. The branch has installed a number of cash drawers, each of which has its own responsible cashier, from which the client can withdraw money. The cashier counts his cash drawer at the end of the working day and ensures that the cash is transferred to the central cash drawer. The financial controller can count the cash drawers at any time of day. At the start of the working day, the cashier can fill his cash drawer from another cash drawer, preferably the central cash drawer, if necessary. The branch finally locks up the cash drawers.

The branch can only de-register a client when all the accounts of the client have been closed. The client actually closes the account.

6.3   Active structured sentences

Before we make the models, we transform our textual description into active structured sentences in the order of subject, predicate, direct object, preposition and indirect object.

Subject	Predicate	Direct object	Preposition	Indirect object
A banking organization	To found	A branch		
A branch	To register	A client		
A branch	To open	An account	of	Client
A client	To deposit	In account	at	Cash drawer
A client	To withdraw	From account	at	Cash drawer
A branch	To install	The cash drawer		
A cashier	To count	The cash drawer		
A cashier	To transfer	The cash drawer	to	Cash drawer
A controller	To count	The cash drawer		
A cashier	To refill	The cash drawer	from	Cash drawer
A branch	To lock	The cash drawer		
A client	To close	An account		
A branch	To de-register	A client		

The direct object shows which objects are changed by actions. The list of direct objects therefore also gives us the minimal set of candidate objects. This is as follows.

6.3.1   Candidate objects

These are:

- Branch;
- Client;
- Account;
- Cash drawer.

To arrive at a complete list of candidate objects we must check whether there are any objects among the indirect objects and subjects of sufficient importance to include. We see here that the indirect objects have already been included in the total list of direct objects, which means that we do not need to expand the initial list.

When we look at the subjects, we arrive at the following list.

6.3.2   Subjects

These are:

- Banking organization;
- Branch;
- Client;
- Cashier;
- Controller.

The branch and client have already been included in the list of direct objects. Within the scope of our proposed system, we decide not to include any further actions for banking organization, cashier and controller. These subjects will therefore be considered as purely regulating subjects for which no object attributes will be maintained. The list of subjects thus remains the same as the original list of subjects.

The eventual list of candidate actions is the total collection of verbs. For each action we write a short description of the changes it makes.

6.3.3   Candidate actions

These are:

- To found   To found a branch of a banking organization
- To register   To register a client at a branch
- To open   To open an account by a client
- To deposit   To deposit cash into an account at a cash drawer
- To withdraw   To withdraw cash from an account at a cash drawer
- To install   To install a cash drawer for a branch
- To count   To count a cash drawer for a branch
- To transfer   To transfer a cash drawer to another cash drawer
- To refill   To refill a cash drawer from another cash drawer
- To lock   To lock a cash drawer at a branch
- To close   To close an account by a customer
- To de-register   To de-register a client at a branch

6.3.4   Synonyms and homonyms

In reality, matters are not always clearly defined, so we must test the above lists of candidate objects and candidate actions for synonyms and homonyms.

Homonyms are words that are identical but have different meanings. For the sake of clarity no homonyms have been included in the example. In practice, homonyms are frequently present when modelling and they can only be discovered by indicating the precise definition of the specified action for each structured sentence.

Synonyms are different words with the same meaning. This sameness must be evaluated relative to the area of attention. In this way words which at first glance seem to be totally different may yet be identical within the area of attention because they are equal to each other for a number of relevant highlighted aspects.

In this example 'To transfer' and 'To fill up' are examples of synonymous actions. Both represent a transfer of money between two cash drawers in the branch. The inclusion of two actions for this is superfluous. We suggest therefore that 'To transfer' be used as the action in the model.

6.3.5   Object/action matrix

For the objects and actions noted above we create a matrix in which the actions found are related to the objects from the grammatical analysis. We do this by placing the actions on the vertical axis and the objects on the horizontal axis. In the matrix we indicate with a cross the relationships isolated from the structured sentences (Table 6.1).

Table 6.1 Object/action matrix.

	Branch	Client	Account	Cash drawer
To found	×			
To register	×	×		
To open		×	×	
To deposit		×	×	×
To withdraw		×	×	×
To install	×			×
To count				×
To transfer				×
To lock	×			×
To close		×	×	
To de-register	×	×		

6.4   Initial object-interaction model

Based on the structured sentences, the grammatical analysis and the object/action matrix, we create an initial object-interaction model for 'bank'. By relating each action type in the candidate action list to the object types with which it is associated, by means of the structured sentences, we arrive at an initial object-interaction model (Figure 6.1).

The initial object-interaction model serves to illustrate the inter-relationships between the candidate objects and actions. With the initial object-interaction model we can also read back the underlying English text. The actions are then the predicate and the objects respectively the subject, direct object or indirect object. By translating back we come across a number of problems because we do not know exactly which role an object will take in the structured sentence. To make this process more precise we must add extra semantics to the initial object-interaction model. This means that the initial object-interaction model does not yet have a definitive character. We still need to validate and flesh out a large number of items.

The first validation of the object-interaction model is performed by modelling the dynamic behaviour of the specified objects in KISS models.

6.5   KISS models for the 'bank' example

The KISS models show the sequence in which actions may be executed by the various objects. The models describe this on a generic level whereby we no longer speak of an individual object and an individual action but of object types and action types. In our example we have used names which are so common that we can simply transfer the names in the candidate object and candidate action lists to the names for the object types and action types.

The object types included in the initial object-interaction model are:

- Branch;
- Client;
- Account;
- Cash drawer.

For each of these object types we create a KISS model.

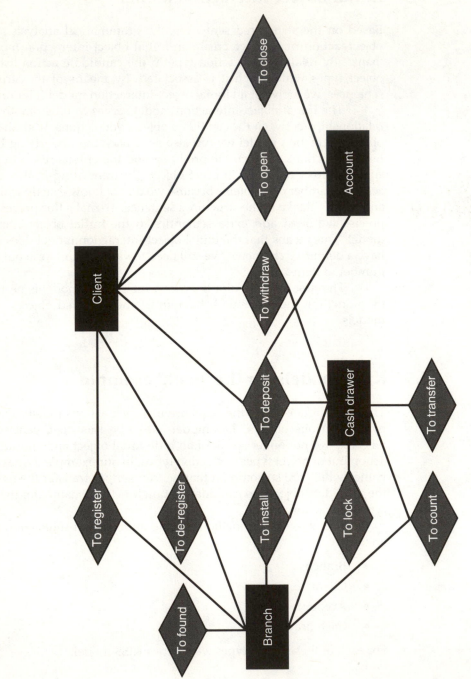

Figure 6.1   Initial object-interaction model for the bank.

6.5.1 Ordering rules

Before we create the KISS model, we show, with ordering rules, what the order is for the execution of actions on one object of an object type. In the ordering rules we may not use conditions on the basis of attribute values of objects.

Ordering rules have the general format:

FIRST one action, THEN (iteratively) the other action.

The ordering rules for the 'bank' example are:

(1)   First found branch, then iteratively register client

(2)   First register client, then iteratively open account

(3)   First register client, then de-register client

(4)   First open account, then iteratively deposit by client

(5)   First found branch, then iteratively install cash drawer

(6)   First install cash drawer, then iteratively deposit by client

(7)   First open account, then iteratively withdraw by client

(8)   First install cash drawer, then iteratively withdraw by client

(9)   First install cash drawer, then iteratively count cash drawer

(10)   First install cash drawer, then iteratively transfer cash drawer

(11)   First install cash drawer, then lock cash drawer

(12)   First open account, then close account

Using the ordering rules above we will create our first KISS models for the four object types. We do this by looking at action types associated with the object type in the initial object-interaction model and ordering rules applying to the action type of an object type. For clarity we will create a KISS model using the behaviour of an object instantiation as an example.

6.5.2 KISS model 'client'

The action types associated in the object-interaction model with the object type 'client' are:

- To register;
- To de-register;
- To deposit;

- To withdraw;
- To open;
- To close.

The object instantiation we use for 'client' is Mr Johnson. The behaviour of client Johnson is:

The very first action of client Johnson is 'To register' himself.
The last action of client Johnson is 'To de-register' himself.

Between 'registering' and 'de-registering', client Johnson can, in random sequence, 'open' and 'close' accounts and he can, in random sequence, 'deposit' and 'withdraw'.

A number of possible action paths for client Johnson are:

- Path A   'register', 'de-register'
- Path B   'register', 'open', 'open', 'deposit', 'withdraw', 'close', 'close', 'de-register'
- Path C   'register', 'open', 'close', 'open', 'deposit', 'deposit', 'deposit', 'withdraw', 'open', 'close', 'close', 'de-register'

We see in Path A that client Johnson does not *per se* need to open an account but can immediately be de-registered. Paths B and C show us that the first subsequent action of a client is the opening of an account, after which the rest of the actions (to open, close, withdraw and deposit) are free choices that may be executed in a random order.

The first KISS model created for 'client' can be seen in Figure 6.2.

We have shown by the first iteration symbol in the KISS model that client Johnson can open 0, 1 or more accounts. In this way we conform to the order in Path A. We also read in the model that the first action after 'To register' can be either 'To open' an account or 'To de-register'.

In Figure 6.2 we see that we have an iterative choice between the actions 'To open', 'To close', 'To deposit' and 'To withdraw'. At first glance this would seem to match closely Paths B and C. Looking back at the ordering rules, we see that not all the rules are satisfied. Specifically, when client Johnson has opened an account then he may also wish to close this account. Additionally, Mr Johnson could in between times deposit and withdraw cash.

The time sequence can be shown in a KISS model by placing underneath the action type 'To open' an iteration of a selection with the action types 'To deposit' and 'To withdraw'. The iteration must be terminated with the action type 'To close'.

Looking now at the possible paths we can follow with the KISS model for 'client', we see the following pattern:

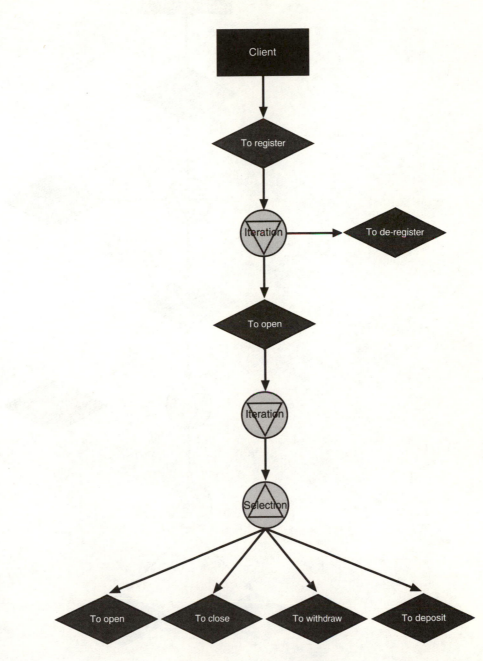

Figure 6.2   KISS model for Client.

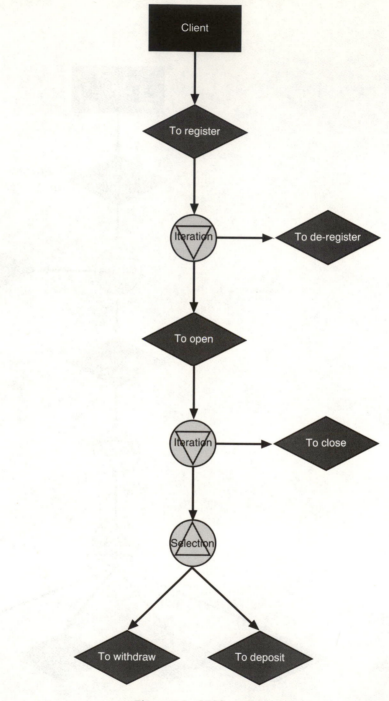

Figure 6.3   KISS model for Client.

- Path D   'register', 'open', 'withdraw', 'deposit', 'withdraw', 'deposit', 'deposit', 'withdraw', 'close', 'open', 'deposit', 'withdraw', 'close', 'de-register'.

We see that it is not possible to simulate Paths B and C with the new KISS model for 'client' because we cannot execute two or more 'to open' actions after each other with the new KISS model. With the new KISS model we can only carry out one action 'to open' immediately after client Johnson is 'registered' or at the moment that client Johnson has 'closed' his existing account. The KISS model for 'client' only permits a maximum of one account to be open at one branch at one moment in time (Figure 6.3).

The problem of having accounts open simultaneously can be solved in the KISS model by including a so-called 'parallel iteration' in the place of the first iteration and selection symbol (Figure 6.4). Parallel iteration says that multiple objects of an object type can be instantiated in parallel with each other by the action of the action type standing underneath the parallel iteration symbol. The condition for this is that a new object type must be defined that starts with the action type underneath the parallel iteration. In our example this is the implicit object type 'account'.

A consequence of the creation of a new object type 'account' is that it is dependent for its existence on the object type 'client'.

With the KISS model in Figure 6.5 we can now follow Paths B and C. The requirement for this is that the status of each of Mr Johnson's accounts be maintained as instantiations of the object type 'account'.

Before creating the definitive KISS model for 'client', we discuss what the KISS model for 'account' looks like.

6.5.3   KISS model for 'account'

In our initial object-interaction model for 'bank' we see that we have already modelled the time sequence of the action types associated with 'account' in the KISS model for 'client'. Therefore we can begin the KISS model for 'account' with the instantiating action type 'to open' and terminate with the action type 'to close'. In between times the actions to deposit and to withdraw can be executed 0, 1 or more times.

The object type 'account' is existence-dependent on the object type 'client'. This makes 'account' a weak object type that is existence-dependent on the existence of 'client'. We show a weak object type by a double rectangle (Figure 6.5).

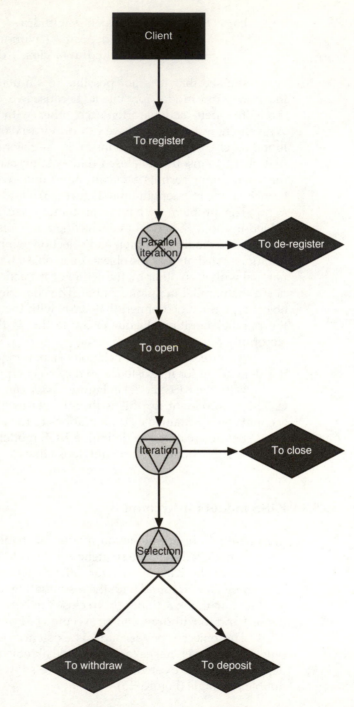

Figure 6.4   KISS model for Client using parallel iteration.

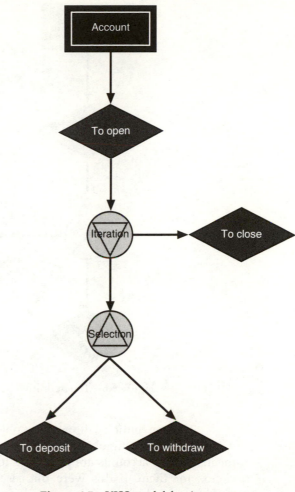

Figure 6.5   KISS model for Account.

6.5.4   Definitive KISS model for 'client'

The KISS model for 'client' looks extremely simple (Figure 6.6). The life of a client begins with an action 'to register' and ends with the action 'to de-register'. In between times the client can iteratively open accounts. The action type 'to open' is thereby the synchronizing action type between 'client' and 'account'. When the opening of an account is carried out by a client, there is also a new object instantiation of the object type 'account' created in the object type 'client'.

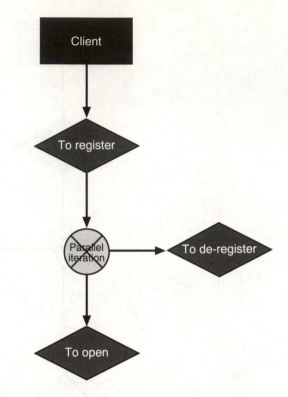

Figure 6.6   The definitive KISS model for Client.

The convention with a weak object type is that it can no longer exist when its strong object type no longer exists. In our example this means that no accounts are permitted to exist when there are no longer clients for them. If this were the case then we would end up with accounts for which we have no client details.

6.5.5   KISS model for 'branch'

Looking at the initial object-interaction model we see that the following action types are associated with the object type 'branch':

- To found;
- To register;
- To de-register;
- To install;

- To close;
- To count.

In the ordering rules is noted that a branch must first be founded before a subsequent action can be executed. Our first KISS model therefore consists of an initial action after which there is iteratively free choice of a large number of other actions (Figure 6.7).

In the KISS model for 'branch' we see that there has not been a terminating action type for the situation where a branch closes. We have decided that this falls outside the scope of the system.

Another interesting point is that we can leave the action type 'to de-register' out of the KISS model for 'branch' because the time sequence following registration is already modelled in the KISS model for 'client'.

According to the ordering rules given at the start this also counts for the action types 'to close' and 'to count' that are executed in time sequence after execution of the action type 'to install'. We can include these integrally in the KISS model for cash drawer, which we will create next.

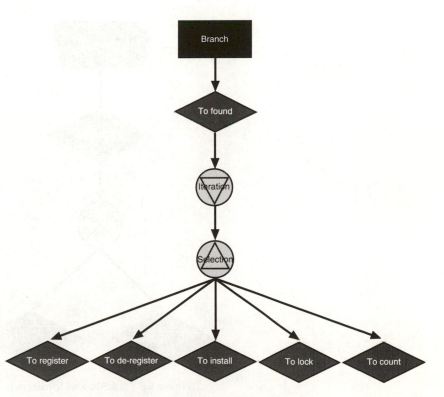

Figure 6.7   KISS model for Branch.

In the KISS model for 'branch' we replace the combination of iteration and selection with a parallel iteration, because a branch can have both multiple clients as well as multiple cash drawers concurrently (Figure 6.8).

We see then that the model becomes markedly simpler with parallel iteration. It should be noted that both KISS models give a correct representation of the real world but that there has been an element of redundancy removed in the second KISS model, by the further modelling of the time sequence of the action types for the weak object types 'client' and 'cash drawer'. The consequence of this is that the object type 'client' becomes existence-dependent on 'branch'. This model for the weak object type 'client' is shown in Figure 6.9.

6.5.6   KISS model for 'cash drawer'

In the initial object-interaction model the following actions are associated with 'cash drawer':

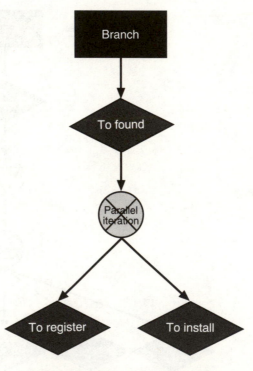

Figure 6.8   KISS model for Branch.

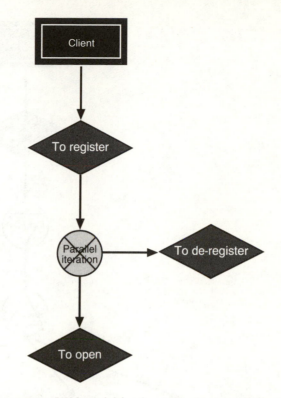

Figure 6.9   KISS model for the weak object type Client.

- To install;
- To lock;
- To transfer;
- To count;
- To deposit;
- To withdraw.

The instantiating action type for the object type 'cash drawer' is 'to install'. The terminating action type for 'cash drawer' is 'to lock'. It is true for 'cash drawer' that all the other actions can be carried out by free choice.

We have already seen that 'cash drawer' is existence-dependent on 'branch' and therefore becomes a weak object type (Figure 6.10).

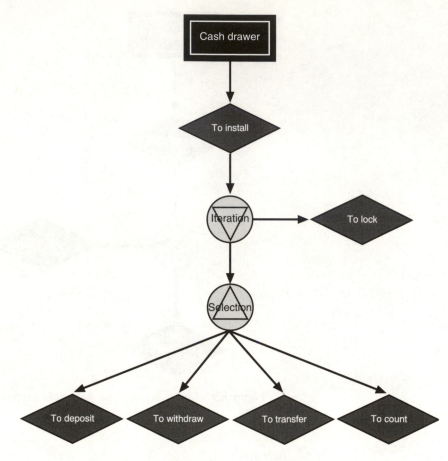

Figure 6.10   KISS model for Cash drawer.

6.5.7   Object-interaction model for 'bank'

Now that we have created all the KISS models for the 'bank' example, we can allow them to interact with each other to form a more definitive object-interaction model (Figure 6.11). The interaction takes place using action types that occur in two or more KISS models of object types. These are the so-called synchronizing action types that ensure that the independent object types are related to each other in an information architecture in the correct way.

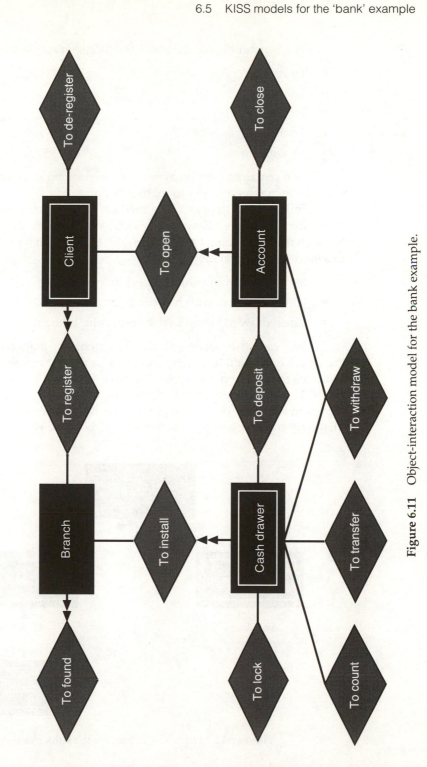

Figure 6.11 Object–interaction model for the bank example.

The synchronizing actions in the 'bank' example are:

- To register;
- To install;
- To open;
- To deposit;
- To withdraw.

The remaining action types are only joined with one line to the object type in whose KISS model they occur.

In Figure 6.11 we can also read off what existence dependencies there are. These are shown by a double arrow on the line segment between the weak object type and the initiating action type. So, we see for this object-interaction model:

- 'Account' is weak with respect to 'client';
- 'Client' is weak with respect to 'branch';
- 'Cash drawer' is weak with respect to 'branch'.

We can also represent the hierarchical relationship between the object types in a hierarchy model. The double arrow in this model indicates the parent object types (Figure 6.12).

The advantage of the hierarchy model is that we can easily represent how the existence dependencies lie between the object types. A hierarchy model provides a better insight because we have suppressed

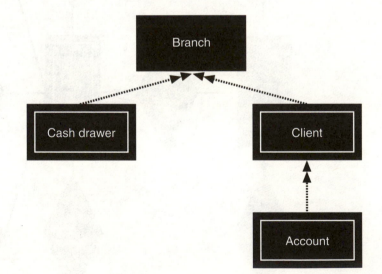

Figure 6.12   Hierarchy model for the bank example.

the action types that we took from the object-interaction model. The hierarchy model can therefore be derived entirely from the object-interaction model by leaving out the action types.

6.6   Extending the 'bank' example

To be able to explain the concepts 'gerund', 'category' and 'specialization' we will extend the 'bank' example with a relation file and an employee.

6.6.1   Description

A branch wishes to use the personal details of clients to set up a relation administration in which both the data and the changes to persons and organizations are recorded.

Since a branch makes use of a central relation administration, we will define a relation as a person or an organization. After registration a relation can open one or more accounts. A registration in the relation file can be de-registered.

A branch employs persons as employees. After the persons have been employed, they can resign. It must be noted that organizations cannot be employed by a branch.

6.6.2   Structured sentences

This gives rise to the following structured sentences:

- Branch   to register   a person as a relation
- Branch   to register   an organization as a relation
- Branch   to de-register   a registration
- Branch   to open   an account for registration
- Branch   to employ   a person
- Branch   to resign   an employee
- Person   is a   relation
- Organization   is a   relation
- Employee   is a   person

6.6.3 Candidate objects

We differentiate the following new candidate objects:

- Person;
- Organization;
- Relation;
- Registration;
- Employee.

6.6.4 Candidate actions

We differentiate the following new candidate actions:

- To employ;
- To resign.

In the lists above we can see a greater number of candidate objects than candidate actions. For all of the candidate objects we need to determine whether or not they will be object types for which we will create a KISS model.

6.6.5 Category

A first glance at the structured sentences leads us to consider Relation in the first instance as a category. The reason for this is that the category Relation can be a person or an organization that allows the action type 'To register' to be reused by both object types. This makes it possible for the action type 'To register' to be included only once in the object-interaction model (Figure 6.13). We will not, therefore, create a KISS model for the category Relation.

The category Relation will in turn place both object types Person and Organization in a state where they can make use of the action type 'To register'.

A category is shown by the same symbol as a gerund except that the lines are dotted.

The characteristic of a category is that it always has multiple object types connected to it each with an ISA symbol. This is necessary because there are always multiple parent object types for a category, each of which is shown by an ISA symbol.

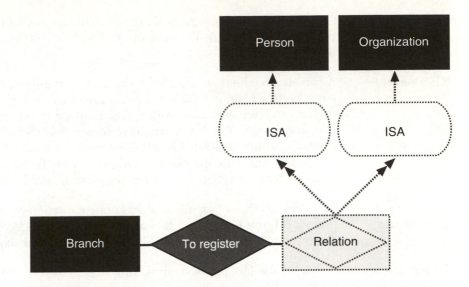

Figure 6.13   Object-interaction model incorporating the category Relation.

6.6.6   Ordering rules

We differentiate the following ordering rules:

(1) First register person at a branch with a registration, then iteratively open account

(2) First register organization at a branch with a registration, then iteratively open account

(3) First register registration, then de-register registration

(4) First employ person, then resign person

(5) First register person at a branch, then employ person

By reading the ordering rules we often come across the grammatical gerund 'registration'. This gerund originates from the subsequent actions on the action type 'To register'. The subsequent actions are to open an account and to de-register a registered person or organization.

6.6.7   Creating KISS models

When creating KISS models we see that the action type 'To register' must be included in the KISS model for Person as well as for Organization.

Owing to the fact that there is only a small number of different action types associated with the new object types, the KISS models will be relatively small.

KISS model for Person

A person must be registered before he can be employed as an employee. After he has resigned, he can be employed as an employee again. A person can have only one working relationship at one moment in time with one branch. This is why we have consciously included an 'iteration symbol' and not a 'parallel iteration' in the KISS model (Figure 6.14).

The subsequent actions 'To register' and 'To employ' are shown respectively in the KISS models for Registration and Employee.

KISS model for Organization

The KISS model for Organization has only one action type, which instantiates it (Figure 6.15). With this action type it is synchronized with the object type Registration, which also takes over the subsequent actions.

KISS model for Employment

Owing to the fact that the employing of a person by a branch directly leads to a gerund, we will give this resulting gerund the name Employment.

The KISS model for Employment (Figure 6.16) shows that a person must be employed before he can resign. By combining this with the iteration symbol in the KISS model for Person we have specified that a person can have only one working relationship at one moment in time.

KISS model for Registration

The KISS model for Registration (Figure 6.17) indicates that it is instantiated by the action type 'To register'. After a person or organization is registered, we can iteratively open accounts. We can do this until we de-register the person or organization.

6.6.8 Object-interaction model

While setting up the object-interaction model we see that two gerunds are included (Figure 6.18). Each gerund is thereby dependent on the associated object types. The gerund Registration is, on one hand, existence-dependent on Branch and on the other, by means of the category Relation, on the strong object types Person or Organization.

6.6.9 Specialization structures

When we consider the current object-interaction model (Figure 6.18) we see that the weak object type Client is no longer included. We also see, however, that the gerund Registration and the category Relation are included in the object-interaction model. Replacing the name

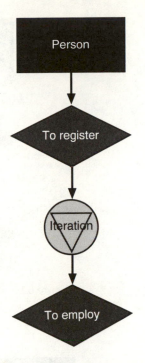

Figure 6.14   KISS model for Person.

Registration by the name Client is not completely justified because a registered person who is employed as an employee has not necessarily also opened an account as a client of the branch.

We can add extra semantics to the object-interaction model by making use of a 'specialization'. A specialization defines a group of objects that carry out a particular action and therefore represents a state

Figure 6.15   KISS model for Organization.

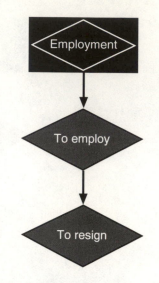

Figure 6.16   KISS model for Employment.

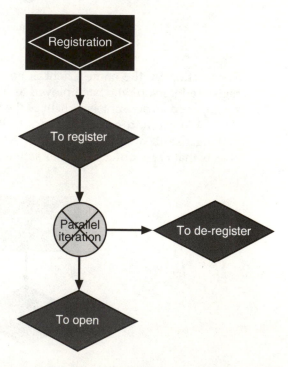

Figure 6.17   KISS model for Registration.

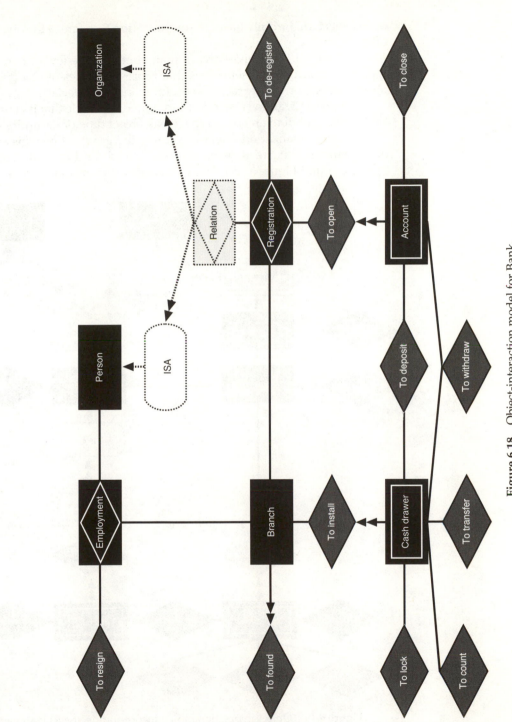

Figure 6.18 Object-interaction model for Bank.

of the object. In the daily life of the organization the state of the object will often be a relevant concept.

The data themselves are all maintained at the level of an object type but for additional semantics that represent states of objects in the object-interaction model it can be useful to include specializations.

A specialization is included as a dotted rectangle that is connected by an ISA symbol to an object type, weak object type or gerund.

The specialization Client is equal to the group of persons and/or organizations that are registered in the branch and have at least one open account (Figure 6.19). We can specify for an object type many

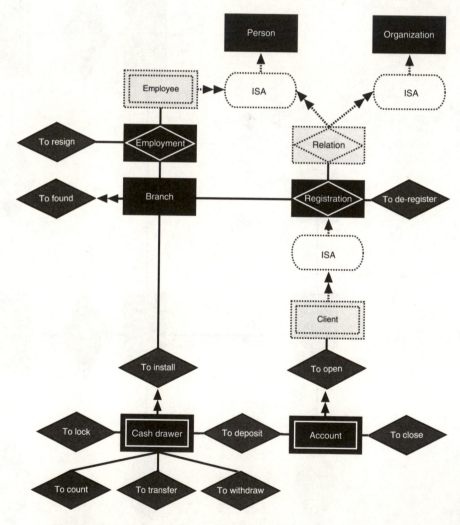

Figure 6.19   Object-interaction model incorporating specializations.

specializations that generally originate from the actions executed by an object type. Therefore we have placed the specialization Employee between the object type Person and the gerund Employment. A specialization is always weak with respect to the object type, weak object type or gerund.

When we can differentiate multiple specializations for one object type, we show this by associating a greater number of specializations with one ISA symbol with the object type. The specializations then always have the same object type as their generalization.

It is useful to note that a specialization can always be left out of the object-interaction model.

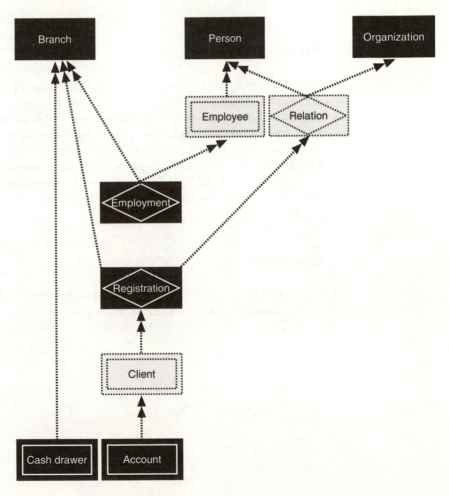

Figure 6.20   Hierarchy model for the bank example.

Since a specialization is not an object type or an existence-dependent object type such as the weak object type and gerund, we do not draw up a KISS model for the specialization.

6.7   Hierarchy model of the 'bank'

By removing the action types and ISA symbols from the object-interaction model of the 'bank' example, which incorporated the object types, gerunds, weak object types, categories and specializations, we can set up a hierarchy model. In the hierarchy model we can see that the strength of the objects decreases as we read in a downwards direction (Figure 6.20).

6.8   Summary

In this chapter we have seen, by using a practical example, how the concepts from the previous chapters can be applied. The method of working is that, after the textual description and grammatical analysis, we create KISS models using an initial object-interaction model. With the definition of the KISS models we see that a very definite validation of the object-interaction model takes place. The object-interaction model is subsequently augmented by one category and two specializations. By using the object-interaction model we can finally set up a definitive hierarchy model.

6.9   Question

(1)   Describe your own organization and perform the activities in the same order as in the 'bank' example.

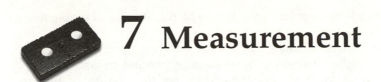

7 Measurement

7.1 Introduction

Measurement is a part of the communication paradigm. To make communication about objects and phenomena possible, the measuring process is of fundamental importance. The basis for object orientation derives from the way in which we observe things in reality. One of the components of observation is the comparison of the observation in reality with a stable reference.

The process of observation and comparison is called the measuring process. By measuring the attributes of objects and phenomena in the real world, we give them particular values that we can interpret and which we can record as attribute values of an information system.

To measure or declare attributes we use five measuring scales. One measuring scale offers more capabilities than another. We will discuss them in the order of their increasing number of capabilities. In this way we will see that more mathematical manipulations are permitted for the frequency scale than for the ranking scale.

It is important for the concepts of object orientation to discuss measuring scales because, for example, the nominal scale provides a fundamental basis for the classification of objects into object classes and the frequency scale lays a theoretical basis for the transfer from an action type to an object type. It is easier to apply multiple measuring scales, units and dimensions in the modelling process when the underlying principles of the measuring process are understood.

7.2 The measuring process

The measuring process is an integral component of the total information provision of an organization. It ensures that we can discover the attributes of objects, and that we can communicate and interpret them.

That this has long been known is shown by the often-used saying that to measure is to know.

The saying indicates that for the building up of knowledge we must give proper attention to the measuring process. In fact, the quality of what we 'know' is fully dependent on the quality of how we 'measure'. It is therefore important for the measuring process to have unambiguous standards that are not subject to change.

Generally used standards for the measuring process are also important for the development of unambiguous communication between persons and organizations. To be able to code and send information about objects in a communication process, it is necessary to have the same standards as the receiving party. After the receiving party has decoded the data, he then also knows in which way the data must be interpreted.

Standardized measuring scales that serve as reference for both the sender and receiver are indispensable for the communication process. In the measuring process, the values of the attributes of objects are determined using one or more reference scales.

Definition of measurement

Measurement is the defining of the values for relevant attributes of objects using fixed rules and defined reference points on a measuring scale.

While measuring is an extremely important part of the total communication process, we usually measure without explicitly considering the basic rudiments of the measuring process itself. This is shown by a number of sentences as follows.

- The item cost $35.
- It is 28 °C today.
- John is taller than Jasper.
- Mr Johnson has put on 3 kilos.
- He goes home at five o'clock.

In the sentences above, measuring with a measuring scale has been included so automatically that it is no longer recognizable as the result of a measuring process. In the sentences we have given explicit and implicit values to the attributes of objects such as weight, price, temperature, height, names and time.

The sentences all consist of measurements for which the values are determined by comparing the values of object attributes against a scale with exact divisions. Not every scale is exactly divided. We can see this in the example: 'The fat man walks across the street'.

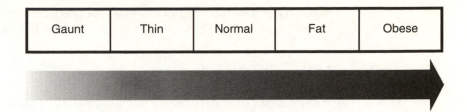

Figure 7.1   Scale division for the girth of a person.

A possible scale division that shows the girth of a person is shown in Figure 7.1.

On this scale we can show where the girth of a particular person lies from our point of view. We can do this, for example, by first gauging the scale by measuring a number of test people. Then we can compare the rest of the people with the scale.

With the scale division above we cannot say that a fat man has a girth four times that of a gaunt man. This scale division does not allow a comparison of specific proportions. What we can say is that an obese man definitely does not fit through a door in which a fat man gets stuck. On the measuring scale for the price of an item we can say that an item with a price of $140 costs four times as much as an item that costs $35. This measuring scale thus would appear to allow this. The difference arises because we use a number of scale types that permit various calculations and comparisons to be made among themselves.

7.3   Scale types

The most common measuring scales we know of are as follows.

- The nominal scale or classes;
- The ordinal or ranking scale;
- The interval or distance scale;
- The ratio or proportional scale;
- The absolute or frequency scale.

Each scale type ensures that the measured results have more or less general attributes. These have to do with, among other things, the reliability, accuracy, validity and the way in which we can use the measurement results for calculations, comparisons, sorts and so forth. We will now look at the various measuring scales in more detail.

7.3.1 The nominal scale or classes

We speak of a nominal scale, or the dividing of objects into classes, when it is possible to group objects according to their attributes. We end up with groups for which it is not possible to define any order. This simplest form of measurement classifies objects on the grounds of their attributes. Such a classification is always possible when we have named or validated the object or action. Classification is not possible when we are talking about complete disorder or about objects or actions that have not yet been named or validated.

Classification is an extremely primitive form of measurement that is not normally viewed as a measuring process. With object-oriented development, classification is, on the contrary, one of the most important principles upon which to build object-oriented information architectures and implement inheritance structures. Particularly in the early stages of setting up an information system, classification systems are of great importance because they are used to gain a global insight into the main structures of an information system.

Definition of classification

Classification is the division of objects into groups or classes according to a specific criterion, in such a way that each object fits into one class. Each class can in turn be a part of a larger group or class, indicated by the term superclass. Each class is given a name.

Examples of commonly used classification systems are:

- Division of the plant and animal worlds according to Linnaeus;
- Division of incomes and expenditures for a business;
- Division of item groups in a catalogue;
- Directories of businesses according to type;
- Division of customers into private, business or government.

An example of division into classes is where we divide animals into vertebrate and non-vertebrate animals. The vertebrate animals are mammals, birds, fish, and so on. The mammals can be further divided into beef cattle, horses, dogs, people, and so on. The beef cattle can be further divided into cows, steers, calves, and so on. An example of this classification is shown in Figure 7.2.

It should be noted that there is no objective ordering indicated by the classification systems. For example, a cow is not better than a calf in beef cattle, and a horse is not higher than a cow in a hierarchy. The only thing that can be said is that the division criterion, on the basis of

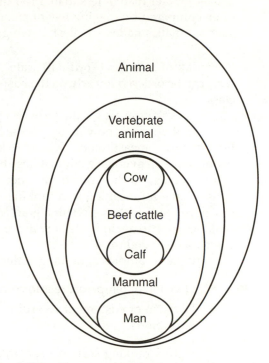

Figure 7.2 A Venn diagram: classification according to the biological dimension.

common attributes, is different. The same is true for directories of businesses where one type of business in the directory is not better than another type, and in a catalogue, one group of items from a department store is not at a higher level than another group. In this way we hope to show that classification only takes place for a group of objects with similar attributes, without any ordering among them.

A class hierarchy must therefore not be interpreted in terms of a hierarchy meaning in the sense of 'order', but rather in the sense of 'more inclusive'.

7.3.2 Ranking scale

To obtain a ranking (ordinal) scale the classes of the nominal scale must comply with an extra condition: the classes must be able to be placed in an order such that their relationship to each other can be defined with equals, greater than or less than. In a ranking scale the attributes are also often compared by making use of a comparative or superlative ladder such as small, smaller, smallest; big, bigger, biggest.

Definition of ranking scale

We speak of a ranking (ordinal) scale when the classes of the nominal scale can be ordered linearly on the basis of a value for the ranking of the class.

A ranking scale for the girth of a person is shown in Figure 7.3.

In it we show how many people have a girth of a particular class. From the total measurement we can discern that the measured group of people have an average girth that lies above 'normal'. The interpretation of the average is difficult to give because the distances between the classes have no meaning in a ranking scale. We see this, for example, in competition with the results 'gold', 'silver' and 'bronze', which are rankings that do not indicate how much faster the winner was than those placed second and third.

Other examples of ranking scales are:

- Division of temperature into cold, warm and hot;
- Division of customers according to credit rating: excellent, good or dubious.

With a ranking scale we sort in ascending or descending order, according to the values of the classes. Sorting on alphabet with a class of

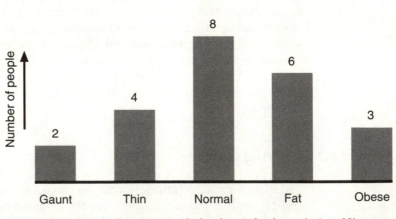

Figure 7.3 Measuring scale for the girth of people ($n = 23$).

items in a catalogue is not a ranking scale for the class of items itself. The name of the item says nothing about the value of the item.

7.3.3   Interval scale

With the interval (distance) scale we measure in random units that are constant over the whole range of the scale. As an addition to the ranking scale we can, with the interval scale, speak of 'that much more' and 'that much less'. The absolute values of the numbers in comparison with a zero point do not have any meaning. There is no 'zero point' present.

Definition of an interval scale

We speak of an interval (distance) scale when we can carry out addition and subtraction operations ($+$ and $-$) on the classes of the ranking scale without reference to an absolute zero point.

Examples of interval scales are the temperature scales in degrees Celsius and Fahrenheit (Figure 7.4). The zero point of the Celsius scale lies at the freezing point of water.

With the temperature scales the measuring scale in degrees Fahrenheit can be translated into a measuring scale for degrees Celsius. This can also be done using the equation:

$$°C = (°F - 32) \times 5/9.$$

Interval scales can therefore be translated into each other by means of calculation formulae.

7.3.4   Ratio scale

With the ratio (proportional) scale we are dealing with an unambiguous zero point where the scale units are defined and constant. With a ratio scale we can compare the relationship of the value of one object with the value of another object.

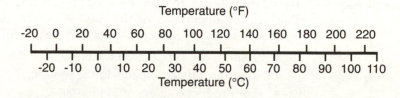

Figure 7.4   Interval scale for temperature: there is no absolute zero point.

Definition of a ratio scale

We speak of a ratio (proportional) scale when we can carry out multiplication and division operations ($\times$ and $\div$) on the classes of the interval scale. There is a definite reference to an absolute zero point. For example: a man of 100 kg weighs twice as much as a man of 50 kg.

It is possible for a ratio scale to carry out all the calculations of the previous scales. Therefore, we also see that for the ratio scale, for example (calculation interval scale), a man of 100 kg weighs 50 kg more than a man of 50 kg. In addition (calculation ranking scale), a man of 100 kg is a heavyweight and a man of 50 kg is a lightweight.

Many natural measures are measured on a ratio scale:

- Height;
- Mass;
- Time;
- Current;
- Absolute temperature;
- Intensity of light.

The use of the ratio scale in more than one dimension is widely practised. Thus we can represent graphically the progression of height from baby through to old age on two ratio scales: 'height' and 'age'.

The proportion between the values for the measures 'height' and 'age' gives us a two-dimensional picture in which we can see a continuous progress (Figure 7.5).

With the values on the ratio scale we can also carry out multiplications and divisions resulting in proportional numbers (ratios) representing the relationship between the various measures.

7.3.5 Frequency scale

The frequency (absolute) scale is based on the counting/identifying of discrete phenomena of a particular object. The values on the frequency scale are therefore also discrete. With the frequency scale we speak of an unambiguous zero point. In addition, the frequency scale contains all the mathematical attributes of the ratio scale.

Definition of a frequency scale

We speak of a frequency (absolute) scale when the measured phenomena have a discrete nature. The observed phenomena are themselves indivisible. All the operations of the ratio scale can be carried out on the frequency scale. We also speak of a definite zero point. For example:

- There are 10 products in the box;
- There are 20 participants in the project;
- The product consists of 234 parts;
- Each product, participant and part is discrete and indivisible.

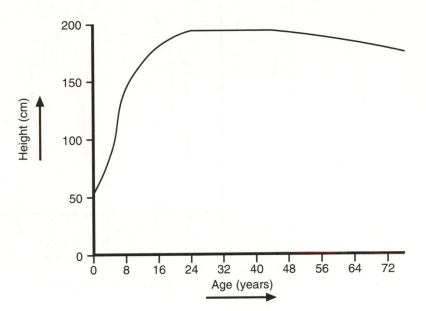

Figure 7.5   Ratio scale for height related to age.

We always come across the frequency scale when an action takes place. The action itself can in fact be seen as an event at one point in time. The action is identifiable and can have attributes with particular values whereby it can become an object. We explain this further with an example of the progress of an inventory of items (Figure 7.6).

The actions we can execute on the inventory are the 'receipt' and 'delivery' of items. The inventory grows with 'receipt' and shrinks with 'delivery'. The 'increase' and the 'decrease' take place at one point in time. In between the 'increase' and the 'decrease' no change takes place in the inventory.

The increase and decrease of the number of items is measured on a frequency scale because we count and manipulate all the items individually. Liquids and crystals are generally more difficult to measure on a frequency scale.

The most typical characteristic of a frequency scale is that all the values are discrete. This means that a measured value can be made into an object. Whether or not we elevate the value of an object to a new object type is dependent on whether it is relevant to the problem area.

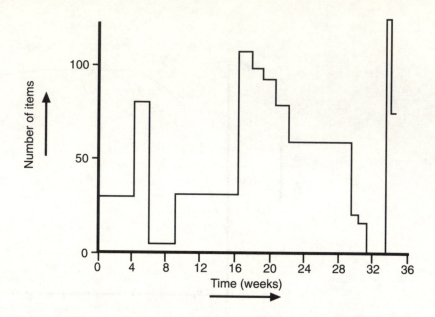

Figure 7.6   Frequency scale for the inventory of an item.

An example is the measurement of weight using a weighing scale or using a balance with discrete weights.

(1) A weighing scale has a continuous scale division from 0 to 100 kg. The scale division makes the weighing scale a ratio scale.

(2) A balance has separate weights. We can use 100 weights of 1 kg, or we can use another assortment of weights, such as:

(a)   3 weights of 25 kg;

(b)   1 weight of 10 kg;

(c)   2 weights of 5 kg;

(d)   5 weights of 1 kg.

In the second example, each weight becomes a new object when we decide to record characteristics that are relevant.

7.4   Scale attributes

All scale types have attributes upon which mathematical calculations can be executed. Depending on the type of scale, we can carry out a greater or lesser number of calculations on the measured values.

The permitted calculations (operations) for the measured values (attributes) are:

=, ≠: Classification becomes possible because the is-equal-to relationship and the not-equal-to relationship indicate that an object with specific characteristics does or does not belong to a particular class. There is no scale, only a classification structure.

<, >: Sorting becomes possible because the unequal relationship indicates whether something is greater than or lesser than a particular reference value. There is no scale unit and there is no zero point. The is-equal-to and not-equal-to relationships are automatically included.

+, −: Ordering of differences by addition and subtraction becomes possible because the scale has constant scale units. There is no absolute zero point but there is a random zero point for the scale to which calculations refer.

×, /: Proportions can be determined because multiplication and division are permitted owing to the fact that the scale has constant scale units and an absolute zero point.

Identification: Frequency additions, identifications and objectivation of characteristics is made possible by the fact that the measurements and scale units are discrete.

The permitted operations for the various measuring scales can be summarized in a table (Table 7.1). The situation in which no classification, identification or naming has yet taken place on the basis of the measuring and dividing into classes is indicated as 'chaos'.

'ID' indicates that a characteristic can be elevated to an object by its own identification and characteristics.

Table 7.1 shows that a ranking scale also has the attributes of the nominal scale, that the distance scale has the attributes of the ranking and nominal scales, and so forth. We can also say that the ranking scale takes over the attributes of the nominal scale, the distance scale takes over the attributes of the ranking and nominal scales, and so forth.

Table 7.1 The scale attributes with their permitted operations.

Permitted operations	=, ≠	<, >	+, −	×, /	ID
0. Chaos	no	no	no	no	no
1. Nominal scale	yes	no	no	no	no
2. Ranking scale	yes	yes	no	no	no
3. Distance scale	yes	yes	yes	no	no
4. Proportional scale	yes	yes	yes	yes	no
5. Frequency scale	yes	yes	yes	yes	yes

In the provision of information, there is a natural inclination to represent the characteristics of objects in a much more exact manner than they are measured in reality. The explanation for this is that when the attributes are entered on, for example, a ratio scale, a greater number of calculations can be executed than when the attribute is entered on a ranking scale. With the ratio scale we can, for example, also execute additions and multiplications in order to furnish a perfect report.

When the reality is such that the maximum scale permitted is a ranking scale without further scale divisions, we can go no further than this ranking scale. Should we go further with our calculations, we end up with false accuracies that can never be realized in reality. The reliability of the reporting often leaves much to be desired after close examination.

7.5 Derived characteristics

It often happens that a characteristic is not measured directly but is calculated by means of a function utilizing other characteristics that have been measured directly. In this way we can calculate the cash balance at the end of the day by calculating the difference between the starting balance and the total received and paid. The actual balance can also be directly measured by counting the final cash.

The cash difference is now a newly derived characteristic that we calculate as the difference between the counted balance and the calculated cash balance. When translating this to an information system we must input the starting balance of the cash as well as all the receipts and payments, in addition to the value of the counted end balance. The derived characteristics 'calculated balance' and 'cash difference' can then be calculated.

To be able to work properly with the derived characteristic, we make a distinction between a fundamental and a derived measuring scale.

Definition of a fundamental measuring scale

A fundamental measuring scale allocates a numeric value directly when measuring a characteristic.

This means that, for an information system, the characteristics measured on a fundamental measuring scale can directly carry over their data to the system without any extra calculations. It is important to note which measuring scale has been used.

Definition of a derived measuring scale

A derived measuring scale allocates a numeric value to a derived characteristic by means of a function. The derived characteristics can be represented on a derived scale. This means that a derived characteristic can only be determined after the calculation of a function. Therefore a function that performs the calculation must be included. In order to record the derived characteristic the best method is to record the original measured data as well as the formula, because then no information can be lost.

Example of the calculation of a derived characteristic

The density d can be determined after the direct measurement of the mass m and the volume V, using the algebraic function for the calculation of the density:

$$d = m/V$$

We can note that the difference between fundamental and derived quantities is the basis of the physical unit system. With the unit system we can show in the relationship between the units, on the basis of an unambiguous structure, how the units of a derived quantity are related to each other.

7.6   Magnitude and object

Two concepts that appear to be very similar are measure and object. In an earlier example we saw that the magnitude 'height' of a person can be related to the measure 'age'. These measures are themselves measured on a ratio scale. Also, we saw that a discrete event can become an object by identification. The 'receiving' thus becomes a 'receipt'. For the receipt we can, for example, maintain the number of products received, in discrete numbers. Each received product can then be seen as a 'receipt'. In this way we arrive at a situation where, by using the frequency scale, we see the objectivation of the characteristics occur. The result of this is that the object itself is used as a reference scale during measuring. The difference between an object on a frequency scale and a measure is that the magnitude is not discretely measured but allows us to indicate the relationship with a discrete reference object.

With the nominal scale and the class division we are at the other extreme because we are talking about a grouping of one or more objects into classes. The class defines the dividing criteria for the characteristics according to how the individual objects are classified. A class thus forms a collection of objects within which the objects remain completely identifiable.

We define magnitude and object below.

Definition of magnitude

Magnitude is a general characteristic that can be measured on at least a ranking scale. Magnitude can have either a qualitative or a quantitative nature. Magnitude is always measurable by relating it to a real reference object that serves as the standard.

Definition of an object

An object is visible, discrete and identifiable in the real world. The object is real or conceptual. It can be divided into classes according to its characteristics.

The difference between a measure and an object is defined implicitly. A magnitude is a measuring criterion according to which attributes can be related to 'standard reference objects'. A magnitude therefore serves as a reference to which we can relate new observations. A magnitude can be regarded as a continuous measuring scale of a reference object. A magnitude can allow the characteristics of new objects to be measurable by showing how the new object is related to the existing standard object.

By definition it is true that the dividing of objects into a class on the nominal scale does not give a ranking scale. There are an additional number of conditions that must be met, such as ranking order, addition-attributes, and so on. It should be noted that the magnitude automatically has the class attributes of the reference objects but that a class does not have the attributes of the other measuring scales. An object can itself be divided into all the other measuring scales by its identifying attributes, whereby it can be used as the basis for reference.

An object in a class occurs as a general value. In the frequency scale the object occurs as a general characteristic that is identified for discrete events.

We can summarize Table 7.2 by saying that we recognize the characteristics of objects by:

- The classification of an object into particular classes;
- The reference of an object to measures;
- The instantiating of an event to object.

The class itself can also have attributes. A class is determined, for example, by aggregation and abstraction of the attributes of the individual objects occurring in the class. The class can be regarded as a domain into which objects can be added when they meet the defined division criteria.

The values of the characteristics are measured on a ranking scale for qualities, and on the other measuring scales for quantities.

Table 7.2 Definitions of scale attributes.

Type of scale	Nominal	Ranking	Distance	Ratio	Frequence
Characteristic type	Class	Magnitude	Magnitude	Magnitude	Object
Value type	Object	Quality	Quantity	Quantity	Quantity
Scale type	Non metric	Non metric	Metric scale	Metric scale	Metric scale

Magnitude is important for the information system because we can always order the values of measure on the basis of a logical ranking. For an object that is divided on a nominal scale into classes it is not possible to define a ranking among the classes. Owing to this, the commonly used names 'superclass' and 'subclass' in object-oriented programming languages gives us an incorrect perception of things. This naming assumes that there is an order to be found between classes, while this, by definition, is not the case for the nominal scale.

The ranking between autonomous classes can be applied to magnitudes on the individual object occurrences that we have found. A magnitude, in fact, implies with the ranking that there is a measuring scale with which measurements can be made.

One of the attributes of existing information systems is that the measures and reference objects are often not explicitly named as a reference scale. In this way the capability of using the generic attributes of the measure or object for the attribute values of objects is not present. Should we wish to reuse the generic attributes of a measure or object, it is necessary that the scale along which the measure is measured, in addition to the division of classes, be explicitly included in the information system as general references for all measured, and still to be measured, characteristics. This is an important part of the semantic aspect of an information system and makes the specification process of systems more general.

Definition of quality

A magnitude is a quality when the measurement takes place on a ranking scale.

With information systems there is often talk of a quality when the measured values refer to subjective measurement criteria using results such as 'pretty', 'good' or 'fine'. In information systems we often come across qualities that process soft and subjective information, and systems where personal preferences and interpretations are recorded.

Definition of quantity

A magnitude is a quantity when the measurement takes place on a distance, proportional or frequency scale.

A quantity can be measured more definitively than a quality. The distance scale is more exact than the ranking scale. An extra point is that calculations can be carried out with quantities. All the calculation characteristics of a measure are therefore defined on the basis of the generic attributes of the measuring scales of the measure.

Definition of metric scales

A scale is metric when the scale has interval attributes.

A class structure is a totally non-metric scale in which only one grouping of the object occurrences takes place, based on the values of their characteristics.

7.7   Unit and magnitude

In physics and economics we work very much with magnitudes that are usually measured in units on ratio scales. Between the various ratio scales there are translation factors, defined as the calculations permitted on the values of measured objects.

For example, the measure 'height' can be measured in the units 'thumb', 'foot', 'yard', 'metre' or 'mile'. All these measurement units can be traced back to the reference objects that serve as standard measurement units. The choice of unit is random in theory except that, for practical reasons, it is important to make agreements and propose standards because the unit and the measure determine how we will calculate the values, from a functional point of view.

7.7.1   History of units

Standard units have been in use throughout the history of mankind. 'Foot' was formerly a standard for the recording of the magnitude 'length' and the gold 'coin piece' was formerly the standard for the measure 'value'.

It would appear that these earlier standards in history were strongly region-oriented, as has been concluded from the fact that almost each region and period had its own 'foot'. These 'feet' could differ from each other in length. The length of a 'foot' was in fact generally determined by the average size of a man's foot in each region. The result of the different 'feet' per region was that the values of attributes between the regions had to be converted from one 'foot' to the other 'foot'. This took time and often caused mistakes with the interpretation of the values. Length, for example, is now almost always measured with the standard metre in continental Europe, while a large number of other magnitudes still need to be converted. Think, for example, of the various monetary units in use in Europe and worldwide.

7.7.2   Foreign exchange rates

If you buy a kilo of apples for £1.89, you do not normally consider what the equivalent value is in French francs, German marks or American dollars. A Dutch person buys the same kilo of apples for Fl5.89 and converts this back to Dutch currency guilders. This is because in general the Dutch make use of and relate to the Dutch guilder for the magnitude 'value'. They are paid in guilders, their salaries are specified in guilders and they pay taxes in guilders.

The noteworthy aspect of the example is that the apples remain the same 'sort' and 'quantity'. The object 'sort' and the magnitude 'quantity' therefore appear to be international standards. For the magnitude 'money value' we use, internationally, a great number of differing monetary units. A class for monetary units has a special name: 'foreign exchange'.

The large number of monetary units leads to an equal number of measuring scales that are used to calculate between them. The conversion factors between the various foreign exchange units are called the 'rate of exchange'. The rates of exchange between the various monetary units can be represented in the form of a table. It must be noted that the exchange rates change from day to day and that Table 7.3 is only a snapshot in time.

Table 7.3   Rates of exchange for various currencies at 11 September, 1992.

	$	DM	FF	£	Fl
$	1.00	1.44	0.20	0.51	1.61
DM	0.70	1.00	3.39	0.36	1.12
FF	0.20	0.29	1.00	0.11	0.33
£	1.95	2.80	9.52	1.00	3.14
Fl	0.62	0.89	3.03	0.32	1.00

One cell in the table gives the conversion of the rate of exchange from one monetary unit to another monetary unit. For reasons of precision this is not the case in many rate of exchange tables. Think, for example, of the Italian lira and the Japanese yen, which have such a low value per unit that 10 000 units are generally used. This can be solved by placing the number of units beside the unit in the table.

In Table 7.3 we see that the various exchange unit columns are headed by symbols instead of the full name. This has a double purpose:

(1) The readability of the table is improved;

(2) The symbols of the units can be used easily in combination with the attribute value, making the attribute easier to interpret.

The different monetary units cannot be added together. Therefore we cannot add guilders to dollars before making the units uniform, by converting the foreign exchange according to the applicable rate of exchange.

The application of foreign currency in an information system can be realized by allowing the measure 'value' to have a large number of 'currency' units that can be converted by means of exchange rate tables.

If these conversions threaten to become imprecise, as for the Japanese yen, there must be the possibility of multiplying the units by a particular power.

A more universal approach for the provision of information is gained by naming the attributes with the assistance of measured magnitudes. This makes the information system less dependent on the technical terms, such as attribute type and value type, used in computing. In this way we create a flexible description of the information architecture. We have the ability to distinguish between the conversions of the various measuring scales, and to incorporate them separately. The expansion of the number of measuring units by new objects will then no longer influence the structure of the information system. It would be simpler if we could avoid the conversions but unfortunately they are necessary. Think, for example, of logistical processes in which a large number of activities take place that change the units of magnitude, such as repacking, mixing and dissolving. Changing the unit for the same measure is more the rule than the exception for logistical processes.

7.7.3   Standardization of units by agreeing upon reference objects

Owing to the growing importance of fast and faultless communication, more and more international standards have been set up for magnitudes with their accompanying units. An example of this is the so-called Système Internationale (SI) that is based on the following fundamental magnitudes and accompanying units. Every unit in the SI is based upon standard reference objects.

The reference objects for the measuring units in the SI are often also physically recognizable. For example, a 'standard metre' that is maintained in Paris is seen internationally as the standard for the reference object with the unit 'metre'.

The big advantage of the SI is that we can make calculations easily because the whole system is based on decimals. A kilometre consists of 10 hectometres, an hectometre of 10 decametres, a decametre of 10 metres, a metre of 10 decimetres, a decimetre of 10 centimetres, and so forth. The measuring scales all calculate by division and multiplication with factors of 10.

The SI is not yet in full use everywhere. Anglicized countries, such as the United Kingdom and the United States, sometimes still use multiple units such as 'mile', 'yard', 'foot', 'inch', 'pound', 'ounce', 'gallon' and 'bushel'. Calculations with these are not so simple, because a yard consists of three feet, a foot of twelve inches. When reading English cookbooks or technical handbooks we must therefore pay attention to the units in which the measures are represented, and the accompanying conversion factors.

Table 7.4   The basic measures and basic units of the Système Internationale.

Measure		Unit	
Name	Symbol	Name	Symbol
Length	l	Metre	m
Mass	m	Kilogram	kg
Time	t	Second	s
Electric current	I	Ampere	A
Temperature	T	Kelvin	K
Intensity of light	J	Candela	cd

7.7.4   Dimension

To make conversions between a reference object or its representing unit and magnitude easier to perform and check we use the concept 'dimension'. The concept 'dimension' in ordinary language means something like 'the same object measured on another measuring scale'. By measuring the object on another measuring scale we arrive at a completely new dimension. We have already seen that by measuring the height of a person against his age we obtained a two-dimensional progression. In Figure 7.5 we measured against the measuring scales for 'age' and 'height'. A measuring scale gives a dimension with which the characteristics of an object can be pictured:

- Magnitude: for example length;
- Reference object: for example the standard metre in Paris;
- Unit: for example metre;
- Dimension: for example (L).

The dimension of a measurement is often represented by a character with which comparisons can be made for a derived dimension. The character used for the measure 'length' is L, for example.

Analogous to the phenomena of derived magnitude and derived unit, we also use the derived dimension. The derived dimension is obtained from the equations for the calculation of the derived magnitude. So we see that the derived dimension for speed measured in metres/second is equal to (LT^{-1}).

The dimension is useful because we can use it to:

(1) Check formulae by determining whether the left-hand side and the right-hand side of an equation have the same dimension, for example, in order to verify that we are not adding cows to horses. An example of an incorrect dimension is: 'The turnover is $900'. This is wrong because turnover is measured in 'money amount per period';

(2) Deduce laws by means of equations for the calculating of derived dimensions. A dimension is useful in definition of the generic formula for a measure by its relation with the reference objects (units) from the SI.

The fundamental dimensions for the SI are shown in Table 7.5.

Table 7.5 Fundamental dimensions for the SI.

Dimension measure	Symbol
Length	L
Mass	M
Time	T
Electric current	I
Temperature	θ
Intensity of light	J

Derived dimensions are defined as functions of the basic measures. Since the SI is a coherent unit system, the dimension of every derived magnitude, X, can be written as:

$$\dim X = L^{\alpha}M^{\beta}T^{\Gamma}I^{\delta}\theta^{\varepsilon}J^{\mu}$$

This is also frequently noted as:

$$[X] = [L^{\alpha}][M^{\beta}][T^{\Gamma}][I^{\delta}][\theta^{\varepsilon}][J^{\mu}]$$

The right-hand element of this dimension equation is given the name of the dimension formula of the magnitude X.

Table 7.6 shows a number of derived magnitudes with their derived dimension formulas and derived units.

The dimension formula defines the derived unit of the derived magnitude in basic units. In this way we gain an easy insight into the meaning of a calculated value and we can validate functions more easily.

Table 7.6 Some derived magnitudes with their dimension formulae, derived units and symbols.

Magnitude	Dimension formula	Unit	Symbol
Surface area	$[L^2]$	Square metre	m^2
Content	$[L^3]$	Cubic metre	m^3
Speed	$[LT^{-1}]$	Metres per second	m/s
Acceleration	$[LT^{-2}]$	Metres per second^2	m/s^2
Force	$[LMT^{-2}]$	Newton	N
Work	$[ML^2T^{-2}]$	Joule	J

For a derived magnitude we can choose derived magnitudes that in some cases also have a specific name. Thus we express power in newtons. One newton is equal to one kg m/s². In Table 7.6 there are two examples from physics, but in daily practice there are many more derived units in use, each of which has its own name.

7.7.5   Business economic units and magnitudes

For business economic magnitudes we can work in an analogous manner with their units. The three best-known basic economic measures are quantity, value and time. The quantity is frequently measured in items, q, although other units are also used. The financial value in the Netherlands is usually measured in guilders, *Fl*. The time in economic activities often has a daily rhythm which is why the unit chosen is often one day, see Table 7.7.

Table 7.7   Economic magnitudes and units.

Magnitude		Unit	
Name	Symbol	Name	Symbol
Quantity	Q	Pieces	q
Value	V	Dollar	$
Time	t	Day	d

With the three magnitudes mentioned above there can be defined an extremely large number of derived measures and units.

- Sales, for example, is equal to the number of items that are sold per time unit. The dimension of sales becomes $[Q][t^{-1}]$ and the unit q/d.

- The dimension of the increase in sales: $[Q][t^{-2}]$ is completely analogous to acceleration in physics: $[L][t^{-2}]$. This is normally not so obvious in economics because the increase in sales is measured in discrete numbers and is represented in previously-defined time periods.

- The dimension of the interest rate can be derived by describing the concept of interest as an amount that is paid per period per money value that a person has available. The dimension analysis then results in: $[F][t^{-1}][F^{-1}] = [t^{-1}]$.

The calculation shows that the dimension for interest is a time period for which the interest is defined. The dimension of interest is not dependent on value.

It would appear that no higher-order dimensions occur for economic magnitudes, unlike the physical magnitudes. For the physical measures we saw that the frequently used magnitudes 'surface area', 'content' and 'acceleration' respectively have two, three and three dimensions. For 'surface area' and 'content' the basic units are identical while for 'acceleration' the basic units are dissimilar.

We often work with figures for the economic measures. In order to form a clearer vision of a particular situation, a large number of economic values are related to each other in the form of fractions.

The time dimension is an important dimension in economics. For the magnitude 'time', we can work with a wide range of possibilities. We can work with the units 'year', 'quartile', 'month', 'week', 'day', 'hour', 'minute', 'second', and so on. To utilize the various units we can, in accordance with the conventions of the Gregorian chronology, swap quickly between measuring scales.

7.8   Object type and magnitude

The object type in the KISS method has much stronger attributes than a reference object, a magnitude and a class. A class is a grouping of objects based on a classification criterion. An object type carries out actions or undergoes actions according to a defined time sequence that is defined in a KISS model. The model thereby gives an ordering in time in which the actions may be executed. It is precisely this action concept and the ordering of actions in time that make it possible for all the attributes of all the measuring scales to be used. We have already commented that each action is a discrete occurrence on a frequency scale whereby the action itself can again become an object of an object type when we are interested in this within the scope of the problem area. In summary this means that the concept 'class' stands orthogonal to the concept 'object type'. The two concepts complement each other.

7.8.1   Ranking scale

Because the actions of an object type can be placed in a specific order in a KISS model, it is possible to refer to a ranking scale for the changes in time. One action will, therefore, take place before, at the same time as, or after another action.

7.8.2   Interval scale

By adding the date and time that an action takes place, an object type can be related to an interval scale. This is of great practical importance because with this we can support the time dimension in which each action records the time it was executed.

7.8.3 Frequency scale

With the execution of an action there is, by definition, a change at one moment in time to one or more object types. We see therefore a very discrete action take place that itself is measured on a frequency scale. The discrete action itself can then again become an object.

7.8.4 Nominal scale

In addition to the scales mentioned above, an object type has the attributes of a nominal scale in any case. We can also group the objects of an object type according to the characteristics of a category. This happens on the basis of common actions that are reused by the object types but also on the basis of identical characteristics of the objects.

In the case of grouping according to identical actions that are reused, we also use the word 'category' in an object-interaction model. The category has the task in the object-interaction model of functioning as a kind of switch element for the diverse object types that can make use of a common action type.

7.9 Summary

In this chapter we have discussed the attributes of the five measuring scales that we use for the measuring of attributes of objects and events in the real world. They are:

(1) The nominal scale;
(2) The ranking scale;
(3) The interval scale;
(4) The ratio scale;
(5) The frequency scale.

The number of possible operations increases from the nominal scale to the frequency scale. With the nominal scale we can indicate whether or not an object belongs to a particular group. With the ranking scale we can indicate whether objects, on the basis of their attributes, are bigger or smaller than each other. With the interval scale we can perform addition and subtraction operations. With the ratio scale we can perform multiplication and division operations. Finally with the frequency scale we can carry out discrete operations on the basis of identification and objectivation of phenomena.

It is possible for the ranking, interval and ratio scales to name a magnitude that makes possible the measuring of object attributes on a continuous scale. The magnitude itself can always be converted into a reference object.

Magnitudes can be measured in units. A unit is generally a reference object. It is possible to show, by means of a conversion table, how one measuring unit can be converted into another measuring unit.

As more and more different measurements are related to each other, the number of dimensions increases. With the use of equations we can check whether the equations have been formulated correctly, and we can determine what the measuring unit for the measured or calculated value must be.

7.10 Questions

(1) Classification is an important task in many object-oriented methods. Where would you position the classification process within the different kinds of measurement processes?

(2) Discuss the different kinds of measurement scales and their importance and use. Give examples.

(3) Describe the relationship between 'knowledge' and 'measurement', and between 'knowledge systems' and 'information systems'.

(4) Discuss the measurement process within the context of the communication paradigm.

(5) What is the distinction between 'magnitude' and 'object' and what is the importance of 'standard reference objects'?

(6) In what way does the measurement process define the foundation for object orientation in general and the KISS method in particular? Describe the dualism between 'action' and 'object'.

(7) What is 'dimension' and how can it be used for the specification of 'magnitudes'?

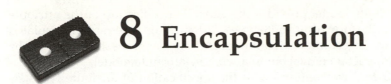

8 Encapsulation

8.1 Introduction

The usefulness of encapsulating details within an object is that we can maintain an overview of the main structure of the information architecture. In the KISS method we have in fact already made use of the principle of encapsulation in creating the KISS models, object-interaction models and hierarchy models, because we excluded all operations, static conditions and attribute types from these models. Hiding the details of objects and the actions that change the objects is done by specifying the attribute types, operations and conditions of actions in separate models.

To model the encapsulated details we use two models:

- Attribute model;
- Action model.

The attribute model shows how the content and naming of the attributes comes into existence in relation to dimensions of measurement and reference objects.

The action model shows how the attributes can be modified by the use of operations. The action model can also show, if necessary, the conditions under which the action may be executed.

8.2 The attribute model

The attribute type specifies the values of the attributes of an object, group of objects or action. The attribute itself specifies, for example, whether something is big or small, whether an action took place early or late or that an object has an identifying name or number.

In a previous chapter we saw how attributes can be identified from adverbs, adjectives and clauses by means of a grammatical analysis of structured sentences.

Definition of the attribute model

The attribute model provides the general specification of the attribute values in the form of attribute types. The attribute types are encapsulated within the object-interaction model and are therefore shown not in the object-interaction model but in a separate attribute model.

Before we continue with the specification of attribute types by means of attribute models we will position this within the more general scope of thought of object orientation. The purpose of this is to further simplify and generalize the specification of attribute types than is possible either by grammatical analysis or by taking stock of all the attribute types. We will therefore explain the principles that apply to object orientation for naming attribute types and defining specific attribute values.

In the introduction to measuring scales it became apparent that the value of an attribute comes into existence at the moment we relate the object to a standard reference object or measuring scale. The measuring scale is in turn also related to a reference object. Depending on the measuring scale used, the value is expressed in the form of reference objects or measuring units. The process of defining the attributes of an object has been described as measurement.

Important for the determination of the general rules for the definition of attributes is the knowledge that an attribute only comes into being by measuring it on a measuring scale, naming the object or comparing it with another object that serves as the reference object.

By measuring object attributes on an appropriate measuring scale, we can determine:

- Whether an object for the attribute is equal to a reference object;
- Whether an object is bigger or smaller than a reference object;
- How much bigger or smaller an object is than a reference object;
- How often an object is bigger or smaller than a reference object;
- How frequently an object undergoes a change.

The reference object is usually a common standard and is often represented as a unit during measurement. So we have, for example, °C or °F as the units for temperature, and the metre, centimetre, inch, mile, yard, as units for length.

The general name for the dimension upon which we conduct all the measurements of object attributes and for which the various measuring units are valid is the measure.

Representation of dimension of measurement

A dimension of measurement defines the general name for the dimension of object attributes upon which the measurements are conducted. A measure is represented by an ellipse drawn with a dotted line (Figure 8.1), while an object is represented by an ellipse with a solid line (Figure 8.2).

Figure 8.1 Dimension of measurement.

The dimension of measurement is equal to an object when the measured object's attributes conform entirely to the discrete reference objects. For cases where this is not possible, we must convert the measured object attributes and the reference object into each other using measuring scales.

A measuring unit defines for a dimension of measurement the measuring scale against which the measuring of attributes has taken place. In many cases the measuring unit is also equal to the reference object. The relationship between objects and dimensions of measurement is shown in Figure 8.3.

Definition of an attribute type

Attribute types give the generic description of the object attributes. An attribute type defines the association between the attributes of an object type and a dimension of measurement by the measurement of the attribute.

An attribute type is shown graphically by a long rectangle containing its name (Figure 8.4).

Definition of an attribute

An attribute is the instantiation of an attribute type by the measurement of characteristics. An attribute of a dimension of measurement is only meaningful when it is associated with the relevant measuring unit.

The sentence 'He is 1.92' expresses too little because we do not know what it refers to. It could be 1.92 metres but it could also be 1.92 seconds. The sentence only becomes meaningful when we include the measuring units.

In an attribute model we connect the attribute type on one side with a line segment to the dimension of measurement or reference object and on the other side with an object type, action type, gerund, weak object type, object class, specialization or category.

The attribute model graphically represents the relationship between dimensions of measurement and/or reference objects via the attribute types with the object types, action types, weak object types, gerunds, specializations, categories or object classes, and we will thus create an attribute model for each of these.

Figure 8.2 Object.

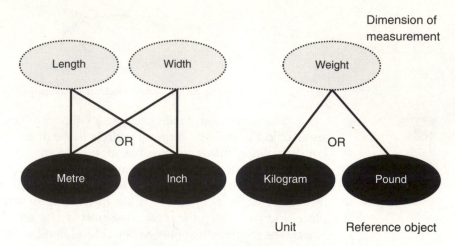

Figure 8.3   Relationship between object and dimension of measurement.

8.2.1   Naming conventions for attribute types

When creating the attribute model we can in many cases automatically generate the name of an attribute type by using the name of the (object) type, action type or (object) class, and combining it with the name of the dimension of measurement or the reference object. The naming convention for an attribute type therefore closely matches the way in which we work in English with the general descriptions of the object attributes using adverbs and adjectives.

In Figure 8.5 we have created the name of an attribute type by combining the name of the object type Person with respectively the dimensions of measurement Height and Weight. We thus end up with the attribute types PersonHeight and PersonWeight.

In English we see that an attribute type is often formed with the words 'of a' which indicate the 'having' of an attribute. The attribute is therefore dependent on the existence of the object type. The example above then becomes:

- Height of a Person;
- Weight of a Person.

Figure 8.4   Symbol for attribute type.

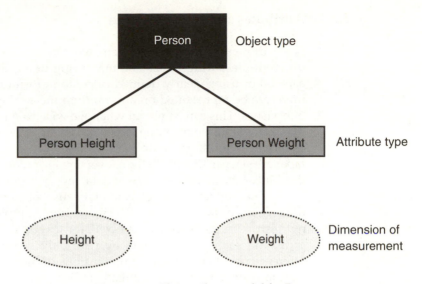

Figure 8.5   The attribute model for Person.

8.2.2   Representation of attributes

The attributes of an attribute type can take on particular values that can be represented in many different ways. Forms of representation often used in information systems, for example, are character strings and numeric representations. The representation of attributes in the form of pictures, colours, graphic measuring scales, graphics, pie-charts, graphic objects, video images, and so on is less commonly used.

Thanks to the now popular GUI (Graphical User Interface) and windows techniques the representation capabilities for attributes continue to grow. Thus we are no longer restricted to a purely textual representation using the 80 positions by 25 lines of a character-oriented screen. Consequently we can increasingly enter the attributes using pictures, graphic measuring scales, graphics, and so forth.

The graphical representation of attributes of object types, action types, weak object types and gerunds provides an extra dimension and attraction to the object-oriented analysis, design and implementation of information systems. The graphical form of representation of attributes provided by GUIs gives us a great number of capabilities that are either not available or only possible to a limited extent with character-oriented screens. The information system can view the pictures, screens, buttons and video images as objects in their own right. The last step necessary to transfer to an object-oriented programming language is then very small.

8.2.3   Attributes and measuring units

For a dimension of measurement we can usually use a great many different measuring units. The measuring units can be converted into each other using clearly defined calculation formulas. An attribute can therefore be represented on any random measuring scale according to our wishes. This can be useful when we wish to represent numbers and measuring units on the same screen according to personal preference, for example in millions of dollars, francs with two decimal places, or Japanese yen per 1000. With the conversion formulas we gain an enormous flexibility between the storage of data and the representation of data.

The reference object can make use of a number of different dimensions of measurement. The metre, for example, can be used without restriction as the reference object for length, breadth, height, depth, girth, and so on. We thus end up with only a very limited number of reference objects to which the dimensions of measurement in the information system directly or indirectly refer.

8.2.4   Attributes, artificial intelligence and the accumulation of knowledge

The accumulation of knowledge of an information system is to an important degree determined by the semantics laid down in the object-interaction model. With an object-interaction model we lay down the overview of the structural semantics of the real world around us for the information architecture.

Knowledge systems are to an important extent implicitly based on the rules with which the phenomena in reality must comply in order to be valid. The encapsulation of knowledge can therefore be considered as populating a reference model with attribute values and rules within an information architecture. The information architecture can, for the sake of the knowledge system, be used with the attribute values and the logic according to which the entered attributes must comply with those of the information architecture. Further decisions can then be taken by the information system.

8.2.5   Connectivity in the attribute model

Analogous to the object-interaction model we can specify connectivity for the attribute model. In the attribute model we specify the connectivity for the relationships defined by the attributes between the dimension of measurement and/or the object and the object type, weak object type, gerund, action type, specialization, category or object class.

The connectivity of an attribute type shows whether a dimension of measurement or an object is used singularly or plurally as the measurement reference by object types, weak object types, gerunds and/or action types. We show the connectivity by letters and numbers in an attribute model.

Upper boundary For the connectivity in the attribute model we specify a lower boundary and an upper boundary. The upper boundary defines the number of instantiations that is maximally included in the relationship with the attribute type. The upper boundary can be limited to 1 but can also be n, in which case it is greater than or equal to 1.

To show the similarity and the difference between the connectivity in the attribute model and the connectivity in the object-interaction model we will look at a bank example. For each figure in the object-interaction model we will separately explain the connectivity of the attribute type in the attribute model. In the object-interaction model we have also included the connectivity for purposes of illustration (Figure 8.6).

The explanation of the connectivity in Figure 8.6 is as follows. The figure shows by the connectivity that a person can be registered many times and that a bank can perform registrations many times. After a person has been registered he or she can open an account many times. The account itself can only be opened once. Deposits can be made into an account many times.

The attribute model is created individually for each figure in the object-interaction model. The specification of the connectivity therefore takes place in the attribute model individually per object type, weak

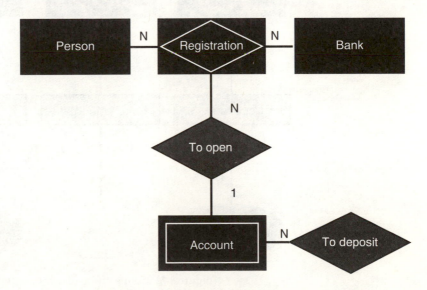

Figure 8.6 Object-interaction model for Bank.

object type, gerund, action type, specialization, category and object class. In this way we uncouple the semantic structure of the object-interaction model from the attribute content of the figures in that model.

In the three attribute models shown in Figure 8.7, connectivity is shown for BankName, RegistrationDate and PersonID. The names of the attribute types are formed by combining the names of the object type or gerund with the dimension of measurement or the reference object.

For BankName we have shown that a bank has one name and that there can be many banks with the same name. 'Name' is a reference object because it is a declaration and we cannot define any ranking for it.

For RegistrationDate we have shown that on one date many registrations can take place and that a registration can only take place on one date. 'Date' is a dimension of measurement of the reference object 'unit of time'.

For PersonID we have shown that ID, an identifier, is valid for one person and that one person also has one ID. As for 'Name' we cannot define a ranking for ID. Every ID is measured against the frequency scale.

When the upper boundary of the connectivity is 1:1, the attribute is an identifier for an object. Whether the attribute type will also be used within the information system as an identifier depends on the specific circumstances of the object within the system. In many cases it might be a good idea to use a systems-generated identifier, to ensure that with the

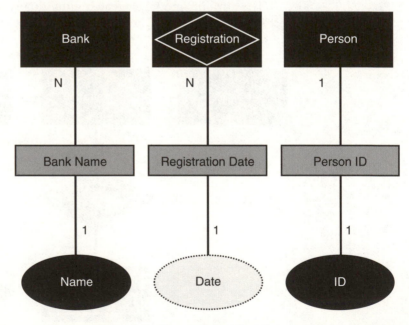

Figure 8.7   Connectivity of attribute types.

growing number of objects in the information system in the future, all objects can be uniquely identified.

For the remaining figures in the object-interaction model we produce the attribute models pictured in Figure 8.8. We will now create the attribute models for the remaining action types and the weak object type.

For ToOpenDate we have shown that an action 'To open' takes place on one date and that on one date many actions 'To open' can take place.

For ToDepositAmount we have shown that one amount belongs to one action 'To deposit' and that one action 'To deposit' belongs to one amount.

When we come to Account we discover a special problem. We have shown by the connectivity in the attribute model that a balance belongs to one account and that one account has many balances. The result of this is that we can measure one attribute type, AccountBalance, against more than one measuring scale without being able to distinguish between the various measured results for the measured attribute type. Consequently we end up with multiple measured results that we cannot represent uniquely and record by the specific name of an attribute type.

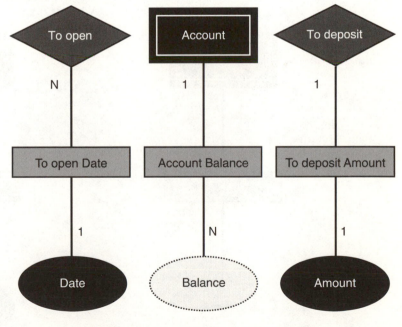

Figure 8.8 Connectivity of attribute types.

We arrive at a solution to the problem when, by further analysis, we incorporate multiple attribute types for the various measured results of the measured balance of an account.

Another solution is to be found when we differentiate one or more object types and/or action types for which we define a specific balance. The consequence of this is that we must further expand the attribute model, and possibly also the object-interaction model, in such a way that a balance is only singularly included with an object type and action type.

The general rule for a connectivity of n for a dimension of measurement or reference object is that there must always be extra consideration given to possible further modelling until the connectivity reaches 1.

To explain the connectivity of $n:n$ we have defined an attribute model with Address as the reference object for the object type Person (Figure 8.9). In the model we have shown that one person has many addresses and that one address has many persons.

When the upper boundary of the connectivity is $n:n$, we must in the first instance check which missing actions we have overlooked and have not yet modelled. The missing actions can then be included so that the upper boundary, the final result of the connectivity for the dimension of measurement or the reference object, is precisely 1. An alternative is to include extra dimensions of measurement or reference objects with which we can create the extra attribute types. In the case of address we decide to create a new object type 'Address'.

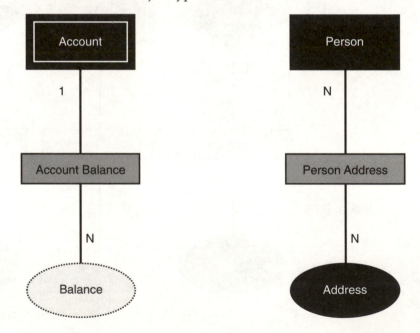

Figure 8.9   Using many dimensions of measurement.

Lower boundary   The lower boundary of the connectivity is complementary to the upper boundary. The lower boundary indicates whether or not a relationship is compulsory. A lower boundary of 0 indicates that a relationship is optional and not compulsory. A lower boundary of 1 indicates that a relationship is compulsory. This is also called a total relationship.

In an attribute model the value for the lower boundary is written in front of the colon and the value of the upper boundary is written after the colon.

The first attribute model in Figure 8.10 shows that it is not compulsory for a bank to have a name and that it is not compulsory for a name to have a bank.

The second attribute model indicates that a date must be included for a registration and that it is not compulsory that a registration exists for a date.

In the third attribute model we show that for each person there must be one ID and that each ID must be related to one person.

If an attribute type is also to be an identifier, the lower boundary for the object type must be 1. If the lower boundary is 0, it is possible that the identifier of an object will not be included with the instantiation of that object, which means that errors will occur.

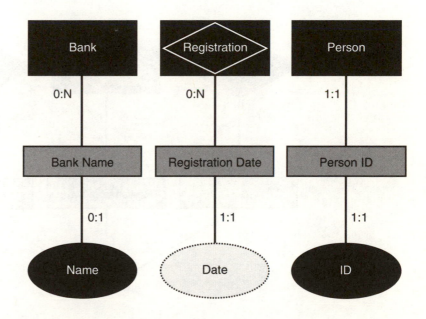

Lower boundary: Upper boundary
0 = partial, 1 = total

Figure 8.10   Lower boundary of the connectivity.

A dimension of measurement or reference object can also be used by more than one object type, weak object type, gerund, action type, specialization or object class (Figure 8.11). The advantage of common use of a dimension of measurement or reference object by various object types and action types is that with limited effort we can define a large quantity of attribute types. We only need to specify the appropriate general characteristics and constraints for a dimension of measurement and a reference object once. When determining the attribute types we can reuse the general definitions of the dimension of measurement or reference object.

We specify the local constraints for the attribute type that apply to the specific combination of an object type or action type with a dimension of measurement or reference object. Thus we can define and specify beforehand the possible occurrences of values for the attribute type, for example the boundary values within which the attribute must lie. In this way we can form a domain of possible values for the attribute.

The generally used forms of representation for the attribute specifications are recorded in the dimension of measurement and the reference object as 'character', 'integer', 'number', 'time', 'date', and so on. In addition we can record the specific representation form of an attribute at the attribute type level. In this way we make a distinction

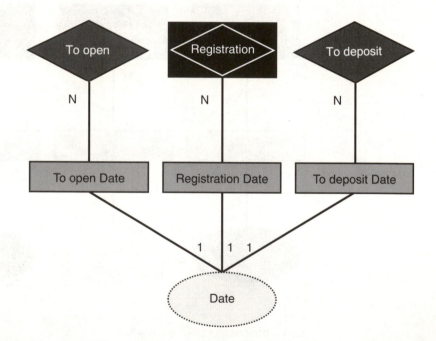

Figure 8.11   Common use of a dimension of measurement.

between the general description of the attribute type from the viewpoint of the dimension of measurement or reference object and the specifically local characteristics of the attribute type that apply to the object type, action type, weak object type, gerund, specialization, category and object class.

8.3   Activating an object into an object type

When relevant actions are to take place on the reference object, it is recommended that the reference object be 'activated' into a new object type. The new object type will then acquire a number of actions that perform instantiation, update and termination. In practice, we see that the determination of new object types occurs quite frequently in information systems.

The activation of a reference object is further explained by means of the example in Figure 8.12 of a Car for which we wish to define the name of the driver in the first analysis by referring to him or her as DriverName. The Car is seen initially as the object type and the DriverName is seen as a reference object. The attribute type is then, according to the described rules, DriverNameCar. At first glance this is not a particularly logical name for an attribute type.

When adding the connectivity between Car and DriverName we discover that this gives us reason to conduct further analysis. Owing to the fact that DriverName can occur many times for one Car and that one DriverName can belong to many occurrences of Car, the upper boundary of the connectivity between Car and DriverName is $n{:}n$. This must be modelled further until we arrive at a connectivity of 1 for the dimension of measurement or the reference object.

In a previous discussion of connectivity we saw that with a connectivity of $n{:}n$ we must continue with further modelling of the attribute model. In our example we can achieve this by activating an object type that is implicitly included in the naming of the reference object. In order to do this we must add the action type 'To drive'.

Using DriverName we introduce the object type Person which is given the attribute type PersonName by relating it to the reference object Name. The connectivity between Person and Name now becomes $n{:}1$, fulfilling the requirement that the connectivity be 1 for a dimension of measurement or reference object.

The action type 'To drive' becomes the interaction between the object types Person and Car, in the new object-interaction model. In this model we can now include all the information for the driving of the car by a person. The person who drives the car is hereby implicitly

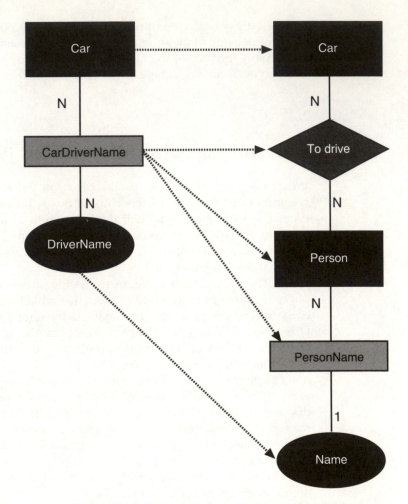

Figure 8.12   Activation of an object to an object type.

the driver. We see that the new object-interaction model offers more possibilities than the old object-interaction model.

The condition for the activation of an object into an object type is that there must be an identifiable object type implicitly included in the naming of the attribute type concerned.

Since the dimension of measurement refers to a measuring scale on which non-discrete objects are pictured, not every dimension of measurement can easily be activated. Reference objects, however, have to be activated when they show a relevant dynamic life.

8.4   The path of an attribute through the KISS paradigm

When we represent the path taken by an attribute through the KISS paradigm, we see that the attribute itself also takes on a number of different states. Thus we can observe particular phenomena in the real world around us, and model them according to the KISS paradigm. In this way we define a structure within which we use the attributes to record the characteristics of objects and phenomena in the real world. The manner in which we can record, use and inquire about the attributes of the phenomena in the real world is handled by discussing the KISS paradigm in detail.

The overview of the KISS paradigm (Figure 8.13) shows globally how the functions, objects, actions, inspections, messages, operations, conditions and triggers are related to each other.

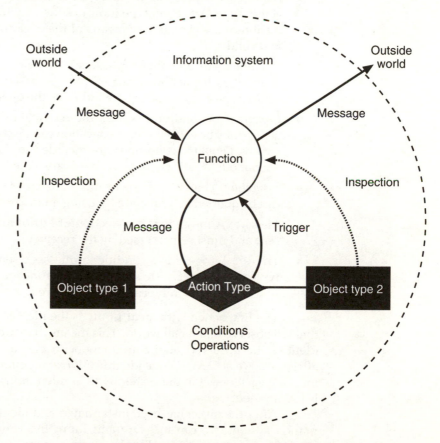

Figure 8.13   The KISS paradigm for object orientation.

The changes that occur in an attribute are caused by the internal treatment of an attribute within the KISS paradigm. In a stepwise manner we will look at how the state of an attribute is changed by the various parts of the KISS paradigm.

The global definitions of the components of the KISS paradigm are:

- *Function*: The function controls, manages and coordinates the execution of actions on objects. A function takes care of the input and output of the attributes for the information system.

- *Object type*: The general behaviour of a group of objects is described by a KISS model for an object type. The object type specifies the state of a real or conceptual object in reality by recording the values of the attribute types of an object within the general scope of the type.

- *Action type*: An action on an object is generally described by an action type. An action type indicates the way in which the object attributes are changed by means of the encapsulated operations and conditions.

- *Operation*: An operation indicates how a specific attribute type changes as the action is carried out. An association between an action type and an object type indicates the operations.

- *Condition:* A condition defines the restrictions under which the action may be carried out. A condition can be static or dynamic in nature. Dynamic conditions are included in the structure of the KISS model. Static conditions are encapsulated in the action type.

- *Inspection*: The state of one or more attributes of a specific object can be queried in a function by using an inspection.

- *Message*: A message is a collection of attribute values which are sent and must be processed by the receiver.

- *Trigger*: A trigger is a conditional message sent from the action type of an object type to a function. The function can activate other functions or action types with it, if desired.

The first action with an attribute is the identification of an object that we observe in the real world. This means that attributes are used to identify the observed object uniquely with one or more identifying attributes. We achieve unique identification in an information system by marking each object in the system with an identifying attribute when it is instantiated.

After the object has been instantiated and identified by the information system, we can measure and input the values of the object's attributes from the real world. The measurement of the attribute types takes place by referring the object in the real world to specific measuring scales for dimensions of measurement or reference objects.

The measured values for the object attributes are initially made known to the information system by a message from the real world to an input function. The input function determines whether the message can be received and decoded by the information system. To do this, the input function performs the first syntax checks on the attribute values. The syntax check is carried out on the basis of the generally applicable attributes defined for the dimension of measurement or the reference object.

After receipt and decoding of the attributes by the input function, the status of the received attributes is changed to that of 'function attribute'. A function attribute can only be observed by us while the function is active. When a function has ended, the attributes of that function cease to exist. Function attributes are therefore extremely transient.

After the input function has received and decoded the message, it sends another message to an action type. Included in this message are the values of the function attributes that have already been syntax-checked by the input function.

The modification of the status of an object of an object type is always done by an action containing the encapsulated operations. It is the action that has the coordinating role in the instantiation of new objects and the modification of the attributes of objects.

The action checks whether or not the identified objects may be instantiated or changed. This is done by checking for all the conditions encapsulated in the action that each object meets the dynamic constraints specified in the KISS models, as well as the static constraints.

When all the action conditions are found to be met, the function attributes are turned into action attributes. At this point, the attributes take on a permanent form and are then known as semi-persistent. From now on the action attributes are used to change the object attributes with predefined operations. When object attributes are formed by operations, the attributes have then acquired a totally persistent form. For purposes of clarity, the action can send the function a 'good' message after acceptance of the attributes, whereby the function knows that the action can be carried out.

An operation is always related to a resulting object attribute and one or more action attributes. It is possible for an object attribute to be calculated by a series of operations with complicated calculations for which the intermediate results are temporarily recorded.

If the static or dynamic conditions of the action are not met, an error message is sent back to the function in the form of a trigger ,with the reason why the specific action could not be performed on the objects.

All changes to the status of the object are checked by the conditions defined for the actions. The action conditions specify the semantic constraints under which a change may take place. Little attention need be paid by the actions to the syntax of the attributes because these have already been checked by the input function. The semantics are mainly specified in the action conditions because they are derived during the modelling process based on the organization's way of working. The actions define the business rules according to which the object data may be changed.

Summarized, this means that the action types function as a semantic filter. The action conditions are principally structure constraints that can no longer be derived from the syntax rules of the attributes. The action conditions therefore define to an important degree the semantics that are incorporated in the information architecture of the information system and therefore its intelligence.

It is semantically depicted in the KISS paradigm that an information system also sends messages to the outside world. It is fairly obvious that this occurs in the form of a report in which the status of objects is represented in the form of an overview. This overview is generally formulated by inspection of the attributes of identified objects in the information system. Then an output function can perform a number of calculations and processes on them before the report is printed.

When composing the report we can make use of the information architecture. In this way the attributes represented in the report are strongly temporary, even though they are a representation of the persistent attributes of the objects in the information system. The temporary nature of the report is caused at the moment that it is produced and printed. After this moment the report attributes are no longer maintained.

8.5   Attribute types of classes

Using the bank example we will explain the difference between the attribute types for an object type and those for an object class. For this we add to the example the requirement that at any time we wish to know the total number of accounts held by a person or the bank itself.

In the example we have turned the attribute type PersonAccount-Total into an attribute type for the object type Person. The dimension of measurement to which we refer is AccountTotal (Figure 8.14).

We see that PersonAccountTotal is made up of the dimension of measurement AccountTotal and the object type Person. AccountTotal can only have whole numbers as values and is measured on a frequency scale.

Because there are not yet objects instantiated for the object type Account, for the action 'To register' a person at the bank, the attribute type PersonAccountTotal cannot be valid for an object instantiation of Account, but is valid at the level of the object type Person.

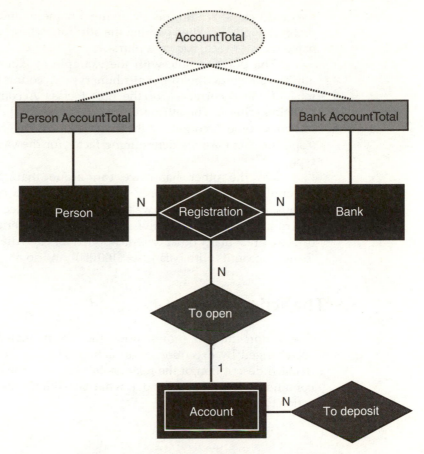

Figure 8.14   Attribute model for Person and Bank.

In the same way we can also specify the attribute type BankAccountTotal for the object type Bank. It will most probably be instantiated by the founding of the bank.

Conditions for the purposeful inclusion of the attribute types PersonAccountTotal and BankAccountTotal are that an object type Account exists for Person and Bank, and that Account is included in the object-interaction model.

In fact, when we look critically at the manner in which the attribute types PersonAccountTotal and BankAccountTotal come to exist, we see that the attribute types can become part of an object class because the data concerns a group of clustered objects of the same person and bank respectively.

Owing to the fact that an object class always has to do with a grouping of one or more objects, we take account of this when naming the object class. We do this by giving a name to an object class that is preferably plural. When naming the attribute type of an object class this name therefore also becomes plural.

The point to note with the example in Figure 8.15 is that the attributes recorded with the attribute type AccountsTotal, describe the total of the occurrences of the object class Accounts for particular selection criteria. The attribute type AccountsTotal does not belong to one object type Account, but the occurrences of the group of accounts of a specific client are the determining factor for the value of the attribute type.

On the other hand we can argue that the attribute type AccountsTotal does not only need to belong to one object Person, because the specific person was only one of the selection criteria for the determination of the class division. Besides the criterion of person, there can be a great many other criteria applied for class division. For example 'bank', 'accounts with balance > $100 000', and so on.

8.6 The action model

The action model shows how the encapsulated attribute types are changed by execution of an action. The action model provides a detailed description of the relationship between the operations and the conditions. It describes under what conditions the operations of an action type can be executed.

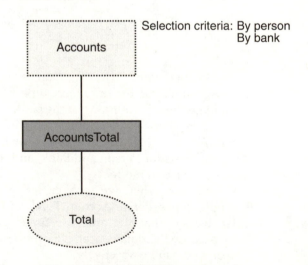

Figure 8.15 Attribute types for a class.

Definition of an
action model

The action model shows the order in which the operations of an action type are executed and under which simple and complex conditions the operations of an action may be executed.

The action model is created as an encapsulated model per action type. For the discussion of the method of creating an action model, we describe the action model for action types in the context of the object-interaction model, with the associations that an action type has in the object-interaction model. To be able to create an action model the associations from the object-interaction model will not be modelled at all.

The elements that are further specified within the action model are the attribute type, the condition and the operation (Figure 8.16). With the discussion of the action model we consider these elements in combination with the components of the information architecture.

8.6.1   Operations

The operations of an action type specify in detail how the attribute types change at the moment that an action is carried out. The statuses of the object types that are directly or indirectly associated with the action type are changed by operations. The action type can also change the attribute types for all object types that are stronger than the directly associated object types. By specifying the maximal set of operations, we define in a stepwise manner the structural functionality that is encapsulated in the information architecture.

The operations themselves are completely encapsulated in the action type. For each action type we define at least one operation that changes an object attribute. When we cannot specify any operations for an action type, we must ask ourselves if the action type is relevant for the information system. An example of an operation we often overlook,

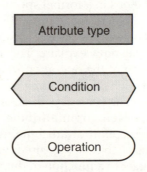

Figure 8.16   Symbols for representing the attribute type, the condition and the operation.

because it occurs so frequently, is the recording of the time and date that an action took place. Another operation that is often considered as self-evident is the identification of a created object.

8.6.2   Specification of operations

The specification of operations can take place in the English language, with action models, as well as in more formal language based on mathematical notation. The operations will eventually need to be implemented in a programming language with a formal notation for which a mathematical notation is used. End users often prefer the specifications to be written both with action models and in clear English, to improve their understanding. In the second instance we can then convert the specifications into a more formal form.

The generally applicable structure of an operation is that there is input which is used to determine the output. Attribute values for the attribute types included in the operation are then used in the operation. Using the input attribute values, the resulting value of the attribute is determined for a defined attribute type.

Definition of an operation

An operation is a description of the way in which the attribute value of a defined attribute type is determined. The resulting attribute value is seen as the output of the operation. An operation receives input of attributes for defined attribute types that possibly undergo processing during the operation.

When we describe an operation in the English language, we indicate with words which changes are caused by an action on the attributes of the objects concerned. The purpose of this is primarily to make the description understandable. When we are dealing with end users who understand a more formal notation, we can directly define the operations in a formal specification.

When we define the operations with a formal specification method we make use of a number of agreements and conventions, which we will now explain. The first agreement has to do with the exact position of the operation in an information system. We do this by once again globally describing the path of an attribute (Figure 8.17).

The general path an attribute follows in an information system is successively input attribute, function attribute, action attribute, object attribute, output attribute. A function can request information on the status of objects, if desired, via inspections. The objects can also provide a trigger to a function to direct particular actions.

The transfer from action attribute to object attribute is actively supported in an information system by the specified operations. Each

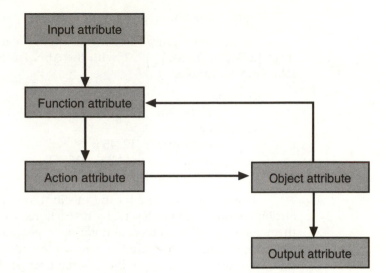

Figure 8.17 The path of an attribute through the information system.

operation defines the transfer of temporary action attributes to persistent object attributes. In this way the operation describes the permanent changes in the information system.

When we have recorded values in an information system as object attributes, we can inquire on them and use them as input to functions. The functions use these values for the direction of actions that carry out the changes on the object attribute using operations. The functions that do this are called the interactivating functions.

8.6.3 Operations for the instantiation and modification of objects

When specifying the operations we have at least three parts. We begin with the operations for the instantiation of the attributes of new objects and the modification of the attributes of existing objects. These are:

(1) The becomes-equal-to character, indicated by ':=';
(2) The output attribute type;
(3) The input attribute type for the (new) attribute value.

The output attribute type is always positioned in front of the ':=' character. The input attribute type is always positioned after the ':=' character. The value for the attribute can also be indicated with the name 'parameter'. The operation thus acquires its basic form:

output attribute type := input attribute type

In the bank example, for the action 'To register' a person with an ID of 12345, on 29 May, 1992, with the ABN-AMRO bank, we have the following operations:

Action:
    To register
Operations:
    PersonID := '12345'
    BankName := 'ABN-AMRO'
    ToRegisterDate := '29 May 1992'

The applied method for the specification of operations with fixed attribute values still has too many restrictions because we cannot apply them generally. The method of notation in general use for the specification of operations is to place the name of the attribute type to be instantiated or modified in front of the ':=' character, and to place the names of the attribute types for the new attribute values, that for example are inputs on a screen using an input function, after it. The values for the input attributes that we input for each attribute type included in the operation must at a minimum conform to the syntax rules that apply to the dimension of measurement or reference object of the attribute type.

When we represent the operations for initialization in graphic form, we see that all the input values are denoted by '?'.

In some cases the names of the attribute types are shortened to keep the action model readable. In the action model the attribute types can be connected by an association line to the object types and the action types within which they are encapsulated. Actually this is redundant because it is already modelled in the attribute model. In the real modelling environment we thus leave attribute connections towards object type, and so on, out of our action model. The arrows between the operations show the data flow of how the value of an attribute type goes from the action type via an operation to the attribute type (Figure 8.18).

The arrows show the direction the attribute types follow in the action model. The association lines between 'To register', Person and Bank are redundant with the attribute model and can be suppressed in the action model .

Action:
    To register
Operations:
    PersonID := '?'
    BankName := '?'
    ToRegisterDate := '?'

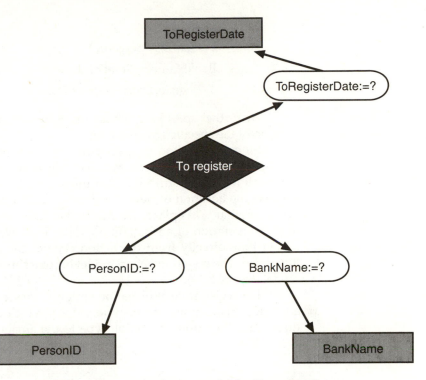

Figure 8.18   Action model for 'To register'.

With the instantiation of a new object and the execution of modifications to existing objects we are dealing very much with the specification of simple operations. The general rule for the specification of simple operations is that the attribute of an object or action becomes equal to the measured value for a dimension of measurement on a measuring scale, or it becomes equal to the specified object. The measured value is received by the action type via a message from the input function, which checks the syntax of the attributes at the time of input. This check can often be made directly by the input screen. For batch functions an error list is generally produced which is then processed in the second instance.

After the syntax check by the input function the attributes have the status of 'function attribute'. Instead of using '?' the status of the input attribute type can be represented in the specification of the operations by the addition of the word 'screen' for the general name of the reference object or the dimension of measurement of the attribute type. The operation specifications then become:

Action:

    To register

Input operations:

      PersonID := ScreenID

      BankName := ScreenName

      ToRegisterDate := ScreenDate

By further specifying the details of the screen we can indicate the location of the specific screen attribute.

Since the method of specifying input attributes described above results in work that can be avoided, we now discuss an alternative approach for action-attributes that initialize attribute values of objects. Because the addition of new attribute values to the objects is the only operation that takes place, we can replace the explicit operation by an implicit operation of an initializing data flow. We do this by drawing a data flow directly from the action type to the attribute types to be initialized. The resulting action model becomes much easier to read and model (Figure 8.19).

For registrative information systems, we see that most operations are just initializations of attribute values, which are modelled with a direct data flow from the action type to the attribute type of the object

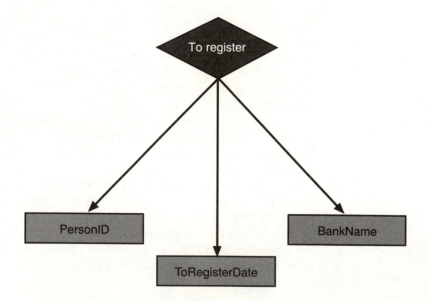

Figure 8.19   Alternative action model for 'To register'.

type. Information systems that have more embedded calculation, like many real-time systems, have much less initialization of attribute values and need to model the operations explicitly more often.

8.6.4 Operations with calculations

The operations we have seen up to now are concerned with initializing the values of attribute types of an object type. In addition to this, we come across both operations made up of simple calculations and operations made up of more complex calculations. The operation itself is often composed of many attribute values, which are manipulated with mathematical operators. Examples of mathematical operators are:

+, −, *, /, log, ln, SUM, AVERAGE, SQUARE ROOT, POWER, MODULUS

The operators always work in combination with one or more values of attribute types. Included in the list above are operators for the values of single attributes and groups of attribute values of the same attribute type. So the SUM and AVERAGE operations always work with a previously defined group of attribute values of the same attribute type. The attribute type must be the same because we cannot add apples to pears. The group itself is made up on the basis of selection criteria.

We make a distinction between operations that work on the attribute types of the object type and operations that work on a group of attributes of one attribute type of, for example, an object class. The operations for the instantiations of the object type are permitted as long as they conform to the conventions of the operators themselves. We can think here of ordering rules such as the general sequence of the mathematical operators, whereby the order is defined as: power multiplication, multiplication, division, finding-the-root-of, addition and subtraction.

Operators for the type level thus become:

+, −, *, /, log, ln, SQR, PWR, e-PWR, MOD

The operators for the type level are all concerned with calculations on single attributes.

We can place the operators next to the data flow. When we add the sequence in which we have to read the input data flow for an operation we have automatically specified the formula of the operation. In order to get a correct formula we have to break the total complex calculation into simple operations, which are connected to each other with direct data flows.

For the class level the calculations are extended to groups of attributes of the same attribute type.

Additional operators for the class are:

SUM, AVERAGE, TOTAL, MEDIAN, MAX, MIN

8.6.5 Operations for object classes

With the operators for the class level we incorporate increasingly more functionality in the information architecture. Analogous to the inclusion of more or less standard operators for the manipulation of the attributes of a group of objects, we can also include calculation functions defined entirely by the end user in the action model. By dismantling the calculation functions we see that they consist of more elementary operators and attributes.

The calculation functions are given a general function name that is specified in the same way as an operator. The description and application of the created calculation functions take place in the action model in a similar way to that of the operators for the class level. The calculation functions are not handled separately in this discussion.

For the purposes of illustration of a simple operation on an attribute type of an object class, we introduce the object class Accounts. Accounts indicate the group of accounts a registered person has with a bank. The operation defined below increases the number of accounts by one by the execution of the action 'To open' an account.

Action: To open
AccountsTotal := AccountsTotal + 1

The general structure of the operation is that the new value of AccountsTotal is equal to the current value of AccountsTotal incremented by one.

A second operation for the 'Opening' of an account is:

AccountBalance := 0

AccountBalance is an attribute type that belongs to the object type Account (watch out, singular!). The attribute type is given the value '0' at the moment that an account is instantiated.

With the action type 'To deposit' we can increase the account balance by the deposited amount. The operations that we include for 'To deposit' are:

Action:
To deposit
Operations:
ToDepositAmount := ScreenAmount
AccountBalance := AccountBalance + ToDepositAmount

For the calculation of AccountBalance we must know the value of ToDepositAmount prior to adding the values of the two attribute types together in a second operation. This is the addition of the current AccountBalance to the value of ToDepositAmount. Before we carry out the operation, we must inquire the current value of AccountBalance.

The attribute type AccountsBalance of the object class Accounts is changed by the action 'To deposit' with the following operations:

Action:

　　To deposit

Operations:

　　AccountsBalance := AccountsBalance + ToDepositAmount

In the action model abbreviations have been used to represent the operations (Figure 8.20).

For the calculation of a new value for AccountsBalance we see that there is a time sequencing between the various operations. It is in fact a requirement first to input the value of ToDepositAmount and then to calculate the AccountsBalance.

The necessary time sequence between both operations can be read in the action model by following the arrows of the data flows. An arrow that points from an attribute type to an operation means that the attribute type provides the input value for the execution of the operation. An outward arrow from the operation to an attribute type indicates that the result is stored away.

An alternative method for the calculation of AccountsBalance is to add all the values of AccountBalance (watch out, singular!) to each other, with the operation:

　　AccountsBalance := SUM (AccountBalance)

This operation is no longer encapsulated by the action type 'To deposit' but is functional by nature. We can determine this by the fact that the operation is not directly fed by an attribute of an action type. For the encapsulation of this operation we could, for example, include the object type Period with an action type 'To close off'. We can then periodically carry out the operation by the action of closing off a period.

The first operation, which adds the deposited amount directly to the total accounts balance of a person, is preferred when we immediately want to know the total balance of all the accounts of a person at any moment in time. The second operation is preferred when we only periodically want to know the current status of the accounts balance of one person. See Figure 8.21.

When we make use of operations that perform calculations on a group of objects we must indicate with defined selection criteria which

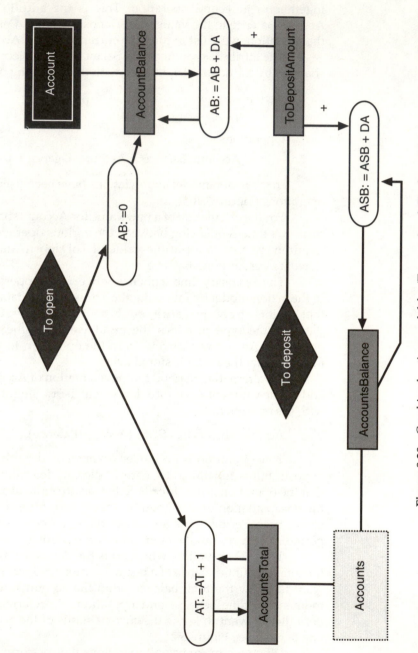

Figure 8.20   Combined action model for 'To open' and 'To deposit'

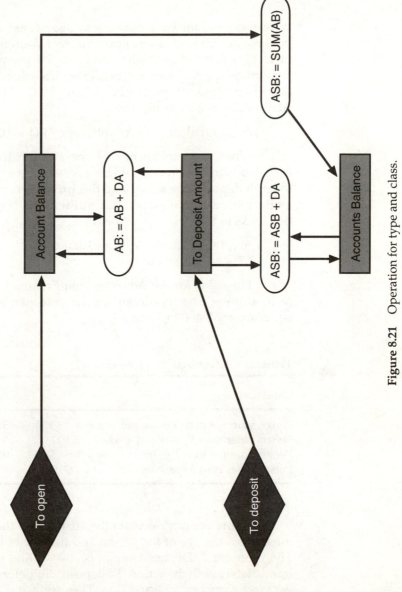

Figure 8.21   Operation for type and class.

objects must be included in the operation. We add the parameters for the selection criteria as conditions to the operation.

8.6.6   Operations with dependent attributes

We can expand the bank example by accepting that the bank carries out periodic advertising campaigns to attract young savers. The advertisement says that the bank gives an extra 5% premium on the deposited amount when the account holder is less than 5 years old and the deposited amount is smaller than $100. The operation for the AccountBalance looks like this:

$$AccountBalance := AccountBalance + (1 + 0.05) * ToDepositAmount$$

When we implement this operation in the information system each deposited amount would be increased by 5%. This is not desirable for each deposit. The solution to this problem is provided when we add a new attribute type AdvertisementPremium (Figure 8.22). The operation looks as follows:

$$AccountBalance := AccountBalance + (1 + AdvertisementPremium) * ToDepositAmount$$

The value for the AdvertisementPremium depends on a number of conditions. The conditions for the percentage of the advertisement premium are listed in Table 8.1.

Table 8.1   Advertisement premium

Condition	Advertisement premium
Person younger than 5 years and amount < $ 100	5%
Person older than 5 years and amount < $ 100	0%
Person younger than 5 years and amount >= $ 100	0%
Person older than 5 years and amount >= $ 100	0%

Before we can calculate the attribute of the AccountBalance, we must know the age of the person and the size of the deposited amount. The value for ToDepositAmount is easy to find out because it is input immediately with the action 'To deposit'. To determine the age of Person we must carry out an inspection. Then we can use the decision table to determine which AdvertisementPremium we must use to calculate the AccountBalance.

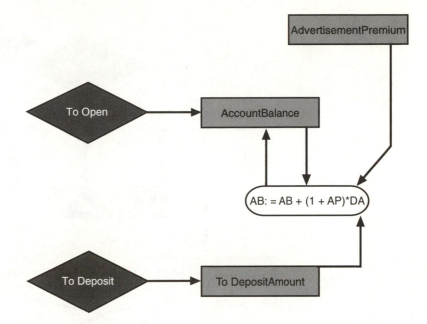

Figure 8.22   Action model for the operation with AdvertisementPremium.

The input of the attribute type AdvertisementPremium leads us to investigate whether Advertisement is a separate object type for which the premium percentage can be modified in the course of time by various kinds of Persons and Amounts. If this is the case and we can distinguish distinct action types for it, then we can incorporate Advertisement as an object type in the object-interaction model.

Using the rules for the creation of operations we specify the structural functionality within the object-interaction model. From this viewpoint we can incorporate an increasing number of operations in the object-interaction model and we can then expand the information architecture in a stepwise manner with, for example, new object classes.

An example of an extension of the information architecture with object classes we have already looked at is the determination of the total balance of the accounts of a person who is registered with a bank. This is recorded with the attribute type AccountsBalance. The initialization of AccountsBalance is specified with the action type 'To register' of the gerund Registration (Figure 8.23):

Action type: To register:

AccountsBalance = 0

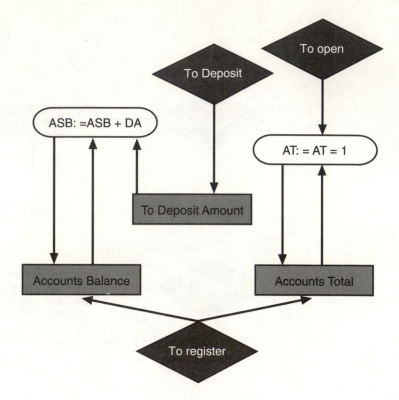

Figure 8.23   Action model for the bank example.

The incrementing of AccountsBalance is recorded with the action type 'To deposit', for which we include the following operation:

Action type: To deposit:
AccountsBalance = AccountsBalance + ToDepositAmount

We can specify in an identical manner an operation for the action type 'To deposit' that increments the total balance for the bank with the deposited amount. This then defines a new object class with a different division criterion for the object class: 'Accounts of the Bank' instead of 'Accounts of a Person'.

The operations for attribute types of object classes are specified in the same way as for the object type, the weak object type and the gerund. There is in fact only a small difference in the location of the initialization of the attribute types for the type and the class.

The general rules that determine whether an operation pertains to the level of an object class or an object instantiation are:

- *Attribute type for object class.* An attribute type is valid for the level of the object class when the attribute type has already been given an intitial value before an object is instantiated.

- *Attribute type for object type.* An attribute type is valid for an object instantiation of an object type when the values of the attribute type come into existence during or after the instantiation of the object.

With this principle and using the object-interaction model we can specify the object classes for which we wish to acquire more information. The object classes are derived from the object types, action types, weak object types and gerunds by the inclusion of the (independent) plural form as names for the object classes. We can define the object classes even more generally by indicating within them the selection criteria with which the attribute values of the object class came to exist.

The operations of the attribute types of an object class are encapsulated in an action type. The changes to the attributes of an object class are of course caused by actions that take place in reality.

8.6.7   Abstract operation

In order to explain the concept of an abstract operation and the situations in which it has to be used we will first extend the bank example with a number of different operations. The operations we can specify for different action types of the bank example are:

Action type:

> To deposit

Operations:

> AccountBalance = AccountBalance + ToDepositAmount
> CashDrawerBalance = CashDrawerBalance + ToDepositAmount
> ClientBalance = ClientBalance + ToDepositAmount
> BranchBalance = BranchBalance + ToDepositAmount

When we take a closer look at a number of different operations of the bank example we can see a high level of redundancy in the operations. The above operations look similar and can be specified at a more generic level by a so-called abstract operation:

> Balance = Balance + Amount

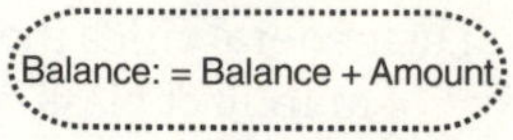

Balance: = Balance + Amount

Figure 8.24   Representation of the abstract operation.

This abstract operation is an operation that we specify at the level of the dimension of measurement. The abstract operation is represented by the same symbol as the operation but with dotted lines (Figure 8.24) and is specified in the attribute model (Figure 8.25).

In the action model the abstract operation is taken up as if it were a normal operation except for the fact that all data flows to and from attribute types do not have to be specified for the abstract operation because this is already specified in the attribute model. The abstract operation can best be specified by a meaningful name without needing to represent the formula text.

When we have specified an abstract operation, we can easily extend the number of action types that make use of the abstract operation just by adding them to the dimension of measurement in the attribute model. Thus there is no need to alter anything for the abstract operation. It is just an addition.

From the attribute model in Figure 8.26 we can read that the abstract operation replaces $3 \times 4 = 12$ operations. These 12 operations had to be specified explicity in the action model for every action type. It is because of the abstract operation that the dimensions of measurement and reference objects have to be specified in a proper way according to the rules.

The advantage of the abstract operation is the reuse of generic operations by different attribute types of different object types. Thus the abstract operation gives the analyst and designer a tool for modelling reuse at the level of operations.

Definition of an abstract operation   An abstract operation is a generic operation that is specified at the level of the dimensions of measurement. The abstract operation takes care of reuse of a specified operation for different object types and action types.

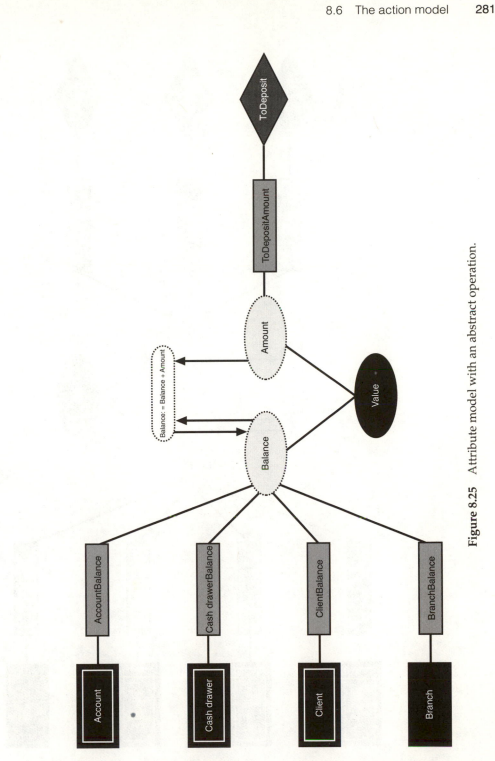

Figure 8.25   Attribute model with an abstract operation.

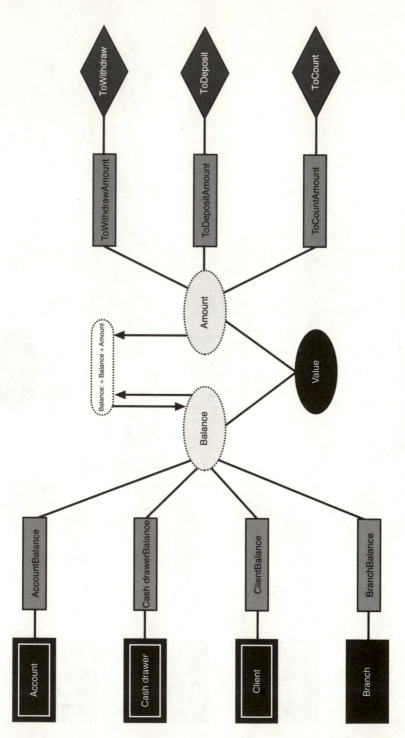

Figure 8.26   Attribute model with an abstract operation.

8.7 Action conditions

The action conditions are important for an action model because they indicate the constraints under which an action or an operation of an action type may be executed. An action condition prevents the processing of the attribute values in a message when the conditions of the action type are not met.

Just as for operations, we can specify the action conditions in the English language as well as graphically in action models (Figure 8.27), in order to communicate with the end user. The closer we get to the actual implementation, the more use we will need to make of formal specifications based on mathematical equation operators.

An action condition is recognizable by one of the following logical operators:

=, ¬ =, <, >, =<, >=, <>.

With a logical operator we specify the individual condition rules. These rules can be combined with each other by the combination operators 'and' and 'or'.

Over the course of this book we have often talked about conditions. In the KISS models we have graphically specified the dynamic conditions under which an object type can execute its actions, and we have indicated by plurality in the object-interaction model how many objects of an object type interact with each other at one moment in time. The conditions included in the various models are the so-called model conditions. The model conditions are completely visible and recognizable in the models we create.

We further expand the model conditions with action conditions. The action conditions can vary from extremely simple to very complex, just as for the operations. They can be entirely independent of each other but they can also demonstrate a strong interrelationship. The action conditions permit an action to be executed. An action condition is specified for the action type as a whole or for independent operations of the action type. To further explain the specification of action conditions we will look at the specification of a number of examples.

Simple action conditions can be combined into two or more condition rules with the words 'and' and 'or', whose use for the specification of action conditions will now be explained.

An example of mutually exclusive conditions is shown in Figure 8.28.

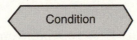

Figure 8.27 Symbol for an action condition.

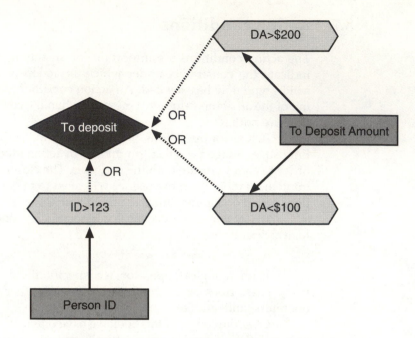

Figure 8.28   Action conditions with an 'or' dependence.

Action type:

>   To deposit

Conditions:

>   ToDepositAmount < $ 100.00 or
>
>   ToDepositAmount > $ 200.00 or
>
>   PersonID > 123.

In the action model all the action conditions are directly connected to the action type 'To deposit'. This means that no logical dependence is indicated between the action conditions themselves.

The creation of an action condition for a range of values can be achieved by use of the word 'and' (Figure 8.29):

Action:

>   To deposit

Conditions:

>   ToDepositAmount > $ 50.00 and
>
>   ToDepositAmount < $ 100.00.

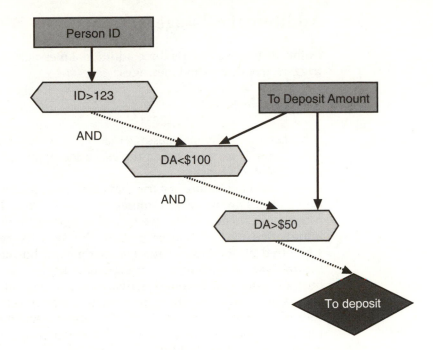

Figure 8.29 Action conditions with an 'and' dependence.

We then wish to show in the action model that the PersonID must also be greater than 123.

In the action model we show the logical 'and' dependence between the conditions by a dotted arrow that goes from the first condition that must be tested to the subsequent condition. The last condition is connected by a dotted arrow to the action type in which it is encapsulated. A dotted arrow indicates a 'condition flow' that shows the sequence of the conditions that must be followed. Thus we first test the condition that retains the fewest occurrences and then we test the conditions for this smaller number of retained occurrences.

There is a logical 'and' dependence between the first two action conditions relating to ToDepositAmount. The two simple conditions deal with the same attribute type and can therefore form one combined condition:

$$ \$\,50.00 < \text{ToDepositAmount} < \$\,100.00 $$

In this case we only need to inspect ToDepositAmount once.

Within a condition we may also perform calculations before determining whether a calculated attribute value meets the condition. This happens in so-called calculated conditions.

8.8   Additional message concepts

In this section we discuss three additional message concepts. These are triggers, inspections and messages.

8.8.1   Triggers

A trigger is a conditional message that is sent when a boundary value for an attribute is reached during the execution of an action. The trigger is always sent to a function.

The main feature of a trigger is that it can send messages from the action types in the object-interaction model to a large number of functions. This means that we can add triggers to the structure of the information system, ensuring that the user is continually better supported on the basis of the knowledge and business rules that are incorporated in the information system. A trigger can be regarded as a business rule that becomes activated when the information system arrives at a particular situation as the result of an action. Triggers take care of the communication from the object-interaction model to the functions which in turn can decide how new messages will be sent to the action types in the object-interaction model.

In the action model we often combine a trigger with the symbol for a condition. The trigger is modelled in exactly the same way as a condition except that the trigger directs a function with a message.

8.8.2   Inspections

When we have instantiated an object we can inspect its status from a function. The function decides which objects to inquire about by means of an inspection, which is done by sending a message to an identified object. The object then sends a return message containing its attribute values to the function. Inspections are part of the function that makes the content of the information system suitable for presentation to the end user.

8.8.3   Messages

The path that an attribute follows through the KISS paradigm is effected by messages. The messages are initiated by a sender and the addressed receiver must always receive and process the message. If this does not happen, the message must be intercepted so that the sender knows what has happened to the message.

A second form of message, which we have already seen, is the inspection, whereby we expect that the attribute values of an object are requested and returned to the inquiring function. The initiative for an inspection comes from the function, so that the function itself keeps track of whether or not a return message has been received.

Each message has at a minimum one address to which it is sent and can optionally have the address from which it was sent. Each inspection always has an address to which it is sent and from which it was sent. If this is not the case, the inspection will not know to which address the reply must be sent.

The attributes of a message must have a structure such that they contain its meaning. This lays down stringent requirements on the semantics of the information system. Thus the information system will need to contain a reference mechanism to which the values of an attribute type can refer. In the previous chapter we catered for this by means of measuring scales. When general measuring scales are missing from an information system, it becomes difficult to work flexibly with attributes when we wish to use them for a representation in another measuring scale.

Sending a message 'The oil drum contains 100' immediately begs the question '100 what?' Unambiguous message traffic is achieved by the addition of the dimension of measurement and the unit. The message in our example would then look like 'The oil drum contains 100 litres'. We can address this to oil drum number 123, in which case we have met the requirement that messages be addressed.

When a message is sent with the measuring unit 'gallon', the receiver of the message must convert the value into litres, using a suitable conversion factor, before it can be stored in the database.

Within information systems it is not necessary to send the measuring units with the messages when we are certain that the receiver knows what the measuring unit is. To make this possible we must define standards for the sending of messages in the information system and for the dimensions of measurement with their accompanying measuring units.

8.9   Summary

In this chapter we have seen how the communication paradigm together with the theory for the measurement of the attributes of objects defines the basis for the specification of attribute types. The method of specification is in fact of such a nature that we obtain a validation of the structure of the information architecture.

We also define a cardinality for the attribute types, using lower and upper boundaries. The cardinality provides on the one hand a validation of the models, and on the other adds constraints to the attribute types. In the case of a connectivity of n:n we must expand, for example, the attribute model by one or more attribute types, or by a new object type with its associated action types.

Operations are specified in the action model. The action model shows by means of data flows the path an attribute follows when it is used in one or more calculations. The calculations that can be performed with mathematical operators are concerned with the type level on the one hand and the class level on the other. It holds true for the type level that the operators are used to calculate values of an object occurrence. It holds true for the class level that the operators are used to calculate values for a group of objects.

The conditions under which an action may be executed are also specified in the action model. We can also model 'and, and, and' and 'or, or, or' structures and combinations of them, by means of 'condition flows'.

We indicate by the modelling of encapsulated attributes how the details of the information architecture will eventually appear. By the encapsulation of the details we are in a position to create an overview of, and maintain an insight into, the information architecture. This is possible because the details never determine the structure of the information architecture, but only indicate its content.

8.10   Questions

(1)   What is the importance of encapsulation and how is it applied in the KISS method? Why are the attributes and the operations not represented in the object-interaction model, KISS model and hierarchy model?

(2)   Describe the use of the attribute model.

(3)   Discuss how and to what level inheritance can be applied in the attribute model.

(4)   Discuss the conventions for naming the attribute type in relation to the grammar of our natural language, the communication paradigm and the measurement process.

(5)   In what ways does the attribute model validate the information architecture?

(6)   Specify in one attribute model the length, height, depth, volume, and surface of the object types Cube, House and Car and the action type 'To paint'.

(7)   Describe the use of the action model with operations, conditions, data flows and condition flows.

(8)   What is the difference between the action type, operation, abstract operation and condition?

(9)   Give examples of 'and, and, and' and 'or, or, or' conditions.

9 Transformation rules

9.1 Introduction

In previous chapters we discussed and illustrated the concepts concerning the building of an information architecture with its encapsulated characteristics. When we create an information architecture we do not make any allowance for the technical restrictions present in the environment where the information system will be implemented. We cater for these technical restrictions in the second phase when we transform the information architecture into the technical restrictions of the implementation environment. During this transformation we make decisions about the way in which we will implement the information architecture.

We can use any number of possible alternative implementation environments and implementation rules. We could, for example, implement the information architecture in a hierarchical, network, relational, semantic or object-oriented DBMS. We could make use of, for example, C, C++, COBOL, BASIC, Clipper or Progress as the programming language. Each specific production environment has its own unique characteristics. In this chapter we will look at the basic ideas and transformation rules for converting the object-interaction model into network, relational and object-oriented database management systems. Then we will look at the transformation rules for converting KISS models into action handlers that control the execution of the information system.

Most of the transformation rules of this chapter are based upon the generic relational transformation. The relational transformation is even discussed for implementations in C++, Smalltalk or an OO database. This is done because most of us are accustomed to the relational transformation. Next to the relational transformation we briefly discuss the object-oriented transformation. This object-oriented transformation is also applicable to any target environment. When reading and studying this chapter you should thus keep in mind that it is just a limited overview of the most commonly used transformation rules.

9.2   General DBMS concepts

In this section we look at the basic concepts behind the definitions used when designing logical data structures and implementing them into database management systems (Figure 9.1). Then we use these common concepts, which lie at the foundation of the network model, the relational model and the object-oriented model. Subsequently we move to a discussion of the rules for transformation to the appropriate logical data model.

For each specific logical data model we denote the various elementary building blocks of the types of DBMS using different geometric shapes (Figure 9.2).

A record type in a network database is denoted by a rectangle with two panels on the left and right which contain the record ID and pointer, respectively. Between these two panels we place the attributes.

A table in a relational database is denoted by a rectangle containing a horizontal and a vertical line. These two lines form a symbolic table of rows and columns. The attributes form the content of the table.

A class in the object-oriented programming environment is denoted by a rectangle containing two horizontal lines. In the banner formed at the top we place the name of the class. In the banner formed at the bottom we place the operations. In the space between we place the attributes. From this general class description we instantiate the individual objects.

To illustrate how we work with logical and physical data models, we will discuss the basic concepts of network, relational and object-oriented database systems, in sequence. We must be careful to allow for the fact that the concepts can be used completely differently when they are implemented in various systems.

9.2.1   Basic concepts for DBMSs

The main characteristic of the concepts of the implementation environment is that they use technical terminology and that the concepts utilized support the specific capabilities of a programming language or database. We look at the most important concepts of the various technical implementation environments without going into great detail. Before we discuss the technical terms we will first introduce the network model.

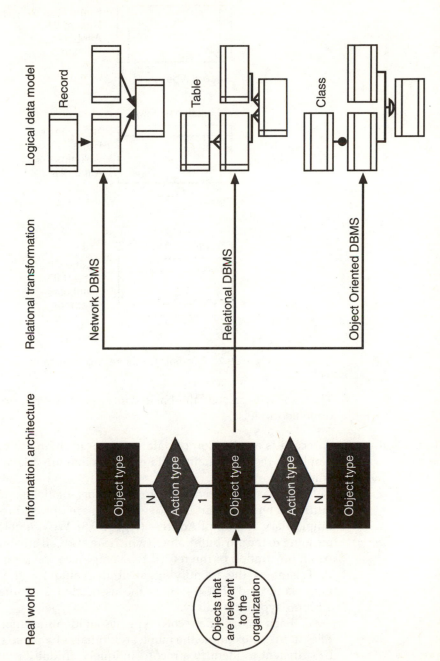

Figure 9.1   Relational transformation of the information architecture into logical data structures for network, relational and OO DBMSs.

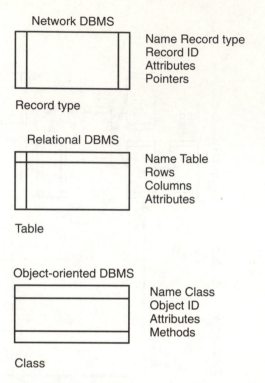

Figure 9.2   Symbols for the record type, table and class.

Then we will discuss the basic concepts of the relational and object-oriented models.

The network model

A record is a collection of data elements in the network model. So an employee record contains data elements that are relevant for a specific employee.

A record is divided into a number of fields. The field names (attribute types) for an employee record are, for example, Emp.Name, Empl.Salary and Empl.Address (Figure 9.3). We use field names to give meaning to the attribute values (which we also call attributes) of a record. As an illustration of the record type employee we see in the figure that P. Tolsma is the identifying attribute value for the attribute type Emp.Name and that $4500 is the associated attribute value for the attribute type Emp.Salary.

Each record of a record type has an identifier that uniquely identifies it. In our example the name and initials of a person would seem to be sufficient to identify a record uniquely. In daily practice this is not usually the case, so we often assign an ascending range of numbers as the identifiers of records.

Record type
Attribute types
Empl.Name
Empl.Salary
Empl.Address
Employee
P. Tolsma
$ 4500
Sneek
Attributes
Field

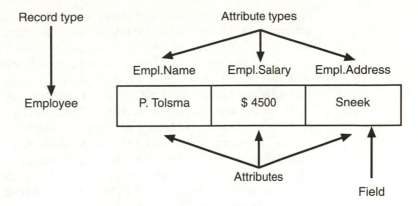

Figure 9.3 Record of one record type.

A file is a collection of records of the same type. We also call a file a record type. An employee file is a collection of employee records (Figure 9.4). The structure and layout of the records in a file can differ widely depending on the type. It is, for example, possible to define records in a network model which have variable lengths, while this is not permitted in a pure relational model.

When the designer models files (record types) he or she will often use the entity concept. In this situation, an entity is the logical description of the things in the real world for which we wish to record data. In this form 'entity' bears a strong resemblance to 'record type'.

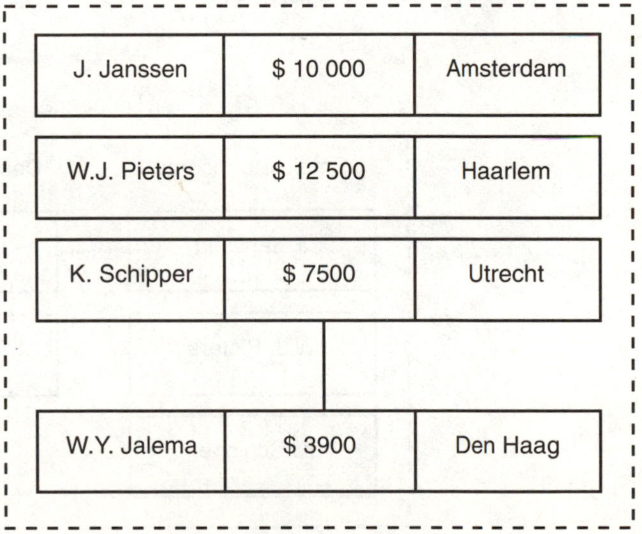

J. Janssen
$ 10 000
Amsterdam
W.J. Pieters
$ 12 500
Haarlem
K. Schipper
$ 7500
Utrecht
W.Y. Jalema
$ 3900
Den Haag

Figure 9.4 An employee file.

We usually find a number of different record types in an information system which are related to each other in a logical manner. We call the collection of records of various types a database.

The records in a database are always connected to each other in a way that allows us to access the data elements in the various records. In this way we can connect all the employee records of employees who work for the same department with each other. Then we can easily check on who works for a particular department (Figure 9.5).

The hierarchy model and the network model (Codasyl) are the oldest forms of record structures for a database management system. The differentiating feature between the hierarchy model and the network model is that a record type in the network model can have multiple parents. In the hierarchy model a record type is restricted to having one parent. We will now continue with the network model.

In a network DBMS we make connections between the records by using pointer structures. Figure 9.6 shows the physical data structure of a database in which the connections between department records and employee records are implemented by means of a chain structure.

A department record has a pointer to the first employee record in the chain. Each employee record in the chain has a pointer to the subsequent employee record in the chain. The last employee record in the chain has a pointer pointing back to the department record.

In the physical data model we can see precisely how the individual records in a database are connected to each other. However, this is much too detailed to be used as a way of communicating the relevant relationships in a database.

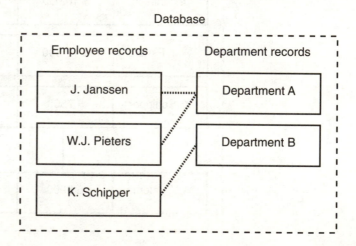

Figure 9.5   Database with the record types Employee and Department.

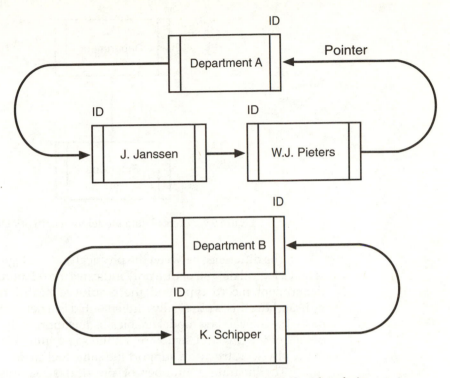

Figure 9.6 Physical structure of a network DBMS with a chain structure.

Since the representation of the physical structures of a database became too detailed to model, there was a move towards the creation of a so-called logical data model. A logical data model is a simple way of representing the record structure of the physical implementation. In the network model we show each record type by a rectangle. The arrow between the record types shows the relationship between the department records and the employee records (Figure 9.7).

The arrow in the logical data model for the network database is called the 'data structure set'. The arrow leaves the owner record type of the data structure set and ends at the member record type of the data structure set. In a data structure set the owner record type may have zero, one or more member records (occurrences). A member record in a data structure set has exactly one owner record.

In our example each department record can be connected to many employee records or to none. Each employee record does, however, need to be associated with exactly one department record. The arrow itself therefore shows a 1:n relationship between the owner record types and the member record types.

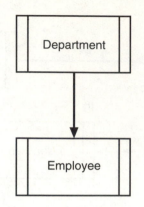

Figure 9.7   Logical data model for a network DBMS.

The difference between the physical and the logical data structure is that a logical data structure only indicates the relationship between the department record type and the employee record type. It does not indicate how this is physically implemented in a network (Codasyl) database. The logical data model enables us to suppress the implementation details of the physical structure. At the same time this also means that many physical structures support the same logical data model.

To illustrate a number of physical structures we describe a number of implementations in a Codasyl (network) database system. There are at least three possible physical data structures that can be used as an implementation of the same logical data model for a Codasyl database (Figure 9.8):

(1) Forward pointers: all employee records for the same department are connected to each other;
(2) Backward pointers: the reverse of forward pointers;
(3) Pointer array: the department record maintains pointers for all the related employee records;

Each of the three physical data structures described for a network DBMS has its advantages and disadvantages:

(1) The structure with forward pointers is simple to realize and is appropriate for sequential processing of employee records;
(2) The structure with extra backward pointers makes it relatively easy to locate the previous employee record in the chain. However, this is at the cost of the extra memory used by the backward pointers (but it does make the deletion process more efficient);
(3) The structure with pointer arrays has the important advantage that all the employee records belonging to one department can be retrieved at one time.

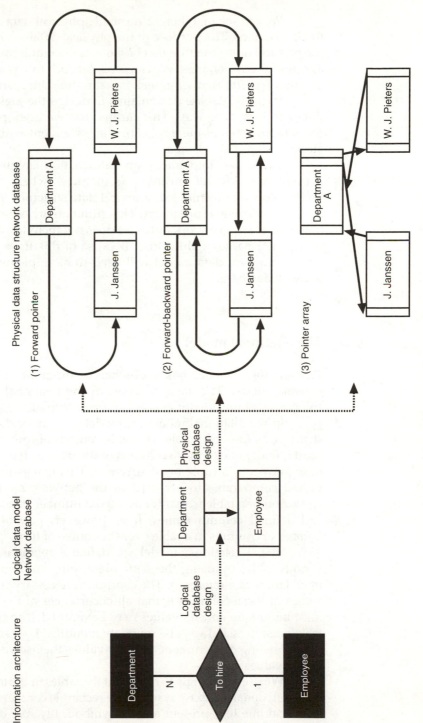

Figure 9.8   Possible physical data structures for a network DBMS.

We can see that there is no single physical data structure optimal in all situations. The purpose of the physical database design is to select the physical data structure that best meets the requirements for the given application environment. We can consider such things as response times, storage capacity, archiving, seek times, redundancy, and so on.

Logical database design aims to design the logical structure of a database in a clear way. This means that we attempt to synchronize the requirements of the application environment with the logical data structure-types of a database.

When we implement an information architecture we must prevent any loss of meaning (semantics) when transforming the information architecture into a logical data structure. We can do this by means of additional programs. This situation arises because the logical data model for a network database does not include all the components of the information architecture. Because of this the semantics missing from the logical data model will need to be implemented outside the network database.

9.2.2   The relational model

The relational model has a number of different premises from the network model. The basic concepts of the relational model are table, column, attribute, identifier (key) and row (tuple).

In the relational model we model a group of data with the same structure as rows of a table. The table consists of rows and columns. We must identify one or more columns of the table as the identifier of a row (also known as a tuple or occurrence). This makes the row analogous to and comparable to a record in the network model. The physical restriction of a table is that it has a fixed number of columns with fixed and defined column names. It is, however, possible to expand the number of columns in a table over the course of time.

In the relational model we define a relationship between the various tables by using the same identifying column name in two or more tables as a reference. The conditions necessary for the identifying values of these columns is that all occurrences of the reference values must be unique and no values may be omitted. The rows (tuples) of a table must in fact always be uniquely identified by a simple or complex key consisting of identifiers. The key values themselves may not consist of null values.

We use a rectangle to represent the tables in the logical data model of the relational database system. The rectangle contains a horizontal and a vertical line to represent a table symbolically. We do this to make a definite distinction between the rectangle symbols for the object types in the information architecture and the tables in the logical data model (Figure 9.9).

The relationships between tables are represented in the logical data model by crow's feet. A crow's foot at the end of a line connected to a table indicates that there are multiple occurrences of that table related to one occurrence of the table where the line started. This makes a relationship in the relational logical data model more or less analogous to the data structure set of the network model. Because the data structure set can have an attribute content, while a relationship between tables cannot, there is a very significant difference between the connecting elements of the two models.

Following on from the logical data model we can physically implement the tables in a number of different ways using the underlying techniques. In general these techniques remain invisible to the programmer.

Just as for the network DBMS, it holds true that we have a number of alternative implementation options for a relational implementation of the same information architecture. We can technically optimize a relational implementation by making use of, for example, normalization and denormalization techniques, conscious duplication of data structures, indexing and so forth.

We always see a substantial loss of meaning (semantics) occurring with a transformation of the information architecture into a relational implementation. We cannot completely represent the meaning of the descriptions in the information architecture in the data storage structure of tables related to each other by means of rows and columns. Thus in a logical data model for a relational implementation we lose, for example, the change rules, the functionality and the constraints. In order to fully implement the semantics of the information architecture we need to take the additional measures of creating programs supplementary to the logical data model of a relational DBMS.

9.2.3   The object-oriented model

In an object-oriented implementation environment an integration takes place between the attributes (instance variables) of an object (instantiated object of a class) and the operations (methods) that are executed on them. The general descriptions of objects with their attributes and operations are recorded in a class. A new object comes into existence when the class instantiates it with a unique identification. The objects themselves refer to each other by sending and receiving messages.

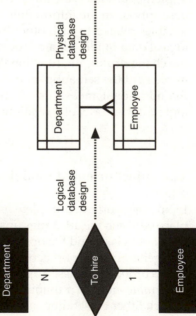

Figure 9.9 Logical modelling for a relational DBMS.

For the creation of a logical data model, the concept of class is analogous to a table and a record type. It must be noted that a class has a much larger content than a table or a record type. This is because a class also describes the change rules and operations which can be executed on the objects of the class.

Just as for network and relational database systems, we can also relate the individual classes to each other. The various classes then form an object-oriented database (Figure 9.10). A multiple relationship between classes is represented in the logical data model by a dot on the relation line between two classes. This conforms to the notation method of Rumbaugh/OMT (1991).

Because classes also have an operation content, we can utilize such principles as generalization, specialization, inheritance and polymorphism in the implementation environment. These principles are implemented by means of 'superclasses'. A superclass indicates which instance variables are generalized to a higher level, allowing us to store them in only one location.

The advantage of implementing superclass structures using inheritance is, among other things, that it leads to the reuse of previously defined attributes and functionality. Applying these principles during the modelling process ensures that the logical data model produced for an object-oriented implementation is semantically richer than the logical data model for a network or relational environment.

It is possible that the physical model of an object-oriented implementation could provide a very cluttered and unclear picture. This happens when we show all the possible relationships between objects communicating with each other by messages. In comparison with the physical models of the network structure we would then obtain a separate implementation picture for each form of an object which communicates with messages for the OO implementation. As a result of this we would in a very short space of time produce a complete confusion of relationships and messages between objects because of its dynamics. It is therefore imperative that modelling for an object-oriented implementation should provide an overview of the details of the structures of the implemented system.

The structure of an object-oriented implementation is primarily effected by means of messages and inheritance. Owing to the fact that messages are of great importance to an object-oriented implementation, we need to introduce a way of distinguishing between messages. We do this in three ways: first, by using the content of the message as the basis for distinction; secondly, we use the method of synchronizing objects; and the third is based on the question of whether the message must be seen as supporting a part of the structure (inheritance, polymorphism and such like).

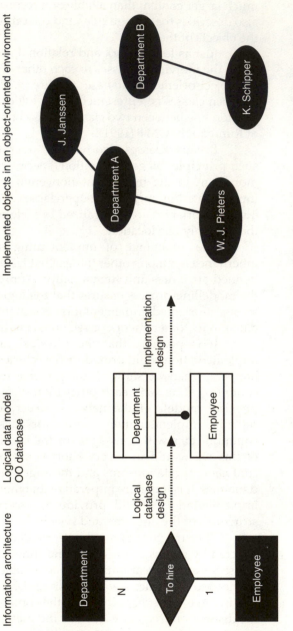

Figure 9.10   Transformation of the information architecture to an object-oriented programming environment.

Given the large variety of implementation alternatives we prefer not to produce any physical models of an object-oriented implementation.

9.2.4   Problems with logical database design

The design of a database is a continuous occupation for which a large number of differing decisions must be taken. When making these decisions the database designer must be responsible for ensuring that the model of the real world is implemented, allowing for the technical restrictions of the specific database system. An additional consideration when making implementation decisions is that the designer must take account of the requirements laid on the information system in the area of retrieval and updating of data in the most efficient way possible. Examples of this are:

- The database designer is restricted by the limited number of data structure types supported by a database system. In most database systems we cannot directly implement many-to-many relationships between two object types, such as between employees and projects. The solution of a relational transformation is to create an in-between object type that is related to the two object types with an *n-n* relationship.

- The database designer will need to define access paths to the attributes in the database by determining how a particular record type, table or object can best be accessed. In the previous examples for the network database it was implied that the employee records would best be accessed via the associated department record.

- The database designer will generally want to make the search and update processes more efficient. This can be achieved by storing the details of an object in the real world as an attribute type in more than one record type, table or class. We could therefore redundantly group the attribute types of an employee into the two record types, tables or classes person and employee.

The problem is that the designer of a logical database must consider a number of issues before he or she can make the correct decision. The problem of designing a logical database is in fact noticeably simplified when an information architecture that represents the organization's way of working has been created first. When designing a logical data model we use the information architecture as the basis for determining the logical and physical database.

The distinction we make between the creation of the information architecture and the creation of the logical database design ensures that the content and the structure of the information system remain understandable for both the end user and the system designer.

The logical data model is a subset of the information architecture that arises from incorporating the technical restrictions of the production environment. This means that it is often not necessary for the experienced information architect to create a logical data model, since he or she will already know what impact the production environment will have on the information architecture. Within this framework it is, however, necessary to know the global rules for the transformation to the various production environments.

9.3   Rules for transformation to a logical data model

In the previous section we saw that the logical data model more closely resembles the physical implementation model of a database than the information architecture. It is not possible to represent in a logical data model the total semantics of the objects and actions that are important for a business. This is why we first create an information architecture in which we represent the objects, actions and attributes from a business viewpoint. These representations are then translated into a logical data model.

In this section we provide a number of ground rules for a relational transformation of object types, action types, weak object types, specializations and gerunds with various connectivities into a logical data model. We will start with action types that are associated with two object types. Then we discuss what happens with more than two object types and with gerunds, and finally we will conclude with specializations.

9.3.1.   Action type with two object types

We will look at an action type that is associated with two object types and has a connectivity of first N:1 and subsequently N:N. We do this by using an example where we indicate the specific database type to which the accompanying logical data model belongs.

The connectivity is N:1

In the information architecture for the example (Figure 9.11) it is shown that a department can employ an employee more than once and that an

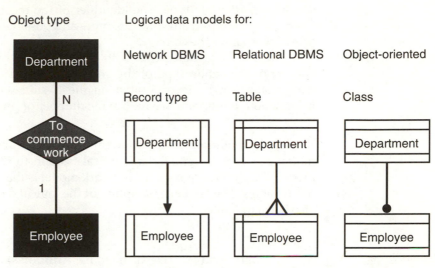

Figure 9.11   Transformation rule N:1.

employee can only commence work once. The connectivity of the object types with the action type is therefore N:1. The result of executing the action 'To commence work' is that at one moment in time there are many employees working for one department. We thus obtain a repeating group of employees who are related to one department. In the logical data model for a network model we show this by an arrow pointing in the direction of Employee. In the relational model we show this by a crow's foot at Employee. And for the OO model we show this by a dot on the line to Employee. When we define the connectivity we must take into account that it goes in an opposite direction in the logical data model to that in the information architecture!

The network model

The implementation of the information architecture into a network model takes place, in principle, by including the attribute content of the action type in a data structure set. As well as this, the identifier of the owner record type must be included as a reference item in the member record type. The general structure of the record types in the logical data model for a network implementation will then look as follows:

Record type	*Content*
Department	(Department ID: Attributes)
Employee	(Employee ID: Attributes, Attribute action, Department ID)

The convention used is that a name with a suffix of ID is an identifying attribute type. The identifier of the record type appears in front of the colon and any attribute types and possible references to other record types after the colon.

It should be noted that with a connectivity of N:1 the attribute content of the action type of the employee record type in the logical data model can be incorporated on the N-side without any loss of information. In this way we reduce the number of physical structures.

The relational model

The implementation of the information architecture into a relational model proceeds in an almost identical fashion to that of the network model. The difference from the network model is that we can only make use of tables. The textual description of the logical data model therefore also looks identical:

Table	*Content*
Departmemt	(Department ID: Attributes)
Employee	(Employee ID: Attributes, Attribute action, Department ID)

When we make a transformation to tables we also see that the attribute content of the action type with a connectivity of N:1 is combined with the attribute types of employee. This is possible because the action attributes do not form a repeating group in the employee table. The advantage of combining the action attributes in the employee table is that we end up implementing fewer tables.

When we attempt to convert the tables in a logical data model back to the action types included in the information architecture, we can easily see that the information we have from the tables, their keys and attribute types is insufficient. This is because the semantics of the action type are not recorded in the relational model.

Object-oriented model

The implementation of the information architecture into an object-oriented model proceeds differently with respect to the allocation of the action attributes. For the action attributes we need to analyse which attribute types specifically belong to one class. In general the action attributes will be applicable for the 1-association in the information architecture, which in our example is employee. In this case the transformation will be identical to the preceding examples. When this is not the case the transformation will proceed by allocating the attribute types of the action to the accompanying classes. This can be derived from the KISS models of the various object types.

Class	*Content*
Department	(Department ID: Attributes, Attributes1-Action)
Employee	(Employee ID: Attributes, Attributes2-Action, Department ID)

The classes are also related to each other by the inclusion of a reference. The reference can further be used by messages to check on the structure between the classes.

In order to describe the logical data structure we can use the notation as above, because this is uniform for the various database types.

The connectivity is N:N

In the information architecture for the example with a connectivity of N:N (Figure 9.12) it is indicated that an employee can manage many times and that a project can be managed many times. The result of

Information architecture

Object types

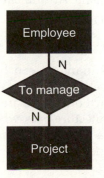

Logical data models for:

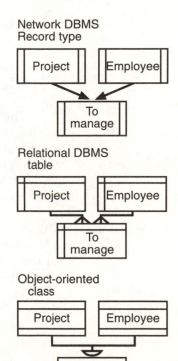

Figure 9.12 Transformation rules N:N.

carrying out the action 'To manage' is that there are many employees for one project at one moment in time and that one employee manages many projects at one moment in time.

The relational transformation rules that apply for the connectivity of N:1 no longer apply to a connectivity of N:N. This is because we would then end up with a repeating group of data within one record type, table or class. We would then have to split this repeating group out of the structure in order to correct it.

It is simpler to make use of the transformation rule that transforms the action type to a record type, table or class respectively. The attribute types of the action type continue to form part of the newly-formed group of data. The way in which the logical groups of data are related to each other is discussed briefly for the various DBMS types.

The network model   With the network model the action type with an N:N connectivity is converted into a record type to which two arrows are directed. The references to the owner record type must be included in the new record type.

Record type	Content
Employee	(Employee ID: Attributes)
Project	(Project ID: Attributes)
To manage	(Employee ID, Project ID: Attribute action)

The new record type 'To manage' can be implemented in a network database as a so-called 'set', which indicates that it relates two or more owner record types to each other. We are then in a reasonable state to trace the information architecture back when 'To manage' is in fact implemented as a set structure. The loss of semantics can be reduced by the use of set structures in the network model.

The relational model   With the relational model we convert the action type with a connectivity of N:N into a table which has two lines with crow's feet connected to it. For the key values of the rows in the new 'To manage' table we use a combination of the keys from the tables 'Employee' and 'Project'.

Table	Content
Employee	(Employee ID: attributes)
Project	(Project ID: attributes)
To manage	(Employee ID, Project ID: Attribute action)

We see with the relational implementation that the table originating from the action type also includes the attribute types of the action type.

Should we wish to convert the logical data model, with its tables, back into an information architecture, we will need to do this by interpreting the tables and their associated applications. The information about the action itself cannot in fact be derived from the logical data model.

The object-oriented model

The transformation of an action type into a logical data model for an object-oriented implementation can take place using two transformation strategies. First, we could incorporate it in a logical model with an 'associative class'. Or we could incorporate it as a class that has two relationships connecting it to the initial classes, analogous to the relational transformation with a connectivity of 1:N. The associative class is shown by a semicircle on top of the class. The associative class and the class both have the attribute types of the action type. Both classes are also uniquely identified by the combination of object identifiers of the classes 'Employee' and 'Project'.

Class	Content
Employee	(Employee ID: Attributes)
Project	(Project ID: Attributes)
To manage	(Employee ID, Project ID: Attribute action)

The inclusion of an associative class enables us to include more of the semantics of the information architecture in the logical data model. It is then also easier to trace the path back from the associative class to the action type than if we were to use an ordinary class instead of an associative class.

9.3.2   Three object types and one action type

It is also possible in an information architecture to have more than two object types associated with one action type. The action type 'To supply' has three associated object types in the example in Figure 9.13: 'part', 'supplier' and 'project'. Parts are supplied to a particular project by a particular supplier. The rules for transforming the ternary action type into a logical data model follow the same principles as for a binary action type with a connectivity of N:N. When transforming a ternary action type to a logical data model the connectivity is no longer relevant. We must in all cases ensure that we include all the possible relationships in a new record type, table or class. The logical data structure will then look as follows:

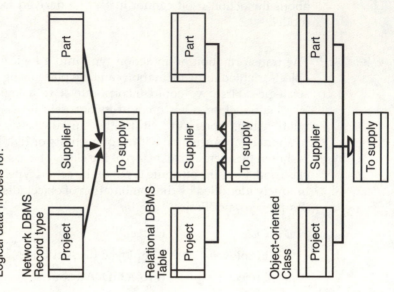

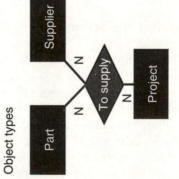

Figure 9.13   Transformation rules for ternary action type.

Record type or Table or Class	Content
Supplier	(Supplier ID: Attributes)
Project	(Project ID: Attributes)
Part	(Part ID: Attributes)
To supply	(Supplier ID, Project ID, Part ID: Attribute action)

When we transform the ternary action type to the logical data model for a relational database it also holds true that we retain the smallest quantity of semantics. We must therefore, for a relational database, store the semantics of the ternary structure from the information architecture in another location.

When we create a logical data model without using an information architecture with its object types and action types as a basis, it is very easy to omit the ternary action types during the analysis and design. We would then end up modelling them as three binary relationships. The logical data model that results will give faulty structures that no longer reflect reality.

To be able to explain why the table of a ternary action type (Figure 9.14) cannot be replaced by three binary relationships, we will disassemble the table 'To supply' into the three tables Part supplier, 'Supplier project' and 'Project part' (Figure 9.15). We can use these to record the three possible binary relationships between the three tables. In the initial table we trace the existing relationships between the columns of the tables. If we then combine the three tables of the binary relationships into one table with a three-way relationship, we see that it results in a number of non-existent events that have never taken place. These are indicated in rows 2 and 3 of the table (Figure 9.16).

Part No.	Supplier No.	Project No.
25	4	1
25	5	2
10	4	2
10	4	3
17	2	1
17	5	1

Figure 9.14 Table of ternary action type.

Part No.	Suppl. No.
25	4
25	5
10	4
17	2
17	5

Suppl. No.	Proj. No.
4	1
5	2
4	2
4	3
2	1
5	1

Proj. No.	Part No.
1	25
2	25
2	10
3	10
1	17

Figure 9.15   Three derived binary tables.

When we restrict ourselves to only making use of logical data modelling we could end up with modelling problems. This can be prevented by creating a complete information architecture before we move on to the transformation into a logical data model. In the information architecture we record in addition the reason for the existence of the ternary action type. By using meaningful action names in the information architecture we have the added advantage that the action tables automatically assume the name of the action type. This makes us less inclined to use artificial names for the combination tables such as Pro-Sup-Prt instead of To supply.

	Part No.	Supplier No.	Project No.
	25	4	1
*	25	4	2
*	25	5	1
	25	5	2
	10	4	2
	10	4	3
	17	2	1
	17	5	1

Figure 9.16   Combined ternary table.

9.3.3 Weak object type

When we created the information architecture we saw that the weak object type is existence-dependent on another object type. For each of the database types we have rules that are used to create the logical data models.

In the discussion of the weak object type we saw that it is identified by the parent object type on which it is existence-dependent. In addition, a weak object type has its own identifier with which we can uniquely identify it for a parent object type.

The transformation rule for a weak object type is that the identifying value of the equivalent record type, table or class is made up of a combination of the identifier of the parent object type and the identifier of the weak object type. The logical data structure for our example (Figure 9.17) then looks as follows:

Client	(Client ID: Attributes)
Order	(Client ID, Order ID: Attributes)

The attribute types of the action type tend to become weak when we minimize the number of data structures. This is the case for any value of connectivity.

Information architecture

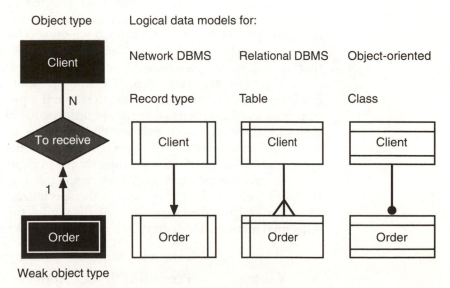

Figure 9.17 Transformation rules for weak object type.

When we want to convert the logical data model back into the information architecture we discover a problem, which is that the key formed for the equivalent data structure of the weak object type is identical to the key formed for the data structure of a binary action type with an N:N connectivity. This means that we can confuse the weak object type and the action type with each other in the logical data model when we attempt to determine their origin.

To be able to preserve the integrity of the information architecture with respect to weak object types, we must cater for these additional aspects by writing extra program logic. By integrity we mean such issues as checking for any existing orders before deleting a client.

9.3.4   Specialization

A specialization is the structure that indicates that a group of objects of an object type (generalization) has one or more common actions and characteristics. In the situation where only one occurrence for an object of an object type can exist per specialization, the identifier of the specialization is identical to the identifier of the generalization. This is of course because they are the same object.

When more than one occurrence of the specialization of an object can exist (many identical role processes of an object), we must uniquely identify the specialization with a sequential number.

We can implement a specialization from the information architecture as a completely independent data structure. We can also include in the data structure the characteristic attributes of the specialization. The equivalent data structures of the generalization include the common attributes that apply to all the specializations, unless they are defined elsewhere.

We must also take account of the fact that the specialization is existence-dependent on the generalization: if a person should disappear from our example it is generally of little use to hold on to the data of their specializations 'client' and 'employee'.

The transformation of a specialization into the various database types follows the transformation rules shown in Figure 9.18.

In the logical data model we implement a specialization by identifying all the data structures of the specialization with the same identifier as the generalization. We then give the generalization a sequential number. The logical data model then looks like this:

Person	(Person ID: Attributes generalization person)
Client	(Person ID, Client ID: Attributes client)
Employee	(Person ID, Employee ID: Attributes employee)

Logical data models for:

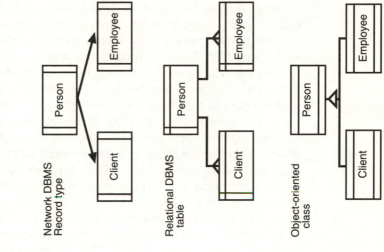

Network DBMS
Record type

Relational DBMS
table

Object-oriented
class

Information architecture

Object type

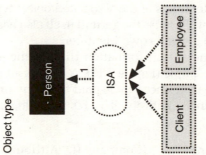

Figure 9.18   Transformation rules for specialization.

At first glance it appears as though the data structures of the logical data model create a great deal of duplication. However, looking at the content of the data structures themselves, we see that the redundancy is minimized, as only the identifier is duplicated.

The specialization structure can be used in a network model and a relational model to make inheritance possible by the addition of some extra program logic. In object-oriented environments we can make use of the inheritance principle by means of the abstract superclasses and subclasses. With the implementation of a specialization we are normally dealing with the principle of single inheritance whereby we can specify that a parent class is a superclass. The specialization is a child and is implemented as a class for the roles of the parent objects.

For some implementations of the specialization we can weigh up the option of implementing all the specializations into a smaller number of tables. The key of the specialization must be expanded by a code for each particular specialization. This implementation strategy is only useful when there is a large degree of commonality between the data structures of the specializations.

The last implementation option we look at for specializations is the implementation in a client/server environment with distributed processing and storage of data. The generalization is then centrally implemented on the server's central database. The specialization is implemented in one or more client locations. The physical separation of the files takes place in the information architecture via the ISA symbols.

9.3.5   The gerund

A gerund is existence-dependent on two or more parent object types. This can be seen in the data structures of the logical data model by the fact that the identifiers of the associated object types are incorporated in the primary key. Because the gerund itself also has all the attributes of the 'type' it is also given its own identifier.

The general transformation rule for the gerund is explained by means of an example (Figure 9.19). A car has an insurance policy with a company. The insurance can be paid for many times and each invoice is always paid in its entirety. The resulting logical data structure is as follows:

Company   (Company ID: Attributes)

Car   (Car ID: Attributes)

Insurance   (Insurance ID, Company ID, Car ID: Attributes)

Invoice   (Invoice ID: Attributes, Insurance ID)

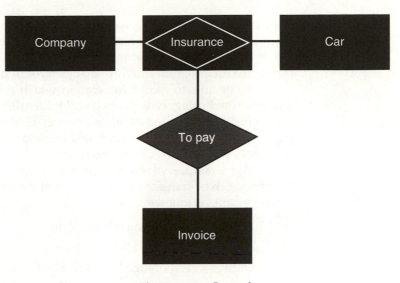

Figure 9.19   Gerund.

The difference between a gerund and an action type is that the gerund has its own object identifier, while this is not the case for an action type.

The logical data model will gain an extra data structure if we could pay an invoice in many instalments (N:N connectivity). The logical data structure would then look like this:

Company	(Company ID: Attributes)
Car	(Car ID: Attributes)
Invoice	(Invoice ID: Attributes)
Insurance	(Insurance ID, Company ID, Car ID: Attributes)
To pay	(Invoice ID, Insurance ID: Attributes)

When transforming a gerund into a logical data model for an object-oriented environment, we could also replace the ordinary association with an aggregation. The concept of aggregation is identical to a gerund in special situations.

An insurance is existence-dependent on both car and company. The integrity of the gerund must be protected in most systems by means of extra program logic.

9.3.6 Category

The category should be viewed as a functional link between the various object types that may make use of a common action type. A category does not, in theory, need to have any attribute content. The category becomes the part of the program structure that ensures that actions can be reused.

To be able to record the way in which action types are reused, a transformed category is given its own identification and description. We include in the category all references to the object types that are parents of the category. In a relational implementation, for example, the references are included as a reference key.

The example where a person can eat an apple, a banana or an orange can be transformed into a logical data model by the use of the category fruit, as follows:

Banana	(Banana ID: Attributes)
Apple	(Apple ID: Attributes)
Orange	(Orange ID: Attributes)
Fruit	(Fruit ID: Banana ID, Apple ID, Orange ID)

When the object types are mutually exclusive to each other we can further simplify the logical data structure of fruit. We would do this by replacing Banana ID, Apple ID and Orange ID by Fruit ID. The attributes of Fruit ID are Banana ID, Apple ID and Orange ID.

Fruit	(Fruit ID: Fruit-type ID)
Fruit type	(Fruit-type ID: Attributes)

The transformation of the category can be further extended by the inclusion of the common attribute types of the parent object types in the logical data structure of the category. By doing this we optimize the logical data structure and reduce the redundancy of stored data. However, we must take care that data in the category always belong to the parent object types. These data have already been defined within the parent object types in the KISS models. Remember that we do not create a KISS model for a category!

With the transformation of a category to a logical data model we must make a number of decisions to arrive at the optimal implementation for the production environment. These decisions primarily depend on the technical restrictions of the implementation environment and on the performance criteria required of the system. The result of the transformation is that we do lose some of the semantics.

The path from a logical data model back to the information architecture is difficult to follow, because the logical data model does not have enough concepts to represent the category principle. This means that information systems must be maintained at the level of the information architecture within the KISS models and object-interaction models.

For an object-oriented implementation, the category provides the basis for the realization of polymorphism. For the category we specify for all action types of the information architecture the manner in which they must be performed on the various object types. This can vary enormously between the various parent object types, leading to the situation where the same action type can produce totally different manifestations.

9.3.7   Hierarchy inversion of category

With a category, particularly for an object-oriented implementation, we see the appearance of the hierarchy inversion phenomenon. Hierarchy inversion occurs with a category because we can specify the common attribute types of the parent objects in the category. We can implement the category with these common attribute types as a separate class. The parent object types can then make use of the common characteristics defined in the category by means of inheritance. The result is an inversion of the inheritance structure, because the inheritance of attributes takes place from the category to the parent object types. This looks paradoxical because the category is by definition existence-dependent on the parent object types. The category in the object-oriented implementation now becomes a superclass and the parent object types become subclasses.

In some object-oriented languages we can make use of the so-called abstract class, which is a class that does not instantiate any objects. This is also the case for the category, specialization and object class. All objects that belong to these concepts are instantiated by the type level. Thus the category will in, for example, Smalltalk be implemented as an abstract superclass from which its subclasses, which are derived from the type level, will inherit.

The conclusion we can make is that from the point of view of the information architecture it is not possible to create a stable class hierarchy based on just the inheritance of attributes from superclasses by subclasses. To be able to obtain a stable information architecture we require more information about the grounds for existence of the super- and subclasses by modelling specializations and categories.

9.3.8   Action types

Each action type can in theory be implemented as an independent logical data structure. The usefulness of this is limited because in most cases the content of the action type is incorporated in the object type as initializations or after the operations of the action model have been executed. The object type is thus transformed into the record type, table or class, which is derived according to the transformation rules, as we have already discussed.

The usefulness of implementing the action types as their own logical data structure will only become obvious when we wish to store the attributes sent by the action type as a message, for security purposes or for future processing. The logical data structure will then provide a reference to the associated objects, processing time and attribute content of the message.

In the event of a disaster we can theoretically use the stored messages to reproduce the original situation.

The messages can also be stored in a separate file for future processing by an action type.

9.3.9 Other transformation rules for a logical data model

The rules we have discussed for the relational transformation of an information architecture into a logical data model or a logical data structure are those most used, but they are not the only transformation rules. We could, for example, also use the simple rule that transforms all the action types into record types, tables or classes, regardless of the connectivity of the association (many-to-many, one-to-many, and so on).

Using this simplified transformation rule the resulting logical data model is more complicated and less efficient in the searching and updating of databases. The advantage, however, of this logical data model is that it provides a higher degree of data independence. By this we mean that programs and database structures do not need to be modified when the connectivity of a specific action type changes from a one-to-many association to a many-to-many association. Using the transformation rules we have discussed for the network model, this change would cause a data structure set to be modified to become a record type or vice versa. If we used the simplified rule, we would not need to carry out the modifications described.

9.4 Improving the performance and storage of the logical data model

After we have created the logical data model from the information architecture by using the transformation rules, we may wish to modify the structure in some situations. The reason for doing this would be to improve the performance of the system or to improve its use of storage space. We will base our discussion of a number of technical aspects on the network model.

One technique we can use to improve performance is to split one logical record type into two record types. By doing this we can, for example, store the generic information in one record type and the specific information in the other. We do, however, need an extra pointer to relate these two record types to each other. We then also need to modify the logical data model.

One of the reasons for splitting one record type into two or three record types is to improve the searching (seek) performance. This technique of splitting records becomes interesting when particular fields are accessed much more often than other fields. There is not much point in searching for data that we do not require, so it is a good idea to divide the record type into two record types.

Another reason for splitting a record type may be when a specific database system has a restriction on the maximum length of the record. In some cases it may be preferable to restrict the length of the record because of hardware or software considerations. An appropriate length may then be fixed at something like 256 bytes, for example. When a 'conceptual' record type is longer than the maximum allowed length of a record, we divide the 'conceptual' record type into two or more record types.

Another technique which is often used to improve system performance is to eliminate repeating groups of data when there is a limited number of values for the attribute types in the repeating group. The consequence of this is that the information system will lose some flexibility and become more difficult to maintain. In addition we must weigh up carefully the advantages of having the data structures and the program structures running parallel with each other. The elimination of repeating groups of data will also affect the resulting functionality.

Combining these data structures into one record type, table or class is a relevant technique when the transformation results in a large number of data structures and when these have been directly derived from many action types between two object types. A necessary condition for this is that the attribute types of the various data structures demonstrate a strong relationship with each other.

Finally, we wish to note that an information architecture can be transformed into many logical data models that vary from each other because of the diverging requirements we have for the processing of data. This is why we recommend that a database design starts with the creation of an information architecture. This information architecture can then be transformed into a logical data model that is adjusted for the specific environment. An extra advantage of creating the information architecture is that it provides for an existing and complete integration between the structural functionality that can be built into an information system and the supporting data structures. This integration is provided by the KISS models and the object-interaction model. The transformation of the information architecture would therefore never be solely carried out as the design and realization of the database; it would always be done together with the transformation of the KISS models into a logical functionality model. We will subsequently refer to this functionality model as the action handler.

9.5   Transformation of the KISS model

A full object-oriented transformation is realized when we start with the transformation of the KISS models into a so-called action handler. We thus do not start with the relational transformation of the structure of the object-interaction model into the different logical data models and implementation environments. Instead we treat every KISS model as an implementation class of its own and add later on the integration and communication aspects between the autonomous implementation classes.

The object-oriented transformation can be applied for any target environment, whether it is a network, relational, or object-oriented database or a conventional or 4GL programming language.

The advantage of applying the object-oriented transformation over the relational transformation is that the resulting structure becomes easier to modify, maintain and extend. This is because the implementation structure is closely related to the KISS model.

The KISS model shows the time sequence in which an object type may execute or undergo its actions. The KISS models describe the dynamic time-sequence constraints regardless of any consideration of the implementation environment. Further analysis shows that the KISS models of the object types can be implemented into any type of implementation environment.

The object types are transformed for a relational database, for example, into tables. The sequence in which, and the conditions under which, the attributes of the objects in the tables may be changed are dealt with per object type by means of an object context table. In the object context table we define the permitted sequence of the execution of actions for the object types.

When we integrate all the object context tables for all the dynamic object models, we end up with a structure that controls the permitted order of all actions. We call this structure the action context table. Before we discuss this any further, we will show how object context tables are created for implementation in relational database systems.

The rules for transforming the KISS model into object context tables and an action context table are as follows:

(1) Add an extra attribute type, the action controller, for a table of each KISS model with the name of the object type plus the suffix -AC. The value type of the action controller is 'character', with an initial value of 0. We use the action controller to represent the dynamic status of the object-model in terms of the last action of an action type that has taken place.

(2) Give each action type in the KISS model a unique identifier or name. It is preferable to give the identifier an ascending number. The identifier is the value of the action controller 'AC'. The attribute determines the status of the object.

(3) For each action type in the KISS model include an operation that gives the action controller 'AC' the value of the status of the action type.

(4) Create an object context table for each KISS model. In the table show for each value of the action controller 'AC' (equal to each action type) what the permitted subsequent action type within that object-model is, and also under which conditions an action may take place (in terms of the action type, action attributes and object attributes).

(5) Combine the object context tables for all the object-models into one action context table. This table shows, for all the action types, for which values of the action controller of an object type the action is permitted.

(6) Optionally create a simplified object context table showing all the various statuses. The individual action types cannot then be recognized by the value of the action controller. The result is a smaller and much-simplified object context table.

(7) Define the return messages for the situation when an action is permitted, or when an action is not permitted. These messages are sent to the function or the input screen. The return messages can be incorporated into a separate table for an implementation of a relational database system.

The object context table is derived directly from the individual KISS models. This can, in principle, be done by an automatic transformation. The following method of working is discussed using the earlier example of the bank, with the object types Cash Drawer, Account, Client and Branch.

We will first carry out steps 1 to 5. After we have explained this we will then carry out steps 6 and 7. In practice we would normally start straight away with steps 6 and 7.

9.5.1   Direct transformation

KISS model for Client   The KISS model for Client (Figure 9.20) shows that after the action 'To register' has taken place, an account can iteratively be opened before the client can de-register himself.

Object type: Client

AC	Action type	Operation
00	To register	AC := 01
01	To open	AC := 02
	To de-register	AC := 03
02	To open	AC := 02
	To de-register	AC := 03
03	–	

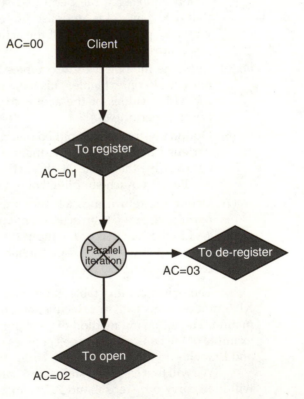

Figure 9.20   KISS model for Client.

The object context table is created by showing with a matrix the actions that are permitted when the Action controller of an object has a particular value.

Object context table Client:

		Action controller			
AC	*Action type*	*00*	*01*	*02*	*03*
01	To register	True	False	False	False
02	To open	False	True	True	False
03	To de-register	False	True	True	False

KISS model for Branch   The KISS model for Branch (Figure 9.21) shows that after a branch has been founded it can iteratively register clients and install cash drawers.

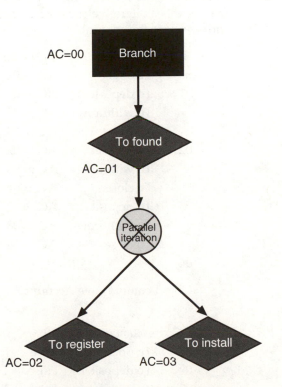

Figure 9.21   KISS model for Branch.

AC	Action type	Operation
00	To found	AC := 01
01	To register	AC := 02
	To install	AC := 03
02	To register	AC := 02
	To install	AC := 03
03	To register	AC := 02
	To install	AC := 03

object context table Branch

		Action controller			
AC	Action type	00	01	02	03
01	To found	True	False	False	False
02	To register	False	True	True	True
03	To install	False	True	True	True

KISS model for Account

The KISS model for Account (Figure 9.22) shows that after opening an account we can iteratively choose to deposit money or withdraw money, until we close the account.

AC	Action type	Operation
00	To open	AC := 01
01	To deposit	AC := 02
	To withdraw	AC := 03
	To close	AC := 04
02	To deposit	AC := 02
	To withdraw	AC := 03
	To close	AC := 04
03	To deposit	AC := 02
	To withdraw	AC := 03
	To close	AC := 04
04	–	

Object context table Account

		Action controller				
AC	Action type	00	01	02	03	04
01	To open	True	False	False	False	False
02	To deposit	False	True	True	True	False
03	To withdraw	False	True	True	True	False
04	To close	False	True	True	True	False

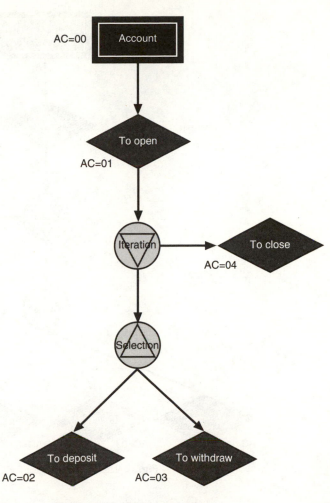

Figure 9.22   KISS model for Account.

KISS model for Cash drawer   The KISS model for Cash drawer (Figure 9.23) shows that we can iteratively deposit, withdraw, transfer and count until the cash drawer is locked.

AC	Action type	Operation
00	To install	AC := 01
01	To deposit	AC := 02
	To withdraw	AC := 03
	To transfer	AC := 04
	To count	AC := 05
	To lock	AC := 06
02	To deposit	AC := 02

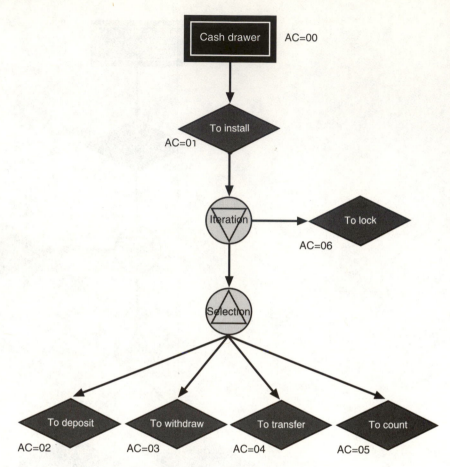

Figure 9.23   KISS model for Cash drawer.

	To withdraw	AC := 03
	To transfer	AC := 04
	To count	AC := 05
	To lock	AC := 06
03	To deposit	AC := 02
	To withdraw	AC := 03
	To transfer	AC := 04
	To count	AC := 05
	To lock	AC := 06
04	To deposit	AC := 02
	To withdraw	AC := 03
	To transfer	AC := 04

	To count	AC := 05
	To lock	AC := 06
05	To deposit	AC := 02
	To withdraw	AC := 03
	To transfer	AC := 04
	To count	AC := 05
	To lock	AC := 06
06	–	

Object context table Cash drawer:

		Action controller						
AC	*Action type*	*00*	*01*	*02*	*03*	*04*	*05*	*06*
01	To install	True	False	False	False	False	False	False
02	To deposit	False	True	True	True	True	True	False
03	To withdraw	False	True	True	True	True	True	False
04	To transfer	False	True	True	True	True	True	False
05	To count	False	True	True	True	True	True	False
06	To lock	False	True	True	True	True	True	False

9.5.2   Simplifying the object context table

We can easily simplify the object context table by only including a new value of the action controller for each status, instead of for each action type. We then arrive at the transformation in Figure 9.24.

KISS model for Branch

The object context table can be simplified by representing the status for the following action controllers.

AC	*Action type*	*Operation*
00	To found	AC := 01
01	To register	AC := 01
	To install	AC := 01

The resulting object context table becomes much simpler. It is, however, no longer possible to trace a specific action type by looking at the action controller.

Object context table Branch:

		Action controller	
	Action type	*00*	*01*
01	To found	True	False
02	To register	False	True
	To install	False	True

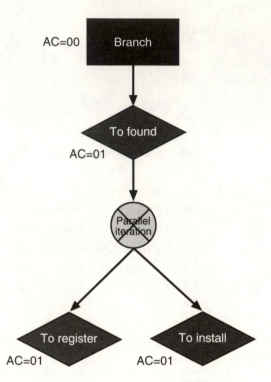

Figure 9.24   KISS model Branch with AC values.

KISS model for Cash drawer   The action controllers that represent the status are shown in the following table:

AC	Action type	Operation
00	To install	AC := 01
01	To deposit	AC := 01
	To withdraw	AC := 01
	To transfer	AC := 01
	To count	AC := 01
	To lock	AC := 02
02	–	

Particularly in situations where we have a choice within the KISS model between a large number of action types, we find it easier to make use of the status (Figure 9.25).

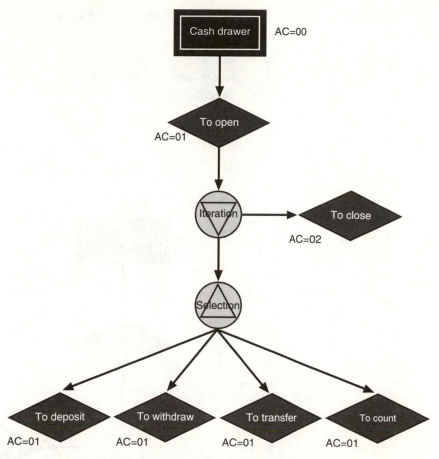

Figure 9.25   KISS model Cash drawer with AC values.

The object context table Cash drawer is as follows (Figure 9.25).

AC	Action type	*Action controller*		
		00	*01*	*02*
01	To install	True	False	False
	To deposit	False	True	False
	To withdraw	False	True	False
	To transfer	False	True	False
	To count	False	True	False
02	To lock	False	True	False

KISS model for Account   The simplified action controllers that result are (Figure 9.26):

AC	Action type	Operation
00	To open	AC := 01
01	To deposit	AC := 01
	To withdraw	AC := 01
	To close	AC := 02
02	–	

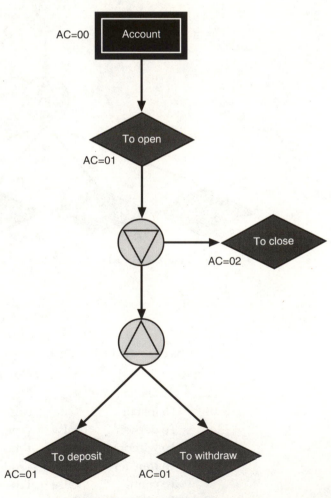

Figure 9.26   KISS model for Account.

Object context table Account:

		Action controller		
AC	Action type	00	01	02
01	To open	True	False	False
	To deposit	False	True	False
	To withdraw	False	True	False
02	To close	False	True	False

9.5.3   General simplified rules for determining the action controller

The following rules are used to determine the values of the action controller:

(1) A sequence results in a new status;

(2) A selection of action types is permitted for the same status;

(3) An iteration does not produce a new status;

(4) A parallel iteration without sequences also does not produce a new status.

Using the rules above, the determination of the status for the action controller becomes simpler than if we were to give a new value to the action controller for each action type.

9.6   Implementation of the action handler

The action type is the basic control element for the input of data into an information system. When a message is sent to the action type, the complete description of the possible subsequent activities is given with the action type. Before we go any further with the discussion on action types we must explain what an action type does with the messages it sends and receives.

For each action type we incorporate an action routine that supports the following functions in the order given:

(1) A syntax check carried out on the basis of the definitions of the attribute types and the domains belonging to the action-attributes. Syntax errors are reported to the outside world by the action routine (the trigger or return message of the action type), and the action is not accepted. The syntax check is necessary when this is not entirely (or not at all) catered for by an input function.

The trigger message to the outside world is usually found in a separate part of the screen for input screens.

(2) A semantic context check carried out on the basis of the object context tables. The information needed for this check regarding the status of the relevant objects (AC-<object>) is gathered by the action routine. Contextual errors are reported to the outside world by means of a trigger from the action type to the input function by the action routine, and the action is not accepted. In addition to the error message, a 'good' message can also be sent to the outside world.

(3) The status of the object defined by the action controller (AC-<object>) is used to formulate the correct message sent to the outside world.

Example:

Action type = To open

Object type = Account

AC-Account = To open, To deposit or To withdraw

Message = 'account is already open'

or

AC-Account = To close

Message = 'account is closed'

Object type = Client

AC-Client = empty

Message = 'client is not yet registered'

or

AC-Client = De-registered

Message = 'client is already de-registered and may no longer open any accounts'

The object context tables are also used to indicate the messages which must be sent to the outside world when we wish to carry out a particular action. The messages summarized for this purpose therefore also form a part of the object context tables.

(4) When the message and the object context table have been accepted, they must also be validated by the conditions of the iteration symbols and the action conditions. For example, the iterations could be executed a maximum or minimum number of times. The values for meeting the conditions are recorded by incrementing a counter.

The action conditions are checked in accordance with the sequence order. This involves the action routine retrieving the attribute values of the action conditions and testing them against the defined action condition.

(5) When all the conditions for the execution of operations on the object attributes have been met, we can move on to actually changing the object attributes as defined by the operations for the action concerned. By this we mean that the action routine retrieves the data of the object concerned, updates it and stores the new result.

(6) The activation of functions for which the concerned action is the trigger. The data for the objects that these functions need are provided by the action routine. The data from objects other than those with which the action is concerned are inspected by the function itself.

An action is the smallest unit of a transaction for input functions. When a function consists of many actions in time sequence, the syntax checks of the action routines that belong to the input function must be carried out first. Then the contextual checks must be carried out, and so forth.

With the implementation of functions, the intermediate results must be stored in buffers in temporary memory space, until all the actions and inspections of the entire function have been completed. By doing this we achieve fewer physical read/write interactions between the function and the implemented database. In addition, we do not need to roll the database back to an earlier state at the moment that one of the conditions is not met during execution of the function.

The integration of the individual object context tables and the representation of the action handler by a matrix provide an overview of the interrelationship between the action types and object types in the implemented information system. The implemented action type/object type matrix is also used to update the information architecture in the information quadrant.

9.6.1 Action handler

	Object types			
Action types	*Cash drawer*	*Account*	*Client*	*Branch*
To install	✕		✕	
To deposit	✕	✕		
To withdraw	✕	✕		
To transfer	✕			
To count	✕			
To lock	✕			
To open	✕	✕		
To close		✕		
To register			✕	✕
To de-register			✕	
To found				✕

When we use the information system we can use the action handler to determine whether or not an action is permitted, given the action controller of various objects. The dynamic aspects are themselves noted in the individual object context tables which must be queried for the respective object types.

9.6.2 Rules for the transformation to program structures

Besides the database for storage of business data and an action handler for the recording of business rules, it is also necessary to implement the functionality as it is described and encapsulated in the information architecture, as program structures. For this transformation of the information architecture into program structures we primarily make use of the content of the action-model. In the action-model we defined the ordering sequence of the operations as they are carried out on the attribute types. We also defined the content of the operation. For the operations we make a distinction between operations that work at type level and, in addition to these, operations that work at class level.

The operations defined at class level lead to separate object classes for recording the results of the operations. The object classes themselves become logical data structures that can be implemented as record types, tables and classes.

We will look at two strategies for the rules of the transformation to program structures. The first strategy is based on a transformation into a conventional programming language. We will then look at how an action-model can be converted into a object-oriented programming language.

Conventional and object-oriented programming languages can be used in combination with network, relational and object-oriented DBMSs. There are no strict guidelines to be given for the decision of which combination to use. An optimal balance between the parts which must be implemented in a conventional or an object-oriented environment can be provided by the information architecture.

Conventional programming language

The group of conventional programming languages consists of all languages that utilize a procedural manner of programming. It includes languages such as COBOL, C, Pascal, Progress and Clipper. It does not make much difference whether the program is written for a mainframe, mini or PC. It makes even less difference whether the programming language is of a higher or lower level. The underlying way of thinking for a 3GL or a 4GL is theoretically the same.

The rule for transforming the action-model in the information architecture to program structures for a conventional environment is:

Each action-model becomes an elementary program module in which the operations are incorporated in the desired order of execution. If there are conditions defined for the execution of the operations then these are totally included in the program module for the action type.

The transformation of the action-model to a conventional environment is then complete. The result is elementary program modules of a relatively small size. The program modules are controlled by functions via messages. The entire error handling takes place in the action handler on the basis of the defined conditions in the KISS models and as action conditions. The reuse of the elementary action modules has already been modelled in the object-interaction model because we included singular action types when we created the object-interaction model.

Maintenance of information systems becomes extremely simplified with the simple implementation of elementary program modules. In this situation we of course do not need to check in various programs whether a change has any effect on them. By the minimization of redundancy we gain the added advantage that maintenance can take place in very isolated locations. Extension of existing systems can similarly take place in isolation, according to the idea of building blocks. The KISS method thus creates information systems that can more easily be maintained even in the case where the information architecture is implemented in a conventional programming environment.

Object-oriented programming languages

The basic premise of object-oriented programming languages is that the data component and the program component are written as an integral whole within classes. The classes instantiate objects with instance variables. The objects have lives of their own and communicate with other objects by sending and receiving messages. Besides this, objects can also belong to a particular class structure allowing them, for example, to make use of data defined for generic objects, or to reuse particular methods.

The way of working with object-oriented programming is therefore not a procedural one. The way of thinking required for working with object-oriented programming languages is therefore different from that required for conventional programming languages.

The transformation of the information architecture into an object-oriented programming environment requires a greater number of transformation rules than for the conventional environment. The reason for this is that for a pure object-oriented programming language everything is incorporated into classes that communicate with other classes and in object-oriented languages there is no equivalent to the action types of the KISS method.

The relational transformation of the object types, weak object types, gerunds, categories, specializations and object classes from the object-interaction model into classes has already been covered by the discussion of the transformation rules for database management systems. A full object-oriented transformation is that only the object types, weak object types and gerunds are transformed into classes, whereas the object classes, specializations and categories are transformed into abstract classes because they do not instantiate any objects. We will now further discuss the object-oriented transformation of the action-model into components of the class.

In the object-interaction model an action type is connected to object types by association lines. An association line states that an action type has minimally one operation or initialization data flow that changes the status of an object.

The association line between an action type and an object type is used for the transformation into 'methods' for classes. A method is the implementation of one or more operations specified for the action types. A method is equivalent to one or more operations belonging to the attribute types of classes.

We create the names for the methods in the object-interaction model by combining the name of the action type with the object type for all the associations in the object-interaction model. For the bank example this results in the following summary of methods, sorted by action type and object type:

Methods by action type	Methods by object type
ToCloseAccount	ToCloseAccount
ToCloseBank	ToWithdrawAccount
ToCloseCash drawer	ToDepositAccount
ToCloseClient	ToOpenAccount
ToDepartBank	ToInstallBank
ToDepartClient	ToDepartBank
ToDepositAccount	ToRegisterBank
ToDepositCash	ToFoundBank
ToDepositClient	ToCloseBank
ToFoundBank	ToLockBank
ToInstallBank	ToWithdrawCash
ToInstallCashDrawer	ToTransferCash
ToLockBank	ToDepositCash
ToLockCashDrawer	ToLockCashDrawer

ToOpenAccount	ToCloseCashDrawer
ToOpenClient	ToInstallCashDrawer
ToRegisterBank	ToDepartClient
ToRegisterClient	ToOpenClient
ToTransferCash	ToWithdrawClient
ToWithdrawAccount	ToDepositClient
ToWithdrawCash	ToCloseClient
ToWithdrawClient	ToRegisterClient

Each method belongs to one class. In the object-oriented transformation the action type is divided among the various classes on the basis of its operational content.

The content of the methods is determined by allocating the operations of an action type to the class, where the attribute types are implemented as variables. This could mean that we end up losing a check on the action type; that is, the check on the logical ordering of the execution of the operations between the objects of the various classes according to the specification of the ordering in the action model. To regain the check we must take extra measures to ensure we achieve the desired ordering of the execution of methods. The implementation in object-oriented environments is by synchronizing the sending, receiving and processing of messages. For procedural-oriented applications implemented in an object-oriented environment, we must stress that this check be carried out for the handling of messages.

In a conventional environment the check on the changes is done centrally in the action handler. In an object-oriented environment it is no longer desirable to include the check on the changes of an object in a central action handler. We prefer to do it at the level of the class and its instantiated objects by implementing the object context table in the class. This ensures the coordination between the objects of the autonomous classes. As well as this we add a method to the highest class whose task is to do the generic work of the action handler. By means of inheritance this method becomes available for each level of the class hierarchy to use. With this structure each object can manage its own behaviour.

9.7 Integrity of the database

The integrity of a database is a concept that indicates whether the status of a database is a correct and accurate representation of that part of the real world in which we are interested at a given moment in time. A database's status can change in the KISS method because actions are performed that include the following elementary operations:

- Input of new data;
- Deleting of data;
- Changing of existing data.

By making changes to the database, it is in theory possible to damage the integrity of the database.

We will now look in more detail at three rules for preserving the integrity of a relational database. The rules are:

- Entity integrity;
- Referential integrity;
- Distribution integrity.

(1) *Entity integrity.* In a relational database no single component may accept a null value as a key. All tuples must also be uniquely identified.

(2) *Referential integrity.* The constraint of referential integrity exists in a relational database where a relation implicitly refers to other relations. This is the case, for example, for existence dependencies of weak object types and gerunds.

(3) *Distribution integrity.* Has to be taken care of in database environments where the same data about objects is stored in different locations.

The three integrity rules for a database can be directly derived from the information architecture. The first rule means that all identifiers of objects and classes must be unique and may not contain any null values.

The second constraint of referential integrity has been implicitly included in the object-interaction model because of the definition of all the existence dependencies. The defined existence dependencies can then be transformed into the referential integrity constraints, for example Alter table for a relational implementation. It can also be taken over in an easier way by the action controller routine.

The third constraint of distribution integrity is realized by identifying a location where the control over the different copies of the objects is allocated. In the case of specializations the control for all table or class implementations is taken over by the parent object type.

In the network, hierarchy, semantic and object-oriented database management systems the integrity aspects are better protected than for relational systems. This is because in all these systems there are more semantics implicitly recorded. In the hierarchy and network database management systems these additional semantics are to be found in the limited flexibility. This occurs because the semantics are stored in pointer structures and sets that are difficult to maintain. This problem, on the contrary, does not appear in semantic and object-oriented database management systems, though for these database management systems pointers also define their coherence.

We will explain how the semantics are recorded in an object-interaction model in order to create rules for referential integrity by means of the bank example. In this example we will delete a person from the file and add the data for a deposit.

A person can be employed and he or she can be registered as a relation. The person can have opened accounts.

The object-interaction model indicates that the 'employment' is existence-dependent on both person and branch. This means that the employed person must be 'resigned' before the person-record can be deleted. The object-interaction model indicates that there is also an existence dependence for 'registration' on person. It holds true for 'registration' that 'account' is existence-dependent on it. This means that all the accounts of a person must be closed, and the registration must be de-registered, before the person-record can be deleted.

In a relational environment we need to trace through the cascade to check any possible direct relationships before we can delete a person-record. The rules for referential integrity can therefore be derived directly from the object-interaction model.

To be able to add the data for a deposit into an account, we must follow a path through the object-interaction model in the opposite direction. So, an account must be opened by a person or organization who is registered at a branch. On the other side, the branch concerned must have installed a cash drawer where an amount of cash can be deposited. The conditions under which the action may be executed can be derived from the object-interaction model. The framework of the object-interaction model will therefore also need to be used when specifying the input functionality.

9.8 Summary

In this chapter we indicated how the object-interaction model and KISS models can be converted from an information architecture into various types of database management system by the use of relational and object-oriented transformation rules.

Then we showed how the KISS models are used to implement an action handler to take care of the integrity and the synchronization of actions upon objects.

Besides the integrity of the action handler, we also indicated how the integrity rules can be implemented for a relational database.

9.9 Questions

(1) Describe the implementation characteristics of the different types of database systems.

(2) Describe the relational transformation rules for transforming the object-interaction model to three different database types.

(3) Discuss in what ways we can create the object-interaction model by reverse engineering existing network, relational or object-oriented database management systems. Illustrate it with examples.

(4) Rumbaugh has introduced the concept 'association as a class'. Discuss whether this concept is an object-oriented concept or a relational concept that is implemented in an object-oriented programming language.

(5) Discuss the implementation aspects of existence dependency with respect to integrity, distribution of objects and access of data.

(6) What is hierarchy inversion and how does it relate to existence dependency and inheritance?

(7) Describe the object-oriented transformation of the KISS models into the action handler and persistent data storage.

(8) Describe the transformation rules for transforming the action model into a conventional programming language and an object-oriented programming language.

(9) Describe the transformation rules for transforming the attribute model into different programming languages and database types.

# 10 Functions

10.1 Introduction

Functions form the interface between the user in the real world and the information system. In the information quadrant the input and output functions were defined as the interface between the controlling model of an organization and the information architecture. In the description of the layers of an object-oriented information system the function layer is the outermost layer and it does not determine the structure. The structure is of course determined by the middle layer, where the information architecture is defined. Functions as such are easy enough to add to and remove from the information architecture without damaging the underlying structure of an information system.

A function is always placed under the responsibility of a subject that as such executes the functions.

In this chapter on functions we discuss how we can use the structure of the KISS models and object-interaction models of the information architecture as a basis for creating function models. A function model describes the communication of the user in the real world with the information system. How the function model is related to the KISS model is discussed. We will also take a detailed look at those aspects where function models differ from KISS models. Using a number of transformation rules we provide a framework for the creation and definition of a dialogue, a menu structure and a screen layout for the input and inspection of attributes.

The method of specification of decision functions is discussed in detail by the use of:

- Decision tables;
- Decision models.

Finally we will look at how we can execute actions in time-dependent functions. These functions may be either backdated or postdated as a way of planning future actions.

10.2   Types of function

A function has been defined in the KISS paradigm as that component of the system that directs the execution of actions by action types using messages. A function also requests information using inspections. The functions thus take care of the management and control of the input and output of data to the storage structure of the information system as it is modelled by the object-interaction model (Figure 10.1). The functions are, to all intents and purposes, added to the object-interaction model. The function in general describes the communication of the end user with the information system.

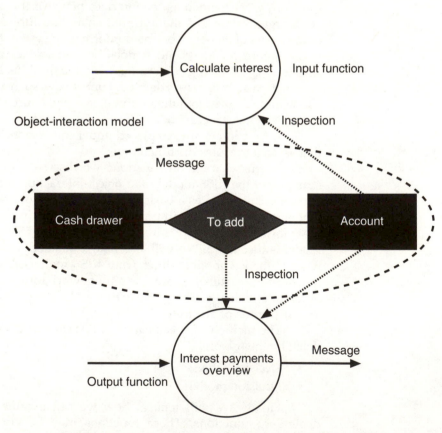

Figure 10.1   Adding functions to the object-interaction model.

When describing the functions we globally separate them into:

- Input function;
- Output function;
- Decision function;
- Time-dependent function;
- System function;
- Dialogue.

10.2.1   Input function

For all of the action types included in the object-interaction model and in the KISS models, we must define at least one input function in the information system. The input functions can vary from very simple to extremely complex.

10.2.2   Output function

Output functions inquire upon the encapsulated attribute types in the object-interaction model by means of inspections. A condition for the supply of information for output functions is that the elementary attribute types must also be included in the object-interaction model. Just as for the input functions, there can be a great variation in complexity.

10.2.3   Decision function

A decision function is more complex than an input or output function. This is because a decision function determines the attribute values with which an action or operation of an action type must be executed, by utilizing decision rules. To do this a decision function carries out inspections on the attributes of objects. The decision function ensures that the static decision rules of an organization are implemented by the information system, in a structured manner.

10.2.4   Time-dependent function

The functions concerned with the planning of future actions or the execution of actions relevant to the past or the future ensure that the time-dimension is taken into account. Time-dependent functions are an extension of the previously described functions.

10.2.5   System function

The various input and output functions are described at different levels. The information system itself can in this way be seen as one enormous function. The system function is the total functionality that takes care of the management of disks, monitors, printers and such like that can be used by a programmer. System functions are therefore generally embedded or woven into the application. We will not go into further detail on system functions because they are specified in the same way as the other functions. The only difference is that they are of a more detailed nature.

10.2.6   Dialogue

The dialogue presents the interrelationship between the different functions of an information system and the end user. The dialogue specifies the generic functional way in which an end user can communicate with the information system. Normally spoken, the dialogue is built up of input and output screens containing data. These screens are supported by extra help screens which offer a choice of selecting subsequent functions on one or more objects.

The dialogue itself can be strongly influenced by the personal preferences of the end user. As the techniques used offer greater possibilities, the user interface will become more complicated. Particularly with the increasing options available for building user dialogues, there is an increasing need to develop standards for the design of screens, menu structures, interactive functions, screen layouts and such like.

The input, decision and time-dependent functions are further explained because of their importance.

10.3   The function model

To describe functions we can use the same techniques as for the description of the behaviour of object types. For the functionality we describe the functional objects in the dialogue with the user using functional KISS models, also referred to as function models. The conventions we used with the KISS models for iterations, selections and sequences also hold true for the function models.

To represent the interaction between function models we create a function interaction model, analogous to the object-interaction model. The difference from the analysis carried out previously is that we are now going to analyse and produce a model of the control of the primary process. The primary process itself has already been described in the object-interaction model.

A function interaction model differs from an object-interaction model in the degree of persistence. In an object-interaction model the encapsulated attributes are totally persistent because the values are stored in a database. An additional criterion for persistence is that the attribute values of the object continue to exist after we turn the power off. This is not the case for the functional objects that result from the analysis of the function. The functional objects disappear after the function has been executed. The attributes of the functional objects also only have a temporary life for the duration of the execution of the function. This makes them transient by nature.

A function takes care of information coming from the information system and processes data before it is sent via a message to an action type. The action type ensures that the data is converted from its transient form into a persistent form. The action type does this by means of encapsulated operations. The concepts of transience and persistence are explicitly used in object-oriented programming languages as extra characteristics of the attribute types. These characteristics are used to make a distinction between permanently stored data and the data that is only used temporarily during the execution of a function.

A function model describes the order in which an end user can utilize the action types and inspections available to him or her. A function model is created using the same symbols for iteration, selection and sequence that we used in the KISS model (Figure 10.2). The symbols for the type level are replaced by the circle symbolizing the function. The ordering rules of the KISS model are also used for the function model.

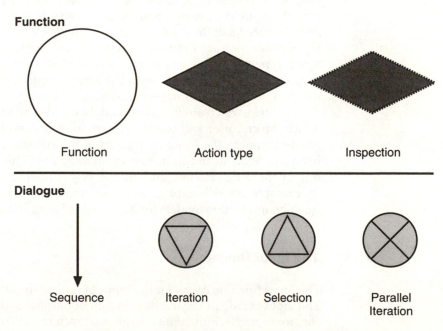

Figure 10.2 Building blocks for the function model.

In a function model we make use of a separate symbol for an inspection. An inspection is symbolized by a diamond with a dotted line.

Definition of an inspection   An inspection is the sending of a message to one or more objects. A return message containing the requested attributes is expected immediately.

We can also, in theory, represent a message to the action type in a function model using a dotted diamond. This is because this message is based on the sending of attributes and in return receiving a message containing the way in which the attributes have been processed. However, it is preferable that we make a distinction in the function model between messages that do or do not result in an alteration of the status of the database. We therefore use the symbol of the action type in the function model to represent the messages which go to an action type.

We sometimes transform the inspection symbols in the function model into action type symbols. We would do this when it is useful to store data, manipulated during the inspection, with an object in the database.

The connection between the functions in the controlling part of an information system and the information architecture is made by the messages to action types and inspections. The action types take care of the change of status of the information system, while the inspections take care of the output of database data to a function. Inspections also take care of output to other functions or to the outside world, via messages. It must be noted that the symbol of the action type within a function model represents a message to an action type, not the execution of actions of the action type itself! The action type is modelled by the action model. An inspection is also modelled with the action model under the condition that no updates of attributes of objects take place.

When we create function models we also specify the manner in which the end user will use the information system. The starting point for determining the function models is the structure that has already been provided in the information architecture. This structure is laid out in the KISS models and in the object-interaction model. Using an example we will explain how we create the function models and function interaction models for a defined information architecture.

10.3.1   The input function

The input function caters for the input of data to the information system. The input of data can be handled in a great number of different ways. We can, for example, input data into an input screen utilizing tools such as a keyboard, a mouse, a light pen, and so on. We can also place data in an input screen by the direct inspection of files by or by exchanging data using batch file transfer or by reading disks. The input function then allows us to view the data in the input screen in different ways. It can also allow us to manipulate the data before it is used to update the database. The input function is therefore a process best described by means of the input screen because it makes the input function relatively easily to visualize.

Input functions that do not make use of an input screen frequently occur. We can think, for example, of measuring in processing plants where all measuring data is directly processed and stored in files without becoming visual in an input screen.

To be able to input data in the correct manner we must validate the data. This is necessary in order to check its syntax before it is used in calculations or to update the database. The validation of input data must take place with reference to the attribute type in a universal information architecture defined by KISS and object-interaction models. The advantage of this is that the input functions are specified inside a framework which is independent of the techniques used to implement a working information system.

10.3.2   Screen dialogue

We base the specification of the handling of screens for inputting data on the object-interaction model. This model provides us with the interactions between the various object types that define the inter-relationships between the data inputs to the information system. The object-interaction model also defines how the autonomous object types are synchronized with each other by their common action types. It is precisely this interaction between object types that is important to providing the structure within which useful screen dialogues can be built.

An example of an integrity rule from the object-interaction model is that data from a weak object type may not be input to the database for as long as the strong object type is not defined. The implications of this for the screen dialogue are that users must first check if the strong object exists when they use a function key indicating that they wish to add one or more objects of a weak object type to the database. If the strong object does not exist, it will first have to be instantiated before the user can return to the screen to add the weak objects.

In reverse this means that the deletion of a strong object can only take place when no existence-dependent objects are associated with the objects to be deleted. If this is the case then the weak objects will first need to be deleted.

We will use the example of an order function to explain in a step-wise manner how an input function is created with the information architecture and the KISS models.

10.3.3   Example of an order function

In the order example an order is placed by a client for items.

Items can be ordered for a client when we have created an order with an order number. On the order lines we record the quantity and the price of the ordered items. An ordered item on an order line can be modified or cancelled. When we progress to delivery, each order line is delivered in its entirety. The KISS model for 'Order line' defines the time ordering of the execution of the actions (Figure 10.3).

We see in the KISS model that an 'Order line' is instantiated by the action type 'To order'. After the instantiation it is possible 'To change' the order line zero, one or more times. Finally the action types 'To cancel' or 'To deliver' are possible. In the KISS model for 'Order line' there are four action types included that in one way or another need to be incorporated into the function model for the order function.

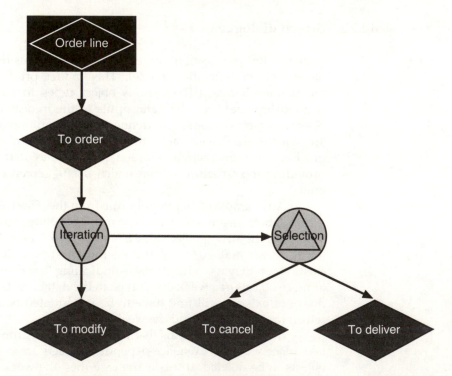

Figure 10.3   KISS model for Order line.

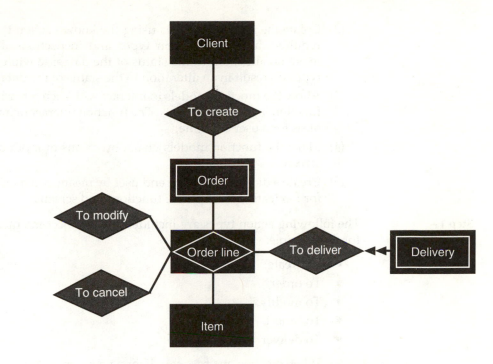

Figure 10.4 Object-interaction model for Order line.

The object-interaction model (Figure 10.4) shows that 'Order line' is a gerund which is existence-dependent on both Item and Order. In turn Order is existence-dependent on the Client. The action type 'To deliver' is the instantiating action type of Delivery.

Using the object-interaction model of the example it is easy to indicate the order in which the various object types can be created and deleted, based on their existence dependencies on each other, for storage in a database. So, for example, it is not possible to store ordered items in a database for which no order has been created and for which no client exists. If this was the case then we would need to ask questions about the integrity of the database.

The steps we follow to create the function model and function interaction model based on the KISS models and object-interaction models are:

(1) Determine which action types from the object-interaction model are to be used for which function model;

(2) Create the function models using the known action types and, if required, additional action types and inspections. Inspections make no alteration to the status of the database while the action types do result in an alteration to the status of the database;

(3) Allow the function models to interact with each other resulting in function interaction models. The function interaction model is the basis for a user dialogue;

(4) Make the function models visual by means of input and output screens;

(5) Create a dialogue with the end user by means of a menu structure for navigation through the functions and screens.

Step 1 –
Action types

The following action types are included in the object-interaction model for the example:

- To create;
- To order;
- To modify;
- To cancel;
- To deliver.

When creating an order the client data is connected with the items that are ordered via order lines. In the example we look at two ways of inputting data in an input screen and the underlying database.

1. Direct singular
input

The first way is to input the data about the ordered items on one order line on the screen for the order function. Each time we input the data on the quantity and price of an item, we write the data to the database using the action type 'To order'. The advantage of this way of working is that the database receives the latest data from the input function.

The disadvantage of ordering per item for an order is that we are frequently writing to the database. In addition the end user loses his or her overview of the order because of having to enter each single order line separately. Also, we must always correct a faulty input by a physical change to the order data in the database. In practice this is generally not a desirable situation because it results in too much interaction in the form of read/write activity on the database.

2. Buffered input

The solution to this is to input a larger number of order lines in one input screen, and to wait until all the order lines have been input before writing the attributes to the database. At the end, all the data input for the order and the ordered items must be sent to the action types 'To create' and 'To order', respectively. The action type 'To create' an order will then only be realized after the amounts for the ordered items have been input to the input screen. For a new order, the action type 'To order' will then always be used in cooperation with the action type 'To create'. The buffered input corresponds to a plurality number in the object-interaction model larger than 1.

When we apply a number of standard transformation rules to the dialogue we can very quickly obtain the structure of a screen. When we create a screen dialogue with the end user we convert the object types from the object-interaction model into screens or parts of screens. We translate the action types into function keys or buttons on the screen. The function keys for the 'order' input screen can be derived from the action types in the KISS model for the order line. We allocate the action types to the following function keys for the screen in our example:

    F2:   To order
    F3:   To modify
    F4:   To cancel
    F5:   To deliver
    F10: To create

Secondly, we derive the function keys themselves from the specification of the action types as elementary functions in, for example, a relational database.

F2:   'To order' means that we create new records for the table 'order line' when we press function key F2.

F3:   Function key F3 for 'To modify' means that we wish to modify the quantity or the price of a record of 'Order line'.

F4:   Function key F4 for 'To cancel' does not mean that we physically DELETE a record, but that the status of a specific record in the table 'Order line' is altered to 'cancelled'.

F5:   Function key F5 for 'To deliver' alters the status of a specific record, just as for F4.

F10:   Function key F10 for 'To create' takes care of the creation of a new record for a client's order.

With 'To cancel' and 'To deliver' we never perform a physical delete because we would then never be able to obtain information about the progress of the status of the objects in the information system. The object no longer exists for the information system after a physical delete.

Step 2 – Inspections and the function model   Generally when we input data into an input screen we also want to know what the status of the existing objects in the database is. To be able to cater for this we need to provide additional function keys in a screen to allow inspection of the status of objects. The input screens of object types can be expanded, for example, with extra functionality whereby the records on the screen are sorted and/or selectively presented in, for example, alphabetic or numeric order. The inspections that provide for this can be seen as elementary information functions.

The following inspections can be seen in the example of the order screen (Figure 10.5):

F1:   Help

F6:   Select order line by order value

F7:   Sort order lines alphabetically by name of item

F8:   Show the full description of the items

F10: Stop. This allows us to leave the order function without writing anything away to the database.

The inspections can become many-faceted by the addition of a little functionality. Inspections need not only be implemented with function keys. We can also make them directly visual in the input part of the screen, for example in the form of choice lists and inquiry screens.

The function key Stop allows the user to cancel all the input to the screen and return to the function choice. The function key Stop could also be implemented by using the Escape key.

The order function is a part of a total information system. The order function itself can only be used after a user has logged onto the system. When he has done this, the user can select the sales function. When he 'stops', the user leaves a function and is returned to a location where he needs to choose a specific function; in our case this can only be the order function. We can also create a separate function model to define the sequence of the action types and inspections of the system functions themselves.

In the function model we have included 'To log on' and 'To log off' as action types (Figure 10.6). We have done this because we think it is important to register the details about the end user and the log-on and log-off times. In order to be consistent we must also include new object types for the newly formed action types. With further detailed modelling we could suggest object types System and User.

Step 3 – Function-interaction model   We define the functions in the function interaction model by tracing through the iterations in the function models. For each iterating group of actions and inspections we include a function in the function-interaction

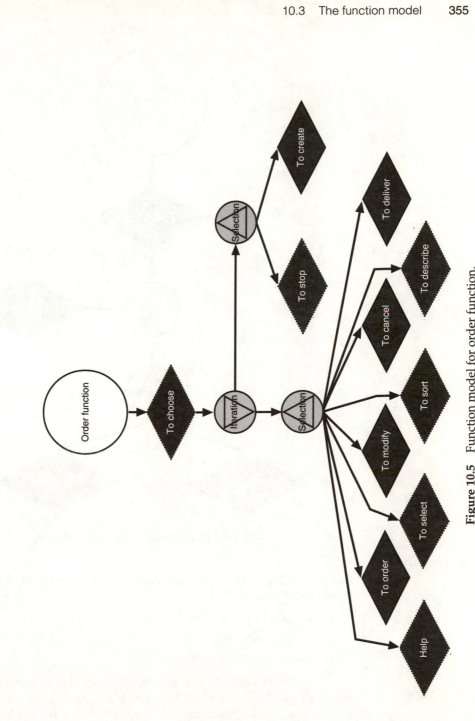

Figure 10.5   Function model for order function.

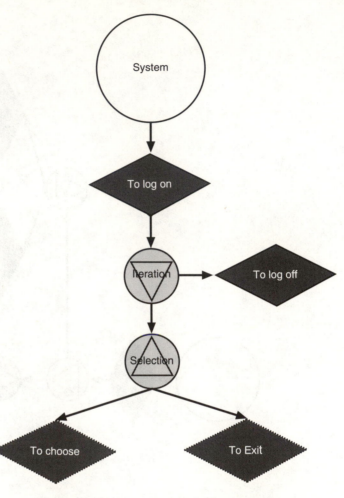

Figure 10.6   Function model for system.

model. In the order function example we arrive at the following functions (Figure 10.7):

- System function;
- Order function;
- Screen function.

Each function has a number of associated action types and inspections. The functions interact with each other by means of action types and inspections. An association line from a function to an action type or inspection means that we can go from one particular

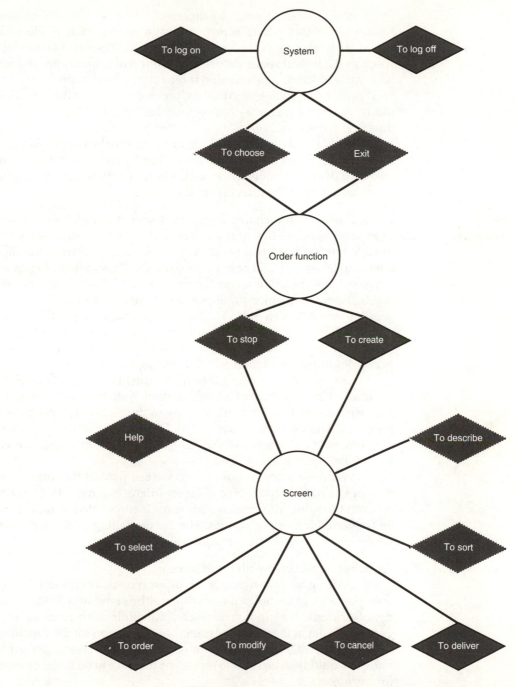

Figure 10.7 Function-interaction model.

function to another function by means of message connections. In some situations an immediate return message is required, while in other situations it remains a one-directional message. The function model itself specifies the logical sequence of the execution of action types and inspections for a function. The function interaction model supports this by the creation of a user dialogue. An easier representation for the user dialogue can be derived by directly connecting the functions to each other with directing arrows.

With an extensive modelling of the internal structure of functions the one-directional messages between functions are often not symbolized by a distinct symbol for an inspection or action type. It is sufficient to use an arrow in the direction of the message.

Step 4 –
Visualizing screens

We will discuss the character-oriented screen because this is still the most-used interface between the core of the information system and the outside world. In a great number of information systems the input of data to a database is still only possible by the direct input of data via the keyboard into the input screen. In recent years it has become possible to use lightpens and mice for input. Even more recently it has become possible for systems to store attributes from input via graphical measuring scales, images, sound and animation. The last forms of graphical input and representation are increasingly based on object-oriented principles for manipulation and data storage.

One of the most important requirements of input screens is that the underlying structure of an information system must be presented in a transparent and understandable way to the end user, who must input his or her data using the input screen. One of the essential aspects of the structure of input screens is that it represents the information architecture of the information system.

When we model input screens we can protect the integrity of the data by basing it on the KISS and object-interaction models. The business rules and existing information structures incorporated in them can then be converted into input screens. For the modelling of the input screens we will look at two transformation rules.

Transformation rule 1

An object type becomes an input screen.

A designer can divide up an input screen according to his or her own preferences, or build it according to the standards of the organization. Standards for input screens could include such rules as having a general header at the top of the screen, and a section for the function keys and error messages at the bottom of the screen. The section left in the middle would then be used to represent the data to be input or modified for the object.

Transformation rule 2

Based on the action type of the object type, we include in the input screen a function key whose task is to send the input message to the action type.

The transformation rule for the input screen is that we include a function key for the action type of an object. The job of this function key is to send the values input to the input screen to an action type, in the form of a message. The function key does not necessarily need to be one of the keys F1 to F10, but could be a field on the screen containing 'OK' or a so-called 'radio button' in windows-type programming environments.

We do not randomly start to include all the action types from the object-interaction model in the input screen. Rather we focus very much on the object type to determine whether the action types make changes to it. We add to the function keys in the screen the inspections that we defined in step 2.

In steps 1 and 2 we have already defined the function keys for the input screen for 'Order'. In the input screen we could, for example, choose to divide it into three parts to include the data for Client, Order and Order line. The advantage of this is that all the data for the objects on which an order line is existence-dependent is then included in one overview on one screen.

To be able to define repeating groups of data for an action type we must examine the plurality in the object-interaction model. The concept of plurality, for an action type, indicates how many objects of an object type can be changed by the action type at one moment in time.

In the example this applies to the action type 'To order', whereby for one order we can perform the action 'To order' an Item several times. The plurality is then 1 for Order and n for Item.

The plurality defines whether the data is sent singly or as a group from the screen to the action type. The plurality therefore also defines the logical sequence. In the example it works best if we first create or select an order and then order one or more items. The order is constant while the item is different for each new order line.

For the input of item data we could inspect the entire assortment of items. When we find that the item data is correct we can then directly input it into the screen.

After we have selected an item for each order line we enter the quantity the client has ordered into the screen (Figure 10.8). If required, we enter the modified price of the item. We can enter the total value for that order line. The value of the order line is a calculated attribute following the equation: value := quantity * price.

The astute reader will have noticed that we have not allocated a function key for writing the data to the database. Until the function key F10 'To create' has been pressed, we cannot associate the data from ordered items with an order (and an order number).

We therefore need to store the data from the screen in a temporary memory or buffer. The data that needs to be temporarily stored is all the attribute values of an order line. When the function key F10 'To create' is

```
┌─────────────────────────────────────────────────────────────────┐
│ Screen number: SCH0101                                            │
├─────────────────────────────────────────────────────────────────┤
│ Client: Name          :XXXXXXXXXXXXXXXXXX                         │
│         First names   :XXXXXXXXXXXXXXXXXXXXXXXXXXXXXXXX            │
│         Address       :XXXXXXXXXXXXXXXXXXXXXXXXXX                  │
│         Post code     :XXXXXXXX                                   │
│         City          :XXXXXXXXXXXXXXXXXXXXXXXXXX                  │
├─────────────────────────────────────────────────────────────────┤
│ Order: Order number   :XXXXXXXXXXXXX                              │
│        Date of creation :XXXXXXXXXXX                              │
├─────────────────────────────────────────────────────────────────┤
│ Order lines:                                                      │
│                                                                   │
│ No     Item-No    Description           Quantity  Price    Value  │
│ 1      23456      Shampoo X             12        $ 0.89   $ 10.68 │
│ 2      34678      Soap Y                20        $ 1.45   $ 20.90 │
│ 3      XXXXX      XXXXXXXXXXXXXXX        XXX       XXXXXX   XXXXXXX │
│ 4      XXXXX      XXXXXXXXXXXXXXX        XXX       XXXXXX   XXXXXXX │
│ 5      XXXXX      XXXXXXXXXXXXXXX        XXX       XXXXXX   XXXXXXX │
│ 6      XXXXX      XXXXXXXXXXXXXXX        XXX       XXXXXX   XXXXXXX │
├─────────────────────────────────────────────────────────────────┤
│ F1: Help        F2: To order   F3: To modify  F4: To cancel  F5: To deliver │
│ F6: Select      F7: Sort       F8: Describe   F9: To stop    F10: To create │
├─────────────────────────────────────────────────────────────────┤
│ Error message:                                                    │
└─────────────────────────────────────────────────────────────────┘
```

Figure 10.8   Example of an input screen.

pressed, the values of Order and Order line can be sent in the form of messages to the action types 'To create' and 'To order', respectively. Pressing the function key F10 'To create' can cause the Function key F2 'To order' to be automatically activated in the dialogue. This automatic activation will continue for as long as there are order lines that can be written to the database via the action type.

Directly pressing the function key F2 'To order' serves no purpose if an order has not yet been created. We cannot store the data for an order line without compromising the integrity of the database. Function key F2 'To order' only becomes relevant when we wish to add order lines to an already created order.

In the method of working described above we see that for the input of data to a screen it is possible to stray from the structure as it is defined in the KISS model. The reason for this is that we want to input the data into the input screen in the quickest, easiest and most understandable way possible. To achieve this we must temporarily store the data before it can be written to the database. Wiping the input data from the temporary memory can be done by, for example, using the function key F9 'To stop' or by pressing the Escape key.

10.3.4 Dynamic screen dialogue

An extra dimension to the modelling of the input screen is given simply by the activation or displaying of function keys that are permitted. We can find out the permitted function keys from the object context tables, which are derived from the KISS models for an object type.

For example, there is no point, for the order line, in having the function keys for 'To cancel', 'To deliver' and 'To modify' for the period of time when there are as yet no items ordered. Pressing these function keys will only lead to an error message with a warning that an item must be ordered before the requested action can be carried out. The object context table supports this by the calling and activating of function keys.

The permitted function keys for the input functions can be represented by a table as shown in Table 10.1.

Table 10.1 Dynamic screen dialogue.

	Action			
Status	To order	To modify	To cancel	To deliver
Status=0	Yes	No	No	No
Ordered	No	Yes	Yes	Yes
Modified	No	Yes	Yes	Yes
Cancelled	No	No	No	No
Delivered	No	No	No	No

The table must be read as follows: when a object has a particular status, then we may or may not carry out the action.

By supporting the end user with a dynamic screen dialogue, the input screen has an improved semantic value for the end user. He is supported by the actions on an object which he is permitted to perform. This is effected by the object controller in the information architecture of the information system.

10.3.5 Menu

A menu is created by summarizing the object types that we have specified for an information system. We can place the object types one after another or we can organize them into groups. By selecting an object type we can immediately be taken to the appropriate input screen where we make use of the elementary input and information functions. The menu structure for our simple example can be seen in Figure 10.9.

Besides giving a summary of the object types, a menu structure can be extended to include output functions that, for example, produce reports or initiate batch functions not directly related to one input screen of an input function.

The main structure of the information architecture can also be presented in a menu according to the hierarchy of the object models. For object types that are existence-dependent on several object types we must choose a way of presenting the hierarchy. One way is to represent the object hierarchy graphically in the menu.

When we go from the menu straight to an input screen for Order line and we want to order items from an assortment, it is easy to see from the graphic menu structure showing the hierarchy that Order, Client and Item must exist before the action 'To order' may be performed (Figure 10.10). We must first define the Order with an order number and order date. The client must also exist. If the client does not yet exist, then the client's details must be input first.

Using an object existence hierarchy we can follow through the whole model to the stronger object types and activate messages for them by pressing local function keys. We subsequently move lower down to the weaker object types. We secondly send the values that were stored in a temporary memory to the action type of the object type in the form of messages. When all the status and dynamic constraints have been met, the change to the weak object type is effected.

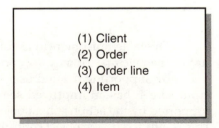

(1) Client
(2) Order
(3) Order line
(4) Item

Figure 10.9   Menu for an information system.

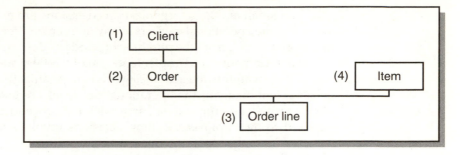

Figure 10.10 Screen with a graphical menu structure.

10.3.6 Screen attributes

In our discussion of input functions we have seen that we can present various attributes on a screen, and calculate them without the necessity of storing them in a database. We have also made a distinction between the attributes that are entered on the screen, the attributes used for screen manipulation and the attributes that are stored in the database to represent the status of an object. We give these attributes a status code to distinguish them from each other. We can even include the status code in the name of the attribute.

For the correct processing of screen attributes during the manipulation of attributes across diverse screens, we often need to create a temporary memory or parking place for the storage of the screen attributes. When particular items have been validated or checked for constraints and attribute values, we can use these screen attributes to update the database. This is done by sending messages to the action type where their content will be used by operations to update the objects in the database.

10.4 Decision functions

Decision functions are more complex to model graphically than the input and output functions. Decision functions are generally strongly regulating and coordinating by nature. They often carry out a great number of inspections on the attribute values of objects before a decision is made. To enable a decision function to be visualized we describe the decision process from the viewpoint of a manager. This makes sense because the manager is the person in the organization who makes decisions using a particularly rational approach. The scope of an organization is in a definite sense of less importance to the way in which decisions are made.

In small and large organizations decisions are made by management and the operational workers at any moment in time. These could be decisions ranging from the purchase of goods or the employment of staff to the determination and implementation of a total strategy.

To streamline the activities within an organization to a greater or lesser extent, many of the operational decisions are taken according to defined rules and procedures. These rules and procedures are constantly referred to by employees. Taking decisions involves making a choice between a number of alternatives.

The decisions in an organization are usually taken by managers, so we will describe how a manager generally makes a decision before we go on to showing how a decision function can be modelled. Using this description we indicate how a decision process can be formally represented.

10.4.1   The decision

We can divide the decision process of the manager into a number of elements. We can view them as a number of steps:

(1) The manager is confronted with an event in the real world for which an adequate reply must be given. The event is the external trigger that requires a decision to be made by the manager. The decision leads to the carrying out (or not) of a particular action, or to a request for more information;

(2) As a result of the question the manager looks for the data that will support him in making the decision. We call this the inspection of the status of objects in the relevant scope of the decision;

(3) When the manager knows what the status is, he can consider the conditions under which he will or will not take action. We call this the definition of the conditions and their associated actions;

(4) During his determination of the actions, the manager can also define the way in which and the intensity with which the action will be performed. We call this the definition of the parameters;

(5) Finally, the manager moves on to giving an order that an action be carried out or not. With this order it should also be specified how the action must be carried out, that is, with which action parameters. We call this the execution of the action. It should be noted that nowhere near all decisions lead to actual actions. A large number of decisions are made that result in a particular action not being executed.

The above description of the decision process shows the flow of decision making in the decision process. Decisions in an organization are often of a repetitive nature, which means that a manager in an identical situation may continually be asked to make a decision for which the result is predictable. We can increase the effectiveness of an organization by analysing and recording all the rules upon which the decision is made, in order to support the manager. The manager then does not need to go through the decision process for each identical situation. The logical result of this is that the way of working of the organization is further formalized.

To record the decision rules we make use of decision tables and function models for the decision function. We use the notation method of the KISS paradigm. When we described the input function we saw how a function model is created using action types and inspections. For the decision function the function models are further expanded to the making of decisions based on complex conditions. To explain this we describe the concepts of the decision table before going on to modelling the decision functions.

10.4.2 The decision table

The purpose of a decision table is to define the rules upon which a decision is based in a simple and understandable way. This is called the decision rule. A decision rule defines which action(s) will be executed when they meet certain conditions for a decision question. A condition is equal to the status of objects relevant to the decision-maker, as they are presented to the decision-maker.

The decision table is not a new technique. The first use of the decision table was in the 1950s, by General Electric and the Sutherland Company. Both organizations developed the decision table at the end of the 1950s, independently of each other, because they were having problems describing complex decision situations. The use of flow diagrams, reports and forms became so complex that they prevented the finding of a solution for describing the decision processes in the organization.

The power of the decision table is that it allows more or less complex decision situations to be mapped in a simple way. A decision table can then be used to support the specification of decision functions that are to be automated.

An example of a decision table is a table with which we answer the questions in a tax return, as shown in Table 10.2.

The simple decision table consists of a main structure with a table with two entry points (Figure 10.11):

- Question;
- Action.

Table 10.2   Example of a decision table for filling in a tax return.

	Table for what to fill in for taxes	1	2	3	4
Question	1. Were you married for all of 1992?	Yes	Yes	No	No
	2. Were you unmarried for all of 1992?	–	–	No	Yes
	3. Did you receive the highest income?	Yes	No	Yes	No
Action	1. Fill in 8 to 19 together	x			
	2. Fill in 20 to 26 individually	x	x	x	x
	3. Fill in 8 to 19 for the married period	x			
	4. Fill in 8 to 19 for the unmarried period	x			

All relevant relationships between the questions and the actions are represented by a double table to the right of the questions and actions. In this double table the possible outcomes for a question are related to the possible actions. Between the question and action sections we draw a double line to make them distinct.

In the question part of the decision table we fill in, for example, the values 'Yes', 'No' and '–'. We fill in a '–' when the answer to the question is not relevant for the action to be carried out. In the action part of the decision table we show with crosses which actions must be carried out when the combination of conditions is met.

The main structure of a decision table consists of four quadrants. These are:

- Quadrant I: the question
- Quadrant II: the possible values of object characteristics
- Quadrant III: the action values
- Quadrant IV: the actions

With the operational use of a decision table we ask the questions for which we expect answers. The answer to the question is found by measuring the characteristics of an object, in reality or by inspecting them in a database. The measured attribute value of the attribute type of an object is used in quadrant II to determine whether the object values meet the criteria of an object class.

In a further detailing of the decision table we see that besides using the Boolean values of 'Yes' and 'No', in the first example, it is also possible to use the values of the object. We do this by defining object classes and determining whether objects belong to the defined object classes.

In the decision table we see the individual decision rules as columns. The part of the column in quadrant II is called the object class entrance. The part in quadrant III is called the action entrance. (See Table 10.3.)

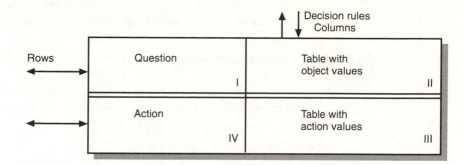

Figure 10.11 Main structure of a decision table.

Table 10.3 Decision rules in a decision table.

Table X	Column	99	= Decision rule
Question	Object class Entrance		
Action	Action Entrance		

A decision rule can also be read as an English sentence by including the word 'if' in the object class section and the word 'then' in the action section. In the action entrance (quadrant III) this is represented in a simple decision table by crosses when a combination of conditions has a particular value. The way we read a decision table is:

When a combination of values for 'object class(es)' is true, then action(s).

In this way we read from the questions in quadrant I via the dividing criteria for the object classes in quadrant II, following the action values in quadrant III to the permitted actions in quadrant IV. The rule for reading through the questions in the decision table is that they are read from top to bottom. The way in which a decision is made is greatly dependent on this. By defining the content of quadrant IV it is recommended that the actions be written in the order they are executed.

When composing the questions we can map the possible object classes and actions systematically. This allows the decision functions to be defined in a compact and clear manner in the form of formal decision rules in a decision table.

The column structure of a decision table also enables us to describe parallel decision rules in an understandable way.

10.4.3   Types of decision table

We can distinguish different types of decision table. The best-known way of differentiating the tables is by the entrance. We look at:

- The limited decision table;
- The extensive decision table;
- The mixed decision table.

After these we will briefly look at the open and closed tables.

The limited decision table

This table only makes use of the values Y (yes), N (no) or – (not relevant) to summarize the possible combinations of object classes. The limited decision table has only two alternative object classes to which an object can be assigned.

The '–' character is used if the question is not applicable or has no meaning given the existence of other questions. This is the case, for example, with implicit decisions that arise from other decisions based on questions answered previously. We saw this in the example of the tax table with the question 'Were you married for all of 1992?'. A Yes answer to this question directly excludes a person from being unmarried at the same time. A '–' character can always be turned into a Yes or No answer.

For the action entrance it is sufficient to use × (execute associated action) or – (do not execute associated action). The dash in the action section is usually left out.

The section at the top left consists of all the questions relevant for making the decision. When we create a limited decision table we must construct the questions in such a way that they can always be answered with a Yes, No or –. The total number of decision rules (N) in a limited decision table in which only Yes and No are used is defined by a formula according to the number of questions (Q).

The formula is: $N = 2^Q$.

The number of decision rules for two questions is $2^2 = 4$ combinations, for 3 questions $2^3 = 8$ combinations, for 4 questions $2^4 = 16$ combinations. Each combination represents a specific decision rule.

When a decision model also contains non-relevant values, we calculate the total number of decision rules by calculating for each column how many decision rules are included in it. The number of decision rules is $2^{(-)}$ per column.

If a column has no non-relevant situations then the total is $2^0 = 1$. The corresponding totals for one and two non-relevant situations, respectively, are:

1       $2^1 = 2$

2       $2^2 = 4$

The table for filling in the tax return is an example of a limited decision table.

The extensive decision table

A practical problem with the limited decision table is that with a large number of questions an exponentially larger number of columns is needed to describe all the possibilities. This quickly leads to very large decision tables. A solution to this problem is to incorporate directly in the table entrance the object classes to which the possible object occurrences belong. In an extensive decision table the object class to which an object belongs is no longer included in the question itself but directly shown in the object class entrance.

The same principle can be applied for the values of actions. These values can be directly included in the table entrance as action parameters. The values are then directly related to the combination of the various object classes to which an object can belong. In this way the decision table gains an expansion of its entrances partly because the entrance to the object classes is expanded. The expansion is also caused by adding to the entrances of the actions the values of the messages that need to be sent to the actions. The result is that the object class entrance can have more expanded values than just the Yes, No and – of the limited table.

Table 10.4   Example of a part of an extensive decision table.

Policy	1	2	3
Q1 Number km per year	< 15 000	15 000–20 000	> 20 000
Q2 Age of driver	< 25	< 25	< 25
Q3 Type of use	private	business	business
A1 Policy per thousand	$ 25	$ 40	$ 50
A2 Type of policy	A	B	C

In the extensive decision table we can find the attributes in the object class and action section in the form of figures, letters, words and other symbols.

To explain the extensive decision table we will use a part of the determination of a policy premium for car insurance. The questions we ask to determine the amount of the premium and the type of policy are with regard to the number of kilometres driven per year, the age of the driver and whether the car is intended for private or business use.

In Table 10.4 we see that there are three alternative policies. We can also see that the decision table is not complete. We will need to establish how many other age categories there are. These could be, for example:

25 years ≤ age < 65 years age ≥ 65 years

Similarly for the private/business use of the car there are a number of other possible alternatives.

The maximum number of combination alternatives in an extensive decision table is calculated by multiplying the number of possible object classes (C) for one condition by the number of possible object classes for the remaining conditions using the formula:

Combination alternatives = C * C * C....

In the example of the premium for car insurance, the number of combination alternatives with three object classes for the yearly kilometres driven, three object classes for the age of the driver and two object classes for the type of use is: $3 \times 3 \times 2 = 18$. We therefore add another 15 decision rules to the original decision table, to cater for all possible combinations between the object classes of the question. For further analysis of this decision table for the premium we will only use a small portion of the table.

An extensive decision table can always be converted into a limited decision table. We can do this by including a separate question for each object class to which an object can belong, and giving it Yes, No or – answers. The consequence of this is that it generally results in an enormous limited decision table.

The extensive table (Table 10.4) can easily be converted into a limited table (Table 10.5).

Table 10.5 Limited decision table.

Policy	1	2	3
Q1 Age < 25 years	Y	Y	Y
Q2 Use private (Y) business (N)	Y	N	N
Q3 < 15 000 km/year	Y	–	–
Q4 > 20 000 km/year	–	Y	–
Q5 > 20 000 km/year	–	–	Y
A1 Premium $25 and type A	×		
A2 Premium $40 and type B		×	
A3 Premium $50 and type C			×

**The mixed
decision table**

This table is a mixture of the two previous forms and has both limited and extensive entrances. Besides Yes, No and – we can use words, amounts, symbols and such like. The mixed decision table can also be converted to a limited table, just as for the extensive table.

**Use and application
of a decision table**

The decision tables seen so far make a limited distinction between object class, object and action with their attributes and associated attributes.

We can include further detail in decision tables by explicitly recording the objects to which the questions refer, what the actions are and on which object types the actions are executed. Within this framework we can also indicate how the attributes should be interpreted and what the valid domain is for the values (value range) of the relevant object characteristics.

The object characteristics are described by means of their attribute types. Each attribute type can have a unit in which it is measured, for example year, $ and km.

A limited decision table can also be presented by making a definite distinction between the various parts included in it. The limited decision table for the determination of the premium would then appear as shown in Table 10.6.

The table is based on a limited decision table and so we see that the question is composed of a number of different components. These are the object type, the attribute type, the object class, the unit and the attributes 'yes' and 'no' that define the validity of a decision rule.

Table 10.6   Detailed limited table.

Policy

Object type	Attribute type	Object class	Unit	1	2	3
Person	Age	< 25	year	Y	Y	Y
Car	Use	Private	Yes/No	Y	N	N
		Business	Yes/No	N	Y	Y
	Distance	< 15 000	km	Y	N	N
	driven	=< 20 000	km	–	Y	N
		> 20 000	km	–	–	Y

Action type	Action parameter	Attribute	Unit			
To take out	Premium	25	$	×		
policy	per thousand	40	$		×	
		50	$			×
Type		A		×		
		B			×	
		C				×

The actions are detailed by defining the attributes of the action parameters for each of possible decision rules. The message necessary to execute an action in the desired manner consists of a collection of action parameters sent to an action from one or more objects.

For extra clarity we show in the decision table for each action the object types for which the action parameters are valid. The main structure of a limited decision table can be represented with the table structure shown in Table 10.7.

Table 10.7   Detailed table.

Table name				1 2 3 4 5 6 x
Object type	Attribute type	Object class	Unit	Object class entrance
Action	Action parameters	Attribute	Unit	Action entrance

We can note that the differences between the object type, the object class and the action with their attribute types and action parameters are much better emphasized in the more detailed decision table shown in Table 10.6.

The expanded decision table (Table 10.8) is much more compact than the limited decision table. This is because the possible classes of objects are included in the object class entrance, and the values for the action parameters are separately specified in the action entrance.

Table 10.8   Detailed extensive table.

Policy					
Object type	Attribute type	Unit	1	2	3
Person	Age	year	< 25	< 25	< 25
Car	Use	Private	Yes	No	No
	Distance driven	km	< 15 000	≤ 20 000	> 20 000
Action type	Action parameter	Unit			
To take out policy	Premium/1000	$	25	40	50
	Sort		A	B	C

The general structure of an extensive decision table (Table 10.9) is now much more compact because the column with the descriptions of the object classes has been totally incorporated into the object class entrance.

Table 10.9 Detailed table.

Table name			1 2 3 4 5 6 x
Object type	Attribute type	Unit	Object class entrance
Action	Action parameters	Unit	Action entrance

Open and closed tables

Decision tables can also be divided according to accessability. Some decision procedures are too complex to be described in one table. If we were to attempt this, the resulting table would be difficult to read and understand. Similar to the idea of a subprocedure, the decision table can usually be split into a number of logical parts. For each logical part we can create a separate decision table. These tables are connected to each other by including references to the other tables. This results in a complete interrelationship between the connected decision tables. The way in which the tables are connected to each other indicates whether these are 'open' or 'closed'.

A table is open when it includes an action that refers to another table without the other table referring back to the original table. We then use the word 'open' in the heading of the table.

A table is closed when another table refers back to a subsequent action in the original table. We either include the word 'closed' in the heading of the table, or we add an extra last action to the table 'reference back to the original table'.

Examples of open and closed decision tables are shown in Table 10.10.

10.4.4 Methods for creating decision tables

We can make use of two different methods for creating a decision table. These are the direct and the indirect method.

The direct method is used when the decision situation is relatively simple and concise. When the decision situation is not so simple and concise, the risk of making mistakes with the direct method is too great. In this case we prefer to use the indirect method.

The indirect method, as the name suggests, produces a decision table less quickly. However the table can be easily validated and checked as it is being built. This immensely reduces the chance of making mistakes.

With the direct method the definitive decision table is built in one go. This will often be done in an interview directly with the manager or

Table 10.10   Example of open and closed decisions.

Table 1 (open)	1	2	3	4
Question 1	Y	Y	Y	N
Question 2	Y	Y	N	–
Question 3	Y	N	–	–
Action 1	×			×
Action 2	×	×		
Go to table 2	×		×	
Go to table 3	×	×	×	×

Table 2 (closed)	1	2	3	4
Question 42	Y	Y	N	N
Question 52	Y	N	Y	N
Action 32	×	×		
Action 42			×	
Action 52		×		
Go back to	×	×	×	×

Table 3 (open)	1	2	3	4
Question 63	Y	Y	Y	N
Question 73	Y	Y	N	–
Question 83	Y	N	–	–
Action 63	×			×
Action 73	×	×		
Go to table 1	×	×	×	×

someone else who has total knowledge of the conditions under which a particular action is taken.

The direct method can be used when the decision situation is relatively simple with a restricted number of questions (3–4) and many mutually exclusive actions. In more complex decision situations the direct method very quickly becomes cluttered and does not consistently produce correct results. In such situations the indirect method is preferable.

The indirect method

For complex situations we use the indirect method, whereby we follow a number of steps to create a complete decision table that consists exclusively of single decision rules. In the second instance all the impossible and irrelevant combinations are eliminated. This is done by combining the irrelevant decision rules with the situations that are possible. We further reduce the table in a stepwise manner by combining single decision rules. The final reduction takes place by indicating which questions are irrelevant for a decision table.

The method of working of the indirect method for the limited decision table is discussed in a number of sequential steps.

Step 1 – Textual description of the decision
To be able to build a decision table we must know what the decision situation looks like. We use a salary administration as an example. Using interviews with the people responsible we have written a textual description of a decision situation. The purpose of the textual description is to record the questions and conditions that form the foundation upon which the action is taken or not taken.

Example
We must build a decision table for the salary administration to define the measures to be taken, which are verbally described as follows:

> In our business the factory workers are paid overtime when they have worked more than 40 hours per week and the general manager has confirmed this overtime in writing. When factory workers have worked more than 45 hours, they are given an extra bonus. Young workers are not allowed to work overtime and are therefore not eligible for overtime or bonus pay.

In the textual description we had for the specification of an information architecture with actions and objects, we focused particularly on the 'what' of the organization. In the textual description above we have looked more at the 'how' of a decision process. It is then also logical that we recognize actions and objects in the textual description that were previously modelled with KISS models and object-interaction models. By the addition of decision functions we specify how we can utilize the previously specified basic structure of the information system.

Step 2 – Question/ action specification
Following the description of the decision situation we move on to the creation of a question/action specification. From the text, five relevant questions are apparent. We will name them Q1 to Q5.

Q1	Is the employee a factory worker?	Yes/No
Q2	Is the employee a young worker?	Yes/No
Q3	Has the employee worked more than 40 hours per week?	Yes/No
Q4	Has the employee worked more than 45 hours?	Yes/No
Q5	Has the overtime been confirmed in writing?	Yes/No

Then we write down the decisions for the possible actions that can result from the measure taken:

A1   Pay the overtime
A2   Pay the extra bonus
A3   Pay no overtime and/or bonus

The questions and actions listed above are not as yet very precise and will become more detailed in the following steps.

Step 3 – Further detailing of the questions

The questions listed can all be answered with Yes or No. So we do not need to modify the questions on this point. We do, however, need to specify which object types, attribute types and object classes with their associated units are involved in each question. The purpose is to specify the question as completely and precisely as possible.

The result of reviewing each question can be seen in Table 10.11.

In the table we can see that the age of young workers can be more exactly defined as younger than 18 years. The object class then becomes '< 18' with the associated unit 'years'.

The overview of the object types with the accompanying object classes is:

Object type	Object classes
Person	Employee; not employee
Person	Younger than 18 years; 18 years or older
Person	=< 40 hours worked; > 45 hours worked; between 40 and 45 hours worked
Overtime	Confirmed; not confirmed

Table 10.11 Result of further detailing the questions.

Object type	Attribute type	Object class	Unit
Person	Employee	Worker	Yes/No
	Age	Young	Yes/No
	Hours worked	> 40	hour
	Hours worked	> 45	hour
Overtime hours	Confirmed	Written	Yes/No

By reviewing the object classes we see that all the object classes are covered by the questions.

Step 4 – Further detailing of the actions

Just as for the questions, we also need to further analyse the actions to see what actually happens when it has been decided to carry out a particular action. We need to specify the attribute value and unit for the action parameter and on which object type the action is carried out (Table 10.12).

Table 10.12 Further detailing the actions.

Action	Action parameter	Attribute	Unit
To pay overtime	Overtime	Amount	$
	Extra bonus	Amount	$
Pay no overtime			

To calculate the amount that is paid out as a bonus, we can use a formula in the decision function. This could be based, for example, on 20% for the first 5 overtime hours and 30% for any further overtime hours. The calculation of the bonus amount would be:

Bonus := $(1+0.20) \times$ No. overtime hours $\times$ hourly rate
Extra bonus := $(1+0.30) \times$ No. extra overtime hours $\times$ hourly rate

The calculated bonus amount can be sent as a value for the action parameter to the action.

A further analysis and detailing of the actions and accompanying action parameters often leads to the definition of a number of formulas for calculating the action parameter values. It is important to specify them as accurately as possible for the decision function.

Step 5 – Create decision table

Before we create the decision table, we determine the number of decision rules that will result from the number of questions that can be answered with Yes or No. We have five questions in our example, so we end up with a total of:

$2 \times 2 \times 2 \times 2 \times 2 = 32$ combinations (2^5 combinations).

Each combination represents one situation that could theoretically arise. The combination can thus be regarded as a decision rule for the execution of an action.

With the questions and actions above we obtain Table 10.13.

In the decision table we read that only older factory workers with written confirmation and after they have worked more than 40 hours will receive payment for overtime. All factory workers who have written confirmation and have worked more than five hours of overtime will receive an additional bonus.

Table 10.13 Limited decision table.

Overtime table									Decision rules																						
	1	2	3	4	5	6	7	8	9	10	11	12	13	14	15	16	17	18	19	20	21	22	23	24	25	26	27	28	29	30	31	32
Q1	Y	Y	Y	Y	Y	Y	Y	Y	Y	Y	Y	Y	Y	Y	Y	Y	Y	N	N	N	N	N	N	N	N	N	N	N	N	N	N	N
Q2	Y	Y	Y	Y	Y	Y	Y	Y	N	N	N	N	N	N	N	N	Y	Y	Y	Y	Y	Y	Y	Y	N	N	N	N	N	N	N	N
Q3	Y	Y	Y	Y	N	N	N	N	Y	Y	Y	Y	N	N	N	N	Y	Y	Y	Y	N	N	N	N	Y	Y	Y	Y	N	N	N	N
Q4	Y	Y	N	N	Y	Y	N	N	Y	Y	N	N	Y	Y	N	N	Y	Y	N	N	Y	Y	N	N	Y	Y	N	N	Y	Y	N	N
Q5	Y	N	Y	N	Y	N	Y	N	Y	N	Y	N	Y	N	Y	N	Y	N	Y	N	Y	N	Y	N	Y	N	Y	N	Y	N	Y	N
A1													×		×																	
A2													×																			
A3	×	×	×	×	×	×	×	×			×			×	×	×	×	×	×	×	×	×	×	×	×	×	×	×	×	×	×	×

Step 6 –
Simplification of
the table

We can ascertain very quickly that Table 10.13 can be simplified much. We use a number of rules to simplify decision tables.

For each decision rule we check which simple decision rules can be converted into combined rules. The reduction of the number of decision rules occurs by eliminating the simple rules whose action sections are the same. These simple rules may also have at most one row that is different in the condition section, that is, that contains a Y rather than an N.

After this has been done we can further simplify the table by determining which conditions for a particular answer automatically result in a fixed answer to another question. The answer to this second question is then redundant, so we place a – in the column.

The decision table can be simplified by the following points:

- Columns 17–32 result in action 3: no payment.
  Q1 is the deciding factor: if Q1 = N then A3 results regardless of the values of Q2 to Q5. The values of Q2 to Q5 are irrelevant and can be replaced with –.
- Columns 1–8 result in action 3: no payment.
  The combination Q1 = Y and Q2 = Y is the deciding factor. The values of Q3–Q5 are irrelevant and can be replaced with –.
- Columns 13–16 result in action 3: no payment.
  The combination Q1 = Y, Q2 = N and Q3 = N is the deciding factor. The values for Q4 and Q5 are irrelevant and can be replaced with –.

The table now looks as shown in Table 10.14.

The decision table can be even more simplified into a shortened table by throwing away all double columns (Table 10.15).

- We show only column 17 of columns 17–32.
- We show only column 1 of columns 1–8.
- We show only column 13 of columns 13–16.

Table 10.14   Decision table.

Overtime table																Decision rules															
	1	2	3	4	5	6	7	8	9	10	11	12	13	14	15	16	17	18	19	20	21	22	23	24	25	26	27	28	29	30	31	32
Q1	Y	Y	Y	Y	Y	Y	Y	Y	Y	Y	Y	Y	Y	Y	Y	Y	N	N	N	N	N	N	N	N	N	N	N	N	N	N	N	N
Q2	Y	Y	Y	Y	Y	Y	Y	Y	N	N	N	N	N	N	N	N	–	–	–	–	–	–	–	–	–	–	–	–	–	–	–	–
Q3	–	–	–	–	–	–	–	–	Y	Y	Y	Y	N	N	N	N	–	–	–	–	–	–	–	–	–	–	–	–	–	–	–	–
Q4	–	–	–	–	–	–	–	–	Y	Y	N	N	–	–	–	–	–	–	–	–	–	–	–	–	–	–	–	–	–	–	–	–
Q5	–	–	–	–	–	–	–	–	Y	N	Y	N	–	–	–	–	–	–	–	–	–	–	–	–	–	–	–	–	–	–	–	–
A1									×	×																						
A2									×																							
A3	×	×	×	×	×	×	×	×			×		×	×	×	×	×	×	×	×	×	×	×	×	×	×	×	×	×	×	×	×

Table 10.15 Shortened decision table after elimination of double colums.

Overtime table		1	9	10	11	12	13	17
Q1	Factory worker?	Y	Y	Y	Y	Y	Y	N
Q2	Young worker?	Y	N	N	N	N	N	–
Q3	Worked more than 40 hours per week?	–	Y	Y	Y	Y	N	–
Q4	Worked more than 45 hours?	–	Y	N	N	N	–	–
Q5	Written confirmation present?	–	Y	N	Y	N	–	–
A1	Payment of overtime		×		×			
A2	Payment of extra bonus		×					
A3	No payment of overtime/bonus	×		×		×	×	×

To check that the table is still accurate we perform several tests.

Step 7 – Check on the decision table   With the creation and subsequent simplification of a decision table not everything always goes right. It could happen that a particular situation is overlooked or that a careless mistake is made. To check on this we perform a number of tests. These are:

- Test for conflict;
- Test for redundancy;
- Test for completeness.

Test for conflict   If two columns (decision rules) have the same combination of Ys and Ns and result in different actions, we have a conflict. The reverse, that different decision rules lead to the same action, of course does not apply.

Test for redundancy   When two decision rules display the same combination of Ys and Ns and lead to the same action, we have redundancy.

Test for completeness   The test for completeness serves to check whether all the possible decision rules have in fact been discovered. To test completeness we follow this procedure:

(1) Count the number of dashes in one decision rule;
(2) Calculate for each decision rule the number of combinations by exponentiating 2 to the power of the number of dashes;
(3) Add the results of all decision rules together;
(4) Check this against the theoretical number of alternatives using the number of possible conditions.

For the shortened decision table we have created we have:

Column 1 : 3 dashes, $2^3 = 8$
Column 9 : 0 dashes, $2^0 = 1$

$$
\begin{aligned}
\text{Column 10}: &\quad \text{0 dashes,} &\quad 2^0 &= 1\\
\text{Column 11}: &\quad \text{0 dashes,} &\quad 2^0 &= 1\\
\text{Column 12}: &\quad \text{0 dashes,} &\quad 2^0 &= 1\\
\text{Column 13}: &\quad \text{2 dashes,} &\quad 2^2 &= 4\\
\text{Column 17}: &\quad \text{4 dashes,} &\quad 2^4 &= 16\\
&& &\overline{32}
\end{aligned}
$$

The number of possible combinations of five conditions that can each have values of Y or N is $2^5 = 32$.

Each shortened decision table must be checked using these three tests. The tests for conflict and redundancy work in the same way for the extensive and mixed decision tables as for the limited table.

10.4.5   Extensive and mixed decision tables

The test for completeness with an extensive or mixed decision table uses a slightly different calculation. This is:

(1)   Determine the number of values a condition can have;

(2)   When a condition in a column has a defined value, we use 1 in the calculation;

(3)   When a condition in a column is irrelevant and this is shown by a –, we use the number of possible values the condition can have in the calculation;

(4)   Calculate for each column the number of combinations by multiplying the number of alternatives;

(5)   Calculate the total number of combination alternatives by adding up the totals for each individual column;

(6)   Compare this with the calculated theoretical number of combination alternatives.

Finally, there are a number of general recommendations for creating decision tables:

- Each decision rule must be unique in the decision table;

- The questions and actions must be noted in the order in which they are carried out;

- The tables must not be too big; guidelines would be 4–7 conditions, 12–16 decision rules and 15–20 actions;

- The name of the table must be written in the table header.

Summary for the creation of a decision table

When we create a decision table we can make use of a number of rules. In practice the decision table will be created on the basis of a piece of text that is written, for example, after an interview has taken place. The decision table is then preferably created by following a number of steps:

Step 1 – Textual description of the decision:
Describe in text the questions and conditions upon which it is decided to carry out or not carry out an action.

Step 2 – Question/action specification:
Write down the questions and actions that are included in the textual description of the decision situation.

Step 3 – Further detailing of the questions:
Write the question in the form of:

> object type, attribute type, object class and unit

Define for which characteristics of objects a decision must be made.

Step 4 – Further detailing of the actions:
Describe the decision in the form of an action as:

> object type, action, action parameter, attribute and unit

Write down upon which object type the action must take place with a specified intensity defined by the values of the action parameters.

Step 5 – Create decision table:
Place the questions with all the decision rules and the associated actions in the entrances to the decision table.

Step 6 – Simplification of the table:
Check for duplication and/or complementary occurrences in the decision rules and/or actions.

Step 7 – Check on the decision table:
Check the resulting table for:
(1) conflict;
(2) redundancy;
(3) completeness.

10.4.6   Advantages and characteristics of the decision table

We now give a summary of a number of characteristics and advantages of the decision table:

(1) The decision table makes it possible to describe a decision situation with parallel decision rules;

(2) The consistency, completeness and absence of redundancy can be analysed in a formal manner;

(3) A decision table provides a compact and simple way of imagining the decision situation, even when this situation is complex;

(4) A decision table is simple in design and in use, and is simple and flexible to modify for changes;

(5) The decision table provides a good basis for communicating decision processes to all layers in the organization;

(6) The decision table promotes the modular building of decision functions. A decision table allows for a shorter processing time of programs and less space in memory;

(7) The coding of the decision function can take place by a direct transformation of the decision table into a programming environment.

10.5   The decision model for a decision function

To graphically represent the decision function we make use of the drawing conventions of the KISS paradigm for object orientation. In the KISS paradigm we represent functions with a circle. A function can send and receive messages, control actions and inspect objects. The distinguishing feature of the decision function is that it serves to make decisions based on a number of questions. Earlier in this chapter we saw how this decision process is depicted by a decision table.

To increase our insight into the modelling of decision functions we will look at the way in which a decision table can be converted into a decision model. To do this we will go back once more to the short example of the determination of the premium for an insurance policy (Table 10.16).

Table 10.16   Decision table for a policy.

Policy			1	2	3
Object type	Attribute type	Unit	Object class	Object class	Object class
Person	Age	year	< 25	< 25	< 25
Car	Use	Private	Yes	No	No
	Distance driven	km	< 15 000	≤ 20 000	> 20 000
Action type	Action parameter	Unit	Attribute type	Attribute type	Attribute type
To take out	Premium	$ 1000	25	40	50
policy	Type	character	A	B	C

We convert a decision table to a decision model by regarding each question in the decision function as an independent function within the decision process. A message is sent to each subsequent function containing the attribute values of the answers to the questions that have already been answered. When we follow a different path in a decision model the resulting answer is also different. We explain this further using the insurance example. We show the decision function graphically in a decision model (Figure 10.12).

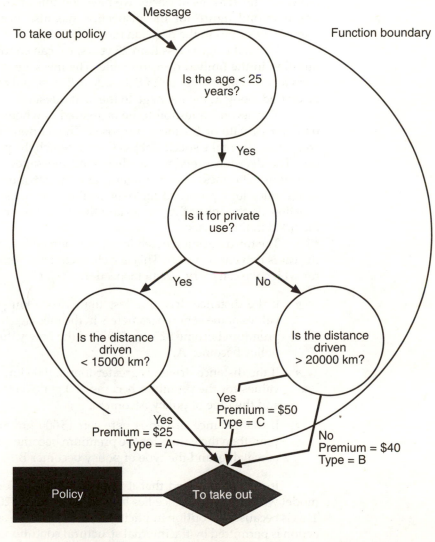

Figure 10.12   Function model for taking out a policy.

The decision model shows that the table gets a message with a request for the policy to be taken out. In the decision model this is shown by a message that comes from outside.

The first question in the decision table that must be answered is whether or not the person's age is less than 25 years. For this the function inspects the value of the object characteristic Age. This could be done, for example, by inspecting the input value on the input screen, or by requesting the value of Age in the person's file. We can show this by a dotted arrow between the object type Person and the decision function. However, for reasons of clarity we have left this arrow off the diagram. The diamond figure for the inspection has also been left off for the internal messages in the decision model.

When the age is less than 25 years, we can continue with the next question in the limited decision table. The message is represented by a solid arrow with the value 'YES' beside it. The actual age of a person can be carried along in the message to the next question.

The second question to be answered is whether the car is to be used for private or business purposes. This is done by inspecting the characteristics of the specific object Car for which the policy is to be taken out. The decision function can then send messages to the subsequent questions. The messages can again take the attributes of the answers to the questions posed so far over to the next question in a decision function. So the age of the person and the type of use of the car would be included in the message.

The third question noted in the decision table is about the distance the car is driven each year. This is a characteristic of the object type Car, for which we can carry out an inspection on Car.

- If the distance driven is less than 15 000 km per year, then the values of the action parameters in the message to the action for the premium become $25 per $1000 of the new value, and the type of policy becomes A.
- If the distance driven is greater than 20 000 km per year, then the values for the premium become $50 per $1000 of the new value, and the type of policy becomes C.
- If the distance driven is between 15 000 km and 20 000 km per year, then the values for the premium become $40 per $1000 of the new value, and the type of policy becomes B.

It should be noted that it is not explicitly asked in the function model whether the distance lies between 15 000 and 20 000 km per year. This is because this option implicitly follows from the answers. When the action is permitted by the internal structural conditions of the object type Policy, the action parameters are used to update the status of the policy by using the action parameters in the operations. The action parameters do not need to be restricted to the values of Premium and Type but can also make use of the values carried through from previous decision functions. In the policy example this would be the values for Age and Type of use.

It should be noted that the result of the decision 'YES' or 'NO' can also be a value that is carried along inside the function.

The final result of the decision function is that there are three alternatives that can be sent as a message to the action 'To take out'.

10.5.1   The influence of the order of questions on a decision model

To show how a decision model changes its visual representation by changing the order of the questions, we have created the decision table for taking out a policy, but with the questions in a different order (Table 10.17).

Table 10.17   Decision table with the questions in a different order.

Policy			1	2	3
Object type	Attribute type	Unit	Object class	Object class	Object class
Car	Distance driven	km	< 15 000	= < 20 000	> 20 000
Person	Age	year	< 25	< 25	< 25
Car	Use	Private	Yes	No	No
Action type	Action parameter	Unit	Attribute value	Attribute value	Attribute value
To take out	Premium/1000	$	25	40	50
policy	Type	character	A	B	C

When we compare the new decision table for the function of taking out a policy with the previous table, we see that the tables are almost identical: there have only been two questions switched. The influence on the graphical image of the decision model is, however, much more definite (Figure 10.13). In this decision model, too, we have left out all the inspections on object values because they negatively influence our overview of the decision model.

The final result of the decision model with a different ordering of questions is completely identical to the result of the previous decision model. In the second decision model the same question has in fact been included a greater number of times. With the question sequence in the second alternative the decision model cannot be further simplified, because the result of a previous decision determines the final values of the action parameters that are sent to the action. It can be seen that the order of the questions defines the history of decisions that have been made. This history is also implicitly locked into a shortened decision table by the ordering of the questions. The preference is therefore to use decision tables instead of decision functions.

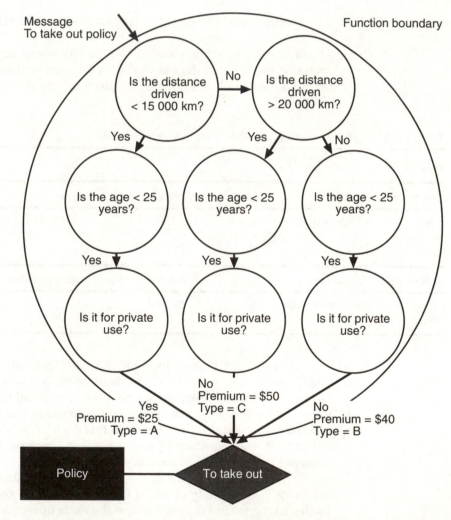

Figure 10.13   Alternative decision model with a different ordering of questions.

10.5.2   Optimizing a decision function

Often during the designing of information systems the question of how a decision function can be carried out in the optimal manner is asked. This question can be reformed into the question of how we can make a decision in a defined problem situation in the quickest and most direct way. To be able to give an answer to this we will look further at the structure of the decision function itself, by using a simple example.

Example

A billing department must calculate discounts for customers' bills for the delivery of items. The items have a variable discount percentage that is dependent on the quantity purchased. The table for the discount percentages is shown in Table 10.18.

Table 10.18   Discount percentage.

No. of items purchased	Discount percentage	Class
1–4	2%	A
5–9	3%	B
10–24	4%	C
25–49	5%	D
50–99	6%	E
≥ 100	7%	F

Two possible alternatives are represented in Figures 10.14 and 10.15.

We can easily read from the function that there are five questions to be answered before we know whether the purchased quantity is between 50 and 99 or that it is greater than or equal to 100.

We only have a smaller number of questions when we choose a different ordering of the questions. A decision function that starts from the middle of the total range of possibilities will result in a smaller number of questions. A decision function that starts from the beginning or end of the range will result in a greater number of questions. We illustrate this alternative with a second decision model for the same decision function.

From the model in Figure 10.15 we see that only three sequential decisions are needed to determine whether the quantity lies between 50 and 99 or is greater than or equal to 100.

To show the difference in figures, we place the total number of decisions for the two alternative functions beside each other in a table (Table 10.19). The situation where from one decision a 'Yes' arrow and a 'No' arrow go to an action is regarded as one decision.

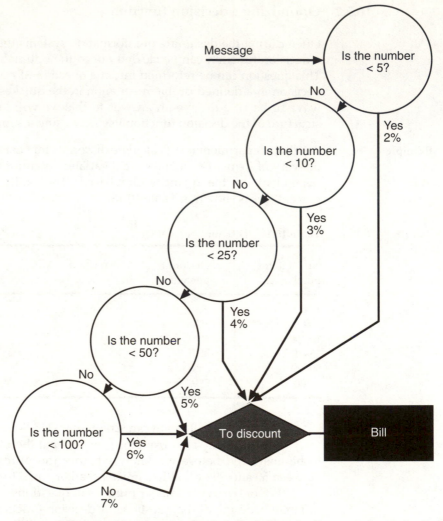

Figure 10.14   Decision function for the calculation of a discount: alternative I.

Table 10.19   Number of decisions required for each alternative.

No. of items purchased	Discount percentage	Alternative I	Alternative II
1–4	2%	1	3
5–9	3%	2	–
10–24	4%	3	2
25–49	5%	4	2
50–99	6%	5	3
≥ 100	7%	–	–
	Total	15	10

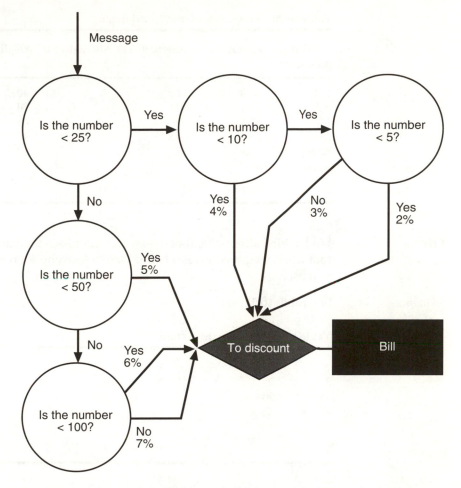

Figure 10.15   Decision function model for the calculation of a discount:
alternative II.

From the table we read that for alternative I the total number of
decisions is 15, while for alternative II it is 10: a difference of 5 to the
advantage of alternative II.

For the previous decision function we still need to indicate the
frequency of purchased items to obtain a correct picture of the best
construction of the function (Table 10.20).

In the calculation we must use the total of the frequencies as the
weighted number for the possibilities with which the decision is
concerned. Having made the calculation we can see from the total that
alternative I is better than alternative II.

Table 10.20   Frequency of purchased items.

No. of items purchased	Frequency	Alternative I	Alternative II	Weighted I	Weighted II
1–4	40%	1	3	40	195
5–9	25%	2	–	50	–
10–24	15%	3	2	45	30
25–49	10%	4	2	40	20
50–99	5%	5	3	50	30
≥ 100	0%	–	–	–	–
	Total	15	10	225	275

Exercise: Find a third alternative that uses fewer questions than alternative II, and that when weighted gives a better result. Also check on which algorithm you used.

Solution: See Table 10.21.

Table 10.21   Solution to exercise.

1	< 10	Y	Y	N	N	N	N
2	< 5	Y	N	N	N	N	N
3	< 50	–	–	Y	Y	N	N
4	< 25	–	–	Y	N	N	N
5	< 10	–	–	–	–	Y	N
1	%	2	3	4	5	6	7

10.6   Time-dependent functions

The time dimension, along with the action and attribute dimensions, is one of the three dimensions of an object that we need to specify further. We use natural language as the basis for the specification of the time dimension.

By using our natural language we can easily describe when an action will take place, is taking place or has taken place. The time aspects of the past, present and future are implemented in our natural language by the tenses of the verb.

The time dimension is added to information systems with an attribute type that says when the action will be carried out, is carried out or was carried out. To be able to record the temporary data of objects it will in any case be necessary to indicate the time that an action caused a change to the object. Only when this has been done are we in a position to secure the elementary aspects of a temporary recording of data.

The concept of time can be divided into the following both in the real world and in an information system:

- The present;
- The past;
- The future.

The time in the real world can be regarded as a 'frame' that views a constant stream of changes. The changes are only caused by actions that are executed now, in the present. The past is the residue of all the actions that are executed now, in the present. The future is the certainty that actions will still be executed and that changes will continue to happen. The certainty of the future is that things change and that nothing stays the same!

In this changing world, information systems must provide support for the end user by producing the correct information to enable him to make correct decisions. The time dimension must therefore be an integral part of the information system. The elements in which time aspects are present are:

- History;
- Error correction;
- Planning functions.

We shall discuss these one at a time.

10.6.1   History

When we make decisions it is often more important to know what the progress of changes has been over a particular period of time than it is to get an absolute value for a single momentary situation. The progress of changes in relation to the executed actions provides an insight into the way actions eventually cause specific effects on objects. The historical statuses of objects thus form the substance of the progression of time.

To bring together the history we make use of two principles. These are:

(1) *Record the status*. Define the history by bringing together all the statuses of an object from the past. This means that the progress of the status of an object must be recorded in a temporary database. In a relational database, for example, we add a new record to the

table for each new status of the object. The record is then no longer uniquely identified by the identifier of the object. In addition to the identifier we now include the time in the key. The record, of course, contains the status of an object from the moment in time an action took place until the time that the next action caused a change of status.

(2) *Reconstruct the actions.* Reconstruct the past by using the actions that were executed on the object types. To do this we must store the messages that were accepted by an action type in a separate file. We need to know what the actual status of the objects is. And we need to know how the stored messages can be replayed with inverse operations starting from the current status of the database as our base.

The complexity of the second method is greater than the first method. This is because we need to define the inverse operations for the total information architecture. Our discussion will therefore continue with the first method.

We base the building of the history on the information architecture. We add a time-dependent attribute type to identify the object uniquely in combination with the object identifier. This attribute type is added to all the files created from the information architecture and for which we wish to update and inquire on historical data. For each weak object type and gerund we must also include the time dimension of all the strong object types, in order to be able to represent the progress of their status over time.

To further explain how we work with the concept of time, we will use the example where cash is deposited into a client's account at a cash drawer.

Example of client's account
'To deposit' is an action type that takes place on Account and Cash Drawer. It holds true for Account that at one moment in time it is Opened. After the account has been Opened we can record the status of Account by recording all new statuses of Account in a temporary database. The progression of the actions that have taken place on an Account with number 123456 could look like this:

Account ID	Action type	ActionDate	AccountBalance
123456	To open	21 January	$0
123456	To deposit	21 January	$200
123456	To deposit	23 January	$1200
123456	To withdraw	28 January	$800

123456	To deposit	31 January	$2000
123456	To withdraw	5 February	$1000
123456	To deposit	10 February	$3000
123456	To close	13 February	$0

We can see from this progression, written in table form, that the status of an object cannot be uniquely identified with the key 'Account ID, ActionDate'. The first two actions in the list would then have the same key value. This is because the time indication in days is not specific enough. We could solve this by adding a sequence number to each identical date, or by giving the key a continually increasing sequence number. The progress of the account balance for account 123456 can also be graphically represented (Figure 10.16).

We also add to the table for the above the attribute value of the action controller (AC), which shows the temporary status of an object within the KISS model for the object type. We will use the KISS model for Account with the action controllers from Figure 10.17.

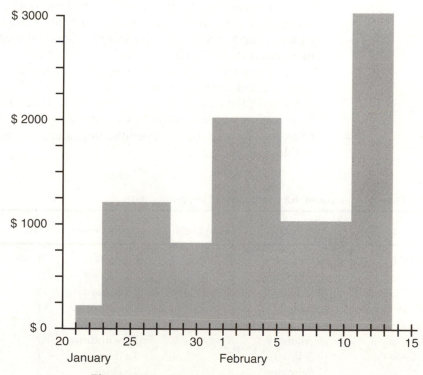

Figure 10.16 Progression of AccountBalance.

KISS model for Account

The simplified action controllers are as follows:

AC	Action type	Operation
00	To open	AC:= 01
01	To withdraw	AC:= 01
	To deposit	AC:= 01
	To close	AC:= 02
02	–	

Object context table Account

AC	Action type	Action controller		
		00	01	02
01	To open	True	False	False
	To deposit	False	True	False
	To withdraw	False	True	False
02	To close	False	True	False

The table for Account with the attribute values for account 123456 becomes as shown in Table 10.22, with the action name, the action controller and an absolute sequence number. In the table the key is made up of Account ID, ActionDate and SequenceNr.

The increase and decrease of the AccountBalance is caused by the encapsulated operations of the action types 'To deposit' and 'To withdraw'. For reasons of completeness we add to the table the attribute type ActionAmount, which shows the amount by which the balance changes with an action of opening, depositing, withdrawing or closing (Table 10.23).

Table 10.22 'Account' for the storage of temporary data.

Account ID	ActionDate	SequenceNo.	ActionName	AC	AccountBalance
123456	21 January	1	To open	1	$0
123456	21 January	2	To deposit	1	$200
123456	23 January	3	To deposit	1	$1200
123456	28 January	4	To withdraw	1	$800
123456	31 January	5	To deposit	1	$2000
123456	5 February	6	To withdraw	1	$1000
123456	10 February	7	To deposit	1	$3000
123456	13 February	8	To close	2	$0

Table 10.23   The addition of ActionAmount.

Account ID	ActionDate	SequenceNo.	ActionName	AC	AccountBalance	ActionAmount
123456	21 January	1	To open	1	$0	$0
123456	21 January	2	To deposit	1	$200	$200
123456	23 January	3	To deposit	1	$1200	$1000
123456	28 January	4	To withdraw	1	$800	$400
123456	31 January	5	To deposit	1	$2000	$1200
123456	5 February	6	To withdraw	1	$1000	$1000
123456	10 February	7	To deposit	1	$3000	$2000
123456	13 February	8	To close	2	$0	$3000

The action controller in the table is used by the object in the action context table to determine whether a subsequent action type may be executed according to the general structure of the KISS model for the object type (Figure 10.17). According to the action context table, the action type 'To open', for example, may no longer be executed after the instantiation of account 123456 on 21 January. We are also not permitted 'To deposit' any more money into account 123456 after 13 February. These actions are prevented by the action context table because an action 'To close' has already been executed which has set the action controller to the value '2'.

10.6.2   Delayed provision of action data

In the situation above we have assumed that the time the action was executed in the real world is the same or close enough to the time the attribute values of the action were processed in the information system. There are other situations where we must take account of a difference between the time that the action occurred and the time that the action data was provided to the information system to be processed. To show this we have included an extra attribute type in the table for the date that the actions were processed.

To further explain the way of working, we will expand the example with a new action for which the processing date is later than the action date (Table 10.24).

The bank uses a computer system to process their administration with some delay. In the table we have noted the times in the column ProcessDate that the forms for opening, depositing, withdrawing and closing were given to a data-entry person, who then input them into the information system. The action dates themselves can of course be very different from the processing dates of the action type data. The order of processing is not automatically the same as the order in which the actions were executed in reality.

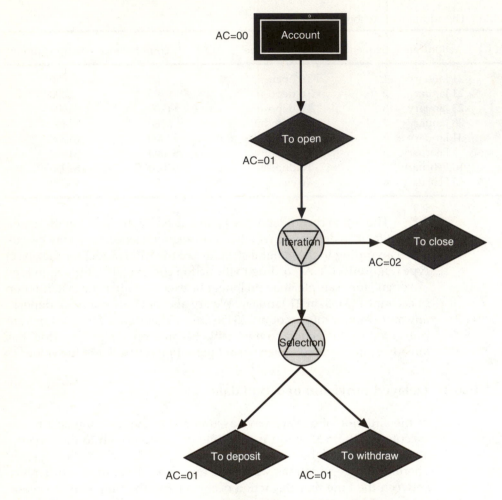

Figure 10.17   KISS model for Account.

Table 10.24   Delayed processing of actions.

Account ID	ActionDate	SequenceNo.	ProcessDate	ActionName	AC	AccountBalance	ActionAmount
123456	21 January	1	25 January	To open	1	$0	$0
123456	21 January	2	27 January	To deposit	1	$200	$200
123456	23 January	3	26 January	To deposit	1	$1200	$1000
123456	28 January	4	28 January	To withdraw	1	$800	$400
123456	31 January	5	7 February	To deposit	1	$2000	$1200
123456	5 February	6	6 February	To withdraw	1	$1000	$1000
123456	10 February	7	15 February	To deposit	1	$3000	$2000
123456	13 February	8	13 February	To close	2	$0	$3000

When we rebuild the table in the order that the attributes of actions were provided to the system and processed, we end up with Table 10.25. The attributes of the actions are provided to the information system in the order of the processing date. The accumulation of historical data then will also be in the order of the provided messages.

Table 10.25   Table in the order of processing date.

Account ID	ActionDate	SequenceNo.	ProcessDate	ActionName	AC	AccountBalance	ActionAmount
123456	21 January	1	25 January	To open	1	$0	$0
123456	23 January	2	26 January	To deposit	1	$1000	$1000
123456	21 January	3	27 January	To deposit	1	$1200	$200
123456	28 January	4	28 January	To withdraw	1	$800	$400
123456	5 February	5	6 February	To withdraw	1	($200)	$1000
123456	31 January	6	7 February	To deposit	1	$1000	$1200
123456	13 February	7	13 February	To close	2	$0	$1000
123456	10 February	8	15 February	To deposit	1	$2000	$2000

In Table 10.25, we see that after the action controller has acquired the value '2', meaning that no subsequent actions may be executed, an action is executed regardless. This is the action 'To deposit' executed on 10 February, for which the data was provided on 15 February. This is after the time that the data for 'To close' (the account) was provided. When the account was closed on 13 February the final balance of $1000 was paid out to the client.

The explanation given for the late supply of the data for 'To deposit' is that there was a delay in the internal mail caused by sickness.

Despite this plausible explanation it is still preferable that the client is given the final balance when he closes his account, which is his by right. At this point there is $2000 which has not been paid to the client, and we also need to check if the last action type 'To deposit' was permitted.

The test for whether the action type is permitted is carried out at the time the action was executed in reality, and not at the time the data for the action is received by the information system. In our example, we must check whether the date of the action 'To deposit' occurs before the date of the action 'To close'. The last action 'To deposit' happened on 10 February and since this is before 13 February, the action 'To deposit' $2000 may be executed.

When this happens, the value of the action controller becomes 1. We can then look at which subsequent actions take place in reality after the deposit of $2000 on 10 February. The deposit of $2000 into the account increases the balance of $1000 from before 10 February, to $3000. This $3000 would then be paid to the client when he closes his account.

Since the action 'To close' has already taken place, with a payment of $1000, we need to correct the action that has been executed.

The steps for correcting an action are:

(1) Go back in time to the moment the action was executed in reality;
(2) Check whether the action is permitted by referring to the object context table. In our example, 'To deposit' is permitted;
(3) Execute the action type on the known status of the object at the moment in time the action took place in the real world;
(4) Execute the subsequent actions that were done in the real world after the previously executed action. When the action type is permitted, according to the action context table, we use the new starting status of the object type;
(5) Determine the difference between the new status and the original status. In our example we need to pay an extra $2000 as a correction to the first payment made for the closing of the account;
(6) Add an extra status for the object containing the correction;
(7) When the action type may not be executed, according to the object context table, an error message must be produced. The organization must then investigate how the action in reality was able to take place. The action must then be undone by the organization in the real world;
(8) In the information system the data for the corrected status must be noted by a correcting action in the action controller. In our example we do this by adding a 'C' to the action controller. The corrected action remains unchanged for the rest of the data in the table because of the actual payment of $1000 made on 13 February.

The new table is shown in Table 10.26.

Table 10.26 Table with correction action.

Account ID	ActionDate	SequenceNo.	ProcessDate	ActionName	AC	AccountBalance	ActionAmount
123456	21 January	1	25 January	To open	1	$0	$0
123456	23 January	2	26 January	To deposit	1	$1000	$1000
123456	21 January	3	27 January	To deposit	1	$1200	$200
123456	28 January	4	28 January	To withdraw	1	$800	$400
123456	5 February	5	6 February	To withdraw	1	($200)	$1000
123456	31 January	6	7 February	To deposit	1	$1000	$1200
123456	13 February	7	13 February	To close	C	$0	$1000
123456	10 February	8	15 February	To deposit	1	$2000	$2000
123456	13 February	9	15 February	To close	2	$0	$2000

The status of the correction action for the closure of the account is input to the information system by once again executing the operations of the action type 'To close' on the last status of Account in the information system. The status of account in our example is an account balance of $2000. By once again executing the action type 'To close' an extra payment of $2000 will be made. To record the status after the correction action has been executed, we add an extra record with sequence number 9, containing the values of the correction action 'To close'.

The progression of the actual account balance in the real world can be seen when we determine the balance by tracing through the actions as they were executed in the real world. The result of this is that the table is read in the time sequence the actions were executed in the real world.

When we also check for the static conditions, a delay in the processing of data can cause the wrong decisions to be made. In the example we could test for the static condition that when we want to withdraw money the remaining balance must be greater than or equal to zero. When we then wish to withdraw $1000 on 5 February, the information system tells us that this is not permitted because there are not sufficient funds in the account. The information system reports a balance of only $800, while the client says that his balance is $2000. This is because a deposit of $1200 made by the client on 31 January has not yet been processed by the system.

The conclusion is that as the size of the delay in processing the data from actions increases, the difficulty in supporting employees with information systems that determine by means of conditions and rules what is and is not permitted also increases. The time delay causes a definite degree of unreliability of the information system. Our goal for the provision of information is aimed at processing the changes to the objects in the real world as quickly as possible in the information system. This is not always possible, and so we need ways to process actions on objects that lie in the past.

10.6.3   Future actions theory

Similarly to the processing of actions in the past, we can also process actions in the future. This means that the actions have an action date that occurs after the processing date. The procedure for processing future actions is identical to that for processing historical actions.

For the processing of future actions we must check whether the object has a valid AC value according to the object context table at the moment in the future that the action will be executed. To decide on this we trace through all the statuses of the object in the time sequence that the object would undergo them in the future. At the last moment in time of the execution of the action, we check the status. After we have found the AC value to be correct, we execute the action on the object type. We then check what consequences the execution of the future action has on the actions that have already been executed even further into the future. We may need to make a correction to these future actions, and include the new future status of the object at a particular moment in time, in the information system.

We can clarify the processing of future actions by expanding the example of the account. We will execute the action 'to close', not on 13 February, but at a later point in time. The table with future actions shown in Table 10.27.

Table 10.27   Table with future actions for the system date 16 February.

Account ID	ActionDate	SequenceNo.	ProcessDate	ActionName	AC	AccountBalance	ActionAmount
123456	21 January	1	25 January	To open	1	$0	$0
123456	23 January	2	26 January	To deposit	1	$1000	$1000
123456	21 January	3	27 January	To deposit	1	$1200	$200
123456	28 January	4	28 January	To withdraw	1	$800	$400
123456	5 February	5	6 February	To withdraw	1	($200)	$1000
123456	31 January	6	7 February	To deposit	1	$1000	$1200
123456	10 February	7	15 February	To deposit	1	$3000	$2000
123456	22 February	8	15 February	To deposit	1	$3500	$500
123456	12 March	9	15 February	To deposit	1	$5000	$1500
123456	30 March	10	15 February	To withdraw	1	$2500	$2500
123456	01 May	11	15 February	To close	2	$0	$2500

In the example the values of the future actions in the real world have a 100% guarantee that they will be executed. They can therefore be input into the information system. In this way we can see the future progression of the account balance, based on the current level of the account balance.

When we withdraw an amount of $700 from the account on 16 February, the new account balance becomes: $3000−$700 = $2300. To correct the progression of the account balance in the future we will need to reduce the account balance by $700 for all future actions. With an eventual closure of the account the amount paid will be $1800 and not $2500. We can alter the statuses of the object for the object's new status by carrying out the future actions once again. The actions themselves can be checked against the object context table. When an action is not permitted, we must ask whether the action will be permitted to be executed in the future.

This method of including all future actions in the same table has the advantage that we maintain an overview of the total progression of the status of an object, seen in time. For objects with many future actions this means that for each action executed now, a complete update process must be carried out to record the future statuses. For the future actions, the newly calculated object status can overwrite the previous object status in the database.

10.6.4   Planning function

The planning of activities is, for the management of many organizations, a functional area that information systems must take care of. Information systems are increasingly required to support the organization in taking correct decisions on the basis of actions that will take place in the future. This is, of course, in addition to the other requirement of supporting the daily activities. The planning and management of future events can be supported by a planning function. The planning function projects in time the actions that we expect to take place in the future. The time dimension is an important factor in this.

With the planning of actions in the future we again make use of the KISS models. A KISS model indicates which actions can be performed on an object, and in which order this may happen. Using the example of a parts workshop, we will show how a KISS model can be used in the planning of actions.

Example

In a parts workshop the mechanical processing of parts takes place. The processing activities are milling, turning, grinding, drilling and polishing.

The parts are ordered from a supplier and can be delivered in any number of deliveries. Only after all the ordered parts of an order have been received can the processing of the parts begin. If the delivered parts are faulty, they are repacked in the delivery storeroom and returned to the supplier. When the parts have been processed they are packaged and sent to the customer.

The KISS model (Figure 10.18) for ordering parts includes the attribute types that we find relevant for our planning function. These are the measures Quantity and Date. We illustrate the progression of the values of the attribute types for the action types in the KISS model by the examples of the date and the quantity.

A planning trajectory for 100 parts ordered on 2 January, to be delivered and processed in two processes, is described below.

To order:

Order Quantity:	100 pieces
Order Date:	2 January

Plan Receipt 1

Plan Receipt Quantity:	40 pieces
Plan Receipt Date:	15 January

Plan Receipt 2

Plan Receipt Quantity:	35 pieces
Plan Receipt Date:	20 January

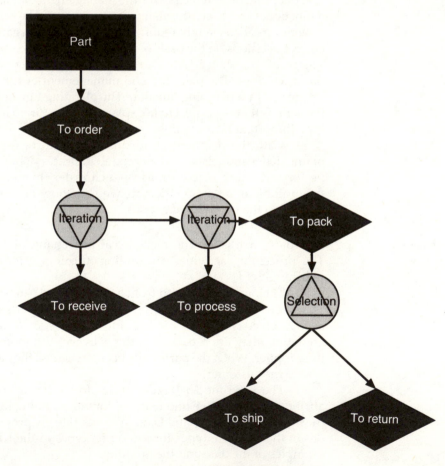

Figure 10.18   KISS model for Part.

Plan Receipt 3
Plan Receipt Quantity: 25 pieces
Plan Receipt Date: 25 January

Plan Process 1
Plan Process Quantity: 50 pieces
Plan Process Date: 26 January

Plan Process 2
Plan Process Quantity: 50 pieces
Plan Process Date: 3 February

Plan Packaging:
Plan Packaging Quantity: 100 pieces
Plan Packaging Date: 10 February

Plan Returning:
Plan Returning Quantity: –
Plan Returning Date: –

Plan Sending:
Plan Sending Quantity: 100 pieces
Plan Sending Date: 17 February

We can note from this example that including a date for the receipt of a delivery when parts have been ordered is not sufficient. This is because according to the KISS model we can receive many deliveries. This is also true for the processing of items. The attribute types for the planning of receipts must then form a repeating group to be included with the ordered part. This leads directly to a more complex situation for the creation of a record structure or a table. For our original example we will limit the table structure to planning for a maximum of three receipts and two processes. The table is as shown in Table 10.28.

Table 10.28   Table for the planning for parts.

Part ID	Number ordered	Date ordered	Plan 1 number received	Plan 1 date received	Plan 2 number received	Plan 2 date received	Plan 3 number received	Plan 3 date received	Plan 1 number processed	Plan 1 date processed	Plan 2 number processed	Plan 2 date processed	Plan number packaging	Plan date packaging
123456	100	2/1	40	15/1	35	20/1	25	25/1	50	26/1	50	3/2	100	10/2

We can also transform the planned actions from the KISS model into a storage structure in a simpler and more flexible manner. We do this by making a distinction between the PlanDate, PlanActionDate and the ActionDate.

- The PlanDate is the date on which the action is planned.
- The PlanActionDate is the date the action is planned to be carried out.
- The ActionDate is the date the action was actually carried out.

By comparing the PlanDate with the PlanActionDate we can see if a particular planned action still needs to be executed, or has already been executed. We can tell when the PlanActionDate lies further ahead in time than the PlanDate because then the action still needs to take place. Besides this we also make a distinction between the planned quantities and the actual quantities of the specific action.

The data for the planning function for the part is given in Table 10.29.

Table 10.29   Data storage structure Planning function KISS model.

Part ID	NameAction	PlanDate	PlanAction Date	ActionDate	Quantity PlanAction	ActionQuantity
123456	To order	2/1	2/1	2/1	100	100
123456	To receive	2/1	15/1		40	
123456	To receive	2/1	20/1		35	
123456	To receive	2/1	25/1		25	
123456	To process	2/1	26/1		50	
123456	To process	2/1	3/2		50	
123456	To package	2/1	10/2		100	
123456	To send	2/1	17/2		100	

The comparison of the planned date and quantity with the actual date and quantity provides the basis for reporting on the quality of delivery and processing of the parts. Differences between planned and actual date, and planned and actual quantity, can be measured. The problems we had in Table 10.28 with the limited number of alternatives for the input of planning data is solved with the new table. In theory we could include the data for an unlimited number of 'receipts' and 'processes', in the new table for the ordered 'part'.

The table for 'part' can also be used to trigger particular activities. So we could use the table to inform the warehouse a week early about the parts to be received. We could also inform the workplace of which parts will need to be processed. We can now use the table to signal large discrepancies in dates or quantities. When the dates and quantities differ too much, a re-planning of actions can take place, using the KISS models in the information architecture.

The general transformation rule for implementing a data structure for a planning function using KISS models is to include a separate column in the table with the name of the action. We include the attribute type PlanDate to indicate the date the action is planned to happen. For the remaining measures that are important for planning we include the attribute type that the measure indicates and its opposite, which represents the planned value:

Measure	Actual	Planning
Date	ActionDate	PlanActionDate
Quantity	ActionQuantity	PlanActionQuantity

The table can now easily be expanded with the derived attribute types for new measures like 'costs' and 'content'. This is done by including two values for each attribute type. These are the planned value and the actual value of the action. In this way we create redundancy in the implemented table. The redundancy can be eliminated by implementing the actual data and the planning data each in separate tables. So we will have a table that records the planning data and a table that records the data for the actions that have taken place.

When we decide to plan all the data of the actions that will be executed, we end up with tables of planning data and action data that are identical in structure (Tables 10.30 and 10.31).

Table 10.30   Data storage structure Planning function KISS model.

Part ID	NameAction	PlanDate	PlanActionDate	PlanActionQuantity
123456	To order	2/1	2/1	100
123456	To receive	2/1	15/1	40
123456	To receive	2/1	20/1	35
123456	To receive	2/1	25/1	25
123456	To process	2/1	26/1	50
123456	To process	2/1	3/2	50
123456	To package	2/1	10/2	100
123456	To send	2/1	17/2	100

Table 10.31   Action table.

Part ID	NameAction	ActionDate	ActionQuantity
123456	To order	2/1	100

With the extensive use of KISS models in a planning function, we make use of the procedural time order in the KISS models for the execution of the actions. This is possible with the future action theory as we have described it. With the planning functions defined in this way, we also make use of the procedures that are defined in an organization for the execution of actions.

In the example of the ordered parts, their receipt is only possible when the parts have been ordered on a date earlier than the planned receipt date. Sending and returning are also only possible after the items have been repacked. The sent date and the receipt date therefore may not occur before the repacking date.

The power of the KISS model is that the planning function can be specified in a simple way. The starting point is that an organization cannot plan any more than the actions it carries out.

Assumption: We cannot plan more activities for an organization than the actions it carries out.

The level of detail for planning can vary significantly from one organization to another. There is often no detailed planning done for actions that deal, for example, with the individual sales of goods with low sales value. If we were to plan for these extreme cases, the planning exercise would cost more in computer time than the extra value gained from the amount of product sold.

In situations of low value and/or relevance the planning takes place at a higher level of aggregation. The planning then generally happens on a collection of actions of a class of objects for a specific time period. The values planned for the higher aggregation level are the expected result from the actions that will take place in the specific period on the class.

The converse of the planned value is the actual value of actions that have taken place in the elapsed period of time. The actual value of an attribute on a higher aggregate level is calculated by tracing through the actions that have taken place, along with their changes on the objects, in the elapsed period. For a higher aggregate level, the actual value is always a derived attribute type. This attribute type is calculated on the basis of the attribute values of the action and the object. The attribute type for planning on a higher level of aggregation must be directly comparable with the calculated attribute type that results for a period. To understand the meaning of the planning numbers, it is helpful to make use of an information architecture in which the semantics are recorded.

The planning numbers for the higher aggregation level can be stored in an object class in the same data storage structure as that in which the calculated period results are stored.

10.6.5 Time aspects of actions on many objects

For action types that work on more than one object type the method of working for the processing of actions in the past and future must be carried out for each individual object. Examples of action types that work on two different object types are 'To deposit' and 'To withdraw' money into and from an Account at a Cash drawer. Both Account and Cash drawer alter their status when an action is carried out.

In our discussion of the content of the temporary database we saw that the content of an action is included with an object. So the deposited amount is included with each status of an account. We can do the same for Cash drawer, whereby the attributes of the Cash drawer also include the deposited amount.

In the data structure we must be able to check for both objects what the common action was that changed both objects. For each status change of an object it is therefore necessary to specify the identifier of the action that changed the objects. We can realize this by recording, in a separate table, which objects of the various object types at which moment in time have undergone changes. The action table takes care of the coordination needed for processing actions relevant to the past and to the future. When building the action table, consideration can be given to either including the attribute values of the action individually with the associated objects or including them for all objects commonly in the action table. Including the action attributes in the object has the advantage of requiring fewer read actions in other tables. The disadvantage is that the same attribute is stored in multiple locations.

10.7 Summary

In this chapter we have shown how function models are created using KISS models from the information architecture. We have shown how a dialogue, input screen and various menu structures can be built using simple transformation rules. Decision functions were discussed by decision tables and decision models. A comparison of the use of these two techniques revealed that a decision table is more quickly and easily modified than a decision model. In addition, a small change to the order of the decisions can result in an extremely large visual change in the decision model. This is not the case for the decision table. It is therefore preferable to make use of the decision table for the specification of complex decision functions.

The time aspects of information systems were discussed using time-dependent functions. By using a time-dependent function we can determine the processing of actions in the past, present and future. This is done with the 'future action theory'. The effect of the future action theory is that all actions that are carried out in the past, present and future have already been modelled in the KISS models and in the object-interaction models of the information architecture.

The addition and removal of a function to and from the information system is relatively simple when the information architecture has been created and implemented in an object-oriented manner. The functions then no longer determine the structure, but are added to handle the interface between the end user and the information system. The functions then maintain the strongly variable character that is often demanded by the managers and employees in an organization.

10.8   Questions

(1)   What is a function? Describe the different types of functions by examples.

(2)   Describe the elements of the function model.

(3)   Discuss the transformation rules of the function model into screens and menus.

(4)   Discuss the decision process.

(5)   Describe the elements of the different types of decision table.

(6)   What is the importance of natural language for the specification and use of decision tables?

(7)   Apply the steps of defining a decision table to a case taken from your own environment.

(8)   Describe the decision model and discuss why it is preferable to make use of a decision table.

(9)   What is optimization of a decision process and what is the advantage of optimizing decision processes?

(10)   What is the importance of time to the supply of information in organizations?

(11)   In what ways does the KISS method provide solutions to time-related questions and aspects?

(12)   Discuss the future action theory.

(13)   Describe how the decision table can be encapsulated in the action model.

11 A clock example

11.1 Introduction

Using a simple clock example we look at how to use the concepts of all the previous chapters. We describe a clock because it is an example that has more similarity with real-time systems. The textual description of a clock with a limited functionality is given. The example does not pretend to give all the detailed implementation aspects of a digital clock. It focuses on demonstrating the way in which we describe the encapsulated characteristics and behaviour of actions and objects with attribute models, action models and decision tables. The subjects of the example add to those of the bank example of Chapter 6.

11.2 Description of the clock example

A person has a digital clock for reading the correct time. The clock displays the time in the order: hour, minute, second (HH,MM,SS). The clock is bought by the person in a shop. After he has bought the clock he places a battery in the clock and sets the time. The battery powers a crystal that pulses every second. The battery is removed after it has stopped powering the crystal. The person resets the time when it is incorrect. He uses the clock until he throws it away. Before the clock is thrown away the battery has to be removed in order to avoid environmental pollution.

11.3 Active structured sentences

Before making any models we transform the textual description into active structured sentences in the order of subject, predicate, direct object, preposition, indirect object.

Subject	Predicate	Direct object	Preposition	Indirect object
A person	to read	time	from	clock
The clock	to display	time	in	HH,MM,SS
A person	to buy	clock	in	shop
A person	to place	battery	in	clock
The battery	to power	crystal		
A person	to set	time	of	clock
The crystal	to pulse	second		
A person	to remove	battery	from	clock
The battery	to stop	power	for	crystal
A person	to reset	time	of	clock
A person	to throw	clock	away	

11.3.1   Candidate objects

The candidate objects are as follows:

Person
Time
Clock
Battery
Crystal
Second
Power
Shop

Person, Second and Power will be removed from this list because the first is a subject and the other two are attributes of Time and Battery.

11.3.2   Candidate actions

All actions are candidate actions and will be modelled further.

To read	to read the time from a clock.
To display	to display the time on the clock.
To buy	to buy the clock in the shop.
To place	to place a battery in the clock.
To power	to power the crystal of the clock.

To set	to set the time of the clock
To pulse	to pulse seconds with the crystal.
To remove	to remove the battery from the clock.
To stop	to stop the power for the crystal.
To reset	to reset the time of the clock.
To throw	to throw the clock away.

11.3.3 Object/action matrix

From the description we set up an initial object/action matrix, as shown in Table 11.1.

Table 11.1 Object/action matrix of the clock.

Action	Clock	Time	Battery	Crystal	Shop
To read	×	×			
To display	×	×			
To buy	×				×
To place	×		×		
To power			×	×	
To set	×	×			
To pulse	×			×	
To remove	×		×		
To stop			×	×	
To reset	×	×			
To throw	×				

In the final action list we do not take up 'To read' because it is seen as an information function.

11.3.4 Initial object-interaction model Clock

Based upon the textual description we define the initial object-interaction model (Figure 11.1). The initial object-interaction model is validated with KISS models for the objects that have a relevant life. When looking at the initial object-interaction model we see that Shop does not have a relevant life and will therefore not be modelled in a KISS model. Shop will be omitted from the list of objects because it lies outside the scope of the problem area.

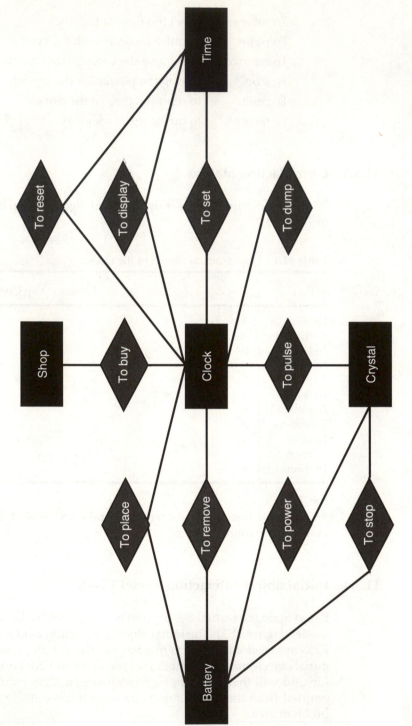

Figure 11.1   Initial object-interaction model for the clock example.

11.4 KISS models

The KISS models show the sequence in which actions may be executed by the various objects. The object types that have to be modelled in KISS models are:

Clock

Battery

Crystal

Time

11.4.1 Ordering rules

Before we create the KISS model, we show by ordering rules what the possible life of the object type is. The ordering rules for the clock example are:

(1) First buy clock, then place battery, then set time

(2) First place battery, then remove battery

(3) First remove battery, then place battery

(4) First set time, then iteratively either remove battery, reset time or display time

(5) First remove battery, then throw clock away

(6) First place battery, then power crystal

(7) First power crystal, then stop power to crystal

(8) First stop power to crystal, then remove battery

(9) First set time, then iteratively either pulse, reset or display time

(10) First power cristal, then iteratively pulse time

With the ordering rules we subsequently specify the KISS models of Clock, Battery, Time and Crystal.

1!.4.2 KISS model for Clock

The action types associated in the object-interaction model with the object type Clock are:

To buy

To place

To remove

To pulse

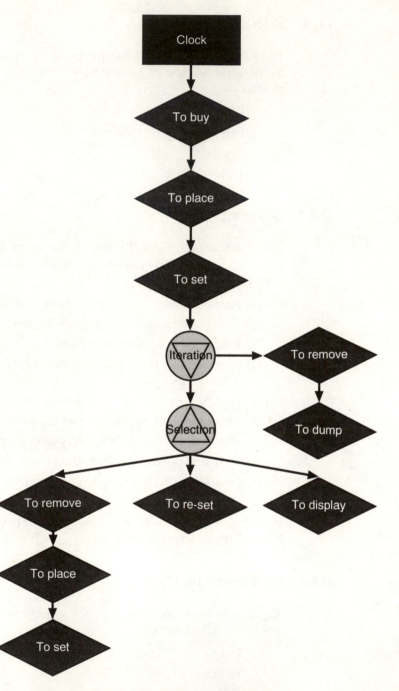

Figure 11.2   KISS model for Clock.

To set

To display

To reset

To dump

In the above description of the ordering rules and the initial text we can conclude that Time is dependent upon the existence of Clock. The action type 'To pulse' will therefore be left out in defining our initial KISS model of Clock. The initial KISS model of Clock looks as shown in Figure 11.2.

From the KISS model we can check that all ordering rules are met. We can also see that no time can be displayed or reset while replacing the battery of the clock. The replacement is a sequential iteration and therefore the sequence of the iteration and selection symbol cannot be replaced by a parallel iteration.

11.4.3 KISS model for Battery

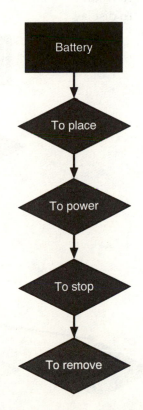

Figure 11.3 KISS model for Battery.

The action types connected in the object-interaction model to Battery are:

> To place
> To power
> To stop
> To remove

The relevant life of a battery is relatively simple in the sense that there is only one possible path sequence for the four action types mentioned above. The KISS model for Battery is shown in Figure 11.3.

11.4.4   KISS model for Time

The action types connected to time are:

> To set
> To pulse
> To reset
> To display

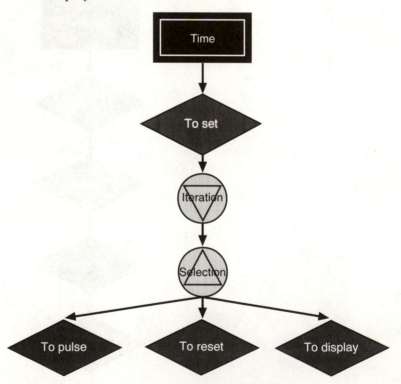

Figure 11.4   KISS model for Time.

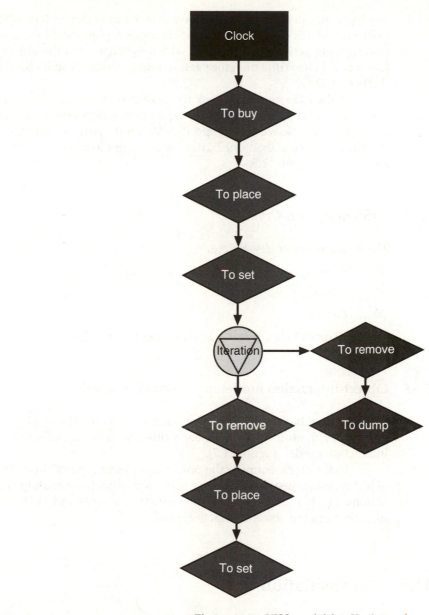

Figure 11.5   KISS model for Clock.

We have already found indications that Time is dependent upon the existence of Clock. The existence dependency is established by the instantiating action type 'To set', which synchronizes the object types Clock and Time. Time therefore gets a double rectangle in its KISS model (Figure 11.4).

In the KISS model of Clock we have to remove the action types 'To reset' and 'To display' because of the existence dependency of Time. In this clock example we have a specific clock with only one battery. When the clock has more than one battery we will get a different KISS model, as shown in Figure 11.5.

11.4.5   KISS model for Crystal

The action types of Crystal are:

>   To power
>   To pulse
>   To stop

The KISS model for Crystal is as shown in Figure 11.6.

11.4.6   Object-interaction model for the clock example

Now that we have created all the KISS models for the clock example, we can let them interact with each other to form a definitive object-interaction model (Figure 11.7).

In the clock example the only weak object type is Time. All other object types are just synchronized with each other by executing common actions. The hierarchy model is therefore very simple and can be derived directly from the object-interaction model.

11.5   Encapsulation

For the explanation of encapsulated characteristics we model Time in more detail. We first model the attributes of time with an attribute model and then the different actions with action models.

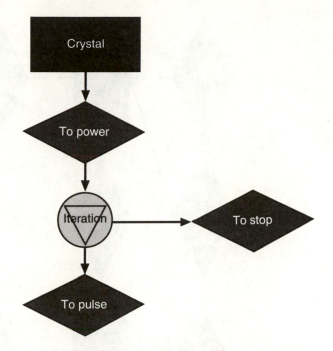

Figure 11.6   KISS model for Crystal.

11.5.1   Attribute model for Time

The attribute types of Time will be:

TimeHour

TimeMinute

TimeSecond

These are specified by relating them respectively to the measures Hour, Minute and Second, as shown in Figure 11.8.

11.5.2   Action models for 'To set' and 'To reset'

The action models of 'To set' and 'To reset' are very simple. The actions are just initializations of the attribute values for TimeHour, TimeMinute and TimeSecond. The initialization is represented in the action model by a direct data flow from the action type to the attribute type (Figure 11.9). No additional operations or conditions are necessary for the execution of the two actions.

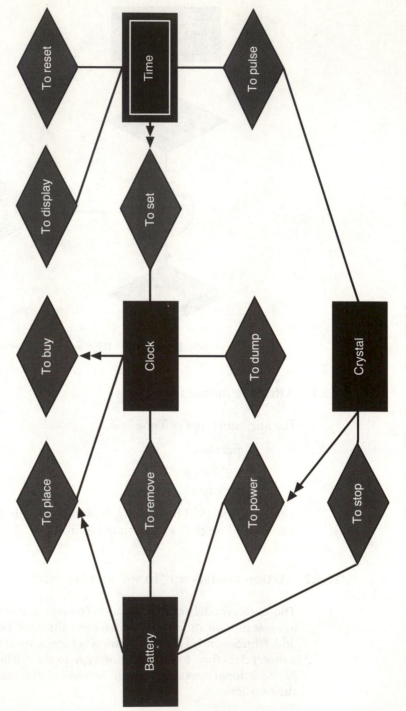

Figure 11.7   Object-interaction model for the clock example.

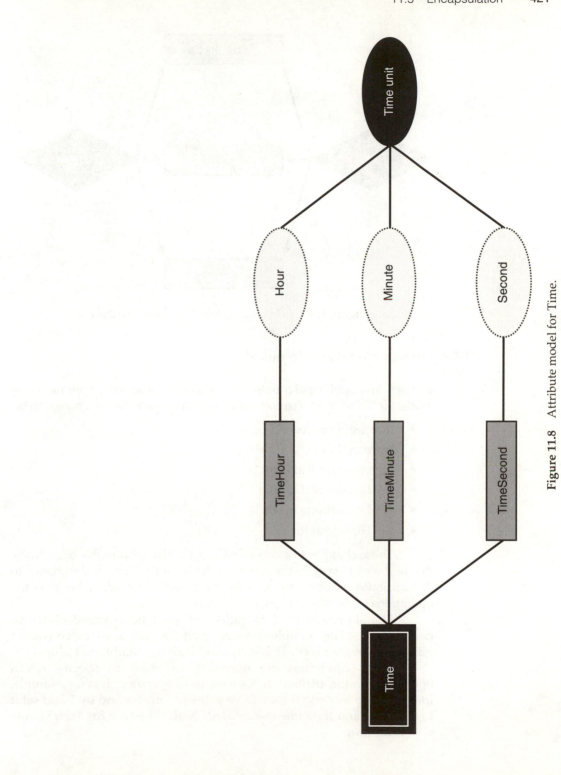

Figure 11.8   Attribute model for Time.

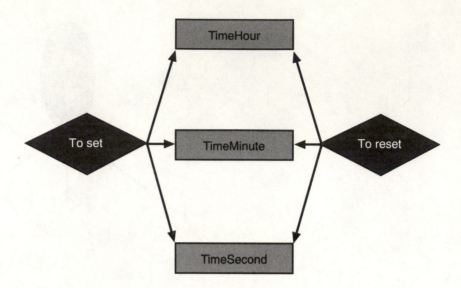

Figure 11.9   Action model for 'To set' and 'To reset'.

11.5.3   Action model for 'To pulse'

The action model for 'To pulse' is not as simple as the previous action model for 'To set' and 'To reset'. That is because the result of a pulse can be:

- Increase TimeSecond by 1;
- Increase TimeMinute by 1;
- Increase TimeHour by 1;
- Set TimeSecond to 00;
- Set TimeMinute to 00;
- Set TimeHour to 00.

These changes to attribute values are also all possible operations. The best way to specify the action model is thus to specify the change to the attribute values first because they will very often become the operations in the action model.

The above-specified operations will not be executed under all circumstances. For example, any operation can only be executed when a pulse has been received. This is checked with the condition: Pulse =?.

Other conditions are necessary in order to specify which operations on the attribute types have to be executed. It is for example, impossible to increase the attribute value of TimeSecond by 1 and set it to 00 at one and the same instant. This is also the case for TimeMinute and TimeHour.

Another condition is that TimeMinute has to be incremented by 1 when TimeSecond is set to 00, and that TimeHour has to be incremented by 1 when TimeMinute is set to 00.

TimeSecond and TimeMinute can only be incremented by 1 until 59 has been reached. TimeHour can be incremented until 23 has been reached. Then the values have to be set to 00.

The operations and conditions of the action type 'To pulse' can be modelled in one action model. The operations are shaken in the action model with abbreviations for the names of the attribute types and the conditions in their appropriate symbols with question marks. We get the following list of conditions and operations:

Conditions: To pulse =? Yes or No
               TimeSecond =? Smaller than 59 or equal to 59
               TimeMinute =? Smaller than 59 or equal to 59
               TimeHour =? Smaller than 23 or equal to 23

Operations: TimeSecond := TimeSecond + 1,   TS := TS + 1
               TimeMinute := TimeMinute + 1,   TM := TM + 1
               TimeHour := TimeHour + 1,   TH := TH + 1

In the action model we have to connect the operation to the attribute types with data flows in order to read and write the attribute values of the attribute types. The data flow is drawn with a solid arrow pointing in the direction of the flow. In order to check the conditions we also have to read the attribute values; this is indicated with data flows from the attribute type towards the condition symbol.

For every conditional operation we then have to draw a condition flow from the condition towards the operation. The condition flow is drawn with a dotted arrow. Next to the condition flow we can place the condition value. In the case of and/and conditions we connect the different conditions in sequence.

When we follow the above rules for the definition of the action model of 'To pulse' we will get the model shown in Figure 11.10.

11.5.4 Action model of 'To pulse' with a decision table

The specification of the previous action model of 'To pulse' requires great insight into the way in which conditions and operations are related to each other. This can lead to serious problems in situations with a few more operations and conditions. Problems arise, for example, with testing the completeness of all conditions and operations. A solution for this problem is to make use of the decision table technique. The decision table is encapsulated within the action model of 'To pulse' and is

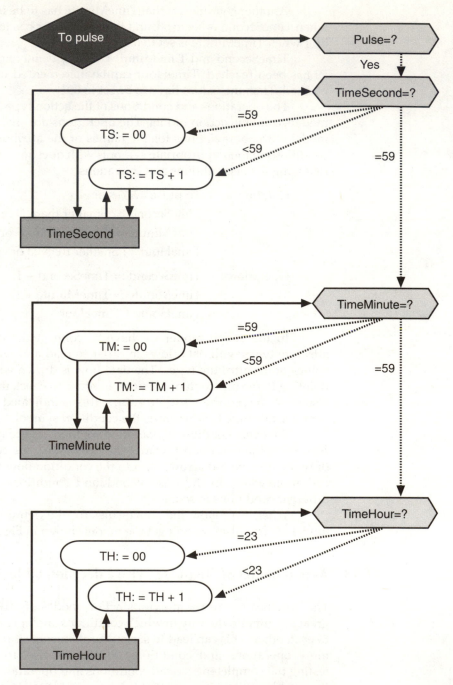

Figure 11.10 Action model for 'To pulse'.

represented by condition symbols glued together underneath each other (Figure 11.11). The and/and condition is replaced by the gluing of the individual conditions. Every condition still reads attribute values of attribute types with ingoing data flows. The condition flows come from underneath the decision table as a whole. Every condition flow is related to one or more columns (decision rules) of the decision table.

In this way knowledge of the outside world is encapsulated in the action model. The more decision rules are encapsulated in the action model with decision tables, the more the model acts as a knowledge base.

Table 11.2 Decision table 'To pulse'.

	1	2	3	4	5	6	7	8	9	10	11	12	13	14	15	16
To pulse = ?	Y	Y	Y	Y	Y	Y	Y	Y	N	N	N	N	N	N	N	N
TimeSecond < 59	Y	Y	Y	Y	N	N	N	N	Y	Y	Y	Y	N	N	N	N
TimeMinute < 59	Y	Y	N	N	Y	Y	N	N	Y	Y	N	N	Y	Y	N	N
TimeHour < 23	Y	N	Y	N	Y	N	Y	N	Y	N	Y	N	Y	N	Y	N
TS := TS + 1	×	×	×	×												
TM := TM + 1					×	×										
TH := TH + 1							×									
TS := 00					×	×	×	×								
TM := 00							×	×								
TH := 00								×								
Nothing									×	×	×	×	×	×	×	×

The decision table shown in Table 11.2 can be simplified by suppressing redundant decision rules (Table 11.3). The decision table can than be represented in combination with the action model (Figure 11.10). The column numbers of the condition table correspond to the numbers next to the decision flow in the action model.

Table 11.3 Simplified decision table of 'To pulse'.

	1	5	7	8	9
To pulse = ?	Y	Y	Y	Y	N
TimeSecond < 59	Y	N	N	N	–
TimeMinute < 59	–	Y	N	N	–
TimeHour < 23	–	–	Y	N	–
TS := TS + 1	×				
TM := TM + 1		×			
TH := TH + 1			×		
TS := 00		×	×	×	
TM := 00			×	×	
TH := 00				×	
Nothing					×

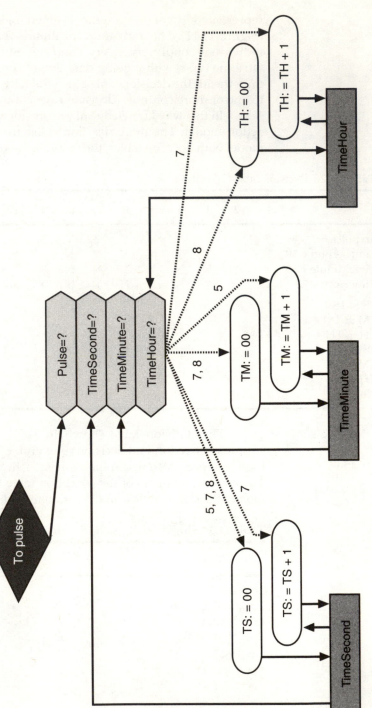

Figure 11.11 Action model for 'To pulse' with encapsulated decision table.

11.6   Summary

In this chapter we have seen how the concepts from the previous chapters can be applied. The method of working is that we start from a textual description, do a grammatical analysis, and define the initial object-interaction model, KISS models and the final object-interaction model. Since the clock example is a very simple structure we have not specified a hierarchy model.

After having defined the information architecture we can specify the encapsulated attribute types, operations and conditions with attribute models and action models. We can also implement decision tables within the action model. In this way we enrich the knowledge of the information system. The information system can thus take away decisions from the outside world and perform them within the action model. By implementing decision tables within action models the description of the functionality of input and output functions gets even less. As discussed in Chapter 10 decision tables give great flexibility and therefore the resulting information system can be adapted more easily to the changing demands of the organization, information needs and techniques used.

11.7   Question

(1)   Apply all the techniques you have learned in a real-world case for realizing an information system.

# 12 System management

12.1 Introduction

In the previous chapters we provided the framework for the management of information and the creation of an information architecture. By using examples we explained the way in which the techniques described can be applied to the realization of information systems.

Along with the knowledge of how to use the techniques described, we need to have a basis from which we can give substance to project management for the life of a project. We also need to know the practical ways in which the KISS method for object orientation can be applied and implemented in a project team.

In order to discuss the effects of applying the KISS method to project management we will use the example of building a ship. At the same time we make a comparison with the project management of more conventional methods of system development.

For the application and implementation of the KISS method in project teams consisting of end users, system developers and the project initiator, we look at how KISS DOMINO provides the common basis for intercommunication between all team members. KISS DOMINO is a tool for the implementation management of object-oriented development.

Finally, by looking at the development of CASE tools over the past 25 years, we discuss the conditions under which CASE tools offer integral support for the design, building and maintenance of information systems.

12.2 Project phases

Project management is just as important for the object-oriented development of an information system as it is for a conventional development. With object-oriented projects we still carry out the activities in a definite logical time sequence. While object-oriented programs are relatively simple to change, it is still better to plan the activities for any project of a reasonable size. In any project requiring two or more people it is sensible to plan, if only to enhance the coordination of the activities.

The main reason for planning is that it gives us the means to adjust the activities when we discern any delay in the completion of activities in comparison with the original plan. In this respect we note no differences between planning for object-oriented systems and planning to build a ship or an office block, or the planning of production in a production plant.

The difference between planning an object-oriented project and planning a conventional project lies much more in the details of the methods used to carry out the activities within the project itself. The difference can be compared with planning the building of a steamship in 1900 and a supertanker in 1970.

12.2.1   The steamship of 1900

The technique used to join the various parts of a steamship together in 1900 was 'riveting'. All the steel parts, such as steel plate, beams and other constructions, were riveted together using rivets. The rivets were heated until they were red-hot and then they were pushed through a hole in both parts and riveted. As the rivets cooled they shrank and pulled both parts tightly together.

In planning the building of the steamship it was primarily the quantity of rivets to be riveted that determined the speed with which the steamship could be built. For each rivet, planning needed to consider whether it was to be placed in an easily accessible location or in a difficult location. In an easily accessible location a rivet could be riveted by one person. For the walls of the ship, however, at least two people were required, and for very inaccessible places more than two people were required.

Besides the construction itself, there was also the necessary supply and heating of the rivets which required logistical planning in the form of rivets, coal and coal ovens. Enormous savings in materials, construction time and money could be made when the design of the ship minimized the number of rivets.

12.2.2   The supertanker of 1970

A supertanker built in the 1970s was no longer riveted but welded instead. The planning for the supertanker can exclude the activities of riveting because they are no longer necessary. Instead of riveting there are activities such as welding and unloading of the welding material. The determining factor for the construction time for a supertanker is the quantity of welding work and the degree of difficulty of the welding.

The planning techniques for the building of a steamship or a supertanker are not the focus of our discussion. Neither is it the order of the design, construction drawings and subsequent building of the ship when we apply different joining techniques. In the construction phase we simply replace the riveting activities with the welding activities. In the design we then need to replace the riveting technique with the welding technique. It would of course not be possible to convert the drawings of a supertanker using rivets to one using welds.

To emphasize the aspects that play a role in the management of projects for the design and building of information systems, we continue the analogy of shipbuilding. All the major activities that must be carried out before a ship can be launched are remarkably similar to the major activities that must be carried out before an information system can go into production.

The major activities for the building of a ship and an information system can be categorized as:

Ship	*Information system*
Capacity planning	Information planning
Ship specification	Requirements definition
Design	Design analysis
Detailed design	Detailed design
Construction	Implementation

12.2.3 Capacity planning

A shipping company will only order a new ship to be built after it has checked the level of demand and where and when it needs to expand or replace its fleet. This is determined by looking at the trend of capacity required. It may be possible to do without such an investment by utilizing the ships in a more efficient and effective manner. However, at some point in time it will be necessary to replace existing ships or add new ships. We can call this the capacity planning process for a shipping company.

12.2.4 Ship specification

When the company knows when a new ship of a specific capacity will be needed, it can work at defining the specifications to which the ship must be built. Issues such as the type of ship, its length, the engine power, speed, type of load, safety requirements and floating capabilities are defined. We can call this the ship specification for a shipping company.

12.2.5   Design and detailed design

Using the specification as a basis, a first design for the ship can be made. This first design brings the specification and a particular architecture together. Any errors in the specification can be corrected in the design, after which the design can be made more detailed.

During the design process it holds true that the more precise and formal the specification supplied, the easier the design process is to carry out. The experience of the person who defines the ship determines the quality of the information used by the designer. The designer formalizes the design process with measurements and by demonstrating the construction and form with drawings.

12.2.6   Construction

When the design is complete, the construction plans need to be clearly drawn showing how the ship is to be constructed. The construction plans must be so precise, clear and formal that a steel worker, mechanic or foreman is unable to interpret them in his own way. When the construction plans are open to interpretation by steel workers, mechanics and foremen, we have absolutely no guarantee of the resulting quality of the ship. This rule applies regardless of how advanced the technology used, such as welding, measurement and cutting apparatus.

After the ship has been launched, we can add the following to the specification, design and construction activities:

Ship	*Information system*
Launch	Take into production
Maintain	Maintain
Redesign	Redesign
Wreck	Pull plug out of the wall

It is clear that a bad design results in extra costs in the form of unnecessary use of fuel, slow speeds, too many crew, too much maintenance, lengthy loading and unloading, poor manoeuvrability, inflexibility for rerouting, and so forth. This could in fact become so bad that the total cost of running the ship is many times greater than the cost of building it. In addition the ship could generate less revenue than the competition. This would occur because the ship has higher tariffs to pay for longer

stays in port for loading, unloading and maintenance. The only econom-
ically viable answer is to redesign the ship to make it productive, or to
take the ship to the wreckers. Some shipping companies in criminal
circles decide to let the ship and its crew sink in order to claim on the
insurance.

12.3   Quality of the project

The degree to which the ship answers to the needs for which it was built
is mainly determined by the extent to which the ship specification and
design allow us to convert the architecture into clear construction
drawings and models. These drawings and models in turn must also be
accurate and simple to build from.

The clarity is determined by the formality of the concepts used in
the design and construction process. If all the concepts have an identical
meaning and are clear and easy to understand from the architecture to
the construction, then we can achieve clear communication between
the designer and the construction worker. The construction worker
transforms the construction drawings into the physical parts of the ship.
The basis of the communication between the designer and construction
worker lies with the 'objects' and the 'actions' that must be performed on
or with the objects. The objects are depicted on the construction plan with
their specific characteristics. Along with the objects and actions there is a
list of materials and the actions to be performed, which are noted on
attached working instructions.

We end up in a different situation when we allow the meaning of
the concepts to change with the wind. In this situation each phase must
be interpreted differently leading to both a breakdown of quality control
and eventually no control possible over the progress of the project.

The interpretation of specifications occurs relatively quickly with
information systems when functions and data are modelled separately.
The application of functional decomposition as a design technique
promotes ambiguity from the very beginning of the design phase with
the drawing of a boundary around the functional areas. The technique of
functional decomposition, in fact, uses a black box approach whereby we
are only interested in the input and output to and from a function. In a
subsequent step the further details of the function are specified by
subfunctions, each of which has its own input and output. This method
of defining the internal structure of functions can of course continue
endlessly.

The disadvantage of this method is that the structure created by
the first division of a function into subfunctions determines the entire
structure for all the sub-subfunctions that result from the subfunctions.

Any change in the first division will make it necessary for all the other divisions to be investigated. We then more or less end up starting the functional decomposition again, and of course the system derived from it will also need to be radically changed. An additional problem is that with functional decomposition there are no formal and testable arguments that can be used to determine the relevance of dividing or not dividing a function into subfunctions. The consequence is that the level of detail provided by the design for the developer can differ greatly.

The result in extreme situations in a conventional project is that a project team creates an information plan which is then interpreted and rewritten by a subsequent project team for the requirements definition. The project team adds a number of additional aspects. Then the requirements definition is passed on to the design, detailed design and implementation phases. In each of these phases the specifications of the previous phase are interpreted and reformulated with different terminology. The chance of introducing mistakes by a wrong interpretation of course increases in each phase. In addition, the project team uses extra time for the interpretation and rewriting of the document supplied.

The result can be called 'horizontal development'. We see that each subsequent step interprets the previous step and only adds a very limited amount of detail with each new specification (Figure 12.1).

The functional decomposition with the black box approach has some benefit when we are talking about the planning of a project. From a top-down approach we see, of course, how easy it can be to divide a project into sub-projects for the subfunctions. In reality, however, there is a big problem with this approach, which is that we need to be aware of the total content before we can start to plan, and that the possible interactions between the subfunctions must be sufficiently analysed. Often it is the interfaces between the subfunctions that turn out to be more complex and larger in size than the subfunction itself.

Lately the word 'prototyping' has been the term that has been given as the answer to the structured analysis, design and implementation of systems. The basic premise of prototyping is to spend as little time as possible on the requirements definition and design, and to move quickly to the development of a working model of a possible application. The system should be specified and developed after a number of iterations. In contrast with 'horizontal development', prototyping can be described as 'vertical development' (Figure 12.2). The advantage of vertical development compared with horizontal development is that it saves time.

The consequence of vertical development, stated in pictorial terms, is that a ship has been constructed but that the architecture and construction plans for the ship have never been made. Because of this the maintenance of large systems will demand a great deal of effort.

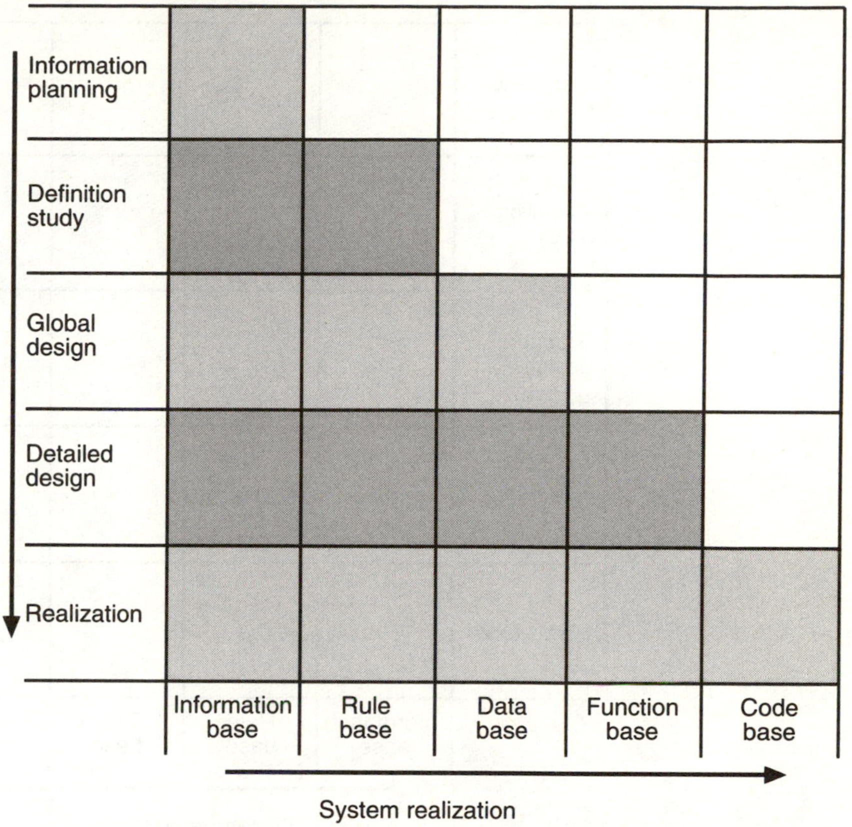

Figure 12.1   Horizontal development.

Nevertheless, to be able to make the systems maintainable, transparent, modifiable and flexible after they have been developed, we must have a design and an information architecture. The requirement of the information architecture is that it be completely transformable into the production environment without any interpretation taking place.

The components of the KISS method at the specification level related to their counterparts in the implementation environment are:

Concept	*Information system*
Information quadrant	Information base
Subject-communication model	
KISS models	Rule base
Object-interaction model	Data base
Attribute model	
Function model	Function base
Action model	
Implementation model	Code base
Distribution model	

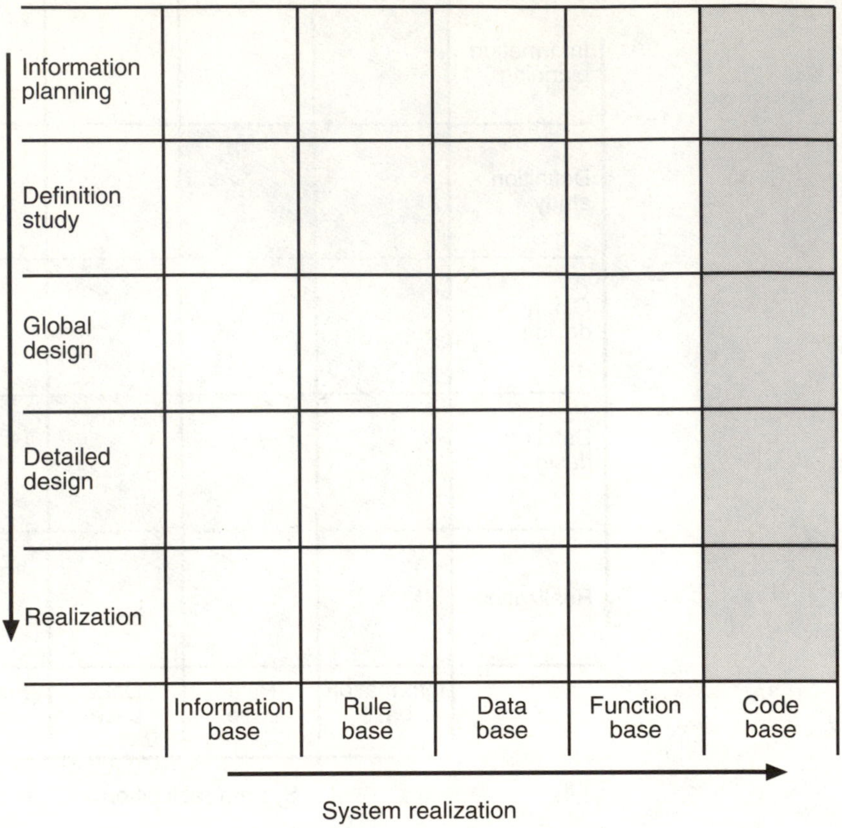

	Information base	Rule base	Data base	Function base	Code base
Information planning					
Definition study					
Global design					
Detailed design					
Realization					

System realization

Figure 12.2   Vertical development.

From the conceptual level the specification, supported by transformation rules, is converted into the components of the implementation environment (Figure 12.3). In this way we can add to the specifications in subsequent steps without having to interpret and rewrite the products of the previous steps. By adding these new elements we gain increased validation and quality control of the model we have developed.

The feature of this stepwise design is that the entire design can in theory be traced through object by object. The size of the project team can then be confined to a small group who incrementally produce and test new elements of the information system.

The KISS approach markedly reduces the stress placed on a project team. On the other hand, the need for the management of the concepts, ideas and agreement increases. The concepts are of course the basis upon which project communication takes place.

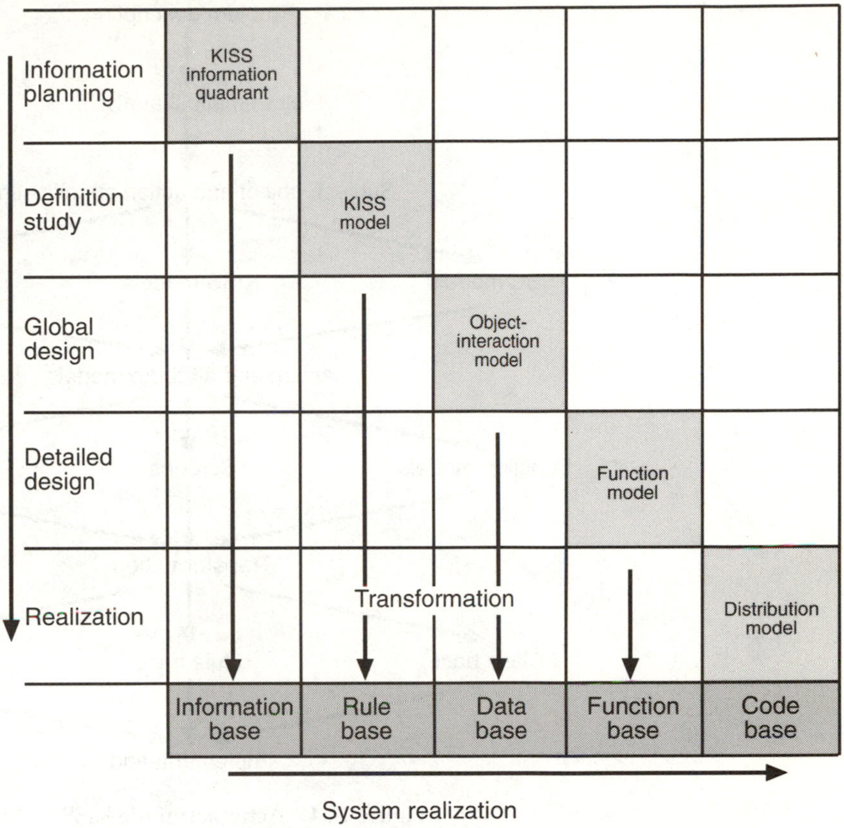

Figure 12.3 Stepwise development.

By the use of formal specifications a design can in theory be converted, with the help of automated transformation rules, into a programming language or database management system.

12.4 Activities of the KISS method

After a global sizing of the problem area has been defined, there are in the KISS method a number of activities that are of an iterative nature. The sequential activities check the specifications produced and add to them. The activities of the KISS method are shown in Figure 12.4.

(1) Description of activities

The describing of the activities aims to record 'what' happens in a particular department or section of an organization. Describing the activities of end users should be done with text using their own words and terminology.

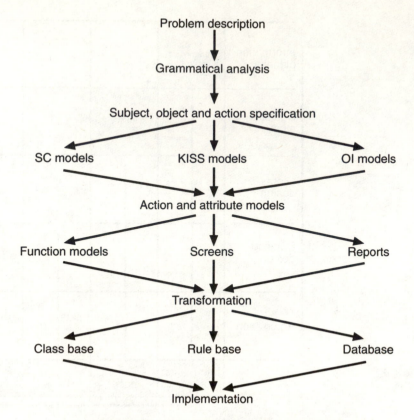

Figure 12.4   Activities of the KISS method.

A description of the activities can be written using notes of interviews, descriptions of existing systems or individual notes made by the end users themselves of their work content.

(2) Make an inventory of forms and administrations
In addition to the description of activities the existing forms and administration must be specified. These show how the business currently operates. They also further define the scope of the work.

(3) Subject-communication model
The subject-communication model shows to whom or from whom, in which system, the various forms or other messages are sent or received. The subject-communication model provides insight into the problem area.

The three steps above are generally carried out once, in order to depict the current situation with an information quadrant. Using the current situation we work in steps towards the eventual desired organizational situation.

(4) Grammatical analysis

Using the textual description we move on to forming simple active structured sentences. The active structured sentences are in the form of:

subject – predicate – direct object – preposition – indirect object – preposition – indirect object.

Using the structured sentences lists of the candidate objects and candidate actions are drawn up.

(5) Action and object descriptions

For each candidate action and candidate object a list is drawn up with definitions. These serve as the basis for further analysis in subsequent phases.

   The basic premise of an action is that it causes a real change to one or more objects at one moment in time. This change must be described as text.

   The basic premise of an object is that it represents a status that can be changed by certain actions.

(6) Object/action matrix

In the object/action matrix we show the details of the object upon which a particular action is carried out. The matrix is a cross-reference between objects and actions.

Steps 4 to 6 provide the basis for further analysis of the problem area.

(7) Initial object-interaction model

Using the defined objects and actions we create an initial object-interaction model. The aim is to incorporate in the model the known existence dependencies and category/classification structures.

(8) KISS models

For each object type included in the object-interaction model we create a KISS model. The KISS model shows the permitted temporary behaviour of an object by means of iteration, selection and sequence. We also describe the procedural way of working with a KISS model.

(9) Object-interaction model

After the individual KISS models have been created we integrate them into one or more object-interaction models. Combined with the KISS models, the object-interaction model defines the information architecture of an organization.

The documentation produced by the preceding steps is reviewed and supplemented by the new insights discovered in steps 7 to 9.

(10)   Attribute models

Based on the available forms and administrations the attribute types are added to the object types and action types. We also check what other new attribute types are needed for the system.

(11)   Action models

For each action type of an object type we show which operations are carried out on the attribute types. For each action type we also define the conditions under which the action can be carried out.

(12)   Domain/value type

For each attribute type we indicate the valid range of its domain using the measures and reference objects. For each attribute type we define its value type.

Steps 10 to 12 provide a description of the lower conceptual level that is encapsulated for an object type. They provide a validation of the KISS models and the object-interation models. The complete structural functionality has now been specified.

(13)   Screens and input functions

We show how the end user can input and inquire on data. This is done by defining screens based on the object-interaction model with its defined attribute types.

(14)   Reports and output functions

The structure of reports is defined. The number of reports defined will depend on the project and the system.

(15)   Dialogue

The way in which end users are permitted to work with the system is defined by a dialogue and the specification of the authorizations. The dialogue defines how the actions are carried out within functions.

Steps 13 to 15 define how the administrative information system is presented to the end user.

(16)   Physical data definitions

For the attributes from the information architecture we note the conventions according to which they will be implemented in a physical structure. It is very important to give thought to the reuse of existing definitions and the standardization of abbreviations.

(17)   Database

The object-interaction model is transformed according to the physical limitations of a specific database structure.

(18)   Rule base/action handler
All the KISS models are transformed to a rule base and action handler, taking into account the static constraints. The rule base/action handler is the core of the eventual information system.

(19)   Screen generation
The screens are implemented in the production environment.

(20)   Prototyping
Using the specifications a prototype which can be used to test the functionality is built.

Steps 16 to 20 deal with the transformation of the specifications to the limitations of a specific production environment. These steps can be further expanded according to the diverse aspects of the implementation. We can think of batch functions, planning functions and system management functions.

The project activities listed above could be divided up differently according to the starting position and the desired goal of the project. In this way, the order of activities for re-engineering an existing application will be different than for a completely new system. With re-engineering there is already a system in existence with screens, procedures, data definitions, database structures and so on. These products could be used as the basis, making the order and emphasis of the activities different.

To plan and estimate the time needed per activity, the general rules and methods that apply to project management also apply to object orientation, as suggested earlier. An important aspect of object orientation that supports project management is that KISS object orientation makes the system development better able to be measured. This is achieved because of the more formal method of working and the fact that the OO concepts used supplement each other. This then fulfils the most important requirement of project management and quality.

12.5   Implementation management for the KISS method

One of the main aims of the KISS method for object orientation is for the information analyst and the end user to define the information architecture and the information system together. The main requirement for actually achieving this is that the information analyst must be able to communicate with the end user in a language the end user understands.

A handicap to this aim is that the end user often does not have much knowledge of the way methods and techniques are applied in order to analyse his information requirements. He expects that the information analyst will support him during the analysis and definition of the structure of the information he requires. The information analyst is then expected to have sufficient ability to communicate the necessary information to the end user.

As well as recording the information architecture and the system specifications it is also the task of the information analyst to communicate the specifications to the programmers in a clear and effective manner.

The way in which communication of information takes place between the end user, the information analyst and the programmer determines how quickly, simply, clearly and methodically an information architecture with its desired information system can be built.

In practice, with a conventional approach the communication between end user, information analyst and programmer is usually limited to written reports and a presentation. The presentation generally takes the form of a monologue, or for the prototype approach, a dialogue in the form of screens and fragments of program code.

12.5.1   Reports as a communication medium

The disadvantage of reports is not only that they take time to write and present but that there is at least as much time again needed to read them and discuss them to a reasonable depth. After the discussion has taken place, any modifications must be incorporated in the report in order to arrive at the definitive version. With a conventional approach this process is repeated many times for the various phases of information plan, requirements definition, design, detailed design and system documentation.

12.5.2   Prototyping as a communication medium

Prototyping has the feature of allowing development of a system to commence before the design is completed. With a pure prototyping approach there is no underlying information architecture available to provide the basis for specifying, developing and managing a system. The application of prototyping can therefore be compared to building a house with no architectural and building plans. The starting point for prototyping is that the house will define itself as it is being built and that it is difficult to tell at the beginning what the house will look like. Enthusiasts claim that the house can be designed much more quickly as it is being built than when using building plans. The building plans themselves are then viewed as unreliable by the enthusiasts.

The prototyping approach does, however, raise some questions about its effectiveness. A much-heard argument is that the restrictions of the technique are catered for far too early on, and not enough thought is given to the problem area itself. In addition, the development and realization of systems occurs in a highly iterative environment, often leading to existing structures having to be rebuilt from scratch.

Despite these disadvantages, prototyping also has many advantages. Prototyping permits a meaningful dialogue with the end user about tangible issues. It makes system development more tangible than all the reports of the conventional approach.

12.5.3   Communication with the end user using the KISS approach

In both the methods of working described above there are a number of advantages we want to hold onto with the KISS approach, while at the same time wishing to eliminate the negative aspects. These are the danger of bureaucratization with the conventional approach and the lack of a design with the prototyping approach.

The requirements we place on the communication process in order to ensure a speedy communication with the end user are:

- *Interactive specification.* System specifications must be created interactively with the end user, without resorting to the production of fat reports. Fat reports are not read by a busy end user anyway. This does not mean that no reports should be written, but that the reports must not become the primary product of any phase of the system development.

- *Immediate validation of specifications.* The specifications must be validated at the same time as they are created. The end user must take responsibility for the specifications.

- *Concepts understood by games.* The end user must quickly be able to understand the techniques with which the information analyst has specified the information system. The end user must be able to apply the concepts by playing a game, with the help of the information analyst.

- *Attract and hold attention of individuals.* The end user must remain interested during the entire process of specification. The specification process must remain fun, interactive and enjoyable. The specification of the information architecture and the information system must not be reduced to a procedural event that is hidden in some other method or CASE tool managed by a few employees.

- *Specification as a group process.* The specification of information systems must be experienced as a group process. This group process must provide support to and improvement on the organization's way of working and not be seen as a technically advanced high-flying activity or hobby of the computing department.

The use of the KISS method in communication with end users demands totally different qualities from those usual in system development. The issues can be summarized briefly by these core terms:

- Independently-working end-user;
- Group method of specification of the information architecture and the information systems;
- Responsibility for the provision of information lies with the end user;
- The end user understands the information system;
- Gradual development and modification of information systems.

Part of the goal is achieved when we let the end users describe 'what' their daily work involves. The resulting text can be formed into structured sentences by the information analyst using a grammatical analysis. The information analyst also produces candidate object lists, candidate action lists, initial object-interaction models, and so on. The analyst can create a subject-communication model and carry out a workflow analysis to gain insight into the effectiveness of the organization's way of working.

When this has been done, there is sufficient material for one or more meetings to be held to discuss the effectiveness of the organization and to decide which object types and action types must be further modelled.

During the period that the KISS models and object-interaction models are being created, end user participation is absolutely crucial. It is the end users who know exactly what the current and/or desired way of working is, and the actions that are permitted to be carried out on objects. They also know how the objects interrelate with each other. A condition for success is the discovery of a way of allowing end users to participate easily in the creation of the models. In fact, the success of an information system is determined by the degree to which the end users can see their work reflected in and supported by the information system.

To bring the end users into the process of creating an information architecture and an information system, the KISS method is supported by the game KISS DOMINO.

KISS DOMINO is a game in which a group of participants can specify an information architecture and an information system in a very visual manner. The game rules for KISS DOMINO are based on the basic rules that apply to the creation of the various models of the KISS method as well as the regularity of the group process. The result is that KISS DOMINO allows for an optimal communication between end users, information analysts and programmers. The end users' threshold to using the KISS method is lowered so that they can effectively participate in the system development. The result is that the system development process takes place with a much greater intensity, faster and with a greatly improved quality of communication.

12.6   KISS DOMINO

While KISS DOMINO can be played by one person, it is intended to be played by many people. The players themselves can have diverse backgrounds and are preferably recruited from the end users' organization, system developers and management. The players must all be connected to the area of interest for which an information architecture or information system is being created. During the game there must be present at least one knowledgeable person from the end users' organization and a game leader who controls the game's progress and game rules.

In preparation for KISS DOMINO the participants must have written on paper in their own words a description of their own activities and those of their colleagues working in the area of interest. These descriptions can be converted by the game leader into simple structured sentences and lists of candidate objects and actions before the game commences.

At the start of the game the general game rules are explained. The candidate objects and candidate actions are randomly divided among the participants. The game rules are explained clearly enough to allow the first model to be developed. The rules for other types of model are explained at a later time.

For the average problem area we are dealing with a total of 15 objects and 45 actions, so that with five participants each is given 12 different items with which to play the KISS DOMINO game. Each participant is given responsibility for maintaining an administration of the changes taking place on his objects and actions, and the attributes that are added to them. At the end of the game the administrations are handed in and processed into a final report.

Besides the candidate objects and actions, the participants also use a number of coloured domino pieces on which the 24 symbols of the KISS method are pictured (Figure 12.5). Each group of symbols that logically belong together is given a different colour. The colours define the following groups:

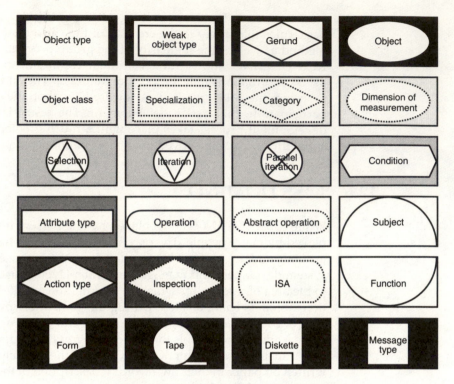

Figure 12.5   Symbols of KISS DOMINO.

(1) Black: object type, weak object type, gerund, object
(2) Pink: object class, specialization, category, measure
(3) Yellow: selection, iteration, parallel iteration, condition
(4) Blue: attribute type
(5) Red: action type, inspection
(6) White: subject, function, operation, ISA symbol
(7) Green: form, tape, disk, message type

12.6.1   The object-interaction model

After the items have been divided up among participants and the domino pieces are at hand, the game can be started. It is preferred with KISS DOMINO that we start by building an initial object-interaction model.

At the start, the game leader picks someone who begins by placing an object type on the game table. The player takes a domino piece with the symbol for an object and places a sticker on it with the name of the object type. The player notes in his administration the time that he placed the object type piece.

After the first player has chosen an object type, the following players must lay action types and object types against the object type. The domino pieces are laid immediately next to each other without worrying about the lines connecting them. The connecting association is implied by laying one piece next to another piece. In some cases the entire side of a piece will not be able to lie against another piece, but only against part of the side.

The placing of the domino pieces invokes the rule that a player placing a weak object type, gerund or specialization on the table may place two pieces in one turn. A player defining a category may even place three pieces in the same turn. The extra pieces do not need to come from the player's own list of items, but the administration must be maintained by the person who places the item on the table.

When the object-interaction model becomes too complex, the players may continue with a new separate model. To make the connection between domino pieces, the players can use special pieces with lines drawn on them. An example of an object-interaction model in KISS DOMINO is shown in Figure 12.6.

Modelling in a group situation means that items, homonyms and synonyms will need to be discussed. The aim of the group process is to gain, step by step, clarification of the concepts used. The administration process for each concept and the changes to the concept over time are therefore of tremendous importance. The better the administration is carried out by the players, the easier the process that created the model can be traced.

The transfer of object type to weak object type and to gerund is of fundamental importance to the further specification of models. The object-interaction model must be in complete accordance with the autonomous KISS models.

12.6.2   The KISS model

Next, a short explanation is given to the group of the game rules for building KISS models for objects. We then start to build a KISS model for each object type in the object-interaction model. The administration of the KISS model is maintained by the player who brought it into the game as an object. In the game, the rule is that all action types that are associated with the object type either directly or via specializations and categories must be incorporated into the KISS model.

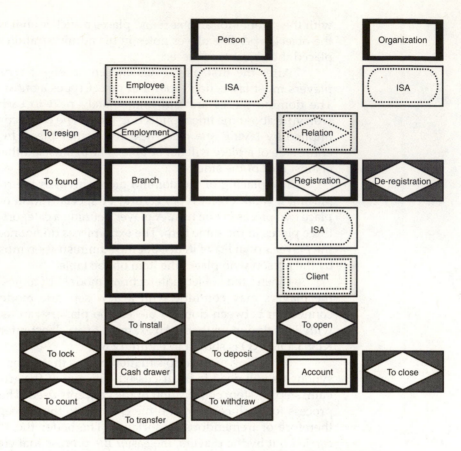

Figure 12.6   Object-interaction model in KISS DOMINO.

When modelling specializations and parallel iterations we place the domino pieces in a row, and possibly in many rows, under the relevant symbol. Subsequent actions on selection, iteration and parallel iteration symbols are placed to the right of the relevant symbol.

The conventions and the way the KISS models are read can be directly applied to the models produced by KISS DOMINO. The players successively build all the KISS models from the object-interaction model. To do this they check whether there are sufficient action types in the initial object-interaction model. When it appears as though action types are missing, they are added to the object-interaction model. An example of the KISS model for cash drawer is shown in Figure 12.7.

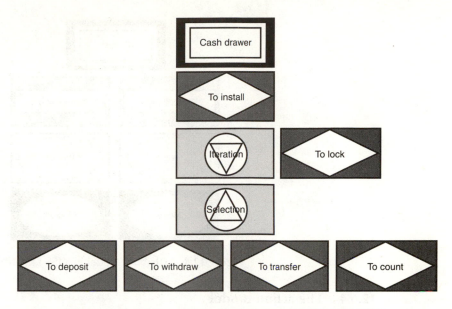

Figure 12.7   KISS model for Cash drawer in KISS DOMINO.

12.6.3   The attribute model

After the main structure of the information system has been defined by KISS models and object-interaction models, the players move on to building attribute models for the specification of encapsulated attribute types. The steps to be followed are to identify the relevant reference objects and measures. Then we determine for which object types and action types 'measurements' must be taken against the reference objects and measures.

The attribute models are created individually for each object type, weak object type, action type, object class, and so forth. The attribute model is built by placing at the top the object type, action type, weak object type, gerund, specialization, category and object class. At the very bottom we place the reference objects. Between the objects and so on at the top and the reference objects we place the attribute types and measures. An example is shown in Figure 12.8.

Because it often happens that there are a large number of attribute types defined for an object type, we can use a horizontal layout of the attribute model instead of a vertical one. We then end up with an ordering from left to right of object type, attribute type, measure, reference object. In this way we can place twice as many pieces at one height as with a vertical construction.

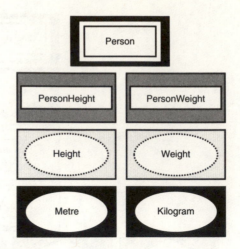

Figure 12.8   Attribute model in KISS DOMINO.

12.6.4   The action model

The action model shows how the attribute types are changed by operations, and under which conditions an action may be carried out. These are the two different sides of the same action model.

In the game the players start by modelling the operations of an action type. By specifying the operations we check the validity of an action type. If there are no operations to be specified for an action type then we must look at whether the action type is valid.

The action model is started by specifying the operations, with the player responsible placing the action type on the game table. First we check which attribute types are directly associated with the action type. An initial operation is named for this. Then we look at the object-interaction model to see which object types and object classes are associated with the action type.

For the attribute types of the associated object types and object classes we look for the operations which change the attribute types. The operations and attribute types are placed in a vertical manner under each other in order of the colours red, white, blue. At the bottom we place the attribute type which comes after most of the operations. In KISS DOMINO we can also directly associate the attribute types with the object types and object classes by placing them next to the attribute types. An example of an action model is shown in Figure 12.9.

A horizontal construction of operations for the action type places all the operations on the attribute types to the right of the action types.

In some cases there are status conditions which must be met before an action can be carried out. For example, the action type 'To

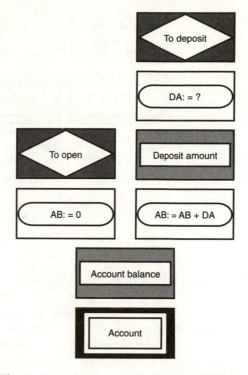

Figure 12.9   Action model in KISS DOMINO.

deposit' may require the ID to be greater than 123 or the DepositAmount smaller than $100 or the DepositAmount greater than $200. The condition lines are connected by 'or, or, or'. In the action model we show an 'or, or, or' situation, in a vertical construction, by placing the conditions beside each other, above the action type (Figure 12.10). Each condition can be placed immediately under the associated attribute type. The operations are placed below the action type. In a horizontal construction the conditions are placed on the left of the action type and the attribute types with the operations on the right.

It can also occur for the action type that the conditions do not exclude one another. We show this in an action model by placing the conditions above one another above the action type. The associated attribute types are then placed to the right of the conditions. Figure 12.11 shows that the ID must be greater than 123 and the DepositAmount must lie between $100 and $200.

In a horizontal construction of the action model the conditions are placed beside each other and are read from left to right.

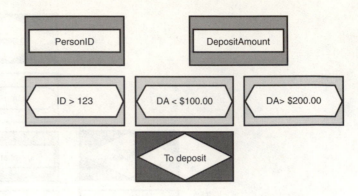

Figure 12.10   Action model 'To deposit' with 'or, or, or' conditions in KISS
DOMINO.

12.6.5   Function model

To build a function model we make use of two domino pieces to
show the function symbol. The rest follows the same rules as the KISS
models. The function model is preferably administered in the game by
one player per round of turns. An example of a function model is shown
in Figure 12.12.

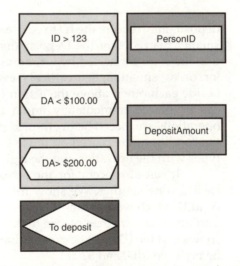

Figure 12.11   'And, and, and' conditions for the action model 'To deposit' in
KISS DOMINO.

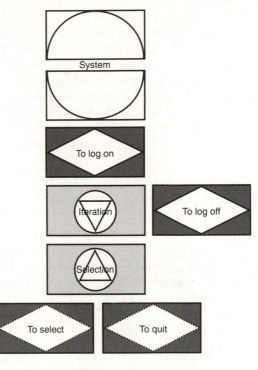

Figure 12.12 Function model.

12.6.6 Other models

The subject-communication model, the hierarchy model and the function interaction model can be built when desired. The determination of the structure has already been done by the KISS models and the object-interaction model. The content is specified with attribute models and action models. Further modelling can be useful for technical implementation aspects but does not necessarily have to be done with KISS DOMINO. When to stop the game is something that must be considered early on. Further development of the models can then be done using a CASE tool.

12.7 CASE tools

Computer-Aided Software Engineering (CASE) was one of the great promises of the past ten years. To make computer-aided software engineering possible, special information systems were designed and built. These were then used to support the design, documentation, realization and maintenance of information systems. All supporting information systems for computing staff are given the name 'CASE tool'.

Despite the initial high optimism with the application of CASE tools, they have the same problems and shortcomings as 'normal' information systems. As far as they go, CASE tools are no different from any 'normal' information system.

In the next section we will try to indicate by describing the development of CASE tools what the requirements are for the successful application of a CASE tool in an organization.

12.7.1   History of the CASE tool

Aids and utility programs to simplify the design and development of information systems were used in the early stages of computing. The large amount of work necessary to write programs in machine code stimulated the creativity of computing staff to search for means to simplify their work.

12.7.2 First-generation CASE

The first generation of utilities and aids ensured that programmers no longer needed to write in machine code. They could make use of a higher-level programming language. The higher-level programming languages, also known as third-generation languages (3GL), can be seen as practical aids. The 3GL allowed a programmer to produce a program in a shorter time, with less work and greater quality. The 3GL also provided the programmer with greater ability to model the structures of a program at the start and then to program in a 3GL. The utilization of higher-level programming languages has increased so enormously that almost all existing information systems are partly or totally based on them in one way or another.

Subsequent to the use of 3GLs, the programmer wanted to be able to model the program structures early, so that they would be well documented for the development and maintenance phases. The models would also provide support for the software design process. The background to this is that the structure of software is much easier to come to grips with when it is visually represented in a model. The model shows the interrelationships between the programs.

To represent the program structures there came into existence in the 1970s a number of representation techniques used in various methods, such as:

- Data flow diagrams;
- JSP models;
- Nassi–Schneiderman diagrams.

The basic premise of the data flow diagrams (DFD) is a top-down specification of the processes. The input and output of the process is shown in relation to other system elements such as files and other processes and systems. At the lowest level the content of the functions is specified and built.

JSP models have a slightly different premise. To build JSP models the structure of input and output is used as the starting point for the specification of the structure of a function. The JSP model defines the structure of a function that processes the input into a defined output.

The Nassi–Schneiderman diagrams have the same premise as the JSP models. The representation of the functions is in fact totally different.

An additional effect of the modelling of functions is that as well as the improved quality of software, function models that are sufficiently formal can also be used for the generation of program code using code generators. The concept of 'formal' is used here to mean that the function models no longer need to be interpreted by an analyst or programmer in order to be converted into program code.

Not every method of modelling conforms to the requirement of 'formality'. So, a DFD model cannot be used for code generation without some extra provisions and agreements. JSP models and Nassi–Schneiderman diagrams do conform to the requirements of 'formality'. JSP models and Nassi–Schneiderman diagrams can therefore also be converted without modification into executable function code. It must, however, be mentioned that the quality of the resulting code is still determined by the original model build by the analyst or programmer.

The first CASE tools that supported the modelling of functions were generally based on one of the modelling techniques mentioned. The CASE tool was often limited to the graphical representation of the structure of a function, the documentation of the function and reporting of the specification. After delivery of the final report of the system specifications, the programmer could then commence programming. The advantage of the CASE tool compared with the old way of working was that the system functions were potentially better documented. This is in comparison with using pen and paper to define the specifications or not defining any specifications at all.

When, for example, JSP or JSD is used in combination with a code generator, in addition to better documentation a portion of the development of the system can also be automated. To be able to carry this out in the best manner, the system analyst must have total insight into the problem area. In addition, the systems development organization must have strict work procedures with a relatively high level of discipline. This is often an organizational shortcoming for which the CASE tool itself cannot provide assistance or a solution. The usefulness of a CASE tool in such situations is restricted to the building of function models which a programmer then codes by hand. The starting point of the first CASE tools was in fact primarily to picture graphically the progress of a program.

In the description of the functionality of CASE tools there is often a distinction made between upper and lower CASE tools. A lower CASE tool is a utility that is intended to generate executable code. An upper CASE tool is intended to produce models and document information systems. The boundary between upper and lower CASE tools disappears when a CASE tool supports the modelling and documenting as well as the generation of program code. When a CASE tool does all of this, we speak of an integrated CASE tool, or I-CASE.

With the passage of time the technical abilities of information systems have been greatly increased, thereby also increasing the requirements placed on I-CASE environments. It is no longer sufficient for an I-CASE to model only the functions and generate programs for them. At this stage, an I-CASE must also, for example, cater for the modelling of database systems and the management and maintenance of applications.

12.7.3   Second-generation CASE

The second generation of CASE tools closely followed the developments in system software. At the time that database management systems became part of information systems on a large scale, there was a need to model the database structure just as there was for the function structure. This modelling takes place in the initial phases and is then used in the development of information systems. The techniques used to do this were, among others:

- Bachman models;
- Entity relationship models;
- NIAM models.

These techniques aim to represent the structure of a database in a clear way. Each database type must make use of techniques that are based on conventions applicable to that database type. The hierarchical, network and relational database systems each have different conventions.

The modelling techniques mentioned above were further supported by the rapidly developing CASE tools. Existing CASE tools were expanded with new techniques for representing data structures.

For the integration of data models and function models in a CASE tool, it was generally decided to integrate at the lowest level. And so, in the underlying database of the CASE tool, integration of the data from the independent data and function models takes place. Second-generation CASE tools have some big problems with consistency between the various models. This is because the methods and techniques used to represent the structure of the functions and the collections of data are not coordinated with each other. As well as this, there is an extra problem with second-generation CASE tools, because the definitions used in the different models are stored in many different locations in the database. When a name is changed in one location, then we must take extra care to change the name in all the locations where it is used in the underlying database. When we omit to do this, we lose, by definition, the total consistency of the specifications in the CASE tool.

There are many diverse possible results from the generation of database diagrams based on the data models created. The facilities for generation are strongly dependent on the modelling techniques used, combined with the database type for which the results are designed. So the generation of SQL tables based on a data structure, in general, produces no problems. On the other hand, the generation of referential integrity rules, optimization of the table structure and the determination of access paths for a relational database produces many more problems because these are not implicitly included in all models. The choice of the correct modelling technique is very important with second-generation CASE tools to ensure that the bulk of the work of system development is taken care of by generation.

Summarized, this means that the introduction of database management systems has increased the complexity involved when using second-generation CASE tools. Where originally he or she only needed to look after function models and their interrelationships, the system analyst is now confronted with the need to design data models that define the structure of the database. The complexity of the problem area can also be recognized, with second-generation CASE tools, in the construction and use of the CASE tool itself.

12.7.4   Third-generation CASE

A third generation of CASE tools was introduced by the further development of 3GL programming environments into the so-called fourth generation languages (4GL). Developments in the 4GL environments have dramatically reduced the programming work for the programmer. Using 4GLs, a programmer hardly needs to think about the full stops and commas of programming languages.

The requirements placed on the function models and data models are changed by the use, in 4GL environments, of program statements at a higher level of specification, and by a different approach to the development of information systems. We see here the graphic building of user interfaces, reports and queries and the building of prototypes.

The extent to which the function models give the necessary support to the details of the programming language is made smaller by a 4GL. In some cases a 4GL provides such readable and understandable code that modelling for small systems becomes unnecessary. The documentation for small systems can also be done to a large extent by the 4GL environment.

The added value offered by the techniques for modelling function structures is reduced when 4GLs are used. The speed with which systems can be built with 4GLs is a number of times greater than the speed of development with 3GLs. This means, too, that any mistakes can be corrected more quickly. A 4GL often needs a data model as a basis upon which to design the database.

As a result of the technical developments of 4GLs, some 4GL environments are now so far integrated with graphical modelling techniques that changes to the programs can only occur with a complete regeneration of the application after the models have been changed. The disadvantage of this is that the application becomes a monolith in which a partial change can only be implemented with difficulty.

Summarized, this means that when we apply the CASE tools of 3GL environments in the same way in 4GL environments, these CASE tools work counterproductively. The net result of the 3GL modelling techniques in comparison with 4GL environments is that too much time is spent creating specifications that are not relevant in a 4GL environment. The reason for this lies in the fact that the modelling techniques used by the CASE tools are too focused on the technical abilities and problems of a 3GL environment. The transferability into 4GL environments is often limited to a conversion of data definitions for a database or data dictionary.

One of the concerns for the optimal use of a 4GL environment is the increase of the effectiveness of the programming effort. The effect of 'building a faulty system ten times faster' with a 4GL is that ultimately there is still no appropriate system available to the end user. The total effectiveness of system development has then not been improved by the application of a 4GL.

12.7.5   Fourth-generation CASE

A fourth generation of CASE tools is introduced by the arrival of object-oriented implementation environments. Just as for the 3GL, 4GL and database environments, it is also true for object-oriented environments that modelling techniques are introduced to cater for the implementation restrictions of the specific object-oriented environment. These modelling techniques can then only be applied to a broad spectrum, in a limited way. For a broader spectrum we must use modelling techniques that are not based on an implementation environment, such as the KISS method.

One of the advantages of object-oriented environments is that the specification of a system element as an object is done in only one place in the database. A change to an object specification means that this is changed integrally for the entire system. The consistency problems of conventional CASE tools can be solved in a much more elegant way with this approach.

Besides the consistency at data level, an object-oriented CASE tool also gives us the ability to preserve consistency between the various models. The quality of the resulting specification is determined entirely by the quality of the method, and the extent to which the method is able to produce formal specifications. These specifications must ensure that the various models tie in with each other perfectly.

A basic premise of the KISS method is that all models are completely consistent with each other and that the models are sufficiently formal that they can be used for the generation of programs and databases. In addition, the KISS method has the basic premise that the specifications can be defined without taking account of any restrictions of the implementation environment. As a result of this we can write transformation rules for the KISS method for the implementation of the models into any desired production environment. Examples could be relational, network, hierarchical, semantic or object-oriented database systems, and conventional and object-oriented programming languages.

This implementation and specification strategy of the KISS method has already been incorporated into the object-oriented CASE tool Paradigm Plus. Using Paradigm Plus the developer can transform the models from the underlying object-oriented repository into code for various production environments using defined transformation rules.

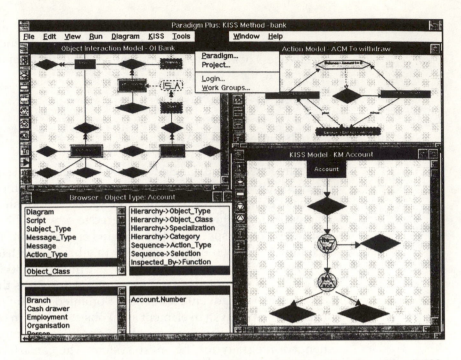

Figure 12.13   Screen example of the OO Meta CASE tool Paradigm Plus/KISS edition.

The experiences from applying Paradigm Plus together with the KISS method lead us to an important conclusion. That is, in theory it is not important to know the syntax of a programming language or database before you can specify an information system. This is because the transformation into a specific production environment is carried out by the CASE tool. With advanced use of the OO CASE tool it can even be possible to reach a situation where a completely parametrized generation takes place, including optimizing for seek times, data structures, and so forth, for a specific production environment.

The requirements placed these days on an I-CASE tool are that the entire development process of an information system be supported from the analysis, design and realization up to and including maintenance. The requirements of the I-CASE tool are so extensive that they can no longer be provided for simply by expanding second- and third-generation CASE tools. Attempts to do this lead to very expensive CASE tools that are so complex that they themselves are unmaintainable. If such a tool does manage to be introduced, then as well as the problem of managing the application there is an extra problem in the form of managing the CASE tool.

The solution to this problem is to make use of object orientation for the fourth generation CASE tools. To become totally I-CASE, the object-oriented CASE tool must have the appropriate interfaces available for models and specifications coming from a less advanced environment. In this way we have a growth path where step by step we move to a more manageable environment for the provision of information.

12.7.6   Implementation of OO CASE tools

When we apply OO CASE tools we must take care to carry out very good preparation. We must check which parts of the existing specification should be transferred to the object Repository. The users of the CASE tool must be trained in the modelling concepts of the KISS method. Without knowledge of the concepts, the OO CASE tool becomes just a very good drawing, documentation and registration utility. In addition, management will need to steer in the direction of greater reuse of object specifications and control of the quality of the specification process instead of steering in the direction of the production of reports, documentation and drawings.

The basis for the management and maintenance of information systems is provided by the object Repository with the models and interrelationships it contains. The consequences of adding to or changing the object Repository are quickly and clearly seen in the CASE tool. The object-oriented foundation of the specifications also means that the additions and changes can be incrementally realized in the information system.

The critical success factors for the application of CASE tools are:

- Knowledge level of the organization;
- Management style within systems development;
- Formality of the method used;
- Extent to which the CASE tool is integrated;
- Openness of the CASE tool;
- Implementation strategy for methods and techniques;
- Medium for a project for the implementation of the method;
- Coordination between the method used and the CASE tool method.

A maximum return on investment with the use of CASE tools can only be gained when all the critical success factors coordinate and co-operate with each other. It is important to devote the necessary attention to preparation with the implementation of CASE tools. The implementation of CASE tools hinges for its success primarily on the small details.

The implementation of new methods and techniques will significantly influence the current ways of thinking and working. When considering whether it is worthwhile to change to a new way of thinking and working the following aspects are evaluated:

- *Productivity?*
  Are we sufficiently productive at the moment to be able to compete with our competitors in the market? How much more productive must we become, in which time frame, to 'survive' in the long term?

- *Speed and flexibility?*
  Can we provide the end users of information systems with the necessary and desired new functionality to improve the competitiveness of the total organization, within acceptable time frames?

- *Ability to manage and maintain?*
  Can we actively manage our information system or can we only manage to keep the information system up by not making any modifications to it?

- *Independent user?*
  Can the user add his own desired functions to the information architecture or must each function be programmed and tested by a programmer?

- *Changes to systems development?*
  Are there aspects of systems development and management where we must actively make changes or do we think that the current way of working is perfect or even totally unable to be changed because of decisions taken in the past?

In addition to these, there are a large number of aspects that when analysed define the path that must be followed. This path defines how the organization will give form to its provision of information in the 3–8 year time frame. Within this scope, the short-term activities will need to be further evaluated.

The general trend is that many system development organizations need to follow a lengthy route before their provision of information will reach the stage where the level of information provision totally supports the organization in the making of decisions. Object orientation provides a path where the desired goal can be reached in a stepwise manner.

12.8 Summary

In this chapter we have looked at the way the KISS method for object orientation leads to a form of project management where the specifications and program structures for objects can be produced. The advantage of the KISS method for object orientation is that we obtain a detailed description of the real world, which serves as the basis for the generation of software.

For the application of the KISS method we indicated the way KISS DOMINO can be used as an aid to the improvement of the communication between system developers, users and project initiators. KISS DOMINO has the important task of getting the players involved, allowing them to visualize the concepts used.

Finally, by looking at the development of CASE tools we discussed how OO CASE tools allow us to grow towards a Repository environment. The complete system specifications are managed by the Repository, and the specifications are used for the realization and maintenance of software.

The three management aspects discussed can be moulded to fit the KISS method for object orientation. Project management, implementation management and Repository management are in fact totally dependent on the system development method used.

12.9 Questions

(1) Discuss the influence on project management of projects with informal and formal specification techniques. Do the same for projects in which techniques that can be easily communicated and understood by system developers and end users are used.

(2) Determine in what ways the KISS method assures the quality of specifications and implementation during the total process. In what aspects does the KISS method differ from conventional approaches?

(3) Discuss the activities of the KISS method and relate them to the different chapters in which the techniques are described.

(4) In what way can the development of information systems become more communicative?

(5) Discuss the history of CASE tools and place known products in the classification given.

(6) Discuss the preconditions for implementing CASE.

(7) Describe the goals of KISS DOMINO and its application in systems development.

Glossary

Abstract operation
An abstract operation is an operation defined on the measure. The abstract operation is valid for all attribute types connected to the measure.

Action
An action is an event that takes place at one moment in time. An action changes the characteristics of one or more associated objects. An action takes place in a very short period in time.

Action handler
The action handler is part of the program that takes care of the coordination and execution of actions within the information system. The action handler also takes care of the authorization of the execution of actions.

Action model
The action model describes the way in which the state of objects is changed by operations. The actions have static conditions that have to be met before an action can be performed. The action model describes the initialization of attributes and the modifying operations as encapsulated to the outside world.

Action type
The action type gives a generic description of the actions. The action type is part of object-interaction models, KISS models, action models, attribute models and function models.

Association
An association is a link between two figures in an object-interaction model. The figures are, for example, object type, action type, object class, attribute type, object, trigger. An association can have extra contents that define the details of the association. We can think of plurality, preposition and connectivity.

Attribute
An attribute is a value of a measured or named characteristic of an object or action. For a measure it is necessary to represent an attribute in combination with a measurement unit.

Attributes represent the characteristics of objects and concepts from real-world objects.

Attribute model
The attribute model specifies the details of the attribute types of all figures of the object-interaction model by relating it to a measure or reference object.

Attribute type
The general description of the characteristics of the attributes are specified by the attribute type. The attribute type is modelled in the attribute model.

Authorization
The authorization relationship describes who is allowed to perform an action or is allowed to demand data of the information system. (*See also* action handler).

Business Process Redesign (BPR)
This is the process of optimizing the current way of working in the organization. Work-flow analysis is used and the subject-communication model supports and represents visually the BPR process.

Button
A button is a part of a screen that becomes active when it is being clicked with a mouse or that is actived by touch.

Cardinality
Cardinality describes the characteristics of an association between object type, weak object type or gerund and an action type. The cardinality determines how many times an action can be executed by an object. The cardinality is composed of an upper and lower bound, which are also called 'connectivity' and 'totality'.

Categorize
Categorization is the technique by which different object types reuse an action type.

Category
A category is part of the object-interaction model. A category takes care of the reuse of action types by different object types, weak object types or gerunds. For a category we always identify two or more parents. For transformation to the implementation environment, the category can incorporate the generic attribute types of its parents, so the attribute types have to be specified only once. In an object-oriented programming

language the category can be implemented as an abstract superclass. The category allows us to model polymorphism.

Characteristic
A characteristic is an attribute type of an object or action.

Class
A class is a concept that is widely used within object-oriented languages for identifying the generic implementation structure for the objects, attributes and operations. We can instantiate individual objects from a class in object-oriented languages.

Class hierarchy
A class hierarchy defines the structure according to which the inheritance of characteristics takes place in an object-oriented implementation environment. The inheritance takes place from a superclass towards a subclass.

Class method
A class method is a piece of code that is executed when a class receives a message.

Classification
Classification is the grouping of objects based upon common characteristics. Classification takes place upon a kind of 'is equal to' association. Classification is the weakest kind of measuring.

Communication process
Communication is the process that transfers information from one person or system to another person or system. The information transfer is dependent upon the knowledge level of the people involved, the quality of the data transportation channels and the common understanding of the semantics of the message.

Concurrency
Concurrency indicates whether more than one object can exist and be active next to each other.

Condition
A condition determines the constraints under which an action can be executed. We make a distinction between static and dynamic conditions.
    Dynamic conditions are represented in a KISS model. Static conditions are specified for, for example, attribute types, action types, iterations and selections.

Connectivity
Connectivity determines in the object-interaction model the maximum number of times an action of an action type can be performed on an object instantiation. The connectivity can be deducted from the KISS model.

Context control
The context control is the part of the action handler that ensures that the dynamic conditions of the KISS model are met.

Context table
The context table is a representation of an implementation of the structure of the KISS models.

Dialogue
The dialogue defines the way in which a user communicates with and navigates in the information system the functions he is responsible for. The dialogue is part of the action handler.

Domain
A domain is a set of attribute values of an attribute type.

Fertility index
The fertility index determines the number of child objects of a parent object. The fertility index is added to the hierarchy model.

Foreign key
A foreign key gives for a relational database a reference of one table to another table in which the foreign key is added as the primary (or part of) key.

Function
Functions are responsible for the coordinating, regulating, calculating and control activities of an information system. A function takes care of the interface with the outside world. The attributes of a function exist during the execution period of the function.

Function interaction model
The function interaction model determines in which way the function models interact with each other.

Function model
With a function model we indicate in what sequence we activate the functions' inspections and actions. The combination of all function models in a function interaction model determines the dialogue of the information system.

Function touch
A function touch is a touch with which the execution of a function will be activated.

Generalization
The generalization is the counterpart of the specialization. A generalization describes the generic characteristics and behaviour of a group of objects.

Gerund

A gerund is an object type that is existence-dependent on two or more other object types. A gerund is created by objectivation of an action type because new actions can take place on the state of the initial action type.

Hierachy model

The hierarchy model determines in which way the object types and object classes are dependent for their existence on other object types. The hierarchy model is the starting point for defining the class hierarchy.

Information quadrant

The information quadrant gives an overview of the relationships between objects, actions, functions and the employees in an organization. The information quadrant supports the control of the information architecture of organizations.

Inheritance

Inheritance is the characteristic that allows attribute types and operations to be specified in a superclass and be reused by objects of subclasses.

Input

Input is the supply of attributes to the functions of the information system and the triggering of functions for the execution of certain tasks.

Inspection

An inspection is a querying of attributes in the information system and from outside the information system. An inspection can be seen as a message to the address of the attribute followed by a message returned to the inspector containing the information.

Instance

An instance is a object that is created by the instantiation of objects of a class.

ISA

An ISA symbol is a structure element that is used for the classification of objects into groups of objects. ISA is derived from 'Is a'. ISA is in a textual description equivalent to a nominal predicate.

Iteration

An iteration is, along with sequence and selection, one of the three basic elements for structuring behaviour. An iteration determines that something can be executed zero, one or more times.

Key

A key is the identifier of a record in a database. The key can be composed of different attribute types.

KISS model

The KISS model gives a description of the behaviour of an object type by modelling its iterations, selections and sequences of the execution of actions of action types.

Logical data model

The logical data model determines in which way data sets are related to each other in a database. In a logical data model we do not model the physical implementation structure. The logical data model has different conventions that are dependent upon the database type that has to be supported.

Man–machine interface

The man–machine interface determines how an information system representents itself to the user. Elements of the man–machine interface are, for example, the screen layout, colours, size of the figures and icons, error messages, and so on.

Measure

A measure is the description of a reference against which we measure the characteristics of objects and actions. A measure will always be measured in combination with a measurement unit.

Measurement scale

A measurement scale gives a reference to which the characteristics of an object can be related in order to determine its attributes.

Message

A message is an addressed set of attributes with a certain internal structure. The message also has the address of the sender of the message.

Message type

A message type is a generic description of the structure and contents of a message.

Method

A method is a piece of code that will be executed when a message is received by executing an operation of an action type.

Multiple inheritance

In an object-oriented programming language, multiple inheritance allows a subclass to make use of the generic characteristics of more than one superclass.

Object

An object is an instantiation of an object type. Each object can also be used as a reference for the measurement of the attributes of another object. In this case the object cannot change its attribute values.

Object class

An object class is a group of objects with common characteristics. For an object class we need to specify the classification criteria according to which we group the objects.

Object hierarchy

An object hierarchy determines in which way objects are dependent on each other with respect to their existence. Object types that are placed lower in the hierarchy are existence-dependent on the object types that are placed higher in the hierarchy.

Object-interaction model

The object-interaction model determines in which way the individual object types interact with each other. The object-interaction model also defines how object classes, specializations and categories are related with ISA symbols to the object types.

Object type

The object type gives a generic description of the life of an object by modelling the sequence in which actions can be executed in a KISS model. When an object type is dependent for its existence upon one parent object type, we call it a weak object type. When an object type is dependent for its existence upon two or more parents, we call it a gerund.

Occurrence

The occurrence is a synonym for an object or an instantiation of an object type.

Occurrence number

The occurrence number determines the number of objects of an object type.

Operation

An operation describes with an equation how an attribute is initialized or modified. The operations are encapsulated in an action type.

Parent relationship

A parent relationship identifies an existence dependency of one or more object types.

Parallel iteration

With a parallel iteration we can model within one KISS model the behaviour and life of different parallel objects. These object act concurrently with each other.

Persistent object

A persistent object is an object whose attributes are stored in the database. The attributes of a persistent object are available until they are removed explicitly.

Physical data model

The physical data model describes the implementation structure of the data sets in a storage structure with possible access paths.

Place association

The place association is an optional characteristic of the association line between the action type and object types in the object-interaction model.

The place association is derived from the preposition next to the active object in a simple structure sentence.

Plurality
With plurality we indicate how many objects of one object type interact at one moment in time with an action of an action type. We add the plurality to the object-interaction model.

Polymorphism
Polymorphism is the characteristic that a group of objects exhibit different behaviour upon execution of the same action type. The action will be activated by a message.

Procedural organization
The set of rules and prescriptions according to which an organization has to keep its administration. The procedural organization gives a description of forms, form flows and administrations, responsibilities and authorizations for employees and functions.

Process
A process is an identifiable group of activities that are executed for a certain goal or purpose. A process is comparable to a function to which we have added the actions it executes on objects. A process regulates, coordinates and controls as well as executes.

Process time
The process time is the time that a subject needs for the processing of a message.

Program
A program is the executable implementation of predefined logic on a machine.

Relationship
A relationship is equivalent to an association.

Response time
The response time is the time that is necessary for getting the requested information from the information system.

Screen
A screen is an aid for the presentation and manupulation of attributes of the information system. A screen can have many different technical characteristics. The screen techniques used determine how far the attributes can be represented with more or less detail.

Security
Security is the set of activities taken to avoid the unauthorized use of the information system. It consists of passive security in order to avoid errors by the end user and active security by access control for the users of the information system (*See also* Authorization).

Selection
A selection is, along with iteration and sequence, one of the three basic elements for modelling the structure of object types in KISS models.

Semantics
Semantics gives an indication of the level to which an information system can deliver and store meaningful information. The semantics are modelled with a number of different models.

Sequence
A sequence is, along with iteration and selection, one of the three basic elements for modelling the structure of object types in KISS models.

Specialization
A specialization represents a group of objects with a common behaviour. The specialization describes the roles of objects because they perform one or more action types in common. A specialization is always dependent upon the existence of one parent object type. For a specialization we will not make any KISS model. We will model the life with the parent object type.

Subclass
For an object-oriented implementation a subclass can inherit the generic characteristics of a superclass.

Subject
A subject is an object that is responsible for regulating and coordinating functions. A subject is identifiable in the real world and has a frame of reference with norms and values with which it interprets, sends and receives messages to and from other subjects. A subject has a certain level of knowledge with which it can independently regulate and control processes to a greater or lesser extent.

Subject type
A subject type is the generic description of a subject.

Superclass
Superclass is a concept that is used in object-oriented environments for specifying generic characteristics on a higher level. Subclasses can make use of the generic specifications by inheritance.

Syntax
Syntax is a concept that defines the correctness of the representation of an attribute. The syntax is checked at the attribute type level. The syntax is specified for an attribute type.

Syntax control
Syntax control checks whether the attribute of an attribute type is represented in a correct way. Syntax control takes place preferably at the input of attributes to the information system. In many cases this is at the input screen.

Transformation
Transformation is the process that transforms the specifications from the information architecture into the technical restrictions of a conventional or object-oriented environment. The transformation process can be automated by CASE tools when the supported method has a formal representation.

Transient
'Transient' is a characteristic of an attribute that indicates that an attribute only has a limited life during the execution of a program. After turning the switch off the information system is dead and the attribute has disappeared.

Transmission time
The transmission time is the time between the sending and receipt of a message between two subjects.

Trigger
A trigger is a conditional message that is sent to a function. The function can vary from very elementary to very complex.

Value
The value is part of an attribute. The value of an attribute is always determined in combination with the measurement unit.

Value domain
The value domain defines the conditions and boundaries for the values of the attributes. The value domains can be checked by syntax control when the attributes are input.

Variable
'Variable' is an often-used concept in object-oriented languages as a synonym for an attribute.

View
A view is a representation of a set of attributes from the information system.

Weak object type
A weak object type is an object type that is dependent for its existence upon one other object type by an initiating action type.

Work-flow analysis
Work-flow analysis determines the intensity of the message traffic of the existing situation in order to determine a more optimal situation. The desired situation is a better starting point for the information architecture.

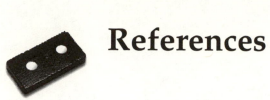

References

Booch G. (1991). *Object-Oriented Design with Applications*. Redwood City: Benjamin/Cummings

Coad P. and Yourdon E. (1991a). *Object-Oriented Analysis*, 2nd edn. Englewood Cliffs, NJ: Prentice-Hall

Coad P. and Yourdon E. (1991b). *Object-Oriented Design*. Englewood Cliffs, NJ: Prentice-Hall

Jacobson I., Christerson M., Jonson P. and Overgaard G. (1992). *Object-Oriented Software Engineering*. Reading, MA: ACM Press, Addison-Wesley

Nolan R.L. and Gibson C.F. (1974). Managing the four stages of EDP growth. *Harvard Business Review*, **52** (1), January-February 76–86

Nolan R.L. (1979). Managing the crisis in data processing. *Harvard Business Review*, **57** (2), March-April, 155–6

Rumbaugh J., Blaha M., Premerlani W., Eddy F. and Lorensen W. (1991). *Object-Oriented Modeling and Design*. Englewood Cliffs, NJ: Prentice-Hall

Shlear S. and Mellor S.J. (1988). *Object-oriented Systems Analysis*. Englewood Cliffs, NJ: Prentice-Hall

Further reading

Budd T. (1991). *An Introduction to Object-Oriented Programming*. Reading, MA: Addison-Wesley

Cameron J. (1989). *JSP and JSD: The Jackson approach to Software Development*, 2nd edn. Silver Spring: IEEE Computer Society Press

CCITT (1988). Specification and Description Language (SDL). *Recommendation Z.100*. Geneva: CCITT

Chen P.P. (1976). The entity-relationship model: towards a unified view of data. *ACM Transactions on Database Systems*, **1** (1), 936

Chen P.P. (1977). The entity-relationship approach to logical database design. Wellesley: Q.E.D. Monograph Series No.6., Q.E.D. Information Sciences

Chen P.P., ed. (1980). *Entity-relationship Approach to Systems Analysis and Design*. Amsterdam, The Netherlands: North Holland

Dijkstra E.W. (1976). *A Discipline of Programming*. Englewood Cliffs, NJ: Prentice-Hall

Eilers H.B. (1989). Systeemontwikkeling op kleinere schaal met SDM. Schoonhoven: Academic Service. (Dutch)

Graham I. (1993). Object Oriented Methods. Wokingham: Addison-Wesley

Helder R. and Whyte R. (1988). Het JSP-boek, een methode voor doelmatig programmeren. Deventer, The Netherlands: Kluwer. (Dutch)

Hoare C.A.R. (1985). *Communicating Sequential Processes*. United Kingdom: Prentice-Hall International.

IBM (1981). Business Systems Planning: Information Systems Planning Guide. GE20-0527-3, IBM Corp., 1133 Westchester Ave., White Plains, NY, 10604

Jackson M.A. (1975). *Principles of Program Design*. London, England: Academic Press

Jackson M.A. (1983). *System Development*. Englewood Cliffs, NJ: Prentice-Hall

Jansen, H. (1984). Jackson Structureel Programmeren. Den Haag: Academic Service. (Dutch).

Kramer N.J.T.A. and de Smit J. (1974). Systeemdenken, Inleiding tot de begrippen en concepten. Leiden: H.E. Stenfert Kroese b.v. (Dutch)

Leeuw A.C.J., de (1974). Systeemleer en Organisatiekunde. Leiden: H.E. Stenfert Kroese b.v. (Dutch)

Meyer B. (1988). *Object-Oriented Software Construction*. Englewood Cliffs, NJ: Prentice-Hall

Perry R.H. and Chilton C.H. (1973). *Chemical Engineers Handbook*, 5th edn. Tokyo: McGraw-Hill Kogakusha, Ltd

Put F. (1988). Introducing Dynamic and Temporal Aspects in a Conceptual (Database) Schema. Leuven, Belgium: Katholieke Universiteit Leuven, Faculteit der Economische en Toegepaste Economische Wetenschappen, Proefschrift Nr 68

Sebus G.M.W. (1981) Business Systems Planning. *Informatie*, March 1981. (Dutch)

Vandenbulcke J.A. (1988). Data base systemen voor de praktijk, 4th edn (in Dutch). Deventer, The Netherlands: Kluwer

Verhelst M. (1987). JSD: een systeemontwikkelingsmethode (in Dutch). *Informatie*, **29** (5), 461–72

Verhelst M. (1980). De praktijk van beslissingstabellen. Deventer: Kluwer. (Dutch)

Wanders A.G.M. (1989). Systeemontwikkelingsmethoden: Vergelijken en kiezen. Schoonhoven: Academic Service. (Dutch)

Ward P.T. and Mellor S.J. (1985). *Structured Development for Real Time Systems*. Englewood Cliffs, NJ: Yourdon Press

Wirfs-Brock R., Wilkerson B. and Wiener L. (1990). *Designing Object-Oriented Software*. Englewood Cliffs, NJ: Prentice-Hall

Yourdon E. and Constantine L.L. (1979). *Structured Design: Fundamentals of a Discipline of Computer Program and Systems Design*. Englewood Cliffs, NJ: Prentice-Hall

Zave P. (1984). The operational versus the conventional approach to software development. *Communications of the ACM*, **27** (2), 104–18

Index